Women Resisting
AIDS
Feminist Strategies of Empowerment

In the series

Health, Society, and Policy

edited by Sheryl Ruzek and Irving Kenneth Zola

Women Resisting
AIDS

Feminist Strategies of Empowerment

BY

Beth E. Schneider

AND

Nancy E. Stoller

TEMPLE UNIVERSITY PRESS
Philadelphia

Temple University Press, Philadelphia 19122

Published 1994

⊖ The paper used in this book meets the requirements of
the American National Standard for Information Sciences—
Permanence of Paper for Printed Library Materials,
ANSI Z39.48 1984

Printed in the United States of America

Text design by Susan Blaker.

Library of Congress Cataloging-in-Publication Data

Schneider, Beth.
    Women resisting AIDS : feminist strategies of empowerment / Beth E. Schneider, Nancy E.
Stoller.
      p. cm.
    Includes bibliographical references.
    ISBN 1–56639–268–3. — 1–56639–269–1 (pbk.)
    1. AIDS (Disease)—Social aspects. 2. AIDS (Disease)—Political aspects. 3. Women—
Diseases. 4. Women—Health and hygiene. 5. Feminism. I. Stoller, Nancy E. II. Title.
RA644.A25S355 1995
362.1'969792'0082—dc20   94–31407

*This book is dedicated to
the memory of
Meredith Eisberg
and
Liz Wolfe*

CONTENTS

CONTRIBUTORS

Priscilla Alexander, BA

Former consultant to the World Health Organization on sex work and prevention of HIV infection and other sexually transmitted diseases; previously, Education Director, California Prostitutes Education Project (CAL-PEP). Alexander is the author or co-author of numerous articles concerning sex industry workers' vulnerability to HIV infection and AIDS-inspired repression; she is also the co-editor of *Sex Work: Writings by Women in the Sex Industry.*

Mabel Bianco, MD, MPH

Fundacion para Estudio e Investigacion de la Mujer, Buenos Aires, Argentina. Bianco is a specialist in public health and development and a member of the steering committee for the 1993 International Conference on AIDS (Berlin).

Rebecca Denison

Founder and executive director of WORLD (Women Organized to Respond to Life-Threatening Diseases), an information and support organization for women with HIV/AIDS. Denison, who was infected over 10 years ago, is a long-term survivor of HIV disease. She has two B.A. degrees from the University of California at Santa Cruz, which is two degrees more than it takes to know that not enough has been done to fight AIDS. She loves backpacking and sea kayaking, and lives in Oakland with her husband, Daniel, and her puppy, Jabu.

Moher Downing, BA, MA (Cultural Anthropology and Women's Studies)

Director, Perinatal HIV Reduction Education Demonstration Activities, San Francisco Department of Health. Downing has extensive experience in AIDS prevention, training, and project administration, especially in programs working with drug users, women, and sex workers;

and is one of the co-founders of Prevention Point, the San Francisco needle exchange program.

Eka Esu-Williams, PhD

President, Society for Women and AIDS in Africa. Esu-Williams is a professor at the University of Calabar, Nigeria.

Marcy Fraser, RN, BA, BSN

Ten years of HIV/AIDS nursing experience including in-patient acute care, home care, hospice, and community advocacy and management.

Cathy Stein Greenblat, PhD (Sociology)

Professor of Sociology, Rutgers University. Greenblat is a specialist in gaming simulations and designer of simulation games, including several related to AIDS. She is the author or co-author of four books on simulation games, including *Designing Games and Simulations: An Illustrated Handbook*. She is the co-author of several books on marriage, family, sexuality, and the life course, including *Life Designs: Individuals, Marriages and the Family*.

Amber Hollibaugh

Director, Lesbian AIDS Project, Gay Men's Health Crisis. Hollibaugh is a long-time lesbian and gay rights activist; she is also an author and critic.

Nan D. Hunter, JD

Professor, Brooklyn Law School. Hunter is the author of numerous articles on health law and constitutional law; she is the editor of and contributor to *AIDS Agenda: Emerging Issues in Civil Rights*.

Valerie Jenness, PhD (Sociology)

Assistant Professor of Sociology, Washington State University. Her work centers on the linkages between gender, social control, and social change. She is the author of *Making It Work: The Contemporary Prostitutes' Rights Movement in Perspective*, as well as articles on prostitution, AIDS education, hate crimes, and gay-lesbian politics.

Diane Jones, RN

Head Nurse on the in-patient AIDS ward at San Francisco General Hospital, where she has worked for the last 10 years.

Diane K. Lewis, PhD (Anthropology), MPH (Epidemiology)

Professor of Anthropology, University of California, Santa Cruz. Lewis is the author of numerous articles on African-American women in regard to health, incarceration, injection drug use, and HIV transmission; she has also written on sexual risk taking in male and female bisexual and heterosexual injection drug users.

Gloria Lockett

Executive Director, California Prostitute Education Project. Lockett is co-chair of COYOTE; a member of the National Minority AIDS Task Force; and director of the CDC research project on HIV prevention for HIV Services, women and infants.

Carola Marte, MD, PhD

Yale University Medical Center. Marte is a specialist on inner city primary care and women's health. Much of her work and writing has been on medical and social issues concerning women with HIV/AIDS and chemically dependent women.

Ntombifuthi Agnes Mtshali, BA, RN (Also certified in midwifery and psychiatric nursing)

South African Youth Health Service. She is a specialist in adolescent sexuality education and life skills for adolescents.

Cheri Pies, MSW, DPH

Associate Professor in Health Science, San Jose State University. Her writing and advocacy are focused on the ethical, social, and political issues in reproductive health and contraceptive technologies. Pies is the author of *Considering Parenthood* and the co-editor of *Face to Face: A Guide to AIDS Counseling*.

Cathy J. Reback, PhD (Sociology)

Project Director, Prototypes/WARN (Women and AIDS Risk Network), Los Angeles. Reback has experience as project director and ethnographer in studies on drug injectors and sex workers; she is the author of articles and presentations on sexuality, ethnographic research, and AIDS prevention.

Helen Rodriguez-Trias, MD, FAAP

Past President, American Public Health Association. Rodriguez-Trias is a specialist on women's, children's, and minority health issues.

Beth E. Schneider, PhD (Sociology)

Professor of Sociology, University of California, Santa Barbara. Schneider is the co-editor and author of *The Social Context of AIDS*; she is also the author of numerous articles on women and AIDS and on sexuality, including issues of sexual assault, workplace treatment of sexuality, and lesbian economics and politics.

Brooke Grundfest Schoepf, PhD (Anthropology)

Schoepf is the author or co-author of numerous articles on gender and economy and on AIDS prevention programs in Central Africa; she is the co-director of the Zaire CONNAISSIDA project in Kinshasa.

Barbara G. Sosnowitz, PhD (Sociology)

Professor and Director of Social Work, Central Connecticut State University. Sosnowitz is the author of articles on neonatal intensive care units, transformations in voluntary AIDS organizations, family AIDS support groups, and social work.

Nancy E. Stoller, PhD (Sociology)

Professor of Community Studies, University of California, Santa Cruz. Stoller is the author of *Forced Labor: Maternity Care in the United States;* she is also the author or co-author of monographs, articles, and brochures on community health, including health of women in prison, AIDS, neighborhood health services, maternity care, and lesbian health.

Beth E. Schneider and Nancy E. Stoller

Introduction: Feminist Strategies
of Empowerment

A major theme of the 9th International Conference on AIDS, held in Berlin in 1993, was the rapid spread of HIV among women. Michael Merson, head of the World Health Organization's Global AIDS Programme, noted with alarm that 45 percent of all new AIDS infections in adults in the world were in women.[1] AIDS is a serious and increasingly complicated medical, political, and social problem, and women are ever more affected and implicated by its presence and its consequences. Women are key to the multifaceted ways in which AIDS is approached on a worldwide scale.

Our experiences as feminist researchers and educators, as well as our work in community organizations, shapes our intentions as editors of *Women Resisting AIDS*. Our feminist understanding of women's place in the AIDS epidemic is complex and contradictory. On the one hand, there is no question that the social, sexual, political, and economic subordination of women structures their vulnerability in the epidemic. Globally, women are poor, with few material resources. When resources are scarce, women are the last to get education, medicine, and food. Women in all countries in the world have limited control over the conditions of their lives, tend to be economically and socially dependent, struggle to protect themselves from violence, and have little say about the circumstances under which they first become sexual or become mothers.[2] These realities of oppression, marginalization, and exploitation need to be thoroughly acknowledged and understood if programs sufficient for women's survival and adequate for social change are to be orchestrated to address the problems of women and HIV/AIDS.

But, on the other hand, as Collins notes, "Oppressive situations are unstable."[3] Those conditions in the wider political economy and culture that shape women's subordination simultaneously foster activism. Consequently, women are in strategic positions to affect the course of HIV's spread. Because of gender segregation in the workplace, women are the vast majority of employees in caregiving and health professions and seem to be the majority of workers in AIDS service organizations in most locations in the world.[4] Women are key actors in sexual negotiation, reproduction,

1

family health care, and cultural transmission of normative behaviors, despite their subordination and exploitation. They are crucial to slowing the spread and managing the consequences of the epidemic. This is true especially in developing countries and in poor communities in industrialized countries, where informal and family networks and community organizations are already the necessary basis for survival.

The assembled essays were prepared specifically for this project at the editors' request. Our contributors address the issues of oppression, survival, empowerment, and social change for women with HIV/AIDS. This collection brings together a respected group of women who are leaders in the area of HIV/AIDS. Each of the authors has first-hand knowledge and is actively engaged in HIV prevention, research, policy making, organizing, or caregiving. Some work as professionals concerned with AIDS; others, as grassroots organizers. Some, including an HIV-positive woman, have, through the process of making a life with HIV, become leaders and community activists in ways they never anticipated. Several of the authors from Africa and Latin America have been leaders of major international AIDS organizations.

The contributors represent a group of women who have many years of experience responding to the AIDS epidemic, as well as in feminist, civil rights, and health advocacy movements. It is a unique group. And, consistent with our hopes, each contributor speaks in a feminist voice of her own. All reject the popular view of women in the epidemic as vessels of disease, and the medical view of women as vectors of infection with no worth of their own. Each author acknowledges women's victimization, but also affirms women's contributions and current or potential leadership.

With two exceptions, the chapters are by women writing from Africa (Nigeria, South Africa, and Zaïre) or the United States. The book focuses primarily on the U.S. experience, with almost all of the chapters addressing activities by, with, or for working-class women and women of color. For readers especially interested in the United States, the international chapters (Alexander, Bianco, and Esu-Williams) or those that focus on a specific region or country (Mtshali, Schoepf) can complement, supplement, or integrate analyses of the activities of women in the United States. Often, the programs set up elsewhere (see Schoepf on Kinshasa, Zaïre) serve as models for what might be accomplished in areas of the United States with large concentrations of women at risk of infection. Collectively, the chapters address regional, class, racial, ethnic, sexual, and national variations on women's experiences with HIV and AIDS.

Women Resisting AIDS presents current social scientific knowledge and theory, coupled with case studies of feminist practice in HIV prevention, caregiving, and organizing. The chapters collectively illustrate formal and informal responses to AIDS that utilize women's culturally shaped skills and activities. It is our hope that the book will meet the needs of a professional audience of policy makers, AIDS prevention and care providers, program planners, medical and public health personnel, sex educators, and criminal justice staff, as well as educated laypeople who are looking for examples of successful programs and explorations of the ethical and policy issues that affect women confronting the HIV/AIDS epidemic.

FEMINIST APPROACHES TO LEADERSHIP IN THE AIDS CRISIS

In preparing this book, we wanted to summarize and highlight four essential themes of feminist approaches to women's leadership in the AIDS crisis.

First is the recognition that *AIDS is a pandemic.* There is virtually no country left in the world, and no county left in the United States, without a case of AIDS. Worldwide, the number of AIDS cases among women is expected to equal the number of men by the year 2000. The World Health Organization estimates that 6 to 8 million women will be infected in that year. Although our focus is primarily on the United States, the broader context of AIDS is global. Particularly when confronting the problem of HIV in women, U.S. organizers and activists learn from and share the experiences of women in many other countries.

In international politics, women historically have not had access to the resources that would enable them to wield influence. Today women are at the bottom of most international hierarchies. In multinational companies women are routinely paid less than even the lowest-paid men. Relative to men, they have lower rates of literacy, and they comprise two-thirds of the world's refugees. Women activists have a harder time influencing struggling ethnic and nationalist movements than do men. And with a few notable exceptions, women have been outside the formal political positions of state power and violence.[5]

The International Conference in Kenya in 1985, marking the end of the United Nations Decade of Women, began a process of building international alliances among women to end men's sole right to vote in many countries and women's exploitation as mothers and prostitutes. There are now a number of areas of political concern being affected by "internationalized feminist organizing"[6]: prostitution, population politics, economic assistance, military alliances, and textile and electronics production. AIDS can now be added to this list.

For many otherwise knowledgeable feminists, AIDS has made visible the plight of women in industrializing countries, beyond those already-familiar faces of factory workers, peasants, and sex workers at military bases. It has also sharpened important differences between women in poorer, less-industrialized countries, by showing the different stakes of middle-class, working-class, and peasant women. At the same time, AIDS has revealed that cross-class alliances can be drawn to effect change in traditional practices.

A second feature of our approach is *sustained attention to the social relations of race, class, sexuality, and culture.* These relations are hierarchically organized, resting on and resulting in social and political inequalities and unequal control over labor, resources, and services. In addition, race, class, and gender are the social factors that most determine a woman's health status and well-being. In concert, these factors affect perceptions of anticipated or real health and illness, kinds and availability of care, access to and modes of care delivery, and interaction with doctors and other health professionals. Race, class, and gender relations also influence the experience of people with AIDS, including community and political reactions, the nature of institutional practice and social control, and the dynamics of social change.[7]

Access to care and services is directly related to ability to pay. In most locales with large numbers of HIV-infected women—among them, New York City, Newark, Baltimore, and Bridgeport, Connecticut—the women most affected are primarily members of racially or ethnically oppressed communities and the poor. Many are also drug users.

> Access to care and services has historically been *marginal* for women with any one of those three criteria. Any two of these . . . essentially put a woman in the *extremely limited* access category. Women with all three of these characteristics fall into the *no access* category.[8]

In addition, access to the care that is available is never certain. In the United States at the present moment, the constitutional right to privacy in matters of abortion is not threatened. However, recent congressional legislation renders any woman who receives government aid a ward of the state who can exercise her constitutional rights only at the state's discretion. Such rights are worthless when the option of abortion is reserved for those who can afford to pay, not necessarily for those who need them most.

In addition to the inequities of the health care system, there are equity gaps in educational opportunities and differential treatment in the legal system in the United States, South Africa, and most developing countries. Many of our contributors attempt to make sense of the ways in which women of color and the white working class struggle against these conditions in managing their lives around AIDS.

The historic experiences of racial and cultural genocide have been, and continue to be, a major concern of women and men in a number of communities. African-American, Puerto Rican, and Native American women in the United States have been subject to racist, coercive, and abusive measures (sterilization, population control, and experimental medical research) over the last hundred years. These, along with slavery, exclusion from citizenship, and loss of land, are not easily forgotten by women or their communities. Though there is certainly variety of opinion about such public health proposals as needle exchange programs and condom use to practice safer sex, many fear that the slow response of the U.S. government to AIDS constitutes another form of genocide. They publicly and actively resist attempts to continue drug use in their communities or limit births.[9]

Finally, the need for alliances across class and race is emphasized by a number of our contributors. Within feminist practice, these coalitions have not come easily. Race and class differences have led to disagreements, alienation, hostility, and separation. In dealing with AIDS, these struggles continue, but the dynamics are dramatically different. It is the experience of women of color and poor women, not white, middle-class women, that must be central to analysis, strategy, and tactics. Still, women of different backgrounds bring different styles and levels of expertise to alliances. To enhance the possibility of coalition, dialogue is needed among HIV-positive women, professional women, and other feminist advocates. Mechanisms for handling internal dissent and for forging alliances that recognize and overcome power differentials are essential.

The *processes of feminist social change* are a crucial third element of women's leadership in the AIDS crisis. These processes begin with a sober examination of the conditions affecting women's lives, including the ideological framing of women. With HIV/AIDS, this has meant viewing women not simply as victims, vectors, or vessels of HIV or solely as recipients of services. Instead, the authors in this volume view women as actors pursuing creative and effective strategies which invariably challenge, even if indirectly, relations of gender inequality and women's enforced passivity. Groups for women with HIV start from the need to honor women and women's place in formal and informal networks and move on to create leaders. Because many women live solitary lives and because the stigma of AIDS sometimes drives them further into solitude, empowerment processes must move to counter women's isolation with community building among women. For HIV-positive women, empowerment begins when they change their ideas about the causes of their powerlessness, when they recognize the systemic forces that oppress them and stop blaming themselves for their situation, and when they begin to act to change the conditions of their lives.

Poor women are often portrayed as unskilled, passive, and uninterested in politics. Like other struggles of poor and working-class women,[10] the political worlds of women affected by the epidemic have been obscured and the activities of white, middle-class women have received most of the attention. In the AIDS epidemic, poor, working-class, and middle-class women are all actively engaged in efforts to change their lives and the institutions that serve them. They engage in what Bookman and Morgen term *empowerment*,[11] a continuum of political activity ranging from acts of individual resistance to mass political mobilizations that threaten the basic power relations of race, gender, class, and sexuality.

The activism discussed in *Women Resisting AIDS* occurs along two dimensions. The first is the struggle for individual and group survival which does not directly challenge structures of oppression. Changing one's sexual relations with male partners to practice safe sex is an example. Here, women use their spheres of influence—at the workplace, in the home, at church, and in other community organizations—to sustain life and foster self-definition and self-direction.[12] Becoming self-directed fosters empowerment. The second kind of activism is the struggle for institutional change, efforts to alter the existing systems of legal, medical, and other oppression.

In most of the chapters, our contributors focus on the practice of social change and leadership. They emphasize effective techniques of self-empowerment and organization, mobilization, and alliance. This emphasis on consciousness and social change, always keeping the issues of culture and class in the forefront of the analysis, results in theoretical and evaluative studies that are situation-specific, grounded, and clearly located in their applicability.

The fourth and final element of our approach to leadership is an *emphasis on women's skills and activities.* These are at the heart of any strategy to fight AIDS. Women do the work of holding families together, caring for the sick, healing the unhappy, dealing with grief, teaching the young. These are the tasks women are socialized to do in their families—as daughters, sisters, and mothers—and in the workplace. In some societies, these are the primary tasks women are permitted to do. In learning to express their gender in and through these activities, women learn the social practice of mothering reflective of their history, race, and class. Although the experience is not the same for everyone, similarities in the responsibility for relationships do exist across vast cultural differences. Women also build networks with other women to accomplish these activities in formal and informal settings, such as in "othermother" roles among African-American women.[13]

Although we come from many race and class backgrounds and a variety of countries, as women we bring to our leadership in activism, caring, research, and teaching a distinctive perspective, one that works differently in practice than one men might use. Our female perspective is not invariant across time and place, nor does our experience of gender lead to a unified view of justice, equality, or nurturing. Women's political consciousness is certainly influenced by their concerns as mothers, but it is also very deeply affected by aspects of gender not rooted in childbearing or family relations— in the experience of being vulnerable, poorly paid workers, in being politically disenfranchised.

How particular women have used their skills to fight AIDS transmission or to do AIDS care reflects their social location and what they have learned in their families, communities, and occupations. Some become leaders of health and social welfare institutions. Others organize through political activity in health and education reform movements or in feminist and women's rights organizations. In the AIDS crisis, women have been challenged more than ever before to share their knowledge, teach leadership, and listen attentively to one another.

A BRIEF EPIDEMIOLOGICAL GUIDE TO AIDS IN WOMEN

When we wrote this introduction in the summer of 1993, the problem of AIDS for women was being examined even more seriously than it had been in the first 12 years of the pandemic. The numbers were frightening, and despite the work of thousands of people over the last decade, with and for HIV-infected women (including the work of the contributors to this volume), many people were just beginning to realize the magnitude of the situation.

In the United States, AIDS is spreading at a faster rate among women than men. During 1990, for example, AIDS cases increased 29 percent among women, compared to 18 percent among men. And there were substantial increases in the number of reports of AIDS in 1993, with the increase for women far greater (151 percent) than for men (105 percent).[14]

By 1993, AIDS was already the leading cause of death for African-American women, ages 15 to 24, in two states, New York and New Jersey, and the third highest cause of death for all women in that age group in those states. AIDS is becoming the fourth leading cause of death for all women in that age group nationwide. There are major HIV epidemics in women who reside in Bridgeport, Brooklyn, Miami, and Baltimore. Epidemiologists expect that, by 1995, there will be more women than gay men diagnosed with AIDS each year in New York State.[15]

For the U.S. cases, AIDS among women is a disease primarily of African Americans and Latinas. African Americans, who constitute 12 percent of the nation's population, are 31 percent of the nation's cases. Overall, Latinos constitute 17 percent of the nation's AIDS cases and are contracting the disease faster than any other ethnic group in the United States. Latino AIDS cases have increased 11 percent between 1991 and 1993. Of women with AIDS, 21 percent are Latina and 53 percent are African-American. In New York State, 53 percent of the women with AIDS are African-American and 30 percent are Latina. Nationally, the rate of deaths among African-American women is nine times greater than among white women.[16]

On a worldwide basis, and within most countries, there are various populations of women with different risks; that is, with different relations to AIDS.[17] Risk is heavily skewed by economic class. Half of the cases among U.S. women are the result of drug injection, an activity highly correlated to poverty. Another 20 percent of the cases have resulted from sexual contact with men who are drug users. However, the more recent the infection, the more likely it will be the result of sexual transmission, not drug use. Sexual relations with men who are bisexual constitute only 3 percent of the total. In most of the world, injection drugs are less of a problem for women, and most women are infected through heterosexual contact with their husbands or partners or with customers in the sex industries. In certain African cities, over 20 percent of childbearing women are HIV-infected;[18] in several towns in India, HIV infection rates continue to escalate wildly. In Thailand, there is an epidemic of AIDS among the women who provide sexual services to the large tourist trade. In Mexico since 1984, the ratio of HIV infection in men compared with women has decreased from 25:1 to 4:1 in 1990.

Most medical attention to women in the epidemic has actually been on pregnant women and pediatric AIDS cases. There is virtually nothing known medically about AIDS in nonpregnant women. Until recently, U.S. women have not been included in clinical trials. And many of the opportunistic infections associated with HIV in women, such as invasive cervical cancer and pulmonary tuberculosis, became part of the U.S. Centers for Disease Control "official" definition of AIDS only in 1993. As medical practitioners, Mitchell et al. note that there are no answers for a variety of important questions: Does the natural history of the disease differ in women and in men? How, if at all, does HIV infection affect female reproductive organs and endocrine function?[19] What is a normal T-cell count? Why is cervical cancer associated with poverty? What are the effects of pregnancy on the development of HIV disease? These questions could be answered if women were considered important in their own right and if countries outside the United States with sizable numbers of cases could afford to support the research required to get at these answers.

In sum, the impact of the epidemic on women is "increasing dramatically."[20] The data on the natural history of HIV in women is minimal. Throughout the world, women are grossly underrepresented in research programs and clinical trials.

RATIONALE FOR THE CHAPTER ORGANIZATION

We have organized this book into four sections focusing on unique aspects of the work that is necessary in confronting AIDS: describing the problem, preventing transmission, organizing for social change, and anticipating issues and developing social policy for the future. Each author, no matter what her particular approach, training, or location, touches on at least some of the elements in a feminist approach to leadership that we have identified as crucial to making sense of women's relationship to HIV/AIDS.

Any effort to understand the education and social change practices of women dealing with AIDS must address the particular challenges and constraints of unique cultures and societies. The contributors to Part I, "Women Confront the Problem of AIDS," examine a variety of the most complicated dilemmas and institutional practices confronting any effort to improve women's capacities to respond to AIDS. Collectively, their focus is on those institutions and historical and cultural contexts that make women's HIV prevention and survival so problematic. Particularly important here are principles and interpretations of law that systematically disadvantage women, either by treating women differently by exclusion or coercion; schooling that systematically narrows options for women; and, of course, equity gaps in basic medical services in both industrializing countries and segments of the industrialized countries. One example is the government neglect of social services during the Reagan/Bush administrations which heightened income and resource gaps and further marginalized segments of already-oppressed groups, with severe consequences for women now dealing with AIDS in major U.S. cities.

Of particular importance to the authors of this part, as well as elsewhere in this book, are the effects of (1) traditional patriarchal relations; (2) socialization to femininity and heterosexuality; and (3) group experiences with racial genocide. Several authors are specifically concerned about potentially coercive or genocidal measures that have been proposed to deal with HIV infection and women's reproductive capacities.

Gender relations are central to women's vulnerability, dependence, limited resources, and limited power. An analysis of the multiple interlocking effects of the social relations of race, gender, and class on women dealing with AIDS make clear that women need methods of protecting themselves, access to materials they are frequently denied, and integration into policy development. Women facing AIDS are confronting further discrimination, marginalization, isolation, and poverty. Indeed, poverty is, as Hunter notes in her chapter, the major access problem for women.

Part I begins with Eka Esu-Williams, president of the Society for Women and AIDS in Africa (SWAA) and a member of the Steering Committee of the Global AIDS Policy Coalition. In "AIDS in the 1990s: Individual and Collective Responsibility," initially presented as the keynote address of the 8th International Conference on AIDS (Amsterdam, 1992), Esu-Williams conveys her observations about the growing pandemic and women's roles on behalf of themselves and others in Africa and elsewhere in the Third World. She argues that AIDS has changed women's consciousness of their own situation and gender inequality. Since recognizing the necessity of providing prevention targeted to women, the African women who founded SWAA in 1988 came to understand that numerous social, cultural, and economic factors made women vulnerable to HIV infection and limited women's participation in AIDS work. Esu-Williams provides an important discussion of the interplay of socioeconomic and cultural contexts that shapes women's vulnerability and defines the arenas in which women bear the burden of dealing with AIDS. She is the first of many contributors to link the difficulties of dealing with AIDS to economic change and crisis in Africa and globally.

In "Complications of Gender: Women, AIDS, and the Law," Nan Hunter brings a lawyer's perspective to five critical areas in which legal and policy issues are "gender-linked." She examines prevention, access to health care, decision making related to pregnancy, ramifications of testing newborns, and decisions related to parenting. She demonstrates the ways in which legal concepts and practice historically shape our understanding of women and specifically frame the nature of this disease. According to Hunter, the most contentious of these areas surrounds the issue of whether the state can coerce a pregnant woman to abort in order to reduce the number of children born HIV-positive. Hunter discusses the legal rationales that have been or could be used to justify such actions.

Diane Lewis's contribution on African-American women ("African-American Women at Risk: Notes on the Sociocultural Context of HIV Infection") draws on life history research with women drug injectors and challenges myths about African-American women's sexuality. In so doing, she articulates a set of structural and cultural conditions that shape the risky world in which these women live. She argues that poverty and a shortage of men are crucial factors for these women. More specifically, the context of risk for these women includes the pervasiveness of drugs, the integration (rather than rejection) of people in trouble into the community, and the likelihood of sex with a bisexual African-American man. Acutely aware that these conditions exist within a larger context, Lewis develops a criticism of the federal government's slow response to the crisis in African-American communities and touches on the related fear of genocide, a fear pervasive in African-American politics which has raised community suspicion concerning needle exchange and condom use programs.

Historically, epidemics generate calls to legislate and control the problem and its purported perpetrators. In response, the state can take a number of approaches. In "Social Control, Civil Liberties, and Women's Sexuality," Beth Schneider and Valerie Jenness argue that public policy responses to AIDS are structured by gender and sexuality and conversely that policy initiatives may regulate the social organization of gender and sexuality. They illustrate their argument by focusing on public policy for prostitution and sex education for young women. Demonstrating different strategies of social control of legal and educational institutions, the authors seek to show certain contradictions and complexities in policy. For example, although prostitutes are always the target of repressive legislation and treated as criminals, they are also treated as allies of the state in AIDS prevention. Young women's needs are ignored as schools struggle with conservative and religious groups from the New Right or Traditional Values Coalition over the right to offer programs—despite the fact that many HIV prevention programs offered to them are censored, narrow efforts which systematically reinforce heterosexuality and ignore sexual pleasure.

Part II, "Women and the Problems of HIV Prevention," considers the complexities of five HIV prevention efforts with distinctly different women. Collectively, these pieces document how HIV interventions work when they are culturally specific and gender appropriate. The case studies in Part II pay particular attention to the processes of empowerment and politicization. Women's consciousness of their oppression, and their motivation to change the conditions under which they live, are shaped by a complex set of social relations, some of which are highlighted by the emergency of dealing with AIDS. The cases make clear that the development of this consciousness is neither a linear process nor an automatic response to oppression.

Priscilla Alexander's essay, "Sex Workers Fight Against AIDS: An International Perspective," offers a detailed analysis of the prevention of HIV/AIDS among sex workers worldwide. Based on her 17 years of research and writing on the international prostitutes' rights movement, Alexander explains the community-based, HIV-focused organizing model, which places prostitutes at the center of their own education and emphasizes change in normative sexual practices. This model, in contrast to the state's traditional efforts to control sexually transmitted diseases, strengthens prostitutes' abilities to protect themselves. Here, the process of empowerment begins with concern with HIV but moves to larger issues in these women's lives, such as police harassment and access to responsive health care services.

Unlike the prostitutes described by Alexander, many other women are more isolated. For example, writing about the wives of hemophiliacs, Cathy Greenblat ("Women in Families with Hemophilia and HIV") provides a badly needed contribution for service providers who work not only with these women but also with other wives of men with AIDS. Her work identifies their social isolation and describes a program targeted to deal with it and other problems these women confront. The ENCOUNTERS Simulation Approach (used in Canada and the United States by the Women's Outreach Network of the National Hemophilia Foundation) is based on a model of active learning to deal with sensitive topics, such as sex, death, and discrimination. In groups of five, women help each other experiment with situations dealing with family, friends, health providers, and the HIV-infected partner. The groups' activities are structured to recognize that women are at the hub of networks of relationships in which they might alternately advise, act, react, and observe.

Adolescence is fast becoming associated with serious risk of HIV infection. However, as Schneider and Jenness note, when programs are planned for adolescents, whether in high school or college, they are typically one-shot affairs, extending over an hour or two, with no follow-up. Barbara Sosnowitz writes about a different kind of effort. In "AIDS Prevention, Minority Women, and Gender Assertiveness," she describes in detail the resistance to dealing with AIDS that young people from Latino and African-American communities bring to such a program. She then outlines an 11-week, interactive approach used in a urban college classroom with young women who are Puerto Rican, African American, and Asian American. The approach is aimed at personalizing risk and empowering the women in two ways: by altering norms of public discourse about sex and by teaching skills for negotiation of interpersonal relations.

In South Africa and other places in the industrializing world, the possibility of infection among adolescents is greater than in the urban United States.

Ntombifuthi Mtshali ("Transferability of American AIDS Prevention Models to South African Youth") argues that the Africans in South Africa can design their own strategies for dealing with AIDS through a combination of traditional ways of educating and caregiving and modern techniques borrowed from abroad. With grandparents no longer available to provide the culturally prescribed sex education, Mtshali recommends a generational role change in the culture—educating parents to do the sex talk with their own children that was traditionally forbidden to them. In addition, she proposes that indigenous healers be provided training in AIDS prevention education and that traditional support systems be utilized to look after people who are sick, the latter in a manner very much like homecare in the United States.

The nuts and bolts of prevention require careful attention to the rituals and rhythms of a community. Education, particularly for poor women, is often most effective when located in their neighborhoods, sometimes even on the street. In "Constructing the Outreach Moment: Street Interventions to Women at Risk," Cathy Reback tells readers what outreach workers actually do and how they manage interactions with clients. Using the words of six outreach workers with whom she worked (three Latinas and three African Americans), she explores the symbolic factors in developing trust with women at high risk for HIV infection through drug use or sex. Reback describes and analyzes how continuity in the field, knowledge of gatekeepers, up-to-date referrals, shared personal experiences, and gift giving facilitate the process of identification and make effective HIV prevention education possible, even on street corners. She argues that no real change is likely without this identification between outreach worker and client, and that no effort to empower, to provide tools for the woman to reach her goals, will occur without the trust built through interactions.

Part III, "Women Organize AIDS Care and Foster Social Change," begins with chapters by three grassroots organizers and continues with essays on what we are loosely calling "professional activism." The projects and dilemmas discussed by these authors recognize the complex and often contradictory interplay between women's oppression and women's activism.

As Shaw documents in her analysis of community organizing efforts, the course of mobilization for women and racial/ethnic populations in the United States differed from that for the gay community, given aggregate differences in wealth, political power, and ability to marshal other resources and allies.[21] Nevertheless, organizing of and by HIV-positive women occurred in the 1980s throughout the United States, as well as in an increasing number of countries in Africa and Latin America. Efforts in Asia are more recent. In a recent survey of the AIDS service organizations in developing countries, almost all had been organized by women, usually those with health, education, or social service background, and often to help others, not themselves.[22] In the United States and many European countries, women constitute a segment of the leadership of AIDS activism, including ACT-UP, as well as of community organizations, health and human services, and AIDS service organizations.

As this suggests, organizing and care provision can occur in many contexts. These chapters do not cover every aspect of the informal caregiving women do, efforts such as those by U.S. "mothers of people with AIDS (PWAS)," the work of religious orders that care for orphans, grandparents in Mexican-American families who feel responsible for their grandchildren, or volunteers in AIDS service organizations (ASOs). Informal caregivers, kinship systems, and natural neighbors are the prime sources of help available to poor people in distress. Women provide care and mobilization both as part of their paid employment and as unpaid labor. A crucial component of the breakdown of isolation and political powerlessness among women working with AIDS or HIV-infected women is the support these women give one another. Most of the organizers in this part aim for HIV/AIDS work and mobilization spearheaded by the most affected women themselves.

Questions of mobilization and organization are central to some of the contributions in both Part II and Part III. No matter who is being organized—women who partner with women in New York, female drug users, heads of household, prostitutes, or nurses—some important personal and political issues are constants. Repeatedly, our contributors emphasize the need for identification and empathy. Empowerment and empowerment strategies are seen as integral aspects of the prevention and organizing work described by Alexander, Reback, Denison, Schoepf, and Sosnowitz. Although each author discusses women in different cities or countries, the process of empowerment seems similar. Most try to grapple with the problem of difference within the population described; they particularly emphasize the need to recognize that HIV-positive women participate in multiple communities.

Throughout the epidemic, HIV-infected individuals have discovered that the AIDS programs or organizations that existed in their cities or towns did not meet their needs. This was a common experience for women everywhere. For many, the discovery of a lack of place isolated them further from support they knew they needed. Rebecca Denison was one of these women. In "Call Us Survivors! Women Organized to Respond to Life-Threatening Diseases (WORLD)," she describes the process of identifying her own need in San Francisco, where support groups did not seem to exist for an HIV-positive woman not in recovery, or for a lesbian, or for women diagnosed with AIDS. Denison organized one, WORLD, a group of HIV-positive women from around the country, who now receive a newsletter and meet when they can. She describes a retreat in which 30 of these women confronted their own diversity and developed skills to return to their communities as speakers, group leaders, and educators. These empowerment processes involved turning feelings of victimization into feelings of control and moving from isolation to identification with other women as a survival strategy.

The interview with Gloria Lockett ("CAL-PEP: The Struggle to Survive") complements the themes developed in the chapters of Schneider and Jenness and Alexander with an understanding of how prostitutes organized themselves in major cities in the United States—forming alliances, making compromises, and accumulating successes.

The complications of organizing are made abundantly clear in "Lesbian Denial and Lesbian Leadership in the AIDS Epidemic." Here, Amber Hollibaugh is concerned with the denial and resistance to acknowledging AIDS as a health risk for lesbians. Hollibaugh recognizes that a population of women who have sex with women and who are HIV-positive have had to struggle against racism within lesbian communities and against racism and sexism within gay men's groups and AIDS service organizations. HIV-positive lesbians challenge the notions of unity and sisterhood integral to most lesbian communities, since most HIV-positive women who have sex with women are neither middle class nor white. The Lesbian AIDS Project, of which Hollibaugh is the director, aims to end denial of the "lesbian problem," to identify the services needed for women who partner with women, and to include lesbians at all levels of health, young people, women, people of color, and AIDS organizations. Hollibaugh wants to build an HIV-survival movement of women who partner with women from working-class neighborhoods and communities of color.

The lack of recognition of the AIDS problem for any women is the starting point for Moher Downing's "Some Comments on the Beginnings of AIDS Outreach to Women Drug Users in San Francisco." Downing shows how the early processes of defining persons with AIDS excluded women and impeded the struggles of women health educators, researchers, and organizers to deliver AIDS prevention. She notes that only in New York and San Francisco were drug users interviewed about the specifics of their sexual and drug histories early in the epidemic and that traditional drug clinics found such interest bizarre. A large-scale ethnographic research project on injection drug users (IDUs) in which Downing was involved, though not initially designed to educate, did offer considerable information to people who were not otherwise receiving AIDS prevention and thus provided the opportunity for IDUs to think about and do something about their exposure. Downing wonders with the reader about the ethics of bringing AIDS prevention messages to women who do not have the resources to actually change their lives. Finally, she illustrates how coalitions of which she was a part early in the epidemic were limited by race, class, and gender conflict.

Brooke Grundfest Schoepf is another researcher engaged in a massive project, one outcome of which was the organization of groups of women in Kinshasa, Zaïre, to provide AIDS education for themselves and others. In five years of ethnographic research on the unfolding of the epidemic, CONNAISSADA, a transdisciplinary medical anthropology project, gained valuable knowledge of the "pluralistic" nature of the sexual cultures of the country and provided a program in which researchers talked about AIDS and gave biomedical information to groups. Many of these women were illiterate or without any access to mass communication. This action-research model is similar to those used by Sosnowitz and Greenblat in its dependence on oral learning, its focus on moving from what women know to problem solving, and its outcome of enhanced autonomy and power. The first participants were sex workers. These prostitutes, whose new knowledge gained them status in the community, were trained to transmit their education to other women in a society in which most are at risk due to economic disruption and the existence of a variety of multiple-partner arrangements. They then educated churchwomen. Schoepf notes that the groups' performances and discussions involved women in changing their culture. They themselves change through the demonstration of their power and powerlessness.

The last two chapters in this part focus on the organizers/providers and their motivations, problems, and pleasures. In "Lesbian Involvement in the AIDS Epidemic: Changing Roles and Generational Differences," Nancy Stoller delineates four perspectives lesbians in North America take in decisions about whether and how to make AIDS a priority. Unlike Hollibaugh, whose perspective was HIV-infected women, Stoller looks at activists and organizers within the lesbian community who are very much involved in doing AIDS work. She finds differences in motivation for involvement among the lesbians, due in part to some combination of their specific feminist perspective, their relationships to gay men, their occupation, and their age. She compares the beliefs and practices among four groupings of lesbians: those who feel they, as lesbians, have a distinct contribution to make; those who want women to get recognition and equal treatment from AIDS organizations; those who unite with gay men to put forward a wide-ranging social agenda around health care and lesbian and gay rights; and those who eventually reject AIDS work as a lesbian priority.

Nurses are at the forefront of the medical struggle to provide AIDS care in hospitals, hospices, clinics, and homes. Marcy Fraser and Diane Jones, each in AIDS nursing for more than ten years, gathered 25 nurses together to brainstorm for the chapter "Nurses and HIV." They identify two major problems in the changing nature of their work. First is the need to come to grips with the risks to themselves in patient care. Second is the need to rethink their approach as the patient population changes from gay men to poor people, so as not to be seen as "an accomplice to an unjust system" by those who have been effectively abused and neglected by the medical and legal systems. Of special note is the extreme pleasure expressed by all these women, who find the work emotionally compelling and a challenge to their nursing skills. They enjoy acting as "bridges" for their patients to doctors, parents, and lovers.

In Part IV, "Problems and Policies for Women in the Future," our contributors examine some systemic ethical and political issues which will cause trouble for women with HIV/AIDS, activists, and policy makers for the rest of the decade. Each author takes the position that AIDS is a symptom of larger problems in the global economy and in the relationships of gender and race.

Helen Rodriguez-Trias and Carola Marte tackle the health care system in the United States in their chapter "Challenges and Possibilities: Women, HIV, and the Health Care System in the 1990s." They argue that the system is not adequate to meet the needs of HIV-infected women and that advocates for women with HIV must also be advocates for radical change in the health care system. The numerous deficiencies of the health care system in costs, waste, fragmentation, maldistribution of services, and uneven quality of care are barriers for most of the poor and certainly for HIV-infected women. Within this generally problematic framework, the authors outline seven problems specific to women. One example is the fragmentation of services that separates ob/gyn care from other medical services, forcing women either to get insufficient care or to travel from place to place, doctor to doctor. Rodriguez-Trias and Marte describe the work of the comprehensive AIDS care clinic in Chicago, the first of its kind, which offers a solution to this particular problem. One particularly troubling development they identify is "AIDS exceptionalism," which provides exceptional care to people with AIDS but does not offer equivalent care to uninfected people in the same community. To grapple with these and other problems, the authors suggest the development of strong women's peer organizations for HIV-infected women, following models that already exist in New York and Atlanta; the continuation of networks; and the development of new coalitions.

The chapter by Cheri Pies further develops an issue that Rodriguez-Trias and Marte view as unique to women's health in this epidemic. "AIDS, Ethics, Reproductive Rights: No Easy Answers" attempts to weigh the wide range of views among feminists and public health officials regarding the reproductive choices of HIV-infected women. Criticizing public health officials for putting forward a model of the "logical woman" and for their assumption of a "universal woman" with only one way of thinking, Pies outlines the continuing controversy between those who lean toward counseling HIV-infected women to abort, even against their wishes, and those who want these women to make their own choices and control their own bodies. Pies carefully sets forth the various ethical discussions of professionals as well as the moral calculus women must use to make such decisions.

By the year 2000, 90 percent of the world's AIDS cases will be traceable to either heterosexual transmission or the sharing of infected needles. Mabel Bianco, a physician and public health expert, speaks for the developing countries in her chapter, "How AIDS Changes Development Priorities." She is concerned with the consequences of AIDS in the next decades—the economic ramifications of a disease that strikes the reproductive and productive young, the spiraling effects of poverty, the deterioration of health care services, the gap between more and less privileged nations—and proposes a reconsideration of development models that have been based primarily on individual economic gain and consumption. Bianco calls for a more equitable distribution of resources, including "the socialization of power," so that, among other things, women will become participants in decision making at local and national levels.

In sum, the conditions of women's lives in the tight interaction of economy, polity, and culture function as a highly effective system of social control designed to keep women in subordinate conditions and alienated from their own beliefs and sexuality. At the same time, all cultures contain contradictory elements that foster both compliance with and resistance to their oppression. Given the pervasiveness of poverty and despair, racism and sexism in the everyday lives of most women with HIV infection, it should not be surprising that their attempts to deal with AIDS foster innovative methods and approaches to political organizing. Although the changes to individual women's lives may seem small, collective action to deal with AIDS has yielded impressive achievements. It is our hope that the lessons from these initial efforts will provide the raw materials from which still more successful HIV prevention and AIDS services may be fashioned by and for women throughout the world.

A WORD ON AIDS TERMINOLOGY

Many of our authors have been involved with some aspect of AIDS for at least a decade. In that time, most have become quite fluent in AIDS lingo. This is no small matter, since the words used to describe the disease and related public health matters change often. Lest we confuse our readers unduly, we have selected terminology for this volume that reflects some of the most recent thinking about categories and concepts. And we have chosen to shorten the text by allowing certain abbreviations that arise regularly in writing about AIDS. Among those most often used are human immunodeficiency virus (HIV); community health outreach worker (CHOW); Centers for Disease Control (CDC); sexually transmitted diseases (STD); injection drug users (IDU), once known as intravenous drug user (IVDU); and, of course, people with AIDS (PWA). Finally, we have asked our authors to use *Latino* instead of *Hispanic*, except when the author is discussing a specific nationality or ethnicity.

ACKNOWLEDGMENTS

This book was not done in isolation. *Women Resisting AIDS* is an outgrowth of the editors' separate but overlapping experiences working with AIDS. Nancy Stoller, now Professor of Community Studies at the University of California, Santa Cruz, worked for four years as the coordinator of women's programs of the San Francisco AIDS Foundation and supervisor of educational materials development and distribution. At the foundation and in her association with the Women's AIDS Network, she met an extraordinary number of women who worked in many different capacities on the problem of AIDS. Her current research, which focuses on multiple approaches to political organizing in the AIDS crisis, underscores the complex political activity around HIV. She is an expert in the sociology of women's health issues and on the specific concerns of women in prison. Beth E. Schneider, Professor of Sociology and Women's Studies at the University of California, Santa Barbara, views AIDS from a more rural and much less politically organized context than San Francisco, one which has framed much of her research and political work on AIDS. Schneider served for four years as the President of the Board of Directors of the Gay and Lesbian Resource Center, the parent organization for the AIDS Counseling and Assistance Program, the only AIDS service assistance program in her county. She is an expert on sexuality and gender and has written research papers on AIDS organizing in small cities and towns, lesbians' relationship to the epidemic, and the process by which school systems try to control controversy when introducing AIDS education to their students.

The editors' names appear on the book in alphabetical order. They consider their contributions to the overall project equivalent. The conception of the book was Nancy's. She also had most of the connections with the authors. Each editor contributed her own chapter and worked with the authors through initial drafts. Beth worked with most of the authors in the final stages of their documents, drafted the Introduction, and worked with the copy editor. Nancy worked with the manuscript preparation crew on her campus. In the past two years, they made virtually every decision about final content and format together.

Nancy Stoller wishes to thank her research assistants, Wendy Chapkis, Christine Wong, and Kristy Bright, for many hours of organizational work; Wendy Chapkis for editing as well; the University of California, Santa Cruz, Academic Senate for research grants that helped support this project; the UCSC Word Processing Center, especially Zoe Sodja, for editing and manuscript preparation; members of the "Four Tops" study group (Estelle Freedman, Allan Berube, and John D'Emilio) and the participants in the Rancho Sante Fe Conference for their supportive critique of her work; Melessa Hemler for clerical assistance; Cheri Pies and Gwendolyn Shaw for moral support.

Beth Schneider also wishes to thank Wendy Chapkis and Zoe Sodja. At the University of California, Santa Barbara, she wishes to thank her Academic Senate for grants in support of her research; her colleagues Sarah Fenstermaker, Avery Gordon, and Denise Segura for intellectual support; her research assistants, Franci Montell, Alison Streit, Darcie Vandergrift, and Susan Dalton, for doing what needed to be done; Valerie Jenness for moving from research assistant to colleague with a minimum of trouble and for always reminding her it is possible to "clear off your desk"; Martin P. Levine, who until weeks before his death, generated new ways to contribute to the study of AIDS; Rhonda Levine for her help in naming the book, and her love, patience, and consistent encouragement over the years.

Both editors are indebted to Sheryl Ruzek for her faith in our project and her editing advice; to our contributing authors for their insights and time in preparing this volume of original work; and to the Internet for enabling us to communicate day and night.

NOTES

[1]WHO estimates were reported by Sheryl Stolberg, "AIDS Cases Could Triple by 2000, Meeting Is Told," *Los Angeles Times*, 8 June 1993, p. A7. These figures increased from 33 percent three years ago.

[2]Janet Henshall Momsen, *Women and Development in the Third World* (London: Routledge, 1991).

[3]Patricia Hill Collins, *Black Feminist Thought: Knowledge, Consciousness, and the Politics of Empowerment* (New York: Routledge, 1990), 10.

[4]Jeff O'Malley, "AIDS Service Organizations in Transition," in *AIDS in the World: A Global Report*, ed. Jonathan Mann, Daniel J. M. Tarantola, and Thomas W. Netter (Cambridge, MA: Harvard University Press, 1992), 774–787.

[5]Cynthia Enloe, *Bananas, Beaches, and Bases: Making Feminist Sense of International Politics* (Berkeley: University of California Press, 1989).

[6]Ibid.

[7]Beth E. Schneider, "AIDS and Class, Gender and Race Relations," in *The Social Context of AIDS*, ed. J. Huber and B. E. Schneider (Newbury Park, CA: Sage, 1992).

[8]Janet L. Mitchell, John Tucker, Patricia O. Loftman, and Sterling B. Williams, "HIV and Women: Current Controversies and Clinical Relevance," *Journal of Women's Health 1*, no. 1:(1992): 35–39.

[9]Harlon Dalton, "AIDS in Blackface," in N. McKenzie (ed.), *The AIDS Reader: Social, Political, Ethical Issues* (New York: Meridan Books, 1991).

[10]Ann Bookman and Sandra Morgen, eds., *Women and the Politics of Empowerment* (Philadelphia: Temple University Press, 1988).

[11]Ibid.

[12]Collins, *Black Feminist Thought*.

[13]Ibid.

[14]Lawrence K. Altman, "Cases of AIDS Increase Among Heterosexuals," *New York Times* (11 March, 1994): p. A8.

[15]Susan Y. Chu, James W. Buehler, and Ruth L. Berkelman, "Impact of the Human Immunodeficiency Virus Epidemic on Mortality in Women of Reproductive Age, United States," *Journal of The American Medical Association* 264(2):225–229.

[16]United States Centers for Disease Control and Prevention, "HIV/AIDS Surveillance Report" (U.S. AIDS Cases Reported Through September 1993), October 1993 (Vol-

ume 5, No. 3), United States Department of Health & Human Services, Public Health Services, Atlanta, GA.

[17]For a more detailed description of the worldwide demographic picture, see Mann, Tarantola, and Netter, eds., *AIDS in the World*.

[18]See Tony Barnett and Piers Blaikie, *AIDS in Africa*, (New York: Guilford Press, 1992); and Mann, Tarantola, and Netter, eds., *AIDS in the World*.

[19]Mitchell, et al., "HIV and Women."

[20]Mann, Tarantola, and Netter.

[21]Nancy Stoller Shaw, "Preventing AIDS Among Women: The Role of Community Organizing," *Socialist Review* 18 (1988): 76–92.

[22]O'Malley, "AIDS Service Organizations in Transition."

PART I

Women Confront the Problem of AIDS

Eka Esu-Williams

AIDS In the 1990s: Individual and Collective Responsibility

everal years ago, during one of the first seminars on AIDS in Nigeria, a group of health policy experts met to discuss the implications of this new and troubling pandemic. Following a long discussion about whether there was indeed cause for concern and what needed to be done, particularly in terms of prevention, a woman stood up to ask how she could get her husband, whom she knew had other sexual partners, to use a condom. Her question shocked or embarrassed everyone in the room. What happened? Everyone fell silent. No one was ready to pursue the question or provide an answer, and the next question was promptly taken.

That was not the end of it, however. During a break, this same desperate woman approached other women to find out what she should or could do. Again, stony silence. She found it impossible to start a discussion about this subject, even among the women there. No one appreciated the importance of the question in addressing HIV/AIDS.

The fact that this woman, desperate to protect herself and fearful of AIDS, never got an answer from the assembled experts has haunted me ever since. And, years afterward, I am afraid that this situation has not changed. Today, AIDS is forcing questions both old and new from people who fear for the future and lack the power to protect themselves. Questions are being asked by both women and men, persons with HIV/AIDS, the urban poor, gay and bisexual men and women, injection drug users, young people, older people, nearly everyone. They ask: Why is HIV/AIDS still not under control? When will an effective prevention method for women become available? How can behavior change be sustained? Why are persons with HIV/AIDS still highly stigmatized and discriminated against and their rights violated? Can the cost

This paper was originally presented as the keynote address at the 8th International Conference on AIDS/3rd STD World Congress, Amsterdam, The Netherlands, July 19–24, 1992. Three sources were particularly useful in its preparation: Jonathan M. Mann, Daniel J. M. Tarantola, and Thomas W. Netter, eds., *AIDS in the World: The Global AIDS Policy Coalition* (Cambridge, Mass.: Harvard University Press, 1992); World Health Organization, *AIDS Prevention Does Work*, Press Release WHO/44, 22 June 1992; United Nations Development Program, *Human Development Report 1992* (New York: Oxford University Press, 1992).

23

of treatment and care for AIDS be within the reach of patients? Will a vaccine or cure for AIDS be available, and will the poorer nations be able to afford it? Will AIDS orphans and widows be supported, and will communities devastated by the epidemic be rehabilitated? Can a true global response be fostered to face HIV/AIDS? As the pandemic worsens, questions are being asked with greater frequency, by more and more people. Yet we still do not have satisfactory answers.

No matter whether we live in a traditional or a modern society, AIDS threatens us, tests our abilities to answer the basic questions it poses for our lives. Although in many parts of the world today the changed political climate of the 1990s has reduced insecurity about possible nuclear war, AIDS is bringing about personal and collective vulnerability. This vulnerability stems from the rapidly progressing force of the pandemic and a receding, weakening global response. More than ten years after the discovery of AIDS, while there are many good people doing excellent work, many others are getting burnt out and fearful. How, after all our efforts, after all the tragedy and sorrow, can the sense of urgency be maintained? Will AIDS wear us down, or will we renew our resolve to find solutions to the many questions still unanswered? For many of us, surviving the era of AIDS will hinge on our own personal power. But, for many of us, finding the key to defending ourselves against AIDS is a daunting task. Although we know what needs to be done, our vulnerability to AIDS is being increased by societal inequity, discrimination, and indifference, undermining the power of knowledge that we already possess. AIDS heightens our awareness of gender inequity; we know that women, especially in the developing world, bear the burden of care, of increasing infection rates, of the growing magnitude of perinatal transmission, and of intensified social and economic problems, such as stigmatization, abandonment, loss of property, and loss of income source. This inequity is rooted both in the history of our gender and in society's attitudes and inconsistencies. In AIDS research, the concept of involving women is only recently coming into focus as a priority, and women have hardly been placed in key AIDS program and policy positions. Our actions and decisions have denied us a valuable opportunity to use our knowledge to prevent the spread of HIV and to cope with its impact, and in fact have increased our vulnerability and powerlessness.

Today, we ask ourselves what is new since the 7th International Conference on AIDS in 1991. We have heard about some major advances; some drugs have been approved for limited use; there have been announcements about community and targeted intervention programs that have worked; there have been new initiatives—more United Nations agencies and other donor organizations are taking an active interest in AIDS; an international donor initiative to support community-based groups and nongovernment organizations (NGOs) is in progress; the Harvard-based Global AIDS Policy Coalition has been formed to work independently on AIDS; the U.S.

Congress recently organized a forum to hear from field workers, experts, and donors about the scope of the global pandemic. These are welcome developments and should be applauded.

But there are other realities which are not so comforting. For instance, therapeutics available elsewhere are still unavailable in most of the developing world. Unsafe blood is still being transfused in these countries, even though an HIV antibody test has existed for more than five years. There is so little being spent on prevention and care in the developing world, where 80 percent of the global total of those infected with HIV live. Why are persons with HIV not in the forefront of program plans to address the pandemic? What creates the disharmony, lack of coordination, and territorial conflicts among international agencies and governmental and nongovernmental bodies dealing with the HIV/AIDS pandemic? Within the background of these inequities, inconsistencies, and deficient response, let us consider the extent of the pandemic. What is the global picture of the impact of HIV/AIDS?

IMPACT: THE GROWING HIV/AIDS PANDEMIC

Although many communities are deploying impressive preventive and care efforts, the HIV/AIDS pandemic continues to grow and intensify. The pandemic remains a highly dynamic and devastating one. The spread of HIV has not abated in any community or country. For instance, in just five years, the cumulative number of HIV-infected Africans has tripled to over 7.5 million. In the United States, at least 40,000 to 80,000 new HIV infections are anticipated during 1992; in 1991, more than 75,000 new HIV infections occurred in Europe; worldwide, over 1 million children have been born with HIV infection.

HIV/AIDS has not confined itself to places where it was first noted. It is now reported from areas which, until now, had been relatively untouched. It is spreading to new communities and countries around the world, often with greater speed than it did in the initial phase. Thailand, Burma, and India are now being confronted with a large-scale epidemic. The global implications are clear: during the next decade, HIV/AIDS will likely reach most communities around the world. Clearly, rather than providing us with protection, geographic boundaries have showed us how vulnerable all peoples and countries are to HIV/AIDS.

Furthermore, the pandemic is manifesting itself in more complex ways. The global pandemic is composed of many separate and linked community epidemics. In the metropolitan areas affected, the pandemic now contains several subepidemics of HIV going on at the same time—such as in injection drug users, sex workers, gay and bisexual men, street children, migrant laborers, and infants under five. Each of these subepidemics needs to be recognized and approached with specific interventions. In parallel with these subepidemics, HIV is spreading steadily among other sexually active adult heterosexuals. The pandemic evolves over time: in Brazil, the proportion of HIV infections linked with injection drug use has increased over tenfold since the early 1980s; in the Caribbean, heterosexual transmission is now replacing sex between men as the major mode of HIV spread.

Heterosexual transmission now accounts for two in every three HIV infections, and thus the impact of the pandemic on women is increasing dramatically. Worldwide, the proportion of HIV-infected adults who are women has been rising steadily and is now 40 percent.

Nevertheless, the pandemic's major global impact is yet to be seen. During the period 1992–1995 alone, the number of people expected to develop AIDS—3.8 million—will exceed the total number of persons who have had AIDS over the last ten years. The number of children orphaned by AIDS will double in the next three years, from approximately 1.8 million today to 3.7 million by 1995. By 1995, an *additional* 5.7 million adults will become infected with HIV, a 50 percent increase from the number in 1992. During the same period, the number of children infected with HIV will also double, from 1.1 million to an estimated 2.3 million.

The World Health Organization projects that, by the year 2000, 30 to 40 million people will be HIV-infected, while the Global AIDS Policy Coalition puts the number at between 40 to 110 million adults and over 10 million children. These disturbing projections underscore the need to review our response to the pandemic during the past decade.

VULNERABILITY

To look into the future we must first ask why we have made so little impact and why we remain highly vulnerable to this pandemic. We can describe with confidence many of the biological determinants of the epidemic. We have already solved many of the mysteries of how HIV is and is not transmitted, and we are making progress to improve diagnostics. An increasing understanding of the role of STDs as a cofactor in HIV transmission is reflected in the fact that the 8th International Conference on AIDS in July 1992 was the first international meeting to integrate the World STD Congress with the International AIDS Conference.

But we all know that biology alone does not explain why women are being infected at a much younger age than men across Africa, and why, despite being infected, some women choose to have children. It does not explain why women are more likely than men to sell their bodies for money or why many women are unable to leave relationships in which the risk of becoming HIV-infected is a reality. Biology does not explain why men often prefer unprotected intercourse and are more likely to engage in multiple relationships. Also, while HIV infection has declined in well-established gay communities, it continues to rise among more isolated men who have sex with men. All these are not outcomes of biological investigations. We also know that, among relatively unaffected nations and communities, the poor and the marginalized are much more likely to face explosive epidemics than the well established and the well-to-do, but once again, this insight does not come from biomedical science.

At a biological level, all people are vulnerable to HIV infection if exposed to the virus through sexual intercourse or through blood. This biological vulnerability interacts with fundamental behavioral determinants: visible, specific, and concrete risk behaviors. But beyond these two common denominators of biology and behavior lie the forces, factors, and influences that will diminish, sustain, or accelerate the progress of the HIV pandemic throughout the world.

Donors, researchers, program implementers, and policy makers have paid too little attention to the socioeconomic determinants of the HIV/AIDS pandemic. Studies were presented in a plenary session at the 7th International Conference on AIDS describing the epidemiological implications of rural to urban migration in Kenya, older men's increasing preference for young girls, the increased mortality rates of uninfected children born to infected mothers, and the poverty of young women. The presentations were provocative and provided useful illustrations of the issues; they challenged us to investigate further and to develop appropriate programmatic responses. But we have made very little progress in addressing the socioeconomic context of the pandemic. Rather, we have narrowed our response based on a one-sided perspective focused on biomedical and technical issues.

While this virus may not discriminate, the world does. While biology and individual behavior may be the *ultimate* determinants of vulnerability to HIV infection, we know that these factors are mutable, socially determined and controlled, varying over a person's lifetime, changing in response to personal history and experience, and strongly influenced by lovers, friends, families, communities, and even larger societal and cultural entities, such as religions, traditions, and nations. To understand the multiple HIV epidemics, we need to understand the multiple foci of vulnerability. Vulnerability stems from individual circumstances; from social phenomena, such as discrimination, the oppression of women, and marginalization of populations, from denial of basic rights to persons with HIV/AIDS; and from inadequate or inappropriate programmatic responses to the pandemic. As the pandemic deepens, not only will the levels of vulnerability increase, but new foci of vulnerability will come into play, challenging even further our current responses and resources.

Within each of our communities around the world, there is a need not just to accelerate our responses to AIDS, but to take a quantum leap to a new level of understanding, cooperation, and action. We have a responsibility to understand what makes us vulnerable as individuals, as families, and as communities. We need to challenge that vulnerability with strategies and action plans that empower us.

CENTRALITY OF GENDER RELATIONS

What are the factors that contribute to our vulnerability? My experiences in the field point again and again to the centrality of gender relations. Knowledge of HIV transmission and its prevention does little good if women do not have the necessary social status and economic independence to negotiate sexual relations with their partners or to choose not to sell sex. Educational campaigns to promote the recognition of STD symptoms and to encourage treatment-seeking behaviors are inadequate if health care workers lack knowledge of effective treatment protocols and basic antibiotics or if the cost of treatment is inaccessible to patients. However, we know that many important factors can decrease individual vulnerability—such as self-esteem; responsibility toward present and future sexual partners; access to and use of condoms; access to voluntary, confidential testing and counseling; and the availability of STD services. Comparable strategies can be elaborated to decrease individual vulnerability to HIV infection through perinatal transmission or blood products, or to reduce individual vulnerability to inadequate care.

Similarly, one can enumerate a series of factors that make particular societies more vulnerable to the rapid spread of HIV and inadequate care for the infected. Inappropriate censorship must be challenged to allow for the free flow of necessary information. Canadian customs officials have actually censored one imported magazine's description of condom use because it made reference to anal sex! U.S. television networks have disallowed the explicit mention of sex in advertisements to promote condoms. Obstructive regulations which hamper the smooth functioning of nongovernmental organizations have been instituted in many African countries. We must protect basic educational systems and health and social services against decimation in the name of "structural adjustment." Universally accepted standards of human rights must be protected, and the rights of women and other traditionally oppressed groups must be upheld. All the education and knowledge about HIV/AIDS in the world will not help a woman in the Middle East who is impoverished and socially outcast as the result of a divorce. Populations need access to appropriate communication channels for AIDS information and education. Poverty and underdevelopment, be it nationwide or within particular communities, fuel the epidemic.

The magnitude of the challenge before us must not be an excuse for inaction or pessimism. This conviction has prompted the Society for Women and AIDS in Africa (SWAA)[1] to take action at grassroots levels to implement a variety of programs addressing the educational needs of women and the care and support of orphans and women with AIDS. We are looking at ways of more actively integrating women with HIV into policy and program development relating to human rights violations.

All of us have a role to play in challenging vulnerability, and together, united, we can ensure individual and collective empowerment. In a world united against AIDS, scientists will explore intravaginal barrier methods and virucides to prevent HIV infection. In a world united against AIDS, women and men together will take responsibility for protecting their partners from infection. In a world united against AIDS, those responsible for planning and delivery of care services will use HIV not as an excuse for despondency, but as a trampoline to create new initiatives and learn from past lessons. In such a world, researchers will design studies relevant to the needs of a country, and AIDS program managers will support interventions designed and implemented by affected groups and communities. Only in a world united against AIDS will industrialized countries, which earn 85 percent of the world's income but have only 23 percent of its population, support poorer nations to address the pandemic.

CONCLUSION

What is the magnitude of the task that we are faced with? The challenge will be how to expand existing activities, in terms of program and organizational needs, reaching out to women and other vulnerable groups, responding to the needs of the health sector, and addressing the social and economic situations that fuel the spread of HIV/AIDS. Let us find ways to empower the disempowered and to make the vulnerable less vulnerable. Let us create an "enabling" environment for all.

Let me review briefly what we have been doing and ways we can improve on them. Recently, some key projects in AIDS prevention around the world were reviewed by the World Health Organization's Global Program on AIDS. The report showed that AIDS prevention does work. Mass media campaigns, creative condom marketing programs, and the right messages from friends and coworkers have succeeded in behavior modification, slowing the spread of HIV in some areas. Condoms have been distributed widely in Zaïre and Thailand; educational programs have successfully reached long-distance truck drivers in Tanzania; person-to-person AIDS prevention messages are being disseminated in Zimbabwe; and mass media campaigns in the Philippines and Switzerland are stressing positive messages. These programs owe their positive impact to certain key factors: government cooperation and development of favorable policies; specific, culturally sensitive education and promotion campaigns; and intensive education programs directed at identified target groups.

In some areas we have been able to measure the impact of the response. In Kinshasa, Zaïre, and in Calabar, Nigeria, female prostitutes provided with condoms, counseling, and STD services have increased condom use from less than 10 percent to approximately 60 percent in two years. These are excellent examples of intervention programs that have a proven capacity to slow the HIV epidemic. But what of the problems these programs face? What happens when political upheaval, cost cutting, or poor planning and coordination reduce or even stop such a program? Thus, simply talking about the value of distributing condoms is irrelevant if we do not include other elements—the provision of health and social services necessary to ensure that the supply of condoms matches the demand—and the creation of a supportive social environment that not only encourages the use of condoms by men, but provides women with options to protect themselves.

To enable women to protect themselves, there are three issues at stake: improving the social and economic status of women, providing a method over which they have sufficient control, and getting more men to adopt safer sex. This is not an academic exercise in setting priorities, but a question of life and death for many women.

We must find answers to the questions facing us today, which challenge us with the responsibility to get valuable information to the grassroots, where individuals and communities need it most. Of course, the scope of the pandemic is important to all of us for planning. We need to know all we can about the science of AIDS, but let us not forget that science is still searching for vaccines, treatments, and cures, while more and more people are being infected and dying. And let us not rest too long on the satisfaction that a few prevention programs are working here and there. Here and there is just not good enough to combat this pandemic.

We must bring about individual and collective responsibility to face the future with a clear vision and a strong will. We must draw from the strength of those who have clearly demonstrated that something can be done to challenge the spread of HIV/AIDS and those whose daily lives are entwined with the realities of infection and disease. Let us work toward a global approach that matches the global dimensions of the pandemic. Let us forge a response in an urgent manner, not only where the epidemic is already on the verge of spinning out of control, but where it is still young. Let us not focus our concentration on a few favored countries or projects, but instead move toward finding enough new resources to cover all our needs. And let us find the knowledge, logistics, and materials to empower groups, especially women, who have the potential to play a major role in bringing this epidemic under control.

We need a new sense of inspiration and commitment, carefully articulated and thought through, to create a renewed sense of community, national, and global solidarity in the fight against AIDS. Let it be a sense of solidarity that not only unites public health workers and experts, but also brings together communities at the grassroots, so that solidarity has a foundation at every level of our societies. Let us find the inspiration to break down the barriers between biomedical experts, behavioral scientists, and activists to achieve our common goal: controlling the spread of HIV/AIDS in the years ahead. We can no longer evade the questions that are being asked of us, as was the experience of the woman in the Nigerian conference years ago. We must find answers that work for the people who need information and support, so that they can reduce their vulnerability to HIV/AIDS. The global response to this pandemic in the years ahead requires nothing short of our individual and collective responsibility.

NOTE

[1]SWAA came into existence in 1988 to provide a rallying point for African women to respond to the concerns and dilemmas they face from the epidemic. In just four years, SWAA established branches in 25 African countries and became a recognized authority on women-AIDS matters at national, regional, and international levels. Most importantly, SWAA succeeded in refocusing the AIDS prevention and control agenda in Africa to include the impact of AIDS on women and in working to incorporate the sexual, social, cultural, and economic factors limiting women's participation in HIV/AIDS action programs. Specifically, SWAA national programs expanded from a largely female-oriented educational campaign to the establishment of women's support centers and networks, counseling for women with HIV infection and AIDS, youth-targeted activities, rehabilitation and needs assessment of AIDS orphans, and training of media practitioners on women-AIDS issues. SWAA conducted research to determine barriers to women's self-protection against AIDS, their access to information and care, and their knowledge, attitudes, and practices concerning HIV/AIDS. Research and advocacy programs related to AIDS–human rights abuses have been initiated in order to increase women's ability to cope with the impact of the epidemic on their lives. But, like nearly every response to AIDS, SWAA is not keeping pace with the growth of the epidemic.

Complications of Gender: Women, AIDS and the Law

T he popular conception and typical media image of the person with AIDS (PWA) or HIV disease is male—either a gay man or a male injection drug user. Media portrayals of women and AIDS early in the epidemic tended to ignore women entirely or depict them as vectors of transmission[1] or as the victims of bisexual male partners.[2] Only the latter depiction considered women at risk of illness and death, and its emphasis on bisexual men made the risk seem most threatening to middle-class, primarily white women.[3]

In fact, the risk to women has been substantial and is rapidly increasing, but it is heavily skewed by race. It is specifically among women of color in the United States that HIV disease has reached epidemic proportions.[4] The risk is also heavily skewed by economic class. Half of the cases among women are the result of injection drug use, an activity highly correlated with poverty. Another 20 percent of the cases result from sexual contact with men who are injection drug users. Sexual relations with bisexual men comprise less than 3 percent of the total.[5]

Although more accurate media portrayals of women as PWAs have begun to emerge, there is still a tendency to focus on women as *posing* a risk rather than *being* at risk. This chapter approaches women, not as vectors of transmission, but as persons whose lives are at risk and who are entitled to the highest quality of care and treatment.

The impact of HIV disease on women is multifaceted. Although in many respects, HIV-infected women must fight many of the same legal and social battles as infected men, this chapter focuses on five critical areas in which the legal and policy issues for women are strongly gender-linked: prevention, access to health care, decisions related to pregnancy, testing of newborns, and decisions related to parenting.

PREVENTION

One of the major achievements in the gay male community during the 1980s was the creation of innovative educational programs encouraging behavior changes to reduce the risk of HIV transmission. As a result, the incidence of new HIV infections among gay men fell sharply. Women face a challenge at least as formidable in the 1990s—to develop prevention programs that tackle the issue of negotiating safer sex between women and their partners and that are sensitive to the diverse ethnic and cultural backgrounds of women affected by HIV. The primary role of law on this question should be to ensure that the government is not permitted to choke off the most effective programs because of concerns about the controversial nature of their content.

"Explicit communication" has been at the heart of most of the legal battles concerning AIDS education programs. Federal limitations on the use of funds, which in turn set the limits for how state agencies can structure any programs that utilize federal funds, formerly permitted funding only for materials that were not "offensive" to the general public, even if the materials were distributed only to specific groups.[6] Those restrictions have now been declared unconstitutional,[7] but legislative battles over the scope of AIDS education continue at the state and federal levels. Even in communities where there is "a vital public dialogue about sex, the private, intimate conversations between an individual man and an individual woman may be less open and less forthright."[8] An effective educational program will take full advantage of such a "vital public dialogue," using, when appropriate, vernacular language with which community members are comfortable.[9] Public agencies should not limit the content of AIDS prevention programs to materials that are too bland and nonspecific to be effective.

Specifically, it is the negotiation of condom use that many women report may lead to the risk of physical harm or financial abandonment.[10] Such concerns have led some researchers to call for the development of methods for the prevention of HIV transmission that could be used and controlled by women, without requiring, as condoms do, the cooperation of the male partner.[11] Additionally, not all programs concerning heterosexual transmission should be addressed to women alone. Policies that assign to women the full responsibility for safer heterosexual practices continue and reinforce the same assumption of lack of responsibility on the part of men which creates the risk to women. The same message of the need for change in sexual practices should be directed to heterosexual men as is routinely directed toward gay men.

For women who have sex with women, the prevention issues are different. Here, the primary obstacle is a false perception of security. Because there have been so few AIDS cases reported among lesbians, there is a widely held view that lesbians have essentially no risk. One early lesson of this disease, however, was that risk depends on behavior, not status. The woman who has sex with a woman who has used injection drugs or who has had sexual contacts with an HIV-infected person may be placing herself at risk.[12]

The problem of a false sense of security is compounded by scientists' unwillingness to conduct research on transmission to female partners. The research on the risk of transmission from an HIV-infected woman to a sexual partner has assumed that the partner is male. Basic research needs to be undertaken to analyze how that risk differs, if it does, when the partner is also female.

ACCESS TO HEALTH CARE

Meaningful access to health care has been an elusive goal for many persons with HIV disease. For women, special barriers have led to even greater problems in securing the best available treatments, at the earliest possible times. These issues can be divided into two categories: threshold issues of diagnosis, reporting, and study of the disease; and insufficient access to testing and treatment.

Diagnosis, Reporting, and Study of Disease

The social invisibility of women in the HIV epidemic starts at the very beginning of the care process: with diagnosis and data gathering. A failure of diagnosis precludes women from gaining access to medical systems for treating HIV patients; to legal systems that are triggered by an AIDS diagnosis (such as disability benefits); and to resource allocation systems, which allot funding based on the count of AIDS or HIV patients. After diagnosis, basic epidemiological counting of persons with AIDS classifies women somewhat differently than men.

Misdiagnosis of women occurs largely in two situations, one ad hoc and one the result of formal policy. The first kind has occurred because the perception that AIDS is a men's disease has been widespread among health care providers as well as among the general public. Because physicians do not expect women patients to have HIV disease, they are not alert for its symptoms when treating women. Thus, even well-known signs of AIDS, such as *Pneumocystis carinii pneumonia,* tend to be misdiagnosed in women.[13] Delay in accurate diagnosis leads to delays in treatment and missed opportunities for medical intervention early enough in the course of the disease to significantly prolong life. The result can be a brutally faster death.

The second kind of misdiagnosis reflects the history of the very definition of AIDS. The official definition of AIDS is actually a kind of checklist. HIV disease can be present in forms that range from the early, asymptomatic stage to the last stage, in which AIDS is fully developed. The definitional criteria for when this final stage is reached—and thus for a formal diagnosis of AIDS—are a list of possible symptoms and opportunistic infections. However, until 1993, this definitional checklist, developed by the CDC early in the epidemic, when virtually all the people with AIDS were gay or bisexual men, did not include any gynecological manifestations as possible indicators of AIDS or of earlier stages of the disease. The definition changed after several years of pressure exerted by PWA advocates, who cited growing evidence that for many women gynecological symptoms are the first manifestations of HIV disease.[14]

Beyond the point of diagnosis, there is the question of how the disease progresses in women. To date, there has been no study of the natural history of HIV disease in women. Women are missing from every aspect of the study of AIDS.

> Fundamental questions about the progression of this disease in women have not been asked or answered. Is cervical cancer more common in HIV-infected women? How does HIV infection affect pregnancy and childbirth? Do the different hormones in women and men affect the course of HIV infection? Do women fall prey to different opportunistic infections than men do? Do women respond differently to treatment regimens established for male patients? Do women suffer different side effects and toxicities from AIDS medications? Do women survive a shorter time after the diagnosis of AIDS has been made? Are the causes of death in women different than in men?[15]

Related to problems with diagnosis and study of the disease is the question of how CDC statistics count women with AIDS. These numbers affect how the issues associated with women and AIDS are addressed and significantly shape the allocation of resources. There are multiple ways in which undercounting can harm women. One is simply that, if fewer women are recognized as having HIV disease, those institutions treating large numbers of women will receive less funding, and ultimately the patients' care will be diminished.

Another aspect of the counting issue is the relationship between CDC transmission categories and the formulation of and funding for prevention programs. For example, the relative frequency of transmission by drug use and transmission by sexual contact may be misstated by current statistical procedures, because of the CDC's policy of assigning cases to the risk category believed to be most likely. A woman who has used injection drugs herself and who also has had sexual relations with a partner who has used drugs is automatically assigned to the transmission category of drug user, even though there is no way to know by which mechanism she became infected.[16] The conflation of risk behaviors that results from this categorization could mask important information, making it more difficult to assess the effectiveness of prevention programs geared to one set of behaviors or another, for example. It also erases as a category those women who face double exposure risks.

Recasting the perception of who HIV patients really are will mean revising the fundamental structure for diagnosis, data gathering, and other methods of studying the disease. Policy makers can no longer ignore the ways that existing models do not account for the symptoms or situations of women with this disease.

Insufficient Access to Testing and Treatment

Testing and counseling is the first step to treatment. That essential first step will not be available for women unless testing and counseling programs are much more fully integrated into the locales where women, especially those in the low-income urban neighborhoods hardest hit by HIV disease, actually go for medical and social services.

HIV testing programs are a double-edged sword. There was great resistance to testing in the early stages of the epidemic because of discrimination against HIV-infected persons and the absence of treatments. Now, however, treatment prior to the onset of symptoms has become a reality. To amend the slogan, delay and denial equal death. In this context, the absence of access to testing and counseling programs constitutes a denial of care.

By far the biggest access problem for women is poverty. Most women with this disease are in low-income categories and must rely on inadequate public resources for health care. For many poor people with HIV disease, treatment prior to full-blown illness is only a theoretical possibility.

Without ready access to testing, early diagnosis will not occur. According to Marie St. Cyr, former director of the Women and AIDS Resource Network of New York, half of the women with HIV disease counseled by her organization first learned that they were infected when a pediatrician diagnosed their child as having the disease.[17] Other advocates report similar experiences with women having little effective access to diagnosis of HIV disease. Even physicians treating women for other conditions, including childbirth, may be reluctant to recommend testing out of a desire to avoid having to deal with the consequences of learning that the patient has this particular disease.[18] Because of uncertainties about the effects of AIDS treatments such as AZT on a fetus, some pregnant women have experienced difficulty in getting prescriptions for these medications. An Institute of Medicine report in 1991 recommended that women not be denied these treatments during pregnancy.[19]

Family planning and prenatal care facilities are among the locations where low-income women are most likely to seek medical care, and public health resources have been targeted for the establishment of testing and counseling programs in these facilities. But many more points of intervention are possible and need to be prioritized. Other locales where HIV prevention information could be distributed include social services offices, such as those for Aid to Families with Dependent Children (AFDC) and Women, Infants and Children (WIC) nutritional supplement programs. An Illinois law, for example, requires drug-related information and referrals for treatment to be provided in WIC program offices.[20] Free condoms should be available wherever information is disseminated.

One failure in the provision of services deserves special mention. There is an abysmal shortage of drug abuse treatment programs for women, especially in light of the high correlation of drug use and HIV infection. Drug treatment programs are scarce to begin with. As of 1987, only 338,365 slots were available for an estimated 4 million addicts.[21] The majority of the programs that do exist serve only men.[22] The situation is especially critical for pregnant women seeking drug treatment.[23] The highest court in New York State has ruled that a hospital-based drug treatment program that excludes pregnant women may violate that state's antidiscrimination law.[24] Both the shortage of overall services and the lack of facilities for women need to be addressed.

DECISIONS RELATED TO PREGNANCY

One of the modes of transmitting HIV is "vertical," from parent to child. A mother may transmit HIV *in utero*, through the blood system shared by her body and the fetus. The risk that a baby born to an HIV-infected woman will be HIV-infected is approximately 30 percent.[25] Although 70 percent of infants born to HIV-infected mothers are not themselves infected, all such infants test HIV-antibody positive for approximately the first year to 18 months of life because the maternal antibodies are then still circulating in their bloodstreams.[26]

The policy and legal issue related to women and AIDS that has garnered by far the most public attention has been whether coercion by the state is justified as a mechanism to reduce the number of children with HIV disease. The two most common proposals have been for mandatory HIV testing of pregnant women and mandatory testing of newborn children. A number of expert panels have recommended that such testing be widely available and routinely offered and encouraged, but not mandated.[27] Nonetheless, calls for coercive testing of these two groups persist.[28]

As scientists develop new treatments and learn more about the disease in infants, there may be new proposals for other kinds of state interventions. One already suggested is that treatment with AZT during pregnancy may benefit the fetus and prolong the life of the child after birth.[29] If this hypothesis proves true, policy makers will have to consider whether to require pregnant women not only to be tested but also, if seropositive, to take certain treatments.

Finally, criminal laws may apply. Although no cases have yet arisen, a number of statutes that criminalize HIV transmission could apply to a woman who, knowing that she is infected, decides to become pregnant and to carry her pregnancy to term.[30] Women who used illegal drugs have been prosecuted for "distribution" of drugs to their children on the basis of perinatal transmission, or have been subject to child abuse or neglect proceedings to remove the child from their custody. Whether that same kind of prosecutorial strategy will be applied to women with HIV disease, especially those women who also have used injection drugs, is yet to be seen.

Suspicion about the motivation for mandatory testing of either pregnant women or newborns is heightened by the context for such programs. The government has shown no great zeal for taking aggressive steps to ensure the health of babies in the low-income, urban communities that would be the most affected. Infant mortality rates among those communities in the United States compare to the rates in impoverished nations, and normal prenatal and pediatric care is often unavailable.[31]

Testing of pregnant women raises issues particular not only to the race and economic status of the persons to be tested, but also to how medical interventions have been directed against women. To an extraordinary degree, the social role of women—in the family, in the workplace, and in the body politic—has been constructed around the single fact that women, and not men, have the capacity to become pregnant and to give birth.[32] Singling out pregnant women for testing resonates with a history of subordinating women's health to that of others and using women's reproductive capacity as a mechanism for controlling women. For women of color and poor women, it resonates with a history of medical interventions that include forced sterilizations[33] and the threat of coerced contraception, through such modern devices as implants.[34] Against this background, the eagerness to impose by force of law a testing system that also stigmatizes the same women raises questions of whether unspoken motives or, at the least, unconsidered consequences lay beneath the surface of these proposals.

Mandatory Prenatal HIV Testing and Directive Counseling

At the outset it is important to identify the rationale for testing pregnant women. The only result of testing that is unique to pregnant women is the decision to continue a pregnancy or to abort. When CDC officials first addressed the issues related to HIV and pregnancy, they reportedly assumed that post-test counseling would always lead to delay of pregnancy or to abortions, since anyone who was "logical" would abort the pregnancy rather than risk HIV transmission.[35] There is, at least as yet, no treatment that can be administered prior to birth that will cure or substantially ameliorate the disease for the child. This lack of a prenatal treatment distinguishes HIV from syphilis, for which penicillin is a cure for both mother and *in utero* child.[36]

Issues related to the testing of pregnant women have been part of AIDS policy discussions since almost the beginning of the epidemic. In December 1985, the CDC first formally recommended that HIV testing and counseling be made available to pregnant women in five groups: those with evidence of HIV infection; injection drug users; current or past sexual partners of men "in high-risk groups"; women born in countries where heterosexual transmission is thought to be frequent; and prostitutes.[37] In February 1987, the CDC convened a large public conference in Atlanta to discuss the advisability of mandatory HIV testing of several populations, one of which was pregnant women. Conference participants reendorsed the recommendation of offering, but not requiring, testing and counseling at family planning clinics and during prenatal care.[38] Ultimately, after review by higher-level agency officials, the CDC took no new position on testing of pregnant women and left the 1985 guidelines in place.

Although not adopted at the 1987 conference, proposals for mandatory HIV testing have remained under active discussion. Florida and Delaware adopted legislation that mandates testing of pregnant women for sexually transmitted diseases, but neither law specifies whether HIV disease is included.[39] Michigan requires HIV testing of pregnant women unless a physician determines that it is inadvisable or unless the woman refuses to proceed with the test.[40] Two federal health officials predicted in 1989 that the threat posed by perinatal transmission would lead to mandatory testing of all women of reproductive age.[41] A prestigious task force on HIV infection in women and newborns, convened at the Johns Hopkins University School of Public Health, has issued recommendations against policies of forced testing or directive counseling,[42] but clinicians continue to call for their adoption[43] and may be surreptitiously employing such practices, although the extent is unknown.[44] Some ethicists have argued that, although coercion may not be justified, the state should be permitted to exercise its power to engage in directive counseling, to urge—or perhaps, as many fear, to pressure— women to be tested and, if positive, to forego pregnancy.[45]

What drives the debate on mandatory testing for pregnant women is less the set of issues concerning the physical intrusion of the test[46] than the content of the post-test counseling. The demand for such testing is motivated by the desire to prevent HIV transmission by preventing the birth of HIV-infected babies, an intervention that depends on persuading pregnant women to have abortions. Opposition to this kind of testing centers on the question of whether directive counseling regarding abortion infringes on the woman's right to make independent, unpressured decisions.

Indeed, to some extent, the content of the counseling is an entirely separate question from the voluntary nature of the test. Whether an HIV test is mandated by the state or freely sought out by the woman, post-test counseling could be geared to informing the woman of her options and of their relative risks, or designed to influence her more or less strongly to obtain an abortion. The degree of directiveness in the counseling is the primary issue. The CDC's guidelines discuss only preconception decisions and recommend delay or forgoing of pregnancy. During the 1980s, frustrated doctors complained that the antiabortion politics of the Reagan administration had prevented the agency from explicitly recommending discussion of abortion for all HIV-infected pregnant women.[47] The danger of bias cuts both ways, however. Survey data indicate that many doctors support counseling HIV-infected pregnant women in explicitly directive ways to obtain abortions, but would not use such directiveness if conditions other than HIV disease were involved.[48]

Government action to systematically require counseling of HIV-infected pregnant women to encourage abortion might well be constitutional. That is the ironic result of judicial decisions that constrain a woman's right to decide in favor of abortion. In its 1992 opinion reaffirming the core principle that the Constitution protects a zone of privacy that includes abortion, the Supreme Court also permitted more government restrictions on a woman's decision-making process.[49] Unless it presents "a substantial obstacle" to a woman's obtaining an abortion, the Court said, "a state measure designed to persuade her to choose childbirth over abortion will be upheld if reasonably related to that goal."[50]

The same principle of law would permit the government to skew state policies in the opposite direction. Court decisions that diminish the woman's autonomy and enhance the power of the state to achieve the outcome preferred by legislatures could be invoked to justify coercive *pro*abortion counseling as well. The legal outcome of this question will be determined by how the Supreme Court resolves future abortion cases and possibly by future congressional action. The issue of whether the state can intervene to end a pregnancy when a women is HIV-positive dramatically illustrates that at least one right at issue in abortion cases really is that of choice—either for or against abortion.

In addition to the legal issues specific to whether the state may engage in directive counseling, a series of other legal and policy considerations are raised by proposals for prenatal testing which is mandatory or routinized (without a process of informed consent). Courts ruling on the constitutionality of programs involving state coercion engage in a weighing of the burdens and gains associated with the policy in question, including the harms or benefits to the coerced individual; any selectivity in the imposition of those harms; the efficacy of the policy in achieving its stated goals; and whether less restrictive alternatives exist by which the same advantages can be secured. Judged by these criteria, a policy of required HIV testing of pregnant women is seriously deficient.

CONSTITUTIONAL FACTORS: HARM. First, the harms associated with testing are significant enough that *forced* testing cannot be justified. In addition to the personal harm of involuntary physical intrusion, there is substantial risk of serious social harm if a woman is known to be HIV-infected. Widespread irrational discrimination has been directed against persons with HIV disease, including loss of jobs, health care, custody of children, and housing.[51] Fear of such discrimination could impede prenatal care (which already is often delayed) by causing women to avoid the care as a way of avoiding the test. As discussed above, the benefits of testing include early diagnosis and the possibility of treatments which can slow the progression of the disease.

But, because there is no guarantee that a woman will actually receive the benefits of such treatment, the possibility of treatment cannot be invoked to take away her right to decide whether to be tested.

A possible advantage of being tested could be the greater amount of information available to the woman to use in her own decision making. Although one may oppose a program of directive counseling designed to skew the woman's decision toward abortion, it is also true that the information that one has this disease is extremely important for deciding whether to seek immediate treatment or to continue a particular pregnancy. There may be a host of other planning decisions for which this information could be crucial. Still, the fundamental question is whether such a rationale is sufficient to *coerce* testing. For the nonreproductive aspects of decision making, it would seem clear that the state has no greater authority to impose this information on a pregnant woman than on anyone else.

SELECTIVITY. The issue of selectivity varies with the specifics of a proposed testing regime. If mandatory or directive testing programs were adopted for all women, the impact would be selective by gender. The constitutionality of such a program would depend on whether the courts considered males and females to be "similarly situated" with regard to posing a risk of vertical transmission. Although the expectant father may be the original source of HIV infection, testing him will not determine whether the fetus is infected because the father may not have transmitted the virus to the mother. The risk that HIV will be transmitted to the child exists only if the mother is infected. Thus, selectivity by gender is likely to be viewed as acceptable under current law.

Many proposals for prenatal testing, however, do not envision that testing would be required of all women, but only of women considered at highest risk for HIV infection. As one commission pointed out, both sociodemographic criteria and geographic seroprevalence rates—the most common bases for proposed targeting—"become merely thinly veiled proxies for ethnicity and poverty."[52] The inevitable effect would be to impose a burden on women in already-disadvantaged racial, ethnic, and socioeconomic categories, and to exempt women in socially privileged categories. Even ostensibly universal forms of testing fall prey to this bias. A study of reporting data under a Florida law that required testing all pregnant women for illegal drug use found that many positive toxicologies for white women were not reported to the state, whereas drug-positive results in African-American and Hispanic women were.[53] HIV testing of pregnant women poses the same risks of unequal enforcement, against the same communities.

Although differential treatment by race or ethnicity is highly suspect in the law, a successful challenge to testing policies would have to show that the discrimination was intentional, rather than a mere by-product of a facially neutral system.[54] Evidence of the disproportionate impact of such a policy could demonstrate a lack of neutrality, but its defenders would argue that its purpose was beneficent, and thus that differential application could be justified.

A comparison with other conditions leading to serious health problems for certain groups of children, for which tests are *not* imposed, would be more telling of bias. There is no mandatory testing for carriers of traits for Tay-Sachs disease or sickle-cell anemia, serious genetic diseases that can be detected prenatally, but for which, like HIV, there is no prenatal treatment.[55] Amniocentesis, which tests for chromosomal abnormalities and hereditary diseases such as Downs syndrome, is recommended but not required for all women age 35 and older.[56] In all these examples, because there is no effective prenatal treatment for the fetus, prenatal testing is not required. To treat HIV disease differently suggests that a nonmedical reason, such as bias, is operating.

EFFICACY. The third issue to be assessed is whether such testing would actually be effective in reducing vertical transmission of HIV. Any link between testing and reduced transmission depends on an assumption that HIV-infected pregnant women can and will decide to terminate their pregnancies, based on an approximately one-in-three chance that their baby would have HIV disease. Several factors render that assumption untenable in many cases. To a horrifying degree, pregnant women in low-income communities do not even have contact with a doctor for prenatal care, at least until the last trimester of pregnancy.[57] In most states, public funds will cover the costs of an abortion, but many counties have no facility that will perform an abortion.[58] Moreover, abortion providers may discriminate against HIV-infected women.[59] Thus, even if a pregnant woman wanted to have an abortion, she might learn of the HIV infection too late in the pregnancy to do so or be unable to afford to obtain an abortion.

Even more fundamental, however, is the assumption that she would likely want an abortion or would, if not yet pregnant, decide not to become pregnant. Studies to date have shown that women who learn they are HIV-infected do not elect to have abortions at any higher rate than women who are not infected.[60] For women facing the harshness of life in poverty, a 70 percent chance of a healthy baby, coupled with the enhancement of self-esteem associated with motherhood, leads to very different, but no less logical, assessments of what might be the best option.[61] Thus, the very efficacy of mandatory testing in reducing the numbers of HIV-infected babies is open to serious question.

Finally, constitutional analysis incorporates consideration of whether less restrictive alternatives exist by which the same goals could just as readily be achieved. The obvious alternative protocol is one of making HIV testing readily available and routinely offered, but voluntary. This is the policy that has received the widest endorsement.[62]

Forced Treatment and Penalization for Behavior During Pregnancy

The concern over HIV-infected women becoming mothers is arising in a period when law and medicine are confronting a growing number of issues involving maternal-fetal conflict. The rapid sophistication of perinatal medicine has led to the potential for diagnostic procedures and treatments *in utero* that were impossible two decades ago. A substantial body of legal commentary already has been generated as a result.[63]

To date, there is no treatment or cure for HIV disease *in utero*, although trials of the AZT's efficacy in preventing prenatal transmission are underway. Should AZT or some other drug be proven beneficial as an *in utero* treatment, however, the issue will arise of whether pregnant women (presumably after being tested) could be forced to undergo such treatments. The existing law on the question of forced treatment is in development; to date, most of the reported instances concern forced Caesarean sections or blood transfusions. Until 1990, the reported cases had generally resulted in judicial authorization for such procedures.[64] The leading case now on record, however, is a ruling from the District of Columbia Court of Appeals holding that it was improper for a hospital, and for the lower court reviewing the hospital's decision, to attempt to balance the woman's interests against those of the state in enhancing fetal health.[65] The case involved the performance of a Caesarean on a terminally ill cancer patient, in an attempt to save the fetus. Doctors treating the woman knew that the surgery would hasten her death and had only a small chance of saving the fetus. The patient was too heavily medicated to express her own wishes; her family opposed the surgery. The hospital sought a court order nonetheless, conducted the surgery, and both the woman and the fetus died.

The District of Columbia court grounded its holding in a constitutionally protected "right of bodily integrity . . . [which] is not extinguished because someone is ill, or even at death's door."[66] Following the court's decision, the hospital adopted a new policy on treatment of severely ill pregnant patients, which provided that "respect for patient autonomy compels us to accede to the treatment decisions of a pregnant patient whenever possible."[67]

The D.C. decision is more fully reasoned than earlier cases dealing with forced treatments for purposes of fetal health and thus may be considered persuasive by other courts, but it is binding precedent only in the District of Columbia. It is far from clear how courts in other jurisdictions will rule if confronted with similar situations. Given the sparseness of the law on this question, the strongest support for an autonomy-protective outcome may lie in the policies of professional medical associations.

The American Medical Association,[68] the American College of Obstetricians and Gynecologists,[69] and the American Pediatric Institute[70] have all adopted formal positions against forced treatment of pregnant patients. These policies recognize a distinction between an ethical duty on the part of a pregnant patient to maximize fetal health and the general refusal of law to coerce adherence to samaritan principles. In addition, they conclude that utilization of force destroys the foundation of trust between patient and doctor and that judicial proceedings are an inappropriate mechanism for making treatment decisions involving patients who are competent to consent.

It is less clear whether physicians will actually follow the ethical advice proffered in these policy statements. A 1987 survey of directors of maternal-fetal medicine fellowship programs found that nearly half believed that women who refused to follow medical advice, to the danger of their fetuses, should be detained for medical supervision. Less than one-quarter consistently agreed that pregnant women had the right to decline medical advice.[71]

A related question which has also engendered sharp debate about maternal-fetal conflict has been whether pregnant women can properly be punished by criminal prosecution or by civil proceedings alleging child abuse or neglect for engaging in behavior during pregnancy that creates a danger to the fetus. This issue has arisen almost entirely with regard to use of illegal drugs during pregnancy.[72]

As of 1992, 25 states had made it a crime to transmit HIV or to knowingly expose another person to it.[73] Some criminalize only transmission by blood donation or sexual conduct, but some generally penalize conduct likely to transmit HIV. Although no woman has yet been prosecuted for transmission *in utero*, a woman who knew that she was HIV-infected, knew the risk of transmission to the fetus, and proceeded nonetheless to continue the pregnancy could be liable for prosecution under broadly worded statutes. Only Texas specifically exempts perinatal transmission from the scope of its criminal law.[74] The potential for criminal prosecution is certainly clear, and the impact it could have on deterring women from seeking HIV testing, prenatal care, or both is substantial.

As direct precedent, cases involving prosecution of women for using drugs seem largely inapposite to the situation of HIV-infected mothers. In drug use cases, advocates of legal penalties argue that prosecutions serve as a deterrent that will force pregnant women to avoid behaviors known to harm a fetus. Women with HIV disease, by contrast, can do nothing after becoming pregnant to avoid harm to the fetus. For them, as for women who are carriers of genetic anomalies, the only decision is whether to continue a pregnancy. As far as we know now, nothing that occurs during the nine-month gestation alters the risk of transmission.

The cases are nonetheless troubling for two reasons. First, some courts have gone beyond illegal behaviors during pregnancy to approve penalization of lawful but hazardous decisions, such as alcohol use, or even the refusal to follow doctors' directions.[75] Second, the women who are most likely to be subject to prosecution—those who are addicted to illegal drugs—are also most likely to have HIV disease. Thus, in many instances, the women against whom criminal charges are filed will be the same women against whom some penalization for HIV status could be directed. Their HIV status, if known, could constitute an additional, even if unacknowledged, basis for prosecutors to bring drug-related charges. Given the much greater likelihood of state intervention in the lives of poor women and women of color, one cannot disentangle these two potential bases for surveillance and penalty in practice, even if they are logically and legally distinct.

MANDATORY TESTING OF NEWBORNS

In some respects, mandatory testing of newborns is much easier to justify than testing of pregnant women. No physical intrusion at all is involved for the woman. Moreover, the rationale for testing does not involve the *sub rosa* goal of steering the woman's choice about pregnancy or abortion. Coerced reproductive decision making is not at issue.

Until 1993, testing of newborns could identify with certainty only the mothers, and not the children, who were HIV-infected. Moreover, because treating the noninfected children of infected mothers (who are the great majority) posed the risk that toxic anti-HIV drugs would create harm for those in that 70 percent group, even if they helped the 30 percent who were infected, ethicists found it easy to argue against HIV testing of newborns at least until the tests could reliably distinguish infected from uninfected infants (at about 15 months of age).[76]

But the issue of newborn testing does seem, perhaps more than any other current AIDS issue, the most like a constantly moving target because future improvements in the sophistication of testing and treatment techniques are likely to enhance the value of testing. An effective test to pinpoint HIV in newborns was announced in medical journals in early 1993, with licensing expected to follow rapidly.[77] Recent research also indicates that treatment protocols involving drugs less toxic than AZT may become widely adopted as early interventions for very young children.[78]

As these developments occur, there are likely to be renewed calls for mandatory newborn testing. On its surface, drawing the line at birth appears logical. The potential social harm to the mothers is substantially ameliorated. Although some mothers with HIV disease will be identified by the tests on their children, the 70 percent of infected mothers whose children are born uninfected will not be identified against their will because the children will test negative. Further, established law offers more support for newborn testing than for prenatal testing. The child is a separate person, and our society accepts the principle that the state may intervene to insist on medical treatment of a minor, at least in an emergency, against the wishes of the parent.[79] Accordingly, although syphilis is the only condition for which states require prenatal tests, there are from six to a dozen types of tests automatically performed on a newborn, without requiring the parent's consent.[80] Two states now test newborns for HIV. Rhode Island allows HIV testing of newborns without maternal consent.[81] New York Health Department officials proposed, then withdrew, a plan to "unblind" the HIV tests of newborns, which would effectively detect seropositive mothers.

There are still, however, compelling arguments against automatic testing of newborns without a parent's consent. First, unfortunately, one cannot simply assume that identification of the disease will lead only to benefits for the child. Much of the analysis of the newborn testing issue assumes that any reasonable parent would want to have the child tested so that, if she is infected, treatments could begin as soon as possible. Hopefully, this would be true in almost all cases. But there is no vaccination against discrimination, even for the youngest and most helpless of those with HIV disease.

A 1989 survey of neonatologists vividly illustrates this point. Half of the doctors who would otherwise have recommended open heart surgery for an infant would not have proceeded with that operation if it were known that the child was HIV-infected.[82] In cases where a parent might be aware of similar upcoming medical decisions to be made about the child, or of other situations in which identification as HIV-infected might prompt a real risk of discrimination, the reasonable parent might well decide to postpone testing. Coerced testing programs take this decision away from the parent.

Second, because there is a substantial risk—here, of discrimination— associated with HIV testing, it is improper to deny authority to the parent to consent on behalf of the child, in the same manner as if the child were to undergo surgery. None of the other conditions, mostly metabolic disorders, that are the subject of newborn testing programs, carry comparable, if any, stigma. Thus, the more appropriate analogy is not to routine screening programs but to medical procedures with serious risk.

Treating newborns with HIV disease and their parents differently from other family units amounts to another instance of selectivity which masks differentiation based on race and poverty. There is a long history of greater governmental intrusion into the family life decisions of the poor.[83] In the worst case scenario of a parent withholding consent for reasons justified by the best interests of the child, when testing is indicated, the health care facility can seek a judicial order authorizing forced testing and treatment. In other words, the same procedure could be followed in this situation as would be followed if a parent withheld consent for another medical procedure that a child needed.[84]

Third, and perhaps most fundamental, there is no promise that beneficial treatment will actually be available to the child. Even if the newborn testing techniques existed to pinpoint which infants are infected with HIV and even if the treatments existed to prolong their lives, there is no guarantee that children with this disease will actually receive those expensive treatments. Children with HIV disease are likely to be born into families that are African American rather than white, with low incomes, headed by young adults, and living in the central cities—all characteristics of persons without health care coverage, private or public.[85] One could only justify *coerced* testing as a form of treatment, on beneficent or communitarian grounds, if in fact all those who tested positive were assured that they would receive the treatment.[86]

One last practical consideration supports using an informed consent process, rather than an automatic testing approach. The actual accessing of the treatment by a very young child will depend on the cooperation of the caretaker parent, likely the mother. If that parent's status to authorize medical testing and treatment has been ignored by the program itself, it seems extremely unlikely that the kind of cooperation necessary to provide maximum care and treatment for the child will exist.

There are striking similarities between the issues raised by HIV testing and the history of sickle-cell testing. In each case, the first response was to mandate testing, first of adults for carrier status and then of newborns. Widespread discrimination against an already-disadvantaged minority followed. Ultimately, a policy of routinely encouraging the test, but incorporating a consent procedure, has been adopted.

In 1970, a single, inexpensive, and relatively reliable test for sickle-cell hemoglobin became available. Shortly thereafter, a number of states enacted sickle-cell testing programs. Some were compulsory, and none had specific confidentiality provisions. Although well-intentioned, these programs and the attention they generated triggered panicked and discriminatory responses.[87] At the same time incidents of discrimination were erupting, clinicians had nothing to offer sickle-cell carriers except counseling with regard to reproduction. This lack of an effective treatment added to criticism of the testing statutes.[88] In response to this overreaction, legislatures that had passed mandatory testing laws amended them to make the test voluntary.[89] When Congress passed the National Sickle Cell Anemia Control Act in 1972, it expressly limited federal funding to voluntary testing programs.[90]

In 1987, a National Institutes of Health consensus conference recommended that states mandate the offering of sickle-cell disease tests for newborns, based on the preventability of serious episodes of disease, and in some cases of death, by the administration of penicillin. Even in light of this clear and dramatic beneficial treatment, the conference called on states to "mandate the availability of these services while permitting parental refusal."[91] The finding that penicillin is an effective treatment has led to a resurgence of sickle-cell testing for newborns.[92]

The NIH consensus conference can serve as a useful starting point for developing an approach to HIV testing of newborns, if improvements in treatment and testing techniques materialize. Basic components of such a program should include that:

- Future followup care and treatment should be guaranteed, regardless of ability to pay.

- Parental consent should be sought for testing well in advance.
- The parent should be informed that no denial of service, assistance, or any form of public benefit will result if consent is denied.
- If the parent declines testing, the health care provider may seek a court order to authorize a test. The provider will bear the burden of proving that testing is required to provide treatment needed to prolong the life and health of the child.[93]
- Results of such tests shall be disclosed only to the parents or guardian of the child and to the persons providing health care to the child, unless the parents authorize further disclosure.

DECISIONS RELATED TO PARENTING

Although a single parent can be either a mother or a father, more than 80 percent are mothers.[94] Thus, as a practical matter, the problems of single parents who are HIV-infected disproportionately affect women. Perhaps the saddest of these issues is the question of how a single mother with HIV disease provides for the care of her children during her illness and after her death. In New York City, more than 20,000 children have lost their mothers to AIDS, and the overwhelming majority of HIV patients who are women are mothers.[95] Experts predict that, by the year 2,000, there will be 125,000 children under the age of 18 who will have been left motherless by AIDS.[96]

Every state has a mechanism whereby parents can name as guardians the persons whom they wish to assume parental responsibilities for a child after the natural parent's death. The difference with HIV disease is that its symptoms are often episodic; a person may experience recurring bouts of illness and hospitalization followed by relative health, before entering a phase of incapacity leading to death. Most state laws establishing guardianships operate so that, once a guardian is approved by the court, that person takes over from the parent. As a result, many parents with HIV disease are reluctant to execute documents naming a guardian, since they could be unable to regain custody of a child even if they regained their health.[97]

New York has revised its guardianship law to address this situation. A 1992 measure creates a special procedure for the appointment of a "standby" guardian upon the incapacity of a parent. The statute provides that a simple form, witnessed by two persons, can be used by a parent to designate such a guardian, who will assume authority to care for the children when the parent becomes incapacitated, as determined by a court, or becomes debilitated (unable to care for the child) and consents to the commencement of the standby guardian's authority. The parent can later revoke her designation, so long as she has the legal capacity to do so.[98]

Other state legislatures should also consider adoption of "springing" or "standby" guardianship provisions. Such measures would allow a petition for guardianship to be filed and processed while the parent is still well, without requiring any transfer of custody at that time. The guardianship would "spring" into existence when the parent was no longer capable of care. The ideal provision would also "unspring," permitting the parent who regains capacity to once again become guardian of her child.

CONCLUSION

The intersection of gender, race, and class is nowhere more dramatic than in the law's impact on women with HIV disease. Just as advocates for people with AIDS fought creatively in the 1980s to force policy makers to understand the experience of gay men with this disease, advocates in coming years must recontextualize the debates on AIDS policy to underscore the experience of women.

NOTES

[1]One New York Times article typified the tendency to describe women in terms of how they might transmit HIV: women who are "drug addicts . . . are not using condoms that can arrest the spread of AIDS. And they are becoming pregnant despite the knowledge that they could infect a fetus, and bearing children, many of whom will die. But another category of these infected women, the sex partners of men who have injected drugs, are behaving far more responsibly—protecting their mates and avoiding or terminating unwanted pregnancies." J. Gross, "The Bleak and Lonely Lives of Women who Carry AIDS," *New York Times*, 27 August 1987, p. A-1. See also B. G. Schoepf, "Breaking Through the Looking Glass," in *The Politics of Anthropology: From Colonialism/Sexism Toward a View from Below*, ed. G. Hulzer, B. Mannheim (The Hague: Mouton, 1979).

[2]See, e.g., H. S. Kaplan, *The Real Truth About Women and AIDS: How to Eliminate the Risks Without Giving Up Love and Sex* (New York: Simon and Schuster, 1987).

[3]For example, an article in the *New York Times* stated that only a tiny number of AIDS cases in women resulted from sexual contact with a bisexual man but went on to say that "numbers offer little consolation to the individual woman . . ., especially a middle-class woman" who thinks her chance of involvement with an injection drug user is remote. "For this kind of woman, experts say," according to the article, "the figure of the male bisexual . . . has become the bogeyman of the late 1980s." J. Nordheimer, "AIDS Specter for Women: The Bisexual Man," *New York Times*, 2 April 1987, p. A-1.

[4]The rate of death from AIDS is nine times greater among African-American women than among white women, for example. S. Chu, T. Buehler, and R. Berkelman, "Impact of the Human Immunodeficiency Virus Epidemic on Mortality in Women of Reproductive Age, United States," *Journal of the American Medical Association* 264(1990):225, 226.

[5]CDC, *HIV/AIDS Surveillance Report* (hereafter, *Surveillance Report*), February 1993, Table 5 at 11.

[6]55 Fed. Reg. 23414, 7 June, 1990.

[7]Gay Men's Health Crisis v. Sullivan, 792 F. Supp. 278, S.D.N.Y. (1992).

[8]M. T. Fullilove, R. E. Fullilove, K. Haynes, and S. Gross, "Black Women and AIDS Prevention: A View Towards Understanding the Gender Rules," *Journal of Sex Research* 27(1990):47, 62.

[9]Women in different ethnic or racial communities will respond best to materials that respect the values of those communities. V. Mays and S. Cochran, "Issues in the Perception of AIDS Risk and Rise Reduction Activities by Black and Hispanic/Latina Women," *American Psychologist* 43(1988):949; N. Maldonado, "Latinas and HIV/AIDS: Implications for the 90s," *SIECUS Report* (December 1990/January 1991):10–15; N. Freudenberg, *Preventing AIDS: A Guide to Effective Education for the Prevention of HIV Infection* (Washington, D.C.: American Public Health Association, 1989), pp. 148–50, 171, 175.

[10]E. Murray (quoting Dr. Vickie Mays of UCLA), "Report from the First National Women and HIV Conference," *Gay Community News*, 1–13 January, 1991, p. 16; New York State Department of Health, AIDS Institute, *Focus on AIDS in New York State* October 1990, p. 3 (hereafter, *Focus on AIDS*).

[11]Z. A. Stein, "HIV Prevention: The Need for Methods Women Can Use," *American Journal of Public Health*, 80(1990):460.

[12]S. Y. Chu, J. W. Buehler, P. L. Fleming, and R. L. Berkelman, "Epidemiology of Reported Cases of AIDS in Lesbians, United States 1980–89," *American Journal of Public Health* 80(1990):1380. See, generally, Young, G. Weissman, and H. Cohen, "Assessing Risk in the Absence of Information: HIV Risk Among Women Injection-Drug Users Who Have Sex with Women," *AIDS & Public Policy Journal* 7(Fall 1992):175.

[13]*Focus on AIDS*; see, e.g., Ramos v. Community Health Plan, No. 86-4114, AIDS Litigation Rptr. (Andrews Pub.) 15 (Mass. 1986), a case in which a woman successfully sued her physician for malpractice for failure to diagnose her condition as AIDS.

[14]S. Safrin, B. Dattel, L. Hauer, and R. L. Sweet, "Seroprevalence and Epidemiologic Correlates of Human Immunodeficiency Virus Infection in Women with Acute Pelvic Inflammatory Disease," *Obstetrics & Gynecology* 75(1990):666; J. Rhoads, C. Wright, R. Redfield, and L. Burke, "Chronic Vaginal Candidiasis in Women with Human Immunodeficiency Virus Infection," *Journal of the American Medical Association* 257(1987):3105; CDC, "Risk for Cervical Disease in HIV-Infected Women—New York City, *Journal of the American Medical Association* 265(1991):23.

[15]K. Anastos and C. Marte, "Women—The Missing Persons in the AIDS Epidemic," in *The AIDS Reader: Social, Political and Ethical Issues*, ed. N. McKenzie, (New York: Meridian, (1991). Crucial questions about transmission in women also remain unsolved and unstudied, among them, whether cervical tissue or vaginal tissue is more likely to become infected and whether use of oral contraceptives has an impact on transmission. Z. A. Stein, "The Congressional Biomedical Research Caucus Presentation" (Unpublished testimony, 1991).

[16]See Surveillance Report, Table 5 at 11. CDC officials originally assigned gay male IDUs to the category of homosexual transmission. Subsequently, to correct for the same kind of distortion, a distinct category was created for men who had engaged in both kinds of high-risk behaviors.

[17]G. Kolata, "Growing Movement Seeks to Help Women Infected with AIDS Virus," *New York Times*, 4 May, 1989.

[18]According to Dr. Janet Mitchell, director of obstetrics at Harlem Hospital, "We only identify about one-third of potentially HIV-infected women at my hospital. I don't know what the prevalence is at Harlem because I can't get my ob-gyns to refer women to testing programs and get data. If they don't know the woman's HIV status, they don't have to deal with it." R. Murray, "Report from the First National Women and HIV Conference," *Gay Community News*, 7–13, January 1991, p. 9.

[19]L. M. Hardy, ed., *HIV Screening of Pregnant Women and Newborns* (Washington, D.C.: National Academy Press, 1991), 3708 (hereafter, Hardy).

[20]Ill. Rev. Stat. ch. 127, para. 55.44(b), 1989.

[21]A. Malcolm, "In Making Drug Strategy, No Accord on Treatment," *New York Times*, 19 November 1989, p. 1.

[22]"Help is Hard to Find for Addict Mothers," *Los Angeles Times*, 12 December, 1986, p. J-1.

[23]W. Chavkin, "Drug Addiction and Pregnancy: Policy Crossroads," *American Journal of Public Health* 80(1990):483.

[24]Elaine W. v. Joint Diseases North General Hospital, District Court of N.Y. 2d Circuit, 1993.

[25]Working Group on HIV Testing of Pregnant Women and Newborns, "HIV Infection, Pregnant Women, and Newborns: A Policy Proposal for Information and Testing," *Journal of the American Medical Association* 264(1990):2416 (hereafter, "Working Group Policy Proposal"); C. Levine and R. Bayer, "The Ethics of Screening for Early Intervention in HIV Disease," *American Journal of Public Health* 79(1989):1661, 1662 (hereafter, Levine and Bayer). For reasons not yet understood, recent studies have found that the perinatal transmission rate is lower—only about 13 percent—in Europe than in the United States. "European Study Finds Few Babies Get AIDS," *New York Times*, 5 March, 1991.

[26]Levine and Bayer.

[27]"Working Group Policy Proposal"; Hardy.

[28]M. Angell, "A Dual Approach to the AIDS Epidemic," *New England Journal of Medicine* 324(1991):1498.

[29]*Washington Post*, 11 July, 1989, p. A-16. As of late 1990, researchers were planning for a phase III (the final phase) clinical trial of AZT in pregnant women. *CDC Weekly*, 5 November, 1990.

[30]The possible application of the Illinois statute is discussed in S. Isaacman, "Are We Outlawing Motherhood for HIV-Infected Women?" *Loyola Law Journal* 22(1991):479.

[31]See C. Levine and N. Dubler, "Uncertain Risks and Bitter Realities: The Reproductive Choices of HIV-Infected Women," *Milbank Quarterly* 68(1990):321 (hereafter, Levine and Dubler).

[32]The use of women's reproductive capacity to define the entire category of "woman" is notably true in medicine, where the very fields of "obstetrics and gynecology" and "maternal and child health" bespeak both the convergence of the two functions (medical care for childbirth and health care for women) an the prioritization of the first. H. Amaro, "Women's Reproductive Rights in the Age of AIDS: New Threats to

Informed Choice" (Unpublished speech before American Public Health Association, 1989).

[33]Banks, "Women and AIDS—Racism, Sexism, and Classism," *NYU Rev. L. and Social Change* 17(1989–1990):351, 361–365. One trade newspaper for obstetricians, after conducting a telephone survey in 1987, suggested that a proposal for forced sterilizations of HIV-infected women would have considerable support. A. Mitchell, "Women, AIDS and Public Policy," *AIDS & Public Policy Journal* 3(1988):50, 51.

[34]The *Philadelphia Inquirer* suggested in an editorial that women on welfare be given incentives to use a contraceptive implant. "Poverty and Norplant: Can Contraception Reduce the Underclass?" *Philadelphia Inquirer*, 12 December, 1990, p. A-18, col. 1.

[35]R. Bayer, "AIDS and the Future of Reproductive Freedom," *Milbank Quarterly* The CDC's director of AIDS activities was quoted in 1988 as saying that "there is no reason that the number of [HIV-infected babies] shouldn't decline. . . . Someone who understands the disease and is logical will not want to be pregnant." 68(1990):179, 189–191.

[36]A. Acuff and R. Faden, "A History of Prenatal and Newborn Screening Programs: Lessons for the Future," in *AIDS, Women and the Next Generation*, ed., R. Faden, G. Geller, and M. Powers, (1991) (hereafter, Acuff and Faden). Syphilis is the only condition for which prenatal testing is widely required by law.

[37]*Mortality and Morbidity Weekly Report* 34(6 December, 1985):721.

[38]CDC, "Conference on the Role of AIDS Virus Antibody Testing in the Prevention and Control of AIDS, Closing Plenary Session: Reports from the Workshops" (Transcript, 1987), 3.

[39]Del. Code Ann. tit. 16, sec. 708 (1990 Supp.); Fla. Stat. Sec. 384.31, 384.23 (1991 Supp.).

[40]Mich. Comp. Laws Ann. 333.5123 (1991 Supp.).

[41]R. Edelman and H. W. Haverkos, "The Suitability of HIV Positive Individuals for Marriage and Pregnancy," 261 *Journal of the American Medical Association* (1989):993.

[42]"Working Group Policy Proposal."

[43]K. Krasinski, W. Borkowsky, D. Bebenroth, and T. Moore, "Failure of Voluntary Testing for HIV to Identify Infected Parturient Women in a High Risk Population," *New England Journal of Medicine* 318(1988):185.

[44]Several studies have found widespread surreptitious HIV testing in hospitals. Henry, K. Willenbring, and K. Crossley, "Human Immunodeficiency Virus: Analysis of the Use of HIV Antibody Testing," *Journal of the American Medical Association* 259(1988):1819, 1820; P. Hilts, "Many Hospitals Found to Ignore Rights of Patients in AIDS Testing," *New York Times*, 17 February, 1990, p. A-1, col. 1.

[45]J. Arras, "AIDS and Reproductive Decisions: Having Children in Fear and Trembling," *Milbank Quarterly* 68(1990):353 (hereafter, Arras); R. Bayer, "Perinatal Transmission of HIV Infection: The Ethics of Prevention," in *AIDS and the Health Care System* ed. L. Gostin, (New Haven: Yale University Press, 1990), 62 (hereafter, Bayer).

[46]The beginning point, under privacy doctrine, for analyzing the constitutionality of state-mandated blood tests in the Fourth Amendment, which forbids "unreasonable" searches and seizures. An involuntary blood test falls within the scope of a "search and seizure" for the purposes of that amendment. Winston v. Lee, 470 U.S. 753 (1985).

[47]D. A. Grimes, "The CDC and Abortion in HIV-Positive Women," (letter), *Journal of the American Medical Association* 258(1987):1176.

[48]Although 65 percent "agreed" or "strongly agreed" with the statement that "women should not have babies who will be at risk for [AIDS]," there was only 25 percent agreement with that statement when the disease was Tay-Sachs; only 15 percent for cystic fibrosis; and only 9 percent for Downs syndrome. Bayer, 193.

[49]Planned Parenthood of Southeastern Pennsylvania v. Casey, 112 S. Ct. 2791 (1992).

[50]Ibid., 2821.

[51]American Civil Liberties Union Foundation AIDS Project, *Epidemic of Fear*, 1990. Data from the New York City Commission on Human Rights indicate that the percentage of complaints of AIDS-related discrimination filed in that office by women increased from 20 percent to 32 percent from 1986 to 1990. Communication to author, March 1991.

[52]"Working Group Policy Proposal," 2419.

[53]I. J. Chasnoff, H. J. Landress, and M. E. Barrett, "The Prevalence of Illicit-Drug or Alcohol Use During Pregnancy and Discrepancies in Mandatory Reporting in Pinellas County, Florida," *New England Journal of Medicine* 322(1990):1202.

[54]Village of Arlington Heights v. Metropolitan Housing Development Corp., 429 U.S. 252 (1977); Washington v. Davis, 426 U.S. 229 (1976).

[55]Tay-Sachs is a genetic disorder prevalent among Jews of eastern European ancestry. It is a uniformly fatal neurodegenerative disease affecting approximately 1 in 3,600 Jewish children and 1 in 360,000 non-Jewish children. Sickle-cell anemia found in the United States primarily among African Americans, involves a chemical defect in hemoglobins of red blood cells. Approximately 2.2 million Americans are carriers of the genetic trait, and about 1 in 600 African Americans develop sickle-cell anemia. S. Elias and G. J. Annas, *Reproductive Genetics and the Law* (Chicago: Year Book Medical Publishers, 1987), 62–4.

Although no state currently requires prenatal screening for either condition, the history of Tay-Sachs testing is very different from the history of sickle-cell screening. During the 1970s, several statutes mandating the latter kind of testing were enacted but have now been repealed. See notes 87–92 and accompanying text.

[56]U.S. Department of Health, Education and Welfare, "Task Force Report: Predictors of Hereditary Disease or Congenital Defects," Consensus Development Conference on Antenatal Diagnosis (1979), 35–47.

[57]Levine and Dubler, 340; J. Arras, 358; J. Hunger, "Time Limits on Abortion," in *Reproductive Laws for the 1990s*, ed. S. Taub and N. Cohen, (Clifton, N.J.: Humana Press, 1988), 103.

[58]R. Gold and S. Guardado, "Public Funding of Family Planning, Sterilization and Abortion Services," *Family Planning Perspectives* 20(1988):228, 233; S. Henshaw and J. Van Vort, "Abortion Services in the United States," *Family Planning Perspectives* 22(1990):102, 105–106.

[59]City of New York Commission on Human Rights, *HIV-Related Discrimination by Reproductive Health Care Providers in New York City* (New York: Commission on Human Rights), 22 October, 1990.

[60]P. A. Selwyn, E. E. Schoenbaum, K. Davenny, *et al.*, "Prospective Study of Human

Immunodeficiency Virus Infection and Pregnancy Outcomes in Intravenous Drug Users," *Journal of the American Medical Association.* 261 (1989):1289; Bayer, 180; Gross, "New York's Poorest Women Offered More AIDS Services," *New York Times*, 6 March 1988, p. A-1.

[61]For a richly contextualized discussion of the social realities facing women with HIV disease, see Levine and Dubler.

[62]N. Kass, R. Faden, P. O'Campo, and A. Gielen, "Policy Options for Pre-natal Screening Programs for HIV: The Preferences of Inner-City Pregnant Women," *AIDS & Public Policy Journal* 7 (Winter 1992):225; "Working Group Policy Proposal"; Hardy; Levine and Dubler.

[63]See, e.g., M. A. Field, "Controlling the Woman to Protect the Fetus," *Law, Medicine & Health Care* 17(1989):114 (hereafter, Field); Johnsen, "The Creation of Fetal Rights: Conflicts with Women's Constitutional Rights to Liberty, Privacy and Equal Protection," *Yale Law Journal* 95(1986):599; L. J. Nelson and N. Milliken, "Compelled Medical Treatment of Pregnant Women: Life, Liberty and Law in Conflict," *Journal of the American Medical Association* 259(1988):1060; and Nelson, Buggy, and Weil, "Forced Medical Treatment of Pregnant Women: 'Compelling Each to Live as Seems Good to the Rest,' " *Hastings Law Journal* 37(1986):703.

[64]Jefferson v. Griffin Spalding County Hospital Authority, 247 Ga. 86, 274 S.E. 2d 457 (1981) (Caesarean section ordered over religious objection); Raleigh Fitkin–Paul Morgan Memorial Hospital v. Anderson, 42 N.J. 421, 201 A.2d 537, cert. denied 377 U.S. 985 (1964) (blood transfusion ordered over religious objection); In re: Jamaican Hospital, 128 Misc.2d 1006, 491 N.Y.S. 2d 898 (Sup. Ct. 1985) (blood transfusion ordered over religious objection); Crouse Irving Memorial Hospital, Inc. v. Paddock, 127 Misc.2d 101, 485 N.Y.S. 2d 443 (Sup. Ct. 1985) (blood transfusion ordered over religious objection); Contra, Taft v. Taft, 388 Mass. 331, 446 N.E.2d 395 (1983) (vacating an order requiring vaginal surgery, over religious objection, which would have facilitated delivery).

[65]In re: A.C., 573 A.2d 1235 (D.C. App. 1990) (en banc).

[66]573 A.2d at 1247.

[67]L. Greenhouse, "Hospital Sets Policy on Pregnant Patients' Rights," *New York Times*, 29 November 1990.

[68]Board of Trustees, American Medical Association, "Legal Interventions During Pregnancy," *Journal of the American Medical Association* 264(1990):2663.

[69]American College of Obstetricians and Gynecologists, Committee on Ethics Opinion 55, *Patient Choice: Maternal-Fetal Conflict*, October 1987.

[70]American Academy of Pediatrics, Committee on Substance Abuse, "Drug Exposed Infants," *Pediatrics* 86(1990):639, 642.

[71]V. E. Kolder, J. Gallagher, and M. J. Parsons, "Court Ordered Obstetrical Interventions," *New England Journal of Medicine* 316(1987):1192.

[72]Johnson v. Florida, 602 So. 2d 1288 (Fla. 1992) (reversing conviction for delivery of controlled substances to a minor through umbilical cord); People v. Hardy, 469 N.W. 2d 50 (Mich. Ct. App. 1991) (overturning conviction under statute prohibiting drug delivery to children on grounds that it was not intended to include fetuses); State v. Gray, 584 N.E. 2d 710 (Ohio 1992) (child-endangering statute did not include

woman's prenatal conduct); Reyes v. Superior Court, 75 Cal. App. 3d 214 (1977) (barring prosecution on same grounds); State v. Luster, 419 S.E. 2d 32 (Ga. Ct. App. 1992) (barring prosecution on same grounds); In re. Valerie D., 223 Conn. 492 (1992) (child abuse statute not intended to apply where child born with positive toxicology); In re: Monique T., 4 Cal. Rptr. 3d 198 (Ct. App. 1992) (child's positive toxicology creates rebuttable presumption of neglect); In re: Theresa J., 551 N.Y.S. 2d 219 (App. Div. 1990) (same); In the Matter of Nash, 419 N.W. 2d 1 (Mich. Ct. app. 1987) (same); and Cox v. Court of Common Pleas, 537 N.E. 2d 721 (Ohio Ct. App. 1988) (court lacked jurisdiction to compel pregnant woman to take action for alleged benefit of unborn child).

[73]AIDS Policy Center, Intergovernmental Health Policy Project, George Washington University, January 1993.

[74]Tex. Penal Code Ann. § 22.012(a) (Vernon Supp. 1991).

[75]Field, 118.

[76]Hardy, 26–28.

[77]P. Hilts, "Effective Test Is Developed to Find AIDS in Newborns," *New York Times*, 4 February 1993, p. B-8.

[78]CDC, "Guidelines for Prophylaxis Against Pneumocystis Carinii Pneumonia for Children Infected with Human Immunodeficiency Virus," *Journal of the American Medical Association* 265(1991):1637.

[79]Jehovah's Witnesses v. King County Hospital, 390 U.S. 598 (1968) (per curiam) (statute upheld which permitted children to be declared wards of the court, so that the court could consent to medical procedures for them, when parents opposed blood transfusions on religious grounds). See generally V. Sher, "Choosing for Children: Adjudicating Medical Care Disputes Between Parents and the State," *NYU Law Review* 58(1983):157.

[80]A. Acuff, "Prenatal and Newborn Screening: State Legislative Approaches and Current Practice Standards," in *AIDS, Women and the Next Generation*, ed. R. Faden, G. Belber, and M. Powers (New York: Oxford University Press, 1991), 121–165.

[81]Gen. Laws R.I. 23-6-14(a) (1989 Supp.).

[82]B. W. Levin, J. M. Driscoll, and A. R. Fleischman, "Treatment Choice for Infants in the Neonatal Intensive Care Unit at Risk for AIDS," *Journal of the American Medical Association* 265(1991):2976. Moreover, 20 percent of the doctors surveyed would have changed their recommendation for treating the infant had they known only that the mother was HIV-infected.

[83]J. Areen, "Intervention Between Parent and Child: A Reappraisal of the State's Role in Child Neglect and Abuse Cases," *Geo. J. L.* 63(1975):887, 894–910.

[84]Every state has a statute authorizing intervention to override a parent's decisions regarding medical care of a child. C. Jackson, "Severely Disabled Newborns: To Live or Let Die?" *J. Legal Med.* 8(1987):135, 155 n143.

[85]P. Ries, "Characteristics of Persons with and without Health Care Coverage: United States, 1989," *Advance Data from Vital and Health Statistics of the National Center for Health Statistics* 201 (18 June 1991): Table 1 at 2.

[86]Levine and Bayer, 1666.

[87]P. Reilly, *Genetics, Law and Social Policy* (Cambridge, MA: Harvard University Press,

1977), See also M. R. Farfel and N. A. Holtzman, "Education, Consent and Counseling in Sickle Cell Screening Programs: Report of a Study," *American Journal of Public Health* 74(1984):373.

[88]Acuff and Faden.

[89]"Sickle Cell Legislation: Beneficence or 'The New Ghetto Hustle'?" *Journal of Family Law* 13(1973–1974):278, 279 n6.

[90]42 U.S.C. 300b(a)(1). See Culliton, "Sickle Cell Anemia: National Program Raises Problems as Well as Hopes," *Science* 20 October 1972, 283. Congress repealed the legislation in 1981. Pub. L. 97–35, Title XXI, Sec. 2193(b)(1), Aug. 13, 1981, 95 Stat. 827.

[91]National Institutes of Health, Consensus Conference, "Newborn Screening for Sickle Cell Disease and Other Hemoglobinopathies," *Journal of the American Medical Association* 258(1987):1205, 1209.

[92]Acuff and Faden.

[93]If a parent has "undertaken reasonable efforts to ensure that acceptable medical treatment is being provided for the [] child," a court should defer to the parent's reasonable choice of how medical care should be provided. In re Hofbauer, 393 N.E. 2d 1009, 1014 (N.Y. 1979) (finding no medical neglect where parents chose nutrition and metabolic therapy for child with Hodgkin's disease and refused to follow medical advice of the majority of the medical profession, which recommends radiation and chemotherapy). Where a parent refuses to follow any medical advice or where the medical opinion as to diagnosis and treatment of a life-threatening disease is clear and uncontested, courts will refuse to permit a parent's decision to endanger the child. In re Custody of Minor, 434 N.E. 2d 601 (Mass. 1982); In re Custody of a Minor, 393 N.E. 2d 836 (Mass. 1979); In re Hamilton, 657 S.W. 2d 425 (Tenn. Ct. App. 1983).

[94]U.S. Department of Commerce, Bureau of the Census, *Marital Status and Living Arrangements: March 1989* (1990), Table C at 3.

[95]K. Teltsch, "Mothers Dying of AIDS Get Child Custody Help," *New York Times*, 27 August, 1991, p. B-1, col. 2.

[96]F. Lee, "The Scythe of AIDS Leaves a Generation of Orphans," *New York Times* 7 March 1993, p. E-18, col. 1.

[97]Elizabeth B. Cooper, "HIV-Infected Parents and the Law: Issues of Custody, Visitation and Guardianship," in *AIDS Agenda: Emerging Issues in Civil Rights*, ed. Nan D. Hunter and William B. Rubenstein, (New York: The New Press, 1992).

[98]Act of June 30, 1992, ch. 290, 1992 Laws of New York 972 (surrogate's court procedure—standby guardianship).

Diane K. Lewis

African-American Women at Risk: Notes on the Sociocultural Context of HIV Infection

African Americans appear to be the most disproportionately affected of all ethnic groups by the AIDS epidemic.[1] They are 12 percent of the total U.S. population, but comprise 30 percent of all reported AIDS cases.[2] Of every 5 black adult AIDS cases, 1 is a woman, compared to 1 in every 19 white cases and 1 in every 7 Latino cases. The cumulative incidence of AIDS (number of cases per 1 million persons 13 and over) was more than 11 times higher for black women than white women between 1983 and 1988.[3] Moreover, AIDS is the leading cause of death in black women ages 15 to 44 in New Jersey and New York. And, nationwide, black women died from AIDS at 9 times the rate of white women (10.3 per 100,000 versus 1.2 per 100,000).[4] To begin to understand why blacks, particularly poor black women, carry so heavy a burden of disease, it is instructive to compare AIDS exposure categories for African Americans and whites. As shown in Table 1, the major transmission routes are markedly different for the two ethnic groups.

According to the Centers for Disease Control, through December 1992, 76 percent of white cases were attributed to male homosexual sexual contact, compared to 35 percent of black cases. Whereas 45 percent of blacks acquired the disease either through injection drug use (40 percent) or through a combination of injection drug use and homosexuality (6 percent), only 15 percent of whites reported an association with drug injection. Heterosexual sexual contact with a person at risk for AIDS accounted for 8 percent of all black AIDS cases and 2 percent of all white AIDS cases.[5] In reviewing past CDC surveillance reports, we find that the proportion of total AIDS cases attributed to male homosexuality has dropped, and the proportions linked to injecting drugs and to heterosexual sexual contact have steadily increased. As a consequence, the number of minority cases is beginning to approach the number of white cases in this country and, if present trends continue, blacks and Latinos with AIDS may soon outnumber whites. With the decline in exposure through male homosexual sexual contact, the proportion of female AIDS cases has also increased.

Women now make up 11 percent of all AIDS cases. Since more African

TABLE 1. Distribution of Adult AIDS Cases by Exposure Category and Ethnic/Racial Group, October 1991

Exposure Category	White No.	(%)	Black No.	(%)
Homosexual/Bisexual Contact	80,820	76	19,783	35
IV Drug Use	8,943	8	22,076	40
Homosexual/Bisexual Contact and IV Drug Use	7,355	7	3,478	6
Heterosexual Contact	2,380	2	4,332	8
Born in Pattern II Country*	11	0	2,411	4
Transfusion	2,946	3	750	1
Hemophilia Disorder	1,363	1	126	0
Undetermined	2,946	3	2,930	5
Total Cases	106,764	100	55,886	99†

Persons born in countries where heterosexual contact is the major transmission route for HIV.
†*Column does not add to 100 due to rounding.*
Source: *Centers for Disease Control,* HIV/AIDS Surveillance Report, *February 1991, 9.*

Americans than whites appear to contract AIDS through heterosexual contact, it should not be surprising that black women comprise such a high proportion of all women with AIDS (see Table 2). They are over half (53 percent), compared to whites, who comprise one-quarter, of all female AIDS cases. Except for blood transfusions, the pattern of exposure is similar for black and white women: mainly by injection drug use, followed by sex with a man at risk of AIDS (see Table 2). Almost three-fourths of black women's cases are linked to drug injection, either directly (56 percent) or indirectly through sex with a male drug injector (20 percent), compared to 57 percent of the white women who acquired the virus through injecting drugs (42 percent) or sex with an injection drug user (15 percent). Sexual contact with a bisexual man accounted for 2 percent of all exposures among black women and 6 percent among white women; however, according to disaggregated 1990 CDC data tapes on adult males, bisexuality was reported far more often by black than white men infected through homosexual sexual contact. In other words, 30 percent of the black men in the homosexual/bisexual exposure category were bisexual compared to 15 percent of the white men; 36 percent of the black drug injectors who had homosexual/bisexual sexual contact were bisexual compared to 24 percent of the whites.[6]

Patterns of HIV infection in the general population mirror the ethnic imbalances displayed in AIDS incidence reporting. For example, surveys of migrant farm workers, military reservists, prisoners, blood donors, pa-

TABLE 2. Distribution of Adult Female AIDS Cases by Exposure Category and Ethnic/Racial Group, October 1991

Exposure Category	White No.	(%)	Black No.	(%)
IV Drug Use	2,183	42	5,930	56
Heterosexual Sexual Contact	1,616	31	2,913	27
Sex with an IV Drug User	812	(15)	2,133	(20)
Sex with a Bisexual Man	336	(6)	210	(2)
Sex with an Infected Male, Risk Unspecified	281	(5)	473	(4)
Other Heterosexual Contact*	187	(4)	97	(1)
Born in Pattern II Country†	5	0	684	6
Transfusion	1,039	20	342	3
Hemophilia Disorder	28	1	8	0
Undetermined	381	7	785	7
Total Cases	6,868	101‡	13,575	99‡

* Other heterosexual sexual contact includes sex with a hemophiliac, blood transfusion recipient, or person born in a Pattern II country.
† Persons born in countries where heterosexual contact is the major transmission route for HIV.
‡ Column does not add to 100 due to rounding.
Source: *Centers for Disease Control, HIV/AIDS Surveillance Report, February 1991, 10.*

tients in sentinel hospitals, and female clinic patients, as well as among drug injectors and men who have sex with men,[7] all suggest that black Americans have higher rates of HIV infection than white Americans. The CDC estimated that approximately 1 to 1.5 million people in the United States were infected with HIV. Based on recent AIDS incidence ratios and 1990 U.S. Census population figures, this suggests that 1 to 1.5 percent of all African Americans may be infected, compared to 0.2 to 0.4 percent of all whites.[8]

These data indicate that black women (like black men) are at far higher risk of AIDS and HIV infection than white women. The purpose of this chapter is to examine the societal dynamics that underlie their elevated risk. It discusses the sociocultural context of injection drug use and of sexual risk behavior in poor African-American communities in San Francisco and suggests how wider social forces constraining the life experiences of many inner-city black women have contributed to their exposure to the disease. The chapter also reviews the impact of government reactions to the AIDS crisis in black America. As we will see, the responses of both national and local leaders have had far-reaching repercussions on the course of the epidemic.

METHODS

This discussion draws on current research on women drug injectors for insights about the circumstances of drug use and sexual behavior among African Americans. From September 1988 to September 1990, I collected in-depth life histories from 32 black women as part of a larger study of black and white women injection drug users. The women were recruited at the sites of an ongoing survey of seroprevalence and risk factors for HIV transmission in three low-income communities in San Francisco.[9] Those who agreed to provide their life histories participated in open-ended interviews lasting from one and one-half to four hours. The women were asked to talk about past life events, including childhood experiences, history of drug use, sexual behavior, and knowledge about AIDS and AIDS prevention. Informed consent was obtained, and respondents were paid for their participation. One of the goals of the life history study is to gain the women's own perspectives on their lives. For further information on injection drug users and on sexual behavior, I also consulted the literature on minorities and drug use and the scant research on black women's sexuality. Interestingly, many of the observations by women drug injectors about their sexual attitudes and behaviors, as well as the drug-using scene, reflected those of noninjecting women from similar backgrounds found in the literature.

BLACK WOMEN AND INJECTION DRUG USE

Due to a government policy of disruption of social services and neglect over the past 12 years, black inner cities have become increasingly marginalized and crime-ridden. One index of this deterioration is the apparently disproportionate involvement of African Americans in injection drug use, a situation inextricably tied to poverty and racial discrimination.[10] Forced to live in inadequate housing in segregated neighborhoods, poor residents often experience low educational opportunities and high rates of unemployment.[11] For some, sale of drugs may seem a viable option for economic survival.[12]

A COMPETING LIFESTYLE. Although only a small percentage of African Americans are involved in selling and/or injecting drugs, their overconcentration in relatively circumscribed minority neighborhoods results in injection drug use's achieving the status of a "competing and often destructive lifestyle."[13] Addiction to drugs in these circumstances can become "a significant way of life, pervading a community."[14] By contrast, the small proportion of whites who inject drugs are not only less visible in the much larger white community,[15] they also experience privileges denied most African Americans, such as greater access to legitimate jobs and medical care and avoidance of police harassment and arrests.

The black women drug injectors I interviewed, unlike the white women, often talked about the pervasiveness of hard drug use in the areas where they grew up. As one heroin user noted about her childhood, "It seems like everybody in the projects, they was selling something . . . [and] on the way home from school, . . . the people would be out there, near the drug store, selling heroin." Similar accounts of "epidemic levels" of neighborhood drug use appear in a recent study of a more representative group of women from a poor black San Francisco community.[16] Not only were the black women I interviewed exposed, as children, to a highly visible drug scene on the streets, but some eventually discovered that family members, close friends, or boyfriends were themselves engaged in injection drug use. It was often through these personal relationships that many women were introduced to drug injecting.[17]

The black inner cities, inundated by drug users, differed in another respect from white neighborhoods, where drug use was more hidden. HIV was apparently introduced earlier into black injection drug-using areas. Unaware of the danger, infected users spread the virus rapidly in some black neighborhoods due to the accompanying rituals of drug injecting, such as needle sharing and rinsing (rather than sterilizing) of used equipment before reuse.[18]

PERMEABLE BOUNDARIES. The pervasiveness of drugs in these neighborhoods and the proximity of "straight" residents to injection drug users means that the boundaries between drug users and nonusers are relatively permeable in some black communities. Miller, in a study of street women in Milwaukee, also noticed this phenomenon. She found that black women, unlike white women, tended to grow up in domestic arrangements where one or more household members had ties to street life and such illegitimate activities as drug sales and use.[19]

Because of widespread drug use in poor black communities, chances are high that a woman who does not inject drugs will become intimately involved with a man who does, or who has a history of drug injecting. Some of these women may eventually start to inject drugs themselves, as noted above, while others may remain unaware of their partners' drug use. Other women who do not inject drugs may learn that their partner is an injector but may continue the relationship. A poor black woman's greater likelihood of coming into social contact with a man who injects drugs reflects social patterns reported by drug injectors themselves. Research on injection drug users in both San Francisco and New York indicates that African Americans are significantly more likely than whites to have (that is, to apparently show a preference for) sexual partners who are noninjectors.[20] Consequently, even noninjecting African Americans may encounter a greater likelihood of receiving the virus through sexual intercourse with an infected drug-injecting partner.

The increased probability of interaction between black residents who use drugs with those who do not stems in part from a tradition of greater integration into the black community of people engaged in "deviant" behavior. Although such persons usually try to keep their nonnormative behavior secret, greater tolerance may be shown, for example, when they run afoul of the law. This attitude may be based in part on a recognition that black men and women are more likely to be arrested, to be sentenced, and to serve longer jail or prison terms than whites.[21] For example, black women, who comprised about 14 percent of all women in San Francisco, made up half of those serving local jail sentences, a percentage mirroring state and federal incarceration figures.[22] A study of incarcerated women in San Francisco found, however, that most African Americans, despite family disapproval, continued to be in communication with their relatives. These women retained close ties with their children, often cared for by kin while they were in jail, and felt they could rely on relatives for emotional and other support when they were released. Conversely, the overwhelming majority of jailed white women reported that they were out of contact with children or other relatives and stated that they could not depend on family members for help when they got out.[23] A similar difference is emerging in my current study of women drug injectors, with most of the black women, unlike many white women, stating that they are in frequent contact with at least one relative, even though their use of drugs is frowned upon.

The more permeable boundaries in African-American neighborhoods between people who do and do not use drugs provide more conduits for the spread of HIV into the general community, either through sexual relationships with an injection drug user or through street ties, which lead to younger household members' involvement in drug-using lifestyles. Among whites, on the other hand, the boundaries between "deviant" and "respectable" people appear less penetrable. White drug injectors appear more cut off when their lifestyles are discovered, with a lower likelihood of intimate contact between users and nonusers. For example, Schoenbaum et al. not only found that white drug injectors were more likely than African Americans to have sex partners who were drug injectors, but also implied that they more often restricted their social interaction to friends and relatives who injected drugs. The possible greater isolation of white injection drug users from nonusers may result in fewer bridges for HIV transmission into the white community.[24] One consequence for women of the interpenetration of boundaries around injection drug use in the black community is dramatically shown in the CDC figures for cumulative incidence or risk of exposure to AIDS associated with injecting drugs. Black women have 18 times the risk of white women of acquiring AIDS through drug injection, and 22 times the risk of becoming infected through sex with a drug injector.[25] Moreover, black women's risk of infection through sex with a drug injector may be higher than reported by the CDC. Recent research among injection drug users in

San Francisco suggests that HIV may now be transmitted as often through risky sex as through unsafe needle use.[26] These figures lead us to examine more closely the social circumstances underlying black women's sexual behavior and the specific sexual practices that appear to put them at increasing risk for HIV transmission.

BLACK WOMEN AND HIGH-RISK SEX

Epidemiological studies imply that African-American women's greater risk of AIDS and other STDs is due to their earlier initiation of coitus and to their greater involvement in high-risk sexual behaviors such as prostitution.[27] Very little research has been carried out, however, to test these hypotheses. Moreover, the few recent studies that have been conducted challenge earlier assumptions. For example, recent surveys suggest that black women may begin sexual activity on an average of only 5 months to 9 months earlier than whites: age 15.5 years compared to 16.4 years, respectively, in a national study and 16.7 years and 17.2 years, respectively, in a Los Angeles study.[28] A study of women drug injectors found that white women were as likely as black women to report prostitution experience.[29]

While premarital sex may be fairly common among African Americans, "good girls" are distinguished from "bad girls" by their commitment to one partner rather than multiple partners.[30] Nonetheless, "serial monogamy" is not uncommon. In a study of women and teenage girls in a poor black community in San Francisco, researchers found that the women themselves saw their difficulties in maintaining stable relationships as stemming from the scarcity of black men.[31] Mays and Cochran note that there are 75 unmarried men over age 15 for every 100 black women.[32] Although, as some observers claim,[33] these figures may reflect a perennial undercount of black men, black men are clearly far more likely than white men to be incarcerated and to be the victims of homicide.[34] Those men who are available may find it impossible to obtain jobs or may be addicted to drugs or alcohol, leading again to the undermining of stable family and sexual ties.[35] Under these circumstances, some poor black women, although desiring a long-term commitment, may have to settle for a series of relatively short-term relationships with men who may simultaneously be having sexual relationships with other women and who may have backgrounds of imprisonment or drug use.[36]

While "serial monogamy" may characterize the intimate lives of some, available research does not support the notion that black women, generally, have a history of a greater number of sexual partners than white women. Wyatt, in a Los Angeles study of 250 black and white women, based on a random sample, found that, among sexually active women, white women said they had a larger number of sexual partners since they began intercourse than black women.[37] A study of drug-injecting women found a similar pattern. White women significantly more often than black women said they had four or more partners during the year prior to interview.[38]

The few studies of the sexual practices of black women suggest that many prefer and report engaging most often in vaginal intercourse, which they refer to as "normal sex."[39] In the Los Angeles survey, black women were significantly less likely than (half as likely as) white women to report engaging in sexual practices such as oral sex or anal sex with their partners, an ethnic difference also found among injection drug users in general and drug-injecting women in particular.[40]

Although the average black woman may be less likely than the average white woman to engage in high-risk sexual practices such as anal sex, or to have a large number of sexual partners, she may be more likely to report that her partner does not use condoms. According to Mays and Cochran, the lack of eligible men not only propels noninjecting women into sexual ties with high-risk men, it also causes them to yield to male pressures for unprotected sex. Other research suggests, however, that black women themselves may be less willing than white women to ask their partners to use condoms.[41] For example, Wyatt noted that far more of the black women in her survey stated that they "wanted sex to be normal."[42] Moreover, I found that black women drug injectors echoed these sentiments. As one woman observed, when asked about difficulties she encountered in practicing safer sex, "it's not natural."[43] Although many black women drug injectors had significantly reduced their risk of HIV by no longer sharing needles or by sterilizing their needles, they continued to acquiesce in their partners' noncompliance with safe-sex guidelines.

Black women's general unwillingness to insist on condom use may involve more than the notion that sex with a condom is unnatural. Some women may agree with their partners that condoms cut down on sexual pleasure. Others may feel that condom use signals promiscuity or the belief that the partner is not clean. Askia Muhammed, a long-time AIDS outreach worker in San Francisco, notes "a lack of cultural focus for condoms in the low income black community, outside of their association with prostitution."[44]

Sexual risk taking for black women occurs not only in unprotected sex with men with drug injecting histories, but through sexual ties with bisexual men as well. Recent CDC AIDS incidence figures, noted above, suggesting that bisexuality is more widespread in black than white populations appear to be supported by an earlier nationwide study of homosexuality. Bell and Weinberg[45] found that a higher proportion of black homosexuals than whites said they had heterosexual contact in the year prior to the interview. Furthermore, a 1987 survey of AIDS risk behaviors in black communities in San Francisco found that 7 percent of the men were "hidden" bisexuals.[46] Often married to spouses who did not know they had male sexual partners, these men tended to engage in more high-risk sexual behavior than either exclusive homosexuals or heterosexuals (more multiple partners and more high-risk sexual practices with both men and women).

Research suggests that many men who engage in bisexual behavior may view themselves as heterosexual,[47] an identity believed more common among black and Latino than white bisexually active men.[48] In fact, it has been pointed out that African Americans would rather acknowledge they are drug injectors than gay.[49] Jones notes that, in subcultures where homosexuality is greatly stigmatized, some people who acquire AIDS will "invent" a history of injection drug use rather than acknowledge their homosexuality.[50] If cultural values underlying "natural sex" in the African-American community have inhibited men from both acknowledging their sexuality or engaging in safer sex, then the results have been disastrous for their female sexual partners. For example, in addition to the much higher risk of infection from drug-injecting partners, the cumulative risk of HIV transmission through sex with a man who *acknowledges* his bisexuality is almost 5 times higher for black than white women.[51] Recent articles in the popular African-American press display a growing concern with the extent of hidden male bisexuality in the black community.[52]

If the foregoing analysis is correct, then African-American women may substantially more often be exposed to at-risk sexual partners, although they may be less likely than whites to engage in high-risk sexual practices. This exposure, together with their probable lower likelihood of condom use, may help explain black women's higher risk of being infected with the virus through heterosexual relationships. The data presented here suggest that, without rigorous intervention efforts, the secondary transmission of HIV (through unprotected sexual intercourse) will have an increasingly damaging impact on women in the black community.

GOVERNMENT AND COMMUNITY RESPONSES

The nature of the federal government's response to the AIDS crisis in African-American communities has contributed to the heavy toll the disease has taken on black women and men. A brief review of past government policy indicates why a solution requires not only individual behavioral change, but strong government action including allocation of crucial resources.

The government neglect largely responsible for the pervasiveness of drug use in poor inner-city communities has also played an important role in the rapid spread of AIDS in these communities. As Hammonds[53] pointed out, crucial information about the AIDS epidemic was withheld from minority communities by both the federal government and the mass media under the guise that to publish such information would be "racist." Until 1986, several years into the epidemic, when Bakeman and his colleagues wrote on the topic, virtually no attention was paid to the toll AIDS was taking among heterosexuals in black and Latino communities.[54] Without research on at-risk populations or dissemination of information on risk behaviors that need to be changed, the planning of AIDS prevention programs and risk-reduction strategies cannot be carried out. Most importantly, minorities remain unaware of their probable risk.

For too long, AIDS was presented as an exclusively "white gay disease." While white gays successfully organized around the need for AIDS education and prevention, minority men and all women (minority and white), were largely overlooked. Clinical trials and limited government funding were directed at white men, the group initially hardest hit. As a consequence, blacks and Latinos lacked the knowledge they needed to protect themselves. Furthermore, when some public health departments finally did make limited attempts to introduce AIDS prevention programs in African-American communities, they met resistance from community leaders.[55] As Hammonds noted, black leaders, unknowledgeable about the immediate threat of HIV infection and believing they were acting in the best interests of the community, blocked initial intervention efforts. They worried that distribution of bleach and condoms would increase "promiscuity" and drug use in their communities. Aware that stereotypes about African Americans have been used by whites to justify coercive policies, they feared that such programs would increase the stigmatization experienced by all African Americans. As a result of the misunderstandings and delays, mobilization against the spread of HIV in some black communities is just beginning, several long years into the epidemic and amidst incalculable suffering.[56]

NEED FOR PREVENTION AND TREATMENT RATHER THAN PUNISHMENT. This analysis has attempted to contextualize some primary risk factors for AIDS in low-income black women in San Francisco, and to suggest the role that governmental policy and local community leaders have inadvertently played in perpetuating the behavioral risks. Effective and far-reaching AIDS prevention programs are required which are sensitive to these broader community concerns and the need for widespread structural changes. Black community leaders in New York City, for example, opposed distributing bleach to injection drug users, contending that it was a cheap, unacceptable stopgap measure, when what was needed was money for treatment. In fact, many drug-addicted minority women and men desperately want treatment, however they find that government-funded drug cessation programs are lacking. For example, in San Francisco over a six-month period in 1988, almost 4,000 drug users were awaiting enrollment in a drug detoxification or methadone maintenance program.[57] More distressing, President Bush's "War on Drugs" policy allocated very little funding to treatment and directed most of the money toward punishment.[58] Inevitably, the most stringent punishments were meted out for those drugs used primarily by poor minorities, rather than whites (crack cocaine rather than cocaine powder).[59]

African-American women's risk for HIV infection must be understood in relation to broader social and cultural forces. Clearly, culturally appropriate AIDS risk reduction and drug treatment programs are urgently needed in African-American communities. However, measures targeting individual behavioral change will go only so far. Fundamental to AIDS prevention in minority communities will be the reinstitution of disrupted social programs that ensure equitable educational and employment opportunities and a law enforcement system that protects rather than victimizes inner-city residents. Not to implement critically needed social and economic reforms in poor, minority communities in the face of this devastating epidemic will amount to no less than genocide.

I am indebted to John K. Watters, Jennifer Lorvick, and Patricia Case, whose encouragement made this study possible. I am also grateful to Ellen Opie, Christy Ponticelli, Jim Mulherin, Allen Smith, Kenneth Vail, and Deborah Connolly, who provided research assistance. Special thanks to the women who participated in the study and to Askia Muhammed for sharing his insights. This work was supported by grants from the University of California Universitywide AIDS Research Program and the Faculty Research Committee, University of California, Santa Cruz.

NOTES

[1]We recognize the possibility that African Americans may be overrepresented in AIDS statistics due to the greater probability of being poor and processed through the public rather than private medical care systems. In other words, AIDS cases for whites may be underreported because of their ability to shield their medical histories from scrutiny (see Wyatt, in press).

[2]U.S. Bureau of the Census, *U.S. Department of Commerce News*, (Washington, D.C.: Public Information Office, 1991); Centers for Disease Control. *HIV/AIDS Surveillance Report*, February 1993.

[3]K. K. Holmes, J. M. Karon, and J. Kreiss, "The Increasing Frequency of Heterosexually Acquired AIDS in the United States, 1983–88," *American Journal of Public Health* 80, no. 7 (1990):858–863.

[4]S. Y. Chu, J. W. Buehler, and R. L. Berkelman, "Impact of the Human Immunodeficiency Virus Epidemic on Mortality in Women of Reproductive Age, United States," *Journal of the American Medical Association* 264 (1990):225–229.

[5]These figures refer to heterosexual contact cases only and omit persons born in Pattern II countries. (See Holmes, Karon, and Kreiss, 1990; CDC, 1993; and CDC, 1991, pp. 17–18.)

[6]CDC, 1993.

[7]See, on farm workers, Centers for Disease Control, "AIDS and Human Immunodeficiency Virus Infection in the United States: 1988 Update," *MMWR* 38 (Suppl. no. S-4), 1989; on military reservists, D. N. Cowan, R. S. Pomerantz, Z. F. Wann, M. Goldenbaum, J. F. Brundage, R. N. Miller, D. S. Burke, and C. A. Carol, "Human Immunodeficiency Virus Infection among Members of the Reserve Components of the U.S. Army: Prevalence, Incidence, and Demographic Characteristics, The Walter Reed Retrovirus Research Group," *Journal of Infectious Disease* 162, no. 4 (October 1990):827–836; on

prisoners, C. R. Horsburgh, Jr., J. Q. Jarvis, T. McArther, T. Ignacio, and P. Stock, "Seroconversion to Human Immunodeficiency Virus in Prison Inmates," *American Journal of Public Health* 80, no. 2 (February 1990):209–210; and on all others, CDC, 1989, and H. H. Lee, S. H. Weiss, L. S. Brown, D. Mildvan, V. Shorty, L. Saravolatz, A. Chu, H. M. Ginzburg, N. Markowitz, and D. C. Des Jarlais, "Patterns of HIV-1 and HTLV-1/II in Intravenous Drug Abusers from the Middle Atlantic and Central Regions of the USA," *Journal of Infectious Diseases* 162, no. 2 (August 1990):347–352.

[8]CDC, 1993: U.S. Bureau of the Census, 1991; see also V. M. Mays and S. D. Cochran, "Issues in the Perception of AIDS Risk and Risk Reduction Activities by Black and Hispanic/Latina Women," *American Psychologist* 43 (1988):949–957.

[9]The Urban Health Study, directed by Dr. John K. Watters (San Francisco, CA).

[10]Belinda M. Tucker, "U.S. Ethnic Minorities and Drug Abuse: An Assessment of the Science and Practice," *The International Journal of Addictions* 20 (1985):1021–1047.

[11]C. P. Horton and J. C. Smith, eds., *Statistical Record of Black America* (Detroit: Gale Research, Inc., 1990), see 106, 376, 423; also T. Joe, "The Other Side of Black Female-headed Families: The Status of Adult Black Men," *Family Planning Perspectives*, 19 (1987):74–76; and J. Ogbu, *Minority Education and Caste* (New York: Academic Press, 1978).

[12]A. F. Brunswick, "Young Black Males and Substance Use," in *Young, Black and Male in America,* (ed. J. T. Gibbs, A. F. Brunswick, M. E. Conner, R. Dembo, T. E. Larson, R. J. Reed, and E. Solomon (Dover, Mass.: Auburn House, 1988); V. M. Briggs, "Growth and Composition in the U.S. Labor Force," *Science* 238 (1987):176–180; V. M. Mays and S. D. Cochran.

[13]Espada, 293.

[14]Ibid.

[15]Espada; Tucker.

[16]M. T. Fullilove, R. E. Fullilove, K. Haynes, and S. Gross, "Black Women and AIDS Prevention: A View Towards Understanding the Gender Rules," *The Journal of Sex Research* 27 (1990):47–64.

[17]D. K. Lewis, "Living with the Threat of AIDS: Perceptions of Health and Risk among Black Women IV Drug Users," in *Wings of Gauze: Women of Color and the Experience of Health and Illness,* ed. B. Bair and S. E. Cayleff (Detroit: Wayne State University Press, 1993).

[18]See the work of Chaisson and his colleagues on drug users in San Francisco: R. E. Chaisson, A. R. Moss, R. Onishi, D. Osmond, and J. R. Carlson, "Human Immunodeficiency Deficiency Virus Infection in Heterosexual Intravenous Drug Users in San Francisco," *American Journal of Public Health* 77 (1987):169–172; R. E. Chaisson, P. Bacchetti, D. Osmond, B. Brodie, M. A. Sande, and A. R. Moss, "Cocaine Use and HIV Infection in Intravenous Drug Users in San Francisco," *Journal of the American Medical Association* 261 (1989):561–565.

[19]E. M. Miller, *Street Woman* (Philadelphia: Temple University Press, 1986).

[20]D. K. Lewis and J. K. Watters, "Sexual Risk Behavior among Heterosexual Intravenous Drug Users: Ethnic and Gender Variations," *AIDS* 5 (1991):67–73; E. E. Schoenbaum, D. Hartel, P. A. Selwyn, R. S. Klein, K. Davenny, M. Rogers, C. Feiner,

[44]Askia Muhammed, personal communication, 1990.

[45]A. Bell and M. Weinberg, *Homosexualities: a study of diversity in men and women* (New York: Simon and Schuster, 1978), 286.

[46]Polaris.

[47]D. K. Lewis and J. K. Watters, "Male Bisexuality in Intravenous Drug Users: Sexual Behavior, Sexual Identity and AIDS Prevention" (Unpublished paper, 1992).

[48]Peterson and Marin, 1988.

[49]R. Bakeman, J. R. Lumb, R. E. Jackson, and D. W. Smith, "AIDS Risk-group Profiles in Whites and Members of Minority Groups," *New England Journal of Medicine* 315 (1986):191–192, cited in D. Worth, "Minority Women and AIDS: Culture, Race, and Gender," in *Culture and AIDS*, ed., D. A. Feldman, (New York: Praeger, 1990), 121.

[50]A. B. S. Jones, "Sexual Minority Needle Users," in *Aids and Intravenous Drug Use: Future Directions for Community-based Prevention Research*, ed. C. G. Leukefeld, R. J. Battjes, and A. Amel, NIDA Research Monograph Series 93 (Washington, D.C.: U.S. Government Printing Office, 1990).

[51]Selik et al.

[52]L. B. Randolph, "The Hidden Fear: Black Women, Bisexuals and the AIDS Risk," *Ebony*, January 1988, 120–126; L. Norment, "The Truth about AIDS," *Ebony*, April 1987, 126–130.

[53]Hammonds.

[54]R. Bakeman, J. R. Lumb, and D. W. Smith, "AIDS Statistics and the Risk for Minorities," *AIDS Research* 2 (1986):249–252; R. Bakeman, J. R. Lumb, R. E. Jackson, and D. W. Smith, "AIDS Risk-group Profiles in Whites and Members of Minority Groups," *New England Journal of Medicine* 315 (1986):191–192.

[55]D. Carpenter-Madoshi, "AIDS: The Black Community Fights Back," *The Bay Guardian*, 4 October, 1989, p. 17; G. Raine, "Blacks Face up to AIDS," *San Francisco Examiner*, 16 April 1989, pp. A-1, A-9.

[56]See Carpenter-Madushi, 1989, and Raine, 1989; also see G. Kolata, "Black Group Assails Giving Bleach to Addicts," *New York Times*, 17 June, 1990, p. A20.

[57]See Kolata, 1990, on New York City reaction; the San Francisco data are from the public health report, City and County of San Francisco, Department of Public Health, *Strategic Plan for Mental Health, Substance Abuse and Forensic Services* (San Francisco: Division of Mental Health, Substance Abuse & Forensic Services, 1990).

[58]B. Weintraub, "President Offers Strategy for United States in Drug Control," *New York Times*, 6 September 1989, p. A1.

[59]R. London, "Judge's Overruling of Crack Law Brings Turmoil," *New York Times* 11 January, 1991, p. B5.

REFERENCES

Bakeman, R., J. R. Lumb, R. E. Jackson, and D. W. Smith. "AIDS Risk-group Profiles in Whites and Members of Minority Groups." *New England Journal of Medicine* 315 (1986):191–192.

Bakeman, R., J. R. Lumb, and D. W. Smith. "AIDS Statistics and the Risk for Minorities." *AIDS Research* 2 (1986):249–252.

and G. Friedland, "Risk Factors for Human Immunodeficiency Virus Infection i Intravenous Drug Users," *New England Journal of Medicine* 321 (1989):874–879.

[21]J. S. Townsey, "The Incarceration of Black Men," in *Black Men,* ed. L. E. Gar (Beverly Hills: Sage, 1981); D. K. Lewis, "Black Women Offenders and Crimin; Justice: Some Theoretical Considerations," in *Comparing Female and Male Offender* ed. M. Q. Warren, (Beverly Hills: Sage, 1981); C. E. Owens and J. Bell, *Blacks a, Criminal Justice* (Lexington, Mass.: D. C. Heath, 1977).

[22]U.S. Department of Justice, 1980, 20; also D. K. Lewis and L. Bresler, *Is There a W; Out? A Community Study of Women in San Francisco County Jail* (San Francisc Unitarian-Universalist Service Committee, 1981), 30, 127.

[23]Bresler and Lewis.

[24]Schoenbaum et al.

[25]R. M. Selik, K. G. Castro, and M. Pappaioanou, "Racial/Ethnic Differences in the Ri; of AIDS in the United States," *American Journal of Public Health* 78 (1989):1539–1545.

[26]A. Moss, K. Vranizan, P. Bacchetti, R. Gorter, D. Osmond, and B. Broadi "Seroconversion for HIV in Intravenous Drug Users in Treatment, San Francis 1985–1990" (Presented at the VIth International Conference on AIDS, San Francisc June 20–24, 1990), (Abstract F.C. 553).

[27]Holmes, Karon, and Kreiss.

[28]For the national study, see M. Zelnick and J. F. Kantner, "Sexual Activit Contraceptive Use and Pregnancy among Metropolitan-area Teenagers: 1971–1979 *Family Planning Perspectives* 12 (1980):230–237; for the L. A. study, see G. E. Wya "Ethnic and Cultural Differences in Women's Sexual Behavior," in *Women and AID Promoting Healthy Behaviors,* ed., S. Blumenthal, A. Eichler, and G. Weissman, in pres

[29]D. K. Lewis and J. K. Watters, "Human Immunodeficiency Virus Seroprevalence Female Intravenous Drug Users: The Puzzle of Black Women's Risk," *Social Scien and Medicine* 29 (1989):1071–1076.

[30]Fullilove et al.

[31]Ibid.

[32]Mays and Cochran, 1988.

[33]L. F. Rodgers-Rose, "Some Demographic Characteristics of the Black Woman: 19 to 1975," in *The Black Woman,* ed., L. F. Rodgers-Rose, (Beverly Hills: Sage, 1980).

[34]Townsey; E. E. H. Griffith and C. C. Bel, "Recent Trends in Suicide and Homic; among Blacks," *Journal of the American Medical Association* 262 (1989):2265–2269.

[35]Fullilove et al.; Joe, 1987; Briggs, 1987.

[36]See note in Fullilove et al.; Mays and Lochran, 1988.

[37]Wyatt.

[38]Lewis and Watters, 1989.

[39]Fullilove et al., 55.

[40]Wyatt; Lewis and Watters, 1989; Lewis and Watters, 1991.

[41]Mays and Cochran; Wyatt.

[42]Wyatt, 15.

[43]Lewis, 1993.

A Baseline Survey of AIDS Risk Behaviors and Attitudes in San Francisco's Black Communities. San Francisco: Polaris Research and Development and Research & Decisions Corp., n.d.

Bell, A., and M. Weinberg. *Homosexualities: a study of diversity in men and women.* New York: Simon and Schuster, 1978.

Bresler, L., and D. K. Lewis. "Black and White Women Prisoners: Differences in Family Ties and Their Programmatic Implications." *The Prison Journal* LXIII (1983):116–123.

Briggs, V. M. "Growth and Composition in the U.S. Labor Force." *Science* 238 (1987): 176–180.

Brunswick, A. F. "Young Black Males and Substance Use." In *Young, Black and Male in America,* edited by J. T. Gibbs, A. F. Brunswick, M. E. Conner, R. Dembo, T. E. Larson, R. J. Reed, and E. Solomon. Dover, Mass.: Auburn House, 1988.

Carpenter-Madoshi, D. "AIDS: The Black Community Fights Back." *The Bay Guardian,* 4 October 1989, 17.

Centers for Disease Control. "AIDS and Human Immunodeficiency Virus Infection in the United States: 1988 Update." *MMWR* 38 (Suppl. No. S-4), 1989.

Centers for Disease Control. *AIDS public information data set.* June 1990.

Centers for Disease Control. *HIV/AIDS Surveillance Report.* February 1991.

Centers for Disease Control. "Update: Reducing HIV Transmission in Intravenous-Drug Users Not in Drug Treatment—United States." *MMWR* 39 (1990):529–530, 535–538.

Chaisson, R. E., P. Bacchetti, D. Osmond, B. Brodie, M. A. Sande, and A. R. Moss. "Cocaine Use and HIV Infection in Intravenous Drug Users in San Francisco." *Journal of the American Medical Association* 261 (1989):561–565.

Chaisson, R. E., A. R. Moss, R. Onishi, D. Osmond, and J. R. Carlson. "Human Immunodeficiency Deficiency Virus Infection in Heterosexual Intravenous Drug Users in San Francisco." *American Journal of Public Health* 77 (1987):169–172.

Chu, S. Y., J. W. Buehler, and R. L. Berkelman. "Impact of the Human Immunodeficiency Virus Epidemic on Mortality in Women of Reproductive Age, United States." *Journal of the American Medical Association* 264 (1990):225–229.

City and County of San Francisco, Department of Public Health. *Strategic plan for mental health, substance abuse and forensic services.* San Francisco: Division of Mental Health, Substance Abuse & Forensic Services, 1990.

Cowan, D. N., R. S. Pomerantz, Z. F. Wann, M. Goldenbaum, J. F. Brundage, R. N. Miller, D. S. Burke, and C. A. Carroll. "Human Immunodeficiency Virus Infection among Members of the Reserve Components of the U.S. Army: Prevalence, Incidence, and Demographic Characteristics, The Walter Reed Retrovirus Research Group." *Journal of Infectious Diseases* 162, no. 4 (1990):827–836.

Espada, F. "The Drug Abuse Industry and the "Minority" Communities: Time For Change." In *Handbook on Drug Abuse,* edited by R. L. Dupont, A. Goldstein, and J. O'Donnell. Washington, D.C.: U.S. Government Printing Office, 1979.

Fullilove, M. T., R. E. Fullilove, K. Haynes, and S. Gross. "Black Women and AIDS Prevention: A View Towards Understanding the Gender Rules." *The Journal of Sex Research* 27 (1990):47–64.

Griffith, E. E. H., and C. C. Bell. "Recent Trends in Suicide and Homicide among Blacks." *Journal of the American Medical Association* 262 (1989):2265–2269.

Hammonds, E. "Race, Sex, AIDS: The Construction of 'Other.' " *Radical America* 20 (1986):28–36.

Hartel, D., P. A. Selwyn, E. E. Schoenbaum, R. S. Klein, and G. H. Friedland. "Methadone Maintenance Treatment and Reduced Risk of AIDS and AIDS-specific Mortality in Intravenous Drug Users." Presented at the IVth International Conference on AIDS, Stockholm, 12–16 June 1988 (Abstract 8546).

Holmes, K. K., J. M. Karon, and J. Kreiss. "The Increasing Frequency of Heterosexually Acquired AIDS in the United States, 1983–88." *American Journal of Public Health* 80, no. 7 (July 1990):858–863.

Horsburgh, C. R., Jr., J. Q. Jarvis, T. McArther, T. Ignacio, and P. Stock. "Seroconversion to Human Immunodeficiency Virus in Prison Inmates." *American Journal of Public Health* 80, no. 2 (February 1990):209–210.

Horton, C. P., and J. C. Smith, eds. *Statistical Record of Black America.* Detroit: Gale Research, Inc., 1990.

Joe, T. "The Other Side of Black Female-headed Families: The Status of Adult Black Men." *Family Planning Perspectives* 19 (1987):74–76.

Jones, A. B. S. "Sexual Minority Needle Users." In *Aids and intravenous drug use: future directions for community-based prevention research,* edited by C. G. Leukefeld, R. J. Battjes, and A. Amel. NIDA Research Monograph Series 93. Washington, D.C.: U.S. Government Printing Office, 1990.

Kolata, G. "Black Group Assails Giving Bleach to Addicts." *New York Times,* 17 June 1990, p. A20.

Lee, H. H., S. H. Weiss, L. S. Brown, D. Mildvan, V. Shorty, L. Saravolatz, A. Chu, H. M. Ginzburg, N. Markowitz, and D. C. Des Jarlais. "Patterns of HIV-1 and HTLV-I/II in Intravenous Drug Abusers from the Middle Atlantic and Central Regions of the USA." *Journal of Infectious Diseases* 162, no. 2 (August 1990):347–352.

Lewis, D. K. "Black Women Offenders and Criminal Justice: Some Theoretical Considerations." In *Comparing Female and Male Offenders,* edited by M. Q. Warren. Beverly Hills: Sage, 1981.

Lewis, D. K. "Living with the Threat of AIDS: Perceptions of Health and Risk among Black Women IV Drug Users." In *Wings of Gauze: Women of Color and the Experience of Health and Illness,* edited by B. Bair and S. E. Cayleff. Detroit: Wayne State University Press, 1993.

Lewis, D. K., and L. Bresler. *Is There a Way Out? A Community Study of Women in San Francisco County Jail.* San Francisco: Unitarian-Universalist Service Committee, 1981.

Lewis, D. K., and J. K. Watters. "Human Immunodeficiency Virus Seroprevalence in Female Intravenous Drug Users: The Puzzle of Black Women's Risk." *Social Science and Medicine* 29 (1989):1071–1076.

Lewis, D. K., and J. K. Watters. "Male Bisexuality in Intravenous Drug Users: Sexual Behavior, Sexual Identity and AIDS Prevention." Unpublished paper, 1992.

Lewis, D. K., and J. K. Watters. "Sexual Risk Behavior among Heterosexual Intravenous Drug Users: Ethnic and Gender Variations." *AIDS* 5 (1991):67–73.

London, R. "Judge's Overruling of Crack Law Brings Turmoil." *New York Times*, 11 January 1991, p. B5.

Mays, V. M., and S. D. Cochran. "Acquired Immunodeficiency Syndrome and Black Americans: Special Psychosocial Issues." *Public Health Reports* 102 (1987):224–231.

Mays, V. M., and S. D. Cochran. "Issues in the Perception of AIDS Risk and Risk Reduction Activities by Black and Hispanic/Latina Women." *American Psychologist* 43 (1988):949–957.

Miller, E. M. *Street Woman*. Philadelphia: Temple University Press, 1986.

Moss, A., K. Vranizan, P. Bacchetti, R. Gorter, D. Osmond, and B. Broadie. "Seroconversion for HIV in Intravenous Drug Users in Treatment, San Francisco 1985–1990." Presented at the VIth International Conference on AIDS, San Francisco, 20–24 June 1990 (Abstract F.C.553).

Norment, L. "The Truth about AIDS." *Ebony*, April 1987, 126–130.

Ogbu, J. *Minority Education and Caste*. New York: Academic Press, 1978.

Owens, C. E., and J. Bell. *Blacks and Criminal Justice*. Lexington, Mass.: D.C. Heath, 1977.

Raine, G. "Blacks Face Up to AIDS." *San Francisco Examiner*, 16 April 1989, pp. A-1, A-9.

Randolph, L. B. "The Hidden Fear: Black Women, Bisexuals and the AIDS Risk." *Ebony*, January 1988, 120–126.

Rodgers-Rose, L. F. "Some Demographic Characteristics of the Black Woman: 1940 to 1975." In *The Black Woman*, edited by L. F. Rodgers-Rose. Beverly Hills: Sage, 1980.

Schoenbaum, E. E., D. Hartel, P. A. Selwyn, R. S. Klein, K. Davenny, M. Rogers, C. Feiner, and G. Friedland. "Risk Factors for Human Immunodeficiency Virus Infection in Intravenous Drug Users." *New England Journal of Medicine* 321 (1989):874–879.

Selik, R. M., K. G. Castro, and M. Pappaioanou. "Racial/Ethnic Differences in the Risk of AIDS in the United States." *American Journal of Public Health* 78 (1989):1539–1545.

Townsey, J. S. "The Incarceration of Black Men." In *Black Men*, edited by L. E. Gary. Beverly Hills: Sage, 1981.

Tucker, M. Belinda. "U.S. Ethnic Minorities and Drug Abuse: An Assessment of the Science and Practice." *The International Journal of Addictions* 20 (1985):1021–1047.

U.S. Bureau of the Census. *U.S. Department of Commerce News*. Washington, D.C.: Public Information Office, March 1991.

Weintraub, B. "President Offers Strategy for United States in Drug Control." *New York Times*, 6 September 1989, p. A1.

Worth, D. "Minority Women and AIDS: Culture, Race, and Gender." In *Culture and AIDS*, edited by D. A. Feldman. New York: Praeger, 1990.

Wyatt, G. E. "Ethnic and Cultural Differences in Women's Sexual Behavior." In *Women and AIDS: Promoting Healthy Behaviors*, edited by S. Blumenthal, A. Eichler, and G. Weissman. In press.

Zelnick, M., and J. F. Kantner. "Sexual Activity, Contraceptive Use and Pregnancy among Metropolitan-area Teenagers: 1971–1979." *Family Planning Perspectives* 12 (1980):230–237.

Beth E. Schneider and Valerie Jenness

Social Control, Civil Liberties, and Women's Sexuality

"Crises and disasters have always held a special fascination for social scientists, at least in part because they expose the fundamental assumptions, institutional arrangements, social linkages, and cleavages that are normally implicit in the social order."[1] The AIDS epidemic is no exception. The biological and medical imperatives associated with HIV have been effectively translated into a moral panic.[2] This panic has in turn uncovered significant social processes and arrangements related to sexuality, gender, and social control.

Not surprisingly, the AIDS epidemic has brought with it repetitive calls that "somebody do something." Historically, epidemics typically evoke demands for some form of managerial response and some mobilized effort to control identifiable, projected, and even unknown hazards.[3] In particular, epidemics inspire new public policy, as well as the reform of extant public policy. Again, the AIDS epidemic has proven to be no exception.

In this paper we focus on several public responses that have emerged purportedly to assist in the control of "the AIDS problem." Specifically, we focus on those responses that have consequences for the expansion of social control mechanisms and the potential denial of civil liberties. Although the AIDS epidemic in the United States has touched every segment of society, it is increasingly becoming an illness of women, as well as of racial, ethnic, and sexual minorities. There is no reason to presume that this trend will reverse as the epidemic continues through the nineties and into the next century.[4] Thus, our overarching concern is with how public policy responses to the multitude of threats born of AIDS are structured by gender and sexuality.

The AIDS epidemic has inspired and justified interventionist policies on the part of the state to regulate not only the exchange of bodily fluids, but the social organization of gender and sexuality as well. To illustrate, we focus on public policy surrounding prostitutes and sex education for adolescents, both of which have consequences for the civil liberties of girls and women and the social control of female sexuality through the reinforcement of notions of "good girls" and "bad girls." This particular comparison permits an examination of the complexity of state responses to AIDS and illustrates differing strategies of social control undertaken by two institutions: the legal and the educational.

Some public policies implicitly or explicitly seek to control sexuality and gender; these are our concern in the remainder of the chapter. Different laws and other forms of public policy inspired by the AIDS epidemic operate to interrupt, forbid, and often punish the existence or enactment of particular sexualities. We examine two quite divergent cases—policy surrounding prostitutes in the United States and the policy and practice of AIDS education—for what each reveals about the social control of female sexuality through the construction of "good girls" and "bad girls." We conclude with a discussion of the role that law and other forms of public policy play in redefining social control in general and, more specifically, privacy in light of the "AIDS crisis." We consider what places, spaces, and matters remain private and thus outside the purview of the state, for girls and young women, as well as how processes of protection, intrusion, and redefinition are bound by and reflect the fact that AIDS is structured by race, class, gender, and sexuality.[5]

THE AIDS EPIDEMIC AS A DISEASE AND AS A MORAL PANIC

The evolution of AIDS resembles the social construction of such diseases as leprosy, syphilis, tuberculosis, and cholera.[6] In each of these epidemics, the evolution and consequences of the disease were tied not only to its biological characteristics, but also to the socially constructed meanings attached to the disease. From the beginning, many interested parties, including some units of the state, have sought to make their interpretations of HIV and AIDS dominant. Scientists, physicians, afflicted groups, government agencies, religious officials, politicians, social workers, and other claims makers concerned with the disease have been and continue to be quick to formulate and disseminate interpretations of the disease.[7]

The melange of meanings surrounding the AIDS epidemic has merged to produce a "moral panic." In simplest terms, a moral panic can be thought of as a widespread feeling on the part of the public—or some relevant public—that something is terribly wrong in society because of the moral failure of a specific group of individuals. The result is that a subpopulation is defined as the enemy. Cohen describes the evolution and consequences of a moral panic:

> A condition, episode, person or group of persons emerges to become defined as a threat to societal values and interests: Its nature is presented in a stylized and stereotypic fashion by the mass media; moral barricades are manned by editors, bishops, politicians, and other right-thinking people; socially accredited experts pronounce their diagnoses and solutions; ways of coping evolve, or (more often) are resorted to. . . . Sometimes the panic passes over and is

forgotten, except in folklore or collective memory; at other times it has more serious and long-lasting repercussions and might produce such changes as those in legal and social policy.[8]

Such "changes as those in legal and social policy" are necessarily inter-twined with the negotiation of power and morality and, by extension, are consequential for major societal processes of social change.

Moral panics are inevitably linked to, and thus consequential for, formal systems of social control. They explicitly or implicitly challenge existing systems of control by defining them as failing or defunct. The consequence is that mandates for reform in legal and social policy are rendered timely and legitimate. Wars, epidemics, and other such moral panic–generating events have, at different points in history, served to justify the expansion of old or the introduction of new mechanisms of social control. These emergent forms of social control often constitute significant incursions on the rights of individuals or groups.

Calls for reform in legal and social policy that are consequential for individual civil liberties are especially pronounced when moral panics are tied, in some real or imagined way, to issues of sexuality.[9] Gayle Rubin, for example, has argued that "it is precisely at times such as these [the era of AIDS], when we live with the possibility of unthinkable destruction, that people are likely to become dangerously crazed about sexuality."[10] As a consequence, regulations emerge to control public and private spaces associated with sexuality and eroticism (such as attempts to close bathhouses frequented by gay men or refusal to perform abortions for HIV-positive women).

The AIDS crisis has generated contemporary discourses in which the social conditions attached to the epidemic serve to rationalize formal and informal social control mechanisms on sexuality and gender, ostensibly in the name of safeguarding the public's health. But this has not been done without historical precedent and without overcoming material and symbolic obstacles.

In an effort to make sense of the variety of ways in which history, culture, and politics frame responses to AIDS, Moerkerk and Aggleton[11] identify four overall approaches that nations in Europe have taken to deal with AIDS. Three of these approaches—the pragmatic, the political, and the biomedical—have particular relevance for our understanding of the mechanisms put in place in the United States to manage female prostitutes and to educate female adoles-cents. The *pragmatic response* emphasizes provision of crucial education and information, whatever that might be for a group of people, and the need to protect the afflicted. It relies on a cultural consensus and avoids coercive forms of social control. In contrast, the *political response* is based in judgment of what is politically possible and consistent with the beliefs of the nation's leadership. It relies on the law to regulate behavior, and consequently it interprets AIDS prevention as a mechanism for producing behavior it considers desirable. The *biomedical response* is limited; it relies exclusively on medical personnel to determine policy and shows little interest in the involvement of affected groups. As our analyses indicate, each response, often in combination with others, is evident in the United States, especially in the control of young women by educational and legal institutions.

PUBLIC HEALTH AND CIVIL LIBERTIES: A DIFFICULT DILEMMA

The extension of formal social control mechanisms by the state is not done automatically in times of epidemics because, as Brandt has documented, epidemics marshal two sets of values that are "highly prized by our culture": the fundamental civil liberties of the individual and the role of the state in assuring public welfare.[12] From a public policy point of view, individual civil liberties and public health concerns are generally conceived as values in competition with each other. There is a tension between the extension of social control in the name of "protecting public health" and the prohibition of such extension in the name of "preserving individual civil liberties," especially those related to notions of "privacy" as an aspect of personal liberty protected by the Fourth and Fourteenth Amendments of the U.S. Constitution.[13]

This tension is especially pronounced in situations or contexts where sexuality is salient. For example, the state still interferes in the practice of homosexual sodomy and other sexual acts. However, after providing an extensive review of relevant legislation at state and federal levels, Stoddard and Rieman conclude that, under recent Supreme Court decisions, the right to privacy has effectively precluded or sharply limited governmental interference with some personal decisions surrounding sexuality (such as the use of contraception or access to abortion). They warn that this trend is open to reversal in light of the many hazards posed by AIDS: "the government undoubtedly could treat persons who carry the HIV differently from others for some reasons."[14] The same holds for people who are "at risk" for HIV or presumed to be carriers of the virus. Indeed, everything from tattooing on the buttocks to more drastic segregation measures, such as forced quarantining, have been proposed, entertained, and occasionally adopted.[15] As a result, over the course of the epidemic, the rights of the individual have not invariably prevailed and privacy has, at least from a policy point of view, been redefined.[16]

Although it is clear that prostitutes, frequently considered women in need of control, have been particularly susceptible to constraints on their civil liberties, children are rarely understood in these terms. Children's civil liberties are effectively unacknowledged. Indeed,the treatment of children, especially their education and protection, rests far less securely on any right to privacy. Children and adolescents often need, by law, their parents' permission for most of what adults take for granted as sexual—to receive contraceptive devices at school, to attend sex education classes, to seek an abortion. Familial and educational institutions exercise physical and legal control over how young people learn about sexuality and gender. Schools are social control mechanisms that reinforce patriarchal relations of male domination and female submission. In the face of the AIDS epidemic, the ideological apparatus of schools extends social control over its charges by framing, constraining, and ultimately censoring what is thought about AIDS and how it comes to be understood.

PRIVATE SPACES, PUBLIC INTRUSIONS: THE CASE OF PROSTITUTION

There has been a virtual explosion in the formulation of policy designed to control the spread of HIV and the people who are infected. Laws have been passed by the U.S. Congress and state legislatures; the courts have issued various pronouncements; and businesses, government agencies, prisons, schools, hospitals, and other such public settings have developed workplace policy. Policy proposals with implications for civil liberties in general and privacy in particular include, but certainly are not limited to: requiring blood screening of prisoners or military recruits; banning people with AIDS from being restaurant workers; prohibiting seropositive persons from donating blood; closing gay bathhouses; banning homosexual sodomy; quarantining "suspect" groups, especially prostitutes; dismissing from federal jobs employees suspected of being seropositive; and refusing to care for or provide shelter for PWAs.[17] This list, of course, is not exhaustive of the measures that have been proposed or implemented to control AIDS by restricting liberty and, in some cases, redefining privacy. (In this volume, see the chapters by Hunter and Pies for other examples directly relevant to women's lives.)

Throughout the AIDS epidemic, calls for mass and mandatory testing have been put forth. Initial calls for mass testing and an administrative system developed around testing were expanded in a context of considerable ambiguity over test accuracy, counseling procedures, and the relationship between knowledge of test results and behavior or attitudes. Moreover, these calls seem to point in the direction of quarantining and other forms of detention.[18] However, such calls for testing are not equally applicable to all citizens. They have selectively targeted specific groups—usually gay men, intravenous drug users, prisoners, immigrants, pregnant women, and sex workers.

Implicating Female Prostitutes in AIDS

Stereotypes about women—especially African-American women, pregnant women, and female prostitutes—have been infused with policy proposals. Perhaps the most obvious case of social and legal policy embedded in gender and sexuality is that surrounding sex work. From the beginning, legislation supporting forced quarantining, reporting, screening, and prosecution of sex workers has been proposed and adopted. The biological characteristics of AIDS, combined with the way in which the disease has been socially constructed, almost guaranteed that prostitutes would be implicated in the social problem of AIDS. In an article entitled "Prostitutes and AIDS: Public Policy Issues," Cohen, Alexander, and Wofsy concluded that "prostitutes have often been held responsible for the spread of AIDS into the heterosexual population in this country."[19] This is not surprising given that AIDS has been conceived of primarily as a sexually transmitted disease and was, at least originally, connected with "promiscuous" sex and "deviant" lifestyles.[20] The historical association of prostitution with venereal disease, unfettered sex, and moral unworthiness remains strong.[21] The prostitute is either dangerous, bad, or both. In short, the historical and contemporary context within which female prostitutes have operated ensured that they would be implicated in the AIDS epidemic, even prior to epidemiological evidence justifying such a focus.[22]

As early as 1984, medical authorities were investigating the possibility that prostitutes could spread AIDS into the heterosexual population. Meanwhile, the media continued to spread suspicion about prostitution as an avenue of transmission for the disease. For example, on an episode of the nationally televised "Geraldo Show" entitled "Have Prostitutes Become the New Typhoid Marys?" the host offered the following introduction to millions of viewers:

> The world's oldest profession may very well have become among its deadliest. A recent study backed by the federal Centers for Disease Control found that one third of New York's prostitutes now carry the AIDS virus. If this study mirrors the national trend, then the implications are as grim as they are clear. Sleeping with a prostitute may have become a fatal attraction. . . . A quick trick may cost you $20, but you may be paying for it with the rest of your life.[23]

Supporting Rivera's introduction, a New York–based AIDS counselor appearing on the show argued:

> A high percentage of prostitutes infected with HIV pass it on to their sexual partners who are johns or the tricks, a lot of whom are married or have sex with a straight woman. I think this is how the AIDS epidemic is passed into the heterosexual population.[24]

He argued further that working prostitutes testing positive for HIV are guilty of manslaughter and/or attempted murder. In a relatively short period of time, claims like this became commonplace. Moreover, claims focusing on prostitution were and still are focused on female prostitutes to the exclusion of male prostitutes, and on female prostitutes but not their customers.

Legislation as Social Control

Like the media, legislators have turned their attention to female prostitution as an avenue of transmission. In the name of preventing HIV transmission, legislation that intrudes into private, consensual sexual relations has sprung up around the country. A number of proposals have been introduced and adopted that, in one way or another, make it a crime for someone who is antibody positive to engage in sex with anyone else, regardless of the degree to which the behavior is mutually voluntary, the use of condoms, and the failure of the uninfected participant to test seropositive.[25] Luxenburg and Guild have shown that, as early as 1987, more than 140 AIDS-specific laws had been passed across the United States. Approximately a dozen of these criminalized the act of *exposing* another individual to the HIV. In addition to the emergence of new legislation, jurisdictions that have no AIDS-specific criminal laws have begun to rely on traditional criminal laws (attempted murder, aggravated assault, and the like) to prosecute HIV-positive individuals who engage in behaviors that put seronegatives at risk for acquiring the HIV infection—even when the risky contact is conscious and voluntary on the part of the seronegatives.

The introduction of AIDS-related legislation has posed a significant legal threat to female prostitutes. Many governmental and medical establishments have reacted to AIDS with calls for increased regulation of prostitution in the form of registration, mandatory AIDS testing, and prison sentences for those carrying antibodies to the virus.[26] In the mid-eighties and into the nineties, many states considered legislation requiring arrested prostitutes to be tested for HIV infection. By 1988, some states had introduced and passed legislation requiring mandatory testing of arrested prostitutes. Georgia, Florida, Utah, and Nevada were among the first states to legislate the forcible testing of arrested prostitutes; those who test positive can then be subject to arrest on felony charges. These mandatory testing laws in effect create a state registry of infected prostitutes, while the felony charges could create a quarantine situation if prostitutes are kept in isolation while awaiting trial.

Coinciding with the introduction of this legislation, many judges and district attorneys began contemplating and occasionally charging arrested prostitutes who tested positive for HIV with attempted manslaughter and murder. In July 1990, for example, an Oakland, California, prostitute was arrested after *Newsweek* ran a photo of her and quoted her saying that she contracted the deadly virus from contaminated needles but continued to engage in prostitution. According to newspaper reports, Oakland police asked a judge to force the woman to be tested for HIV and pressured the district attorney's office to pursue an attempted manslaughter charge if she tested positive. The arresting officer stated, "I think her actions, with the knowledge that if you're going to get AIDS you're going to die, is a malicious act akin to firing into a crowd or at a passing bus."[27] Although the judge denied the charge, the woman was held for a number of days while the possibility was contemplated. As another example, in Orlando, Florida, an HIV-infected prostitute was charged with manslaughter even though she used a condom with all of her clients and despite the finding that all of her clients who had been tested were negative.[28]

In essence, the AIDS epidemic has led to increased social control of prostitutes, especially in the form of repressive legislation and increasingly punitive legal sanctions. Such changes reflect the commonly held belief that prostitutes constitute a "vector of transmission" for AIDS into the heterosexual population; thus, legislation and increased legal sanctions have been pursued in the name of controlling the spread of AIDS. Female, not male, prostitutes are arrested, even though male prostitutes are much more likely to be infected.[29] Social policy continues to be used to enforce select moral positions[30]—in this case, the control of female rather than male sexuality. Such laws effectively constitute a social x-ray, one that classifies individuals as mainstream or peripheral, normal or deviant.

Resistance

Some have suggested that the introduction and implementation of AIDS-related statutes and "enhanced penalties" is merely an attempt to mollify public fear of AIDS spreading into the "population at large."[31] Whatever the state's intention, this testing of certain special groups without consent, at both the state and the federal level, has not gone uncontested.[32] The existence of resistance underscores the control of women's sexuality; it is a sign that women are directly experiencing either the reality or the threat of constraints on their sexual practice.

In order to resist the scapegoating of prostitutes, COYOTE and other U.S. prostitute advocacy groups, using scientific studies and research to lend legitimacy to their assessment, went public with two main arguments: (1) that the rate of HIV infection among prostitutes, compared to that among other identifiable groups, is relatively low; and (2) that, regardless of infection rates, it is a violation of prostitutes' civil rights to selectively impose mandatory testing on prostitutes if they are arrested. Additionally, they publicly and persistently explained that sex workers are not at risk for AIDS because of sex work per se. As the codirector of the International Committee for Prostitute Rights explained in the late 1980s:

> They [prostitutes] are demanding the same medical confidentiality and choice as other citizens. . . . They are contesting policies which separate them from other sexually active people, emphasizing that charging money for sex does not transmit disease.[33]

An editorial on this issue by COYOTE's media liaison argues a kind of prostitute exceptionalism:

> Many readers are well aware that prostitutes practice safe sex techniques, using condoms for oral services as well as intercourse, and quite often restricting their activities to manual gratification. Many prostitutes emphasize massage, still others combine fantasy stimulation (S&M, etc.) with minimal physical contact. There is much a "working girl" can do to assure her health and the health of her clients, and we have done it. Most of us followed safe sex practices long before the onset of this epidemic.[34]

These assertions suggest that what separates prostitutes from women in general is higher rates of condom use. In essence, these sex work organizations hold that sex work per se is not responsible for the spread of HIV; viruses do not discriminate between those who exchange money for sex and those who do not. When prostitutes are infected, intravenous drug use is the primary cause.

In promoting the notion that prostitutes do not represent a pool of contagion, COYOTE and other sex worker groups regularly distributed public announcements and issued press releases; attended local, state, national, and international conferences on AIDS; and staged protests to oppose legislation requiring the mandatory testing of prostitutes. At legislative hearings they protested mandatory testing of prostitutes for HIV on the grounds that selective testing is discriminatory and a violation of individuals'—in this case prostitutes'—civil rights.

The AIDS epidemic poses a multitude of threats for prostitutes, their organizations, and their movement to decriminalize and legitimate prostitution. It has siphoned personnel and resources from sex work organizations; organizational agendas and activities have shifted in response to the way in which AIDS has been constructed as a social problem implicating sex workers.

But, at the same time, the AIDS epidemic has served to legitimate prostitutes' rights organizations. It has provided prostitutes and their advocates with financial, rhetorical, and institutional resources. The AIDS epidemic has also brought public officials and prostitutes' rights organizations together in direct and indirect ways. As a result of concern over the spread of AIDS into the heterosexual population, government agencies such as state legislatures, the Centers for Disease Control, and local departments of health have turned to prostitutes' rights organizations for assistance.

Those concerned with halting the spread of AIDS have enlisted the help of prostitutes in investigating the role of prostitution in the spread of the disease. For example, COYOTE applied for and received funds to begin an AIDS prevention project for prostitutes. This new entity, the California Prostitutes Education Program (CAL-PEP) is, as its statement of purpose reads:

> an education project developed by members of COYOTE, the prostitutes' rights advocacy organization, to provide educational programs for prostitutes

and the interested public on various aspects of prostitution. Our first project is an AIDS prevention project designed and implemented by prostitutes, ex-prostitutes, and prostitutes' rights advocates to help prostitutes to protect themselves and their clients from AIDS.

CAL-PEP outreach workers go into the stroll districts where street prostitutes work and distribute condoms, spermicides, bleach bottles, and educational materials, and talk to prostitutes about how they can work safely. CAL-PEP outreach workers take a van into the stroll districts, and the prostitutes are invited to come into the van, which is fully equipped with HIV-prevention items, to rest and to talk about how to keep themselves and their clients free of AIDS. In addition, CAL-PEP sponsors support groups and monthly workshops in a hotel room in the stroll district for prostitutes and their regular customers, safe-sex workshops at the county jail, and other programs. (See the interview with Gloria Lockett in this volume.)

This is obviously an outcome replete with contradictions. The state is not dealing with the problem of AIDS and prostitutes in a singular and consistent fashion. It has utilized what Moerkerk and Aggleton call the pragmatic and political responses. Prostitutes are scapegoats and criminals, but also allies with a unique constituency to educate. Women leaders of these organizations, which in certain ways have been made stronger by the struggle around legal control and HIV prevention work, are nevertheless forced to sustain political work at odds with their original intention to free prostitutes from surveillance by health and legal authorities and promote a less constrained sexuality.

SEX EDUCATION: TO BE OR NOT TO BE, AND IN WHAT FORM?

Unlike prostitutes, other young women face a different set of social control mechanisms. Adolescent girls, even from the most privileged backgrounds, do not have the freedom and resources to organize on their own behalf, and rarely do they have strong advocates. Their families and schools, the primary socializing institutions of children, exercise physical and legal control over what and how they learn about sexuality and accomplish gender. In the face of the AIDS epidemic, the ideological apparatus of schools, which contributes to the perpetuation of race and gender inequality, extends social control over its charges by framing, constraining, and in fact censoring what is thought about AIDS and how it comes to be understood. In that process, it specifies some of the parameters of female sexuality.

Sex education is the vehicle through which children and adolescents learn some portion of what they know about HIV/AIDS, and that learning has not been accomplished (when it has occurred at all) unproblematically. Prevention and control of the spread of HIV requires discussions of sexual and drug-using activities, and sex/health education is a primary institution through which youth are advised whether, as well as how and when, to be sexual beings. In the process, it cues them to what is "safer," "safe," and "risky sex."

Schools respond to AIDS with a hybrid of the political, pragmatic, and biomedical approaches. An examination of how these programs come about in schools reveals a systematic preoccupation with heterosexuality and with the social control of young women's sexuality. These are evident in the multiple discourses of community political struggles over the control of the schools' curricula and over the specific content of prevention materials. Some of these extensions of social control are patently obvious, while others are more implicit. Their limitations are revealed whenever they are resisted, when teenagers provide education for each other in the form of theater, make their own AIDS videos, or join with groups like ACT-UP in the distribution of condoms.

Community Struggles, Social Control, and Censorship

AIDS education for young people was initially proposed in a climate of fear that reflected deep social and cultural anxieties about the disease and its transmissibility. Most importantly, homosexuality and its central symbolic attachment to AIDS rendered particularly problematic the matter of the structure and the content of AIDS education in the public schools.[35] School officials anticipated controversy as parents considered the prospects of such programs for their children. The expectations of trouble were not without cause: legislators were publicly unwilling to support mandatory AIDS education packages for children, teachers harbored memories of painful struggles to introduce sex education, and all school administrators wanted to avoid antagonizing community groups who oppose homosexuality and birth control and favor either no sex education programs or teaching of traditional values about sex.[36]

There has not been a consensus about the need for AIDS education programs (nor about their specific content) in the public schools. By the mid-1980s, the Christian Right's campaign to gain control of the nation's school boards was underway. Among the issues around which its efforts to gain control revolve are bilingual education, the teaching of evolution, affirmative action, and the existence or form of AIDS education and condom distribution. For the last decade, conservative parents have been particularly active in banning books and other materials they found offensive.[37] In the 1992–1993 New York City struggle over school board membership, traditional values groups, reaching out to the Latino community—usually one of their targets—argued that the city, through its "elite" school board (and its approval of condom distribution and its Rainbow curriculum), intended to turn their children into homosexuals.[38]

This sort of censorship has a chilling effect on the search by women, including young women, to understand their own sexuality. While early twentieth-century censorship shielded women from knowledge of birth control, the current round is preoccupied with gay and lesbian depictions and expressions of women's rebellion.

In spite of the real and anticipated trouble, most school systems have offered some form of AIDS education to their students. They have engaged in complicated debates and a variety of institutional maneuvers to structure a nonproblematic AIDS education curriculum.[39] A recent study by the Sex Information and Education Council of the U.S. reported that, although every state in 1993 required or recommended AIDS education, students were getting incomplete information from unprepared teachers. Only 11 states provided "balanced information about safe sex" and numerous states prohibited any discussion of homosexuality. Their summary suggests that only three states provided good programs that provided more than biological information, explained sexual orientation, and discussed a range of safe-sex behaviors and strategies.[40]

Our study of a school system in California reveals a variety of these maneuvers, "deflection strategies" taken by accident or design to reduce the probability of criticism and interference.[41] These strategies include special parental permission forms, preview nights for parents, integration of the AIDS materials into already-existing curricula, cooptation of potential student and parent troublemakers, utilizing the "objective" approach in presentations, and avoiding all discussion of homosexuality. Each strategy enhances the influence of parents and diminishes accordingly the power and participation of students. It is the last two strategies that deserve more detailed attention here since they serve very directly to shape the contours and content of the materials presented to young women.

Gender and the Biomedical Model in Sex Education

The discourses of expertise position recipients of educational messages in a way that disables their ability to actually apply information to their lives, and leaves them liable for failing to have understood that they were to have appropriately responded to the "danger" of AIDS.[42]

The dominant view of adolescents' sex education and sexuality, heavily influenced by the fields of medicine and psychology, has shaped HIV prevention practice. Adolescents are often understood as "other," as strange beings, with those from racial/ethnic groups viewed as particularly so. The fields of medicine and psychology put forward essentially deterministic models of social behavior that are simply not flexible enough to capture the variation and dynamism of sexuality and social interaction. The supposedly value-free behaviorism that provides information about anatomy, reproductive physiology, contraception, and a limited variety of sexual practices, assumes that scientific knowledge about sexuality is nonjudgmental and can be used easily by students in making their own choices about sexual behavior. It conveys the message that heterosexual intercourse is normal behavior that can be engaged in responsibly and calmly with the use of contraception and abortions when birth control fails.

This approach is, or should be, unsatisfactory to feminist parents, educators, and young women themselves. We believe that the limits of the debate about what students should and should not have is premised on the view that they are not capable of critical thinking, emotional self-discipline, and intellectual self-direction. It isolates sexuality from other social relations. It focuses on organs or viruses with little link to humans' relationships to one another or the historical context. It tends to ignore the continued, persistent discrepancies between young women and men regarding atttitudes toward birth control, sex, and relationships. As research on classroom interaction continues to indicate, male domination is uncritically accepted as natural, as an important topic but never as one requiring critical discussion or presented as in any way problematic.[43] Hence, most of these efforts ignore the unequal power relations between men and women that structure heterosexuality.

Moreover, the models utilized in public health campaigns teach biomedical safe sex guidelines as the basis of individuals' everyday behavior. But neither of the two prevailing models deals directly with common-sense knowledge about AIDS and its relationship to AIDS prevention. And it is how these youth understand AIDS that is crucial to what they do. For example, Maticka-Tyndale's study shows gender differences in the ways in which young women and men assess the risk of intercourse based on their views of its consequences. As she describes it:

> For women, coitus, even before AIDS, carried a variety of risks; they commonly cited both risks of pregnancy and emotional hurt. Relative to other risks, HIV was the least likely to occur. . . . For men, the experience of coitus generally lacked any prior sense of risk. Lacking a concept of risky coitus, men spoke of risk by ranking coitus against other sexual activities [such as anal intercourse].[44]

Finally, in high schools AIDS is seen as an aspect of health and family services, not as a political or historical matter. Public policy issues and historical debates are typically not discussed. Students consequently are shielded from an understanding of what is controversial in what they may be learning or doing and from a more conscious understanding of the political significance of condoms, contraception, and sex. The passive, "objective" stance of most education prevents the expression of opposing or alternative perspectives. The family life–planning classes, though the site of whatever sex education is offered in California high schools, emphasize pregnancy and disease. They are not about sex; indeed, they de-eroticize sexuality. When schools avoid presenting alternative perspectives, including those that incorporate a discussion of eroticism and pleasure, they continue to perpetu-ate existing class, race, gender, and sexuality hierarchies.

Nevertheless, adolescents have learned the public health information presented to them. Considerable research over the last five years has confidently concluded that adolescents have high levels of knowledge about AIDS and can voice the biomedical position about the role of condoms in AIDS prevention.[45] However, numerous studies show that the major rule they follow to prevent HIV infection is to try not to have sexual intercourse (unprotected and protected) with an infected partner, a determination requiring trust in a specific partner and/or strong faith in one's own ability to judge people based on reputation or appearance.

Gender differences in sexual scripts are also evident. Trust means some-thing different for women and men. Young women expect young men to disclose prior risky sexual activities; men expect that women with whom they are sexual have had no prior sexual activities.[46] That is, they expect them to be "good girls." Since condoms are still seen as primarily for contraception, there are serious gender differences in the ways women and men approach the introduction of condoms. Women, presumed to be using contraception, may be queried about their lack of other birth control and/or about their own or their partners' infection status. Men may introduce condoms in the guise of protecting their partner and in fact be protecting themselves. Young heterosexual women, similar to older women who have been studied in efforts to improve AIDS interventions, fear the regular use of condoms as an insult to their male partner. Most couples—prostitutes with boyfriends included—determine a point in their relationship when they stop using condoms, a point representing deepening trust and commitment. Indeed, the decision to use safe sex is based on perceived HIV status of the partner or on quality of feelings. (For further discussion of these issues in this volume, see the chapter by Sosnowitz.)[47]

AIDS Videos and Social Control

Videos are a major educational tool through which adults bring children AIDS education. In many school systems, a video with an hour or two of discussion may be all the AIDS education students receive.[48] In the best situations, the program around AIDS takes several days, speakers from Planned Parenthood or the local AIDS project appear, and students get to role-play some of what they have learned. But these elaborations on a basic program are rare. The package as a whole usually fosters heterosexism, and every point in the process has its gendered content or outcome.

An examination of four of the commonly used videos available to high schools in the district we studied indicates the variety of ways in which gender inequality and gender difference is reproduced. When given a choice from among these videos, parents tend to select the ones produced by the Red Cross,

"A Letter from Brian, and Don't Forget Sherrie," targeted primarily to white students, and "Don't Forget Sherrie," targeted to their African-Americans counterparts.[49] In each, a young woman or man learns that a former sex partner is HIV-infected and near death. The friends of the just-notified teenager try to figure out what all of them should think and do about their future sexual or drug use behavior in light of the information that one of them might be infected. The two videos carry a long disclaimer on a black screen:

> [This video deals] with teens and others discussing sexual activity and AIDS prevention in frank terms. The film deals with the threat of the disease, AIDS, for teenagers, and how they can avoid getting the disease.

It is followed by the American Red Cross position: Abstinence is highly recommended for young single teenagers, and education regarding sex should be provided within the family with supplementary materials from the schools and community organizations. "Sex education should be based on religious, ethical, legal, and moral foundations."

"Sex, Drugs, and HIV" takes a less apologetic and fearful approach. This video uses popular music, an actress familiar to young people, and an interracial cast. It is divided into three parts: "Relax, AIDS is Hard to Get," a section intended to overcome myths about mosquitoes, touching, and other forms of casual contact; "You Can Get AIDS By Sharing Needles," a brief section whose sole point is that shooting drugs is bad, "so don't shoot up"; and a last section, "AIDS Can Be a Sexually Transmitted Disease."

Each of the videos talks about the "facts" or the "truth" about AIDS. "Sex, Drugs, and HIV," a 19-minute video, goes so far as to conclude with "That's it. That's all you need to know." This is not only simplistic, it is misleading. Most videos take approximately one minute to explain that "AIDS is caused by a virus," one that infects a person and causes the failure of the immune system. And in most videos one confident speaker or the narrator refers to AIDS as a fatal disease.

Even though videos try to use the language of the teenagers to whom they are geared, the language is not believable in its description of risk behaviors. Not only do young girls and boys not use the same language to talk about sex, virtually none call their own practices vaginal, oral, or anal intercourse. Typically only penile-vaginal intercourse "counts" as "going all the way." This is particularly problematic for AIDS education. As Melese-d'Hospital found in her study with adolescents, many are staying "virgins" as a means to avoid HIV. However, the meaning of virginity, what it includes and what it does not, is consequential. The concept is a marker for what is acceptable sexual behavior. For young women, virginity was "located in the vagina" and related to pregnancy, a greater and more visible concern to them than HIV.[50]

Even in those videos that move away from simply telling the facts to more emotion-laden interactions, it is highly unusual to find serious interaction between males and females: males talk to males, females talk to females.

"Sex, Drugs, and HIV" has two such scenes. Three girls are stretching in a gymnasium. They are talking about true love, about whether to have sex, about which birth control to use. One suggests that her friend, who has never before had intercourse, should use the pill; the third counters that pills do not protect against disease or AIDS. The young woman without the experience of vaginal intercourse is convinced to use a condom but worries about being rejected. The friend with the handy condom responds: "Sit and talk to him. He cares about you. . . . If you can't talk to him about birth control, you shouldn't have sex with him. . . . If you're not sure you want to have sex, you should wait." This enactment, one of the best of its kind in this genre, ignores any direct acknowledgment of the normative context of gender inequality and gendered differences in knowledge about sex.

Conversation among the males in both "Sex, Drugs, and HIV" and "A Letter from Brian" show young men trying to persuade one another to use condoms, with one attempting to best the others by claiming always to have used them. This is a positive and important effort to change the norms of the group. Yet it does not deal directly with the variety of myths surrounding condom use or the interactional and emotional matters at stake in sexual encounters.

The videos are not sex-positive. No other sexual practices are discussed, though adolescents engage in a great many other activities. Consistent with the political approach to the control of AIDS, as described in the Moerkerk and Appleton study, no acknowledgment is made of the possibility of same-sex experience or of the existence of gay and lesbian students. And, in these and other videos, vague use is made of such terms as *love, respect, commitment* and *monogamy* without any attempt to operationalize them or recognize their multiple meanings. Adolescents are treated as if they are one group, in spite of the strong evidence of diverse and overlapping communities of youth even within similar schools and neighborhoods.[51]

As many women involved in AIDS prevention work have already noted, women are expected to take responsibility for what happens sexually. Many of the videos are addressed to young women, even when they aren't explicitly targeted to them. For example, in the "Brian" video, the U.S. surgeon general offers this confusing statement:

> There is another way where you don't need to worry about condoms and that's to have a mutually faithful relationship. In other words, find someone worthy of your love and respect. Give that person both and expect the same from him and remain as faithful to him as he is to you. [If you do this] you will never have to read about AIDS again in your life because it doesn't apply to you.

Aside from the head-in-the-sand attitude, the use of the male pronoun implies that women are the only ones likely to be "good," that they have the burden to make men safe in any relational or sexual situation, and that monogamy protects.

Finally, there are the absences. These videos ignore entrenched fears about homosexuals or unconscious fears about death, though these can surely be said to frame the reception of the facts of AIDS education. With the exception of "Sex, Drugs, and HIV," neither compassion nor "complicity with discrimination"[52] are taught in these and most other HIV-prevention videos. Hence, the strategies of deflection used to shape the content, particularly the avoidance of discussion of homosexuality, highlight the hidden curriculum of schools in their transmission of dominant values and beliefs about heterosexuality. Students are sheltered from the controversial nature of the material presented to them and subsequently rendered politically ignorant.

Working from a feminist framework, a good sex education program would not be simply biological; it would be a political program to change gender relations, free women from emotionally and physically debilitating inequality, and foster positive values about sex. If social relations are bad, so are sexual ones. This kind of sex education would provide what young women need: lessons that women are not just victims of sexuality, that they can construct their own sexual identities and pleasures. This would require a significant restructuring not only of the substance of AIDS education, but also of the organizations responsible for delivering it—the schools. This is no small feat, in that it requires greater recognition of institutionalized gender inequality, including that which is routinely affirmed in the classroom.

Although this sort of sex/AIDS education is not available in any complete form anywhere, some student initiatives are moving in this direction. Students often perceive that part of adults' interest in AIDS education is its potential for containing adolescent sexuality.[53] Young women have been integrally involved in, if not actually leaders of, a number of innovative, usually nonschool-based AIDS prevention programs, such as theater groups supported by local Planned Parenthood organizations and off-campus condom distribution efforts initiated by ACT-UP. At the college level, young women are the major players in most AIDS education efforts.

DISCUSSION

While the cultural and economic implications of the AIDS epidemic are certainly far reaching, so are the consequences for the social organization of sex and gender. Through a logic born of the current epidemic, forms of regulatory intervention that might in other circumstances appear excessive can now be justified in the name of prevention. Such justifications are embedded in, and seemingly cannot be divorced from, larger social systems of gender and sexuality.

The social organization of gender and sexuality is policed by laws and public policy that oversee and regulate our sexual desires, exchanges, images, and identities.[54] The AIDS epidemic strengthens, in legal and educational discourses, the rationale for the extension of social control.

Though the special treatment of prostitutes and HIV education of young women in schools may seem wildly divergent, each helps shape the contours of female sexuality, in efforts to contain the "bad girl" and to construct the "good" one. Whether through limits on mutually contracted sex by prostitutes or through limits on balanced information on safe sex for young women, the state is interrupting and forbidding certain sexual practices.

Yet, these processes are not consistent or unidirectional. The combination of political and pragmatic approaches to prostitutes by public health and legal institutions expands social control while legitimizing and in some ways normalizing the existence of prostitutes' organizations. To the extent that prostitutes are organized and in charge of their own HIV education, they are positioned to shape, if not to transform, their own sexuality in their own terms. Still, regulation of this always-suspect group of women continues.

Young women face a different, seemingly more constrained, situation. Schools are forced to confront their own failure to educate, as the rate of new infection in women and adolescents increases in the United States. Because of their use of three approaches to HIV prevention (political, pragmatic, and biomedical), the schools are faced with a continuing series of contradictions. They are the locus of community struggles over the nature and meaning of sexuality. For them, virtually every effort to educate, even in the simple case of supplying just the biological facts, results in challenges to their program, from both interested parties who want more and from those who want less.

Since young women in school are not in charge of their education and are politically disenfranchised, they have severe limits on their privacy and virtually no cultural permission to construct their own sexuality in their own terms. The protection of their "innocence" through the narrowness of the programs presented to them offers some, but rather limited, access to a fuller knowledge of sexuality and the range of sexual options a young woman might have. Moreover, while the few most expansive programs recognize young women as sexual actors and no longer force them to be chaste and modest, almost all still enforce a femininity centered in presumed heterosexuality in appearance and practice.

It is certainly possible that this crisis has the potential for the adoption of a more positive approach to the sexual in talk and in practice. Nevertheless, it will require the leadership of women of all ages, of all cultural and economic backgrounds, with strong feminist motivations, to counter the emergent forms of social control. Such controls do not stop or slow the epidemic and constitute incursions on the rights of individual and specific groups of women.

NOTES

[1]Susan Shapiro, "Policing Trust," in *Private Policing*, ed. Clifford D. Shearing and Philip C. Stenning (Newbury Park, Calif.: Sage, 1987), 194–220.

[2]Watney (p. 43) argues that "we are not, in fact, living through a distinct, coherent

and progressing 'moral panic' about AIDS. Rather, we are witnessing the latest variation in the spectacle of the defensive ideological rearguard action which has been mounted on behalf of the 'family' for more than a century." Simon Watney, *Policing Desire: Pornography, AIDS, and the Media* (Minneapolis: University of Minnesota Press, 1987).

3Allan Brandt, *No Magic Bullet: A Social History of Venereal Disease in the United States Since 1880* (New York: Oxford University Press, 1985); Linda Singer, *Erotic Welfare: Sexual Theory and Politics in the Age of Epidemic* (New York: Routledge, 1993). See also Susan Sontag, *Illness as Metaphor* (New York: Vintage, 1977) and *AIDS and Its Metaphors* (New York: Farrar, Straus and Giroux, 1988).

4William Darrow, "AIDS: Socioepidemiologic Responses to an Epidemic," in *AIDS and the Social Sciences: Common Threads*, ed. Richard Ulack and William F. Skinner (Lexington: University of Kentucky Press, 1991), 83–99; Samuel V. Duh, *Blacks and AIDS: Causes and Origins* (Newbury Park, Calif.: Sage, 1991); Nan D. Hunter, "Complications of Gender: Women and HIV Disease," in *AIDS Agenda: Emerging Issues in Civil Rights*, ed. Nan D. Hunter and William B. Rubenstein (New York: The New Press, 1992), 5–39; Beth E. Schneider, "Women, Children, and AIDS: Research Suggestions," in *AIDS and the Social Sciences: Common Threads*, ed. Richard Ulack and William F. Skinner (Lexington: University of Kentucky Press, 1991), 134–148; Beth E. Schneider, "AIDS and Class, Gender, and Race Relations," in *The Social Context of AIDS*, ed. Joan Huber and Beth E. Schneider (Newbury Park, Calif.: Sage, 1992), 19–43.

5Duh; Hunter; Schneider 1991, 1992; also Richard Ulack and William F. Skinner, eds, *AIDS and the Social Sciences: Common Threads* (Lexington: University of Kentucky Press, 1991).

6The history of epidemics is vast. Some of the books and articles most frequently used in discussions of AIDS include, in addition to Brandt 1975, Sontag 1977, and Sontag 1988. Charles E. Rosenberg, *The Cholera Years* (Chicago: University of Chicago Press, 1962) and William H. McNeill, *Plagues and Peoples* (Garden City: Anchor Books, 1976). See also, Elizabeth Fee and Daniel M. Fox, eds., *AIDS: The Burdens of History* (Berkeley: University of California Press, 1988) and Ilse J. Volinn, "Health Professionals as Stigmatizers and Destigmatizers of Diseases: Alcoholism and Leprosy as Examples," *Social Science and Medicine* 17(1983): 385–393.

7In addition to Watney, see Virginia Berridge, "AIDS: History and Contemporary History," in *The Time of AIDS: Social Analysis, Theory, and Method*, ed. Gilbert Herdt and Shirley Lindenbaum (Newbury Park, Calif.: Sage, 1992), 41–64 and Cindy Patton, *Inventing AIDS* (New York: Routledge, 1990).

8Nachman Ben-Yehuda, *The Politics and Morality of Deviance: Moral Panics, Drug Abuse, Deviant Science, and Reversed Stigmatization* (New York: State University of New York Press, 1990); Stanley Cohen, *Folk Devils and Moral Panics* (London: MacGibbon and Kee, 1972).

9Brandt; Singer.

10Gayle Rubin, "Thinking Sex: Notes for a Radical Theory of the Politics of Sexuality," in *Pleasure and Danger: Exploring Female Sexuality*, ed. Carole S. Vance (Boston: Routledge and Kegan Paul, 1984).

11Peter Aggleton, Peter Davies and Graham Hart (eds.), *AIDS: Individual, Cultural and Policy Dimensions* (London: The Falmer Press, 1990), 181–190.

[12]Brandt, 195.

[13]Larry Gostin, ed., *Civil Liberties in Conflict* (New York: Routledge, 1988); Joel Feinberg, "Harmless Immoralities' and Offensive Nuisances," in *AIDS: Ethics and Public Policy*, ed. Christine Pierce and Donald VandeVeer (Belmont, Calif.: Wadsworth, 1988), 92–102; Thomas B. Stoddard and Walter Rieman, "AIDS and the Rights of the Individual: Toward a More Sophisticated Understanding of Discrimination," in *A Disease of Society: Cultural and Institutional Responses to AIDS*, ed. Dorothy Nelkin, David P. Willis, and Scott V. Parris (Cambridge: Cambridge University Press, 1991), 241–271.

[14]Ibid.

[15]William Buckley, "Identify All the Carriers," *The New York Times*, 18 March 1986, p. 26; Ronald Elsberry, "AIDS Quarantining in England and the United States," *Hastings International and Comparative Law Journal* 10 (1986):113–126; Mark H. Jackson, "The Criminalization of HIV," in *AIDS Agenda: Emerging Issues in Civil Rights*, ed. Nan D. Hunter and William B. Rubenstein (New York: The New Press, 1992), 239–270.

[16]Privacy encompasses "those places, spaces and matters upon or into which others may not intrude without the consent of the person or organization to whom they are designated as belonging" (p. 20); Albert J. Reiss, Jr., "The Legitimacy of Intrusion Into Private Space," in *Private Policing*, ed. Clifford D. Shearing and Philip C. Stenning (Newbury Park, Calif.: Sage, 1988), 19–44.

[17]Jackson; Pierce and Vande Veer.

[18]Buckley; Elsberry; Jackson; Stoddard and Rieman.

[19]Judith Cohen, Priscilla Alexander, and Constance Wofsy, "Prostitutes and AIDS: Public Policy Issues," *AIDS & Public Policy Journal* 3(1988): 16–22.

[20]Edward Albert, "Illness and/or Deviance: The Response of the Press to Acquired Immunodeficiency Syndrome," in *The Social Dimensions of AIDS: Method and Theory*, ed. Douglas A. Feldman and Tom Johnson (New York: Praeger, 1986), 163–178; Edward Albert, "AIDS and the Press: The Creation and Transformation of a Social Problem," in *Images of Issues; Typifying Contemporary Social Problems*, ed. Joel Best (New York: Aldine De Gruyter Press, 1989), 39–54. See also, Ann Giudici Fettner and William Check, *The Truth About AIDS: The Evolution of an Epidemic* (New York: Holt, 1985); Randy Shilts, *And the Band Played On* (New York: St. Martin's Press, 1988); Harry Schwartz, "AIDS and the Media," in *Science in the Streets* (New York: Priority Press, 1984).

[21]For an historical overview see, in addition to Brandt 1985, Beth Bergman, "AIDS, Prostitution, and the Use of Historical Stereotypes to Legislate Sexuality," *The John Marshall Law Review* 211 (1988): 777–830; Barbara Hobson, *Uneasy Virtue: The Politics of Prostitution and the American Reform Tradition* (New York: Basic Books, 1987); Gail Pheterson, *The Whore Stigma: Female Dishonor and Male Unworthiness* (The Netherlands: Dutch Ministry of Social Affairs and Employment, 1986); Gail Sheehy, "The Economics of Prostitution: Who Profits? Who Pays?" in *Sexual Deviance and Sexual Deviants*, ed. Erich Goode and Richard Troiden (New York: William Morrow, 1974), 110–123.

[22]Darrow; Joan Luxenburg and Thomas Guild, "Prostitutes and AIDS: What Is All the Fuss About" (Paper presented at the annual meetings of the American Society of

Criminology in New Orleans, LA., 1992); Valerie Jenness, *Making It Work: The Contemporary Prostitutes' Rights Movement in Perspective* (New York: Aldine de Gruyter, 1993).

[23]Geraldo Rivera, "Are Prostitutes the New Typhoid Mary's?" The Geraldo Show, 1989, Fox Headquarters, 10201 Pico Boulevard, Los Angeles, California.

[24]John Cristallo, "Are Prostitutes the New Typhoid Mary's?" The Geraldo Show, 1989, Fox Headquarters, 10201 Pico Boulevard, Los Angeles, California.

[25]Jackson; Luxenburg and Guild, 1992; Joan Luxenburg and Thomas Guild, "Coercion, Criminal Sanctions and AIDS" (Paper presented at the annual meetings of the Society for the Study of Social Problems, Washington, D.C., 1990).

[26]This parallels what happened to prostitutes in the first half of the twentieth century when "physicians and social reformers associated venereal disease, almost exclusively, with the vast population of prostitutes in American cities" (Brandt, p. 31). Perceived threats like these led to the increased social control of prostitution, primarily in the form of state regulation.

[27]"No Murder-Try Case for Addicted Hooker," *Sacramento Bee*, 18 July 1990, p. B7.

[28]Priscilla Alexander, "A Chronology of Sorts," personal files, 1988.

[29]Darrow, p. 94. He observes, "To date, no HIV infections in female prostitutes or their clients can be directly linked to sexual exposure."

[30]Lord Patrick Devlin, "Morals and the Criminal Law," in *Pierce and Vande Veer*, 77–86.

[31]Carol Leigh, "AIDS: No Reason For A Witchhunt," *Oakland Tribune*, (17 August 1987), p. 1; Carol Leigh, "Further Violations Of Our Rights," in *AIDS Cultural Analysis, Cultural Activisim*, ed. Douglas Crimp (Cambridge, MA: The MIT Press, 1988), an October book, 177–181.

[32]Stoddard and Reiman, 264.

[33]Gail Pheterson, *A Vindication of the Rights of Whores* (Seattle: Seal Press, 1989), 28.

[34]Leigh 1987, 1.

[35]Dennis Altman, *AIDS in the Mind of America* (New York: Anchor, 1987); Paula A. Treichler, "AIDS, Homophobia, and Biomedical Discourse: An Epidemic of Signification," in *AIDS: Cultural Analysis, Cultural Activism*, ed. D. Crimp (Cambridge, Mass.: MIT Press, 1988), 31–70.

[36]Beth E. Schneider, Valerie Jenness, and Sarah Fenstermaker, "Deflecting Trouble: The Introduction of AIDS Education in the Public Schools" (Presented at the annual meetings of the Society for the Study of Social Problems, 1991).

[37]Michael Granberry, "Besieged by Book Banners," *Los Angeles Times*, (10 May 1993), p. 1ff.

[38]Donna Minkowitz, "Wrong Side of the Rainbow," *The Nation*, (28 June, 1993), pp. 901–904.

[39]Douglas Kirby, "School-Based Prevention Programs: Design, Evaluation, and Effectiveness," in *Adolescents and AIDS: A Generation in Jeopardy*, ed. Ralph DiClemente, (Newbury Park, Calif.: Sage, 1992); David C. Sloane and Beverlie Conant Sloane, "AIDS in Schools: A Comprehensive Initiative," *McGill Journal of Education* 25 (1990): 205–228.

[40]John Gallagher, "Why Johnny Can't Be Safe," *The Advocate* 631, (15 June 1993), pp. 46–47.

[41]Schneider, Jenness, and Fenstermaker.

[42]Patton, 99.

[43]Susan Russell, "The Hidden Curriculum of School: Reproducing Gender and Class Hierarchies," in *Feminism and Political Economy: Women's Work, Women's Struggles*, ed. H. J. Marmey and M. Luxton (Toronto: Methuen, 1987).

[44]Eleanor Maticka-Tyndale, "Social Construction of HIV Transmission and Prevention Among Heterosexual Young Adults," *Social Problems* 39 (1992): 238–252.

[45]DiClemente, 1992.

[46]Maticka-Tyndale.

[47]For additional consideration of these issues, see ACT-UP/New York Women and AIDS Book Group, *Women, AIDS and Activism* (Boston: South End Press, 1990); Laurie Wermuth, Jennifer Ham, and Rebecca L. Robbins, "Women Don't Wear Condoms: AIDS Risk Among Sexual Partners of IV Drug Users," in *The Social Context of AIDS*, ed. Joan Huber and Beth E. Schneider (Newbury Park, Calif.: Sage, 1992), 72–94.

[48]Kirby.

[49]These videos were produced in 1988. "Sex, Drugs and HIV," referred to in a later discussion, was produced in 1990 after complaints by parents resulted in revisions to an earlier version, "Sex, Drugs and AIDS."

[50]Isabelle Melese-d'Hospital, "Still a Virgin: Adolescent Social Constructions of Sexuality and HIV Prevention Education" (Paper presented at the annual meetings of the American Sociological Association, Miami, 1993).

[51]Benjamin P. Bowser and Gina M. Wingood, "Community Based HIV-Prevention Programs for Adolescents," in DiClemente.

[52]Patton 1990, 108.

[53]Sloane and Conant Sloane; Schneider, Jenness, and Fenstermaker.

[54]Singer; Watney. See also Jeffrey Weeks, *Sexuality and Its Discontents: Meanings, Myths & Modern Sexualities* (New York: Routledge, Kegan Paul, 1985).

PART II

Women and the Problems of HIV Prevention

Priscilla Alexander

Sex Workers Fight Against AIDS:
An International Perspective

Conceptualizations of "prostitution" and "the prostitute"[1] are likely to affect the way societies respond to prostitution in the context of AIDS. This paper discusses two distinct societal responses: the traditional STD-control model and a newer, community-based organizing model which comes directly from the work of prostitutes. Both responses are born in and affect discourses on prostitution, sexuality, and disease. The paper examines how the discourse is changing as a result of prostitutes' active involvement in the struggle to prevent the spread of this tragic disease. My thinking in this paper is the result of 17 years of research and activism in the prostitutes' rights movement, initially in the United States but, since 1986, increasingly on an international level.

CONCEPTUALIZATIONS OF "THE PROSTITUTE"

The nature of the discourse on prostitution has a profound effect on both the form and the outcome of AIDS prevention interventions, and thus on the course of AIDS. For most of recorded history, societies have defined prostitutes, culturally and through systems of law, as "other," a group often considered necessary for the functioning of society, but one that must be kept apart. Whether the legislative body was religious or civil, governments have often confined prostitutes to certain streets, held them within locked buildings or districts, or outlawed them altogether. During some periods of history, civic leaders have required prostitutes to wear special clothing or marks, whereas in other periods, they have castigated them for the clothes they wore.

Within any culture, religious and political authorities have used the concept of "other" to divide the "good woman," from the "bad." The whore is counterposed to the chaste wife and mother.[2] Deep-seated prejudices distinguish the black, Asian, or Jewish woman from the white or Christian. Defining the prostitute as "other," military victors have forced women

---

I would like to express by deep gratitude to Lyndall MacCowan, who has read an endless number of drafts of this paper and helped me in numerous ways to clarify my thinking. I would also like to thank Karen Booth, who made many valuable suggestions after reading a late version.

captured from conquered and occupied towns or countries to work in brothels, both to "protect" their own country's women and to provide "variety" for their men.[3]

On the other hand, prostitutes have taken advantage of some forms of "otherness" to mask their stigmatized labor. For example, although for the last several thousand years many women have been forced to work in wartime brothels, some have volunteered, to avoid starvation or other consequences of war, to escape from their families or traditions, or even for less desperate reasons. For centuries, women have migrated from rural communities, where their activities (whether as prostitutes or as noncon-forming sexual beings) would be more likely to be observed and commented upon, to cities that provide anonymity and privacy or to other countries where the traditional cultural norms mean less to them. To the extent that prostitutes are rebels against their societies' expectations regarding female sexual and other behavior, this "otherness" can provide the space for an independent and productive life.[4] There is a difference, however, between prostitutes' manipulating "otherness" to protect themselves and policy makers' justifying repressive measures on the basis of prostitutes' "other-ness."

In the context of AIDS, numerous writers in both the medical and the mainstream press have continued to perceive and describe prostitutes as a class with objectifying language (for example, as members of a "core group of high-frequency transmitters,"[5] as "promiscuous," and as "reservoirs" or "pools of contagion").[6] These terms have colored the way health care practitioners provide services, especially those related to sexually transmit-ted diseases (STDs), to women who identify themselves, or are perceived to be, prostitutes. Policy makers who think of themselves as "subject" and of prostitutes as "object" or "other" are likely to try to increase the state's control over "them," in order to protect the clients (who they *may* perceive to be more like themselves, even though such identification may cross class, nationality, and racial lines). They are much less likely to support or strengthen prostitutes' ability to protect themselves, for example, by control-ling their working conditions. Such efforts to control the prostitute are, in turn, likely to increase the marginalization of prostitutes and to drive the world in which they operate underground, away from health promotion interventions.

A second, related conceptualization is the common perception of female prostitutes as intrinsically dirty and diseased. For example, clients com-monly equate sex with prostitutes as "dirty" and therefore somehow more exciting. It is through this ideological equation of prostitutes with dirt and contagion that policy makers, novelists, journalists, medical writers, and others assume that prostitutes are, by definition, responsible for virtually all sexually transmitted diseases, including AIDS.[7] In a rather bizarre twist, however, in countries where prostitutes are required by law to have regular examinations for STD, often including HIV, clients may resist using condoms, justifying their refusal by saying that they know the prostitute is "clean" (that is, has been purified by the clean medical profession).

ONE OPTION, ONE DISCOURSE: THE REGLEMENTORY RESPONSE

The first thing that policy makers, sometimes including public health officials, tend to do in response to the spread of STD is to try to identify all infected prostitutes, treat those infections that are treatable, and bar prostitutes from working while infected. Although such programs could benefit prostitutes (if they reduced the duration of treatable infections and thus the incidence of complications), the primary agenda behind such schemes has always been, and continues to be, to protect the client. Since the current AIDS context is not the first time public officials have tried to control the spread of STD by controlling prostitutes, it may be useful to examine the historic record of such approaches.

The Historical Record

In the nineteenth and early twentieth centuries, governments in England, France, and the United States experimented with various control measures focusing on the prostitute. In 1864, England enacted the Contagious Diseases Acts, authorizing the police in some cities to take any woman suspected of being a prostitute to a special hospital ward, have her examined for sexually transmitted diseases, and, if she was found to be infected, keep her there until the infection was "cured" or, what is more likely, the visible signs of infection disappeared. The legislation made no reference to the clients, who were primarily sailors and other seamen who had sex with, and sometimes infected, prostitutes during their shore leave. The police often arrested women who were not actually engaging in prostitution, but who lived or worked in the same neighborhoods. Feminists became alarmed and objected to the system's stigmatization of working-class women. Led by Josephine Butler, they organized an effective campaign to overturn the Acts.[8]

In the nineteenth century, France established a formal *reglementation* system which required street prostitutes and women who worked in brothels to register with special health centers and report regularly to be examined for syphilis and gonorrhea. Feminists opposed this system as well, arguing that, by institutionalizing prostitution, the regulations kept women trapped in what was, to the feminists, an unacceptable profession. Nonetheless, the system continued to operate until it was dismantled after World War II.[9] Under both schemes, many if not most prostitutes went to great lengths to avoid being identified and registered, preferring to remain "clandestine," a term that continues to be used to refer to the majority of prostitutes who work outside such registration schemes where they exist.

In the United States during the nineteenth and early twentieth centuries, many cities established or permitted zones of toleration where brothels flourished (New Orleans' Storyville, San Francisco's Barbary Coast). The one formal effort modeled after the French reglementation system, in St. Louis in 1879, was stopped very quickly, again in response to community outrage about the institutionalization of prostitution.[10] After the turn of the century, in the period prior to World War I, many cities tried to control STD by closing brothels and brothel districts.[11] When that failed to end either prostitution or STD, one state after another enacted legislation prohibiting prostitution.[12] Although legislators and other officials often used feminists' concerns about "white slavery" to justify their actions, they were in fact responding more to pressure from a military concerned about the potential impact of venereal diseases on the ability to mobilize for the coming war. Of course, Prohibition also failed to reduce the prevalence of STD (which rose slightly), and prostitution continued to flourish underground. As brothels were closed, prostitutes worked increasingly on the street, where, as a result of the increased need to be furtive and to negotiate quickly to avoid coming to the attention of police, they were less able to evaluate the health status of their clients or to insist on condoms or other disease or pregnancy prevention practices (such as vaginal sponges soaked in lemon juice). Closing the brothels also significantly interfered with the women's ability to collaborate to protect themselves from STD, pregnancy, and especially violence, forcing them to rely increasingly on men to protect them.

The Response to AIDS

From the first moment that epidemiologists realized that AIDS might be a sexually transmitted disease, they singled out prostitutes as the primary source of infection. However, men who have sex with prostitutes usually have other nonmarital partners as well. It is often only the assumption that prostitutes are diseased that produces the conclusion that men with HIV who report having had sex with both prostitutes and nonprostitutes could only have become infected through their contact with a prostitute.[13] Moreover, due to the repression of homosexuality in most societies, married men diagnosed with HIV or other STD often claim contact with a female prostitute as "the source," as such behavior is less stigmatized than either homosexuality or injection drug use.[14]

Many countries have enacted new laws or added provisions to existing STD laws, requiring all prostitutes to be tested for HIV infection. The tests are done either following an arrest or a conviction, in countries where prostitution is illegal,[15] or as part of a compulsory registration system. By 1989, mandatory testing of prostitutes was in place in 13 states in the United States,[16] including Nevada, which tests both legal prostitutes, working in brothels, and those who work illegally everywhere else. Sweden, Austria, and Germany, where prostitution is legal in some circumstances, require registered prostitutes to be screened regularly for HIV infection. Sweden quarantined at least one woman who continued to work after testing positive, although no effort was made to determine whether she actually engaged in high-risk practices.[17]

In Asia, several countries have mandatory registration and examination schemes, often tied to carefully carved out exceptions to the prohibition of prostitution (entertainment or hospitality workers). In Thailand, for example, women who work in bars, nightclubs, and brothels must register and have a current health card showing that they have had a recent test. When women test positive for HIV or other STD, the clinics withhold their certificates and tell the women not to work until the infection has cleared up. If women test positive for HIV infection, they are told to stop working permanently, although, with few economic alternatives, it is questionable how many can afford to stop working as prostitutes.[18] Some merely move on to another city and work until they are again examined, after which they may move on again. In any case, the highest rates of infection are among women working in low-income brothels catering to local clients. Many of them are young, working to pay off debt bondage agreements for their families; increasingly they come from the hill tribes that live across the Myanmar border. In 1992, there were widespread reports that the Thai government deported some Burmese women after they tested positive and that the Myanmar police executed them when they returned to their own country.[19]

In the Philippines, women who work in bars and nightclubs serving the U.S. military bases are more likely to register than women working for establishments patronized by Filipino clients.[20] In Singapore, women who work for bars and brothels, most of whom are immigrants with temporary visas, register, whereas at least an equal number of women who work for massage parlors do not.[21] Indonesia requires prostitutes to register and to receive what is called "prophylactic" treatment, whether or not they have a diagnosed STD—although anecdotal reports suggest that fewer than 30 percent of prostitutes actually register.[22]

After finding high rates of infection among women who live and work in brothels catering to local clients in Madras, New Delhi, and, most alarmingly, in Bombay (where more than 70 percent of over 700 women who had been arrested, taken to Madras, jailed, and forcibly tested, were infected), India's first official response was to call for mandatory testing and the arrest and incarceration of women who continued to work after testing positive.[23]

In Latin America, several countries, including Peru and Uruguay, have long-established registration systems, particularly for brothel workers. In Mexico, one project established its own registration system, providing health certificates to women who registered with their project.[24]

Although the authors of papers reporting on registration schemes often claim that registered prostitutes have less STD than unregistered or clandestine workers,[25] and therefore recommend the approach, such claims may not have much meaning. For example, in Indonesia, although the government claims that registered prostitutes have lower rates of STD than unregistered workers, anecdotal reports suggest that the opposite is true, despite the mass treatment.[26] The unregistered prostitutes in Singapore have lower rates of STD, perhaps because they rarely provide more than a hand-job, while the registered prostitutes usually engage in vaginal sex, often without condoms, despite their regular contact with health care workers.[27]

In virtually all registration systems, the majority of prostitutes resist being registered and in many cases avoid STD clinics in order not to come to the attention of the officials who are supposed to register them. For example, in Nevada, approximately 350 women who work in legal brothels are registered and regularly screened for gonorrhea, syphilis, and HIV, whereas an estimated 3,000 continue to work illegally, being tested only if and when they are arrested.[28] In Athens, about 350 of an estimated 3,350 women were registered after they were arrested.[29] In Dakar, Senegal, 800 to 900 out of an estimated 16,000 female prostitutes are registered.[30] This is true even where registration is backed up by the threat of arrest.[31]

Prostitutes resist registration for a variety of reasons, always including the refusal to be officially identified as a prostitute because of the lifelong stigma associated with the label. Since the repercussions of being registered are the same as those resulting from being arrested and jailed for prostitution—for example, the loss of one's children, eviction from one's home, and denial of the right to international travel—most women prefer to take the chance that they will not be caught. Thus, the category of "clandestine prostitute" remains vast, its members beyond the reach of researchers, and data on their STD unavailable, while the authorities delude themselves that they are in control.

Shifting the Focus from Control to Prevention: An Ideological Debate?

Many voices are calling for increased medical interventions, with a little education on the side, to "control" STD, rather than the intensive behavioral change interventions needed to prevent it. This agenda is part of an increasing medicalization of AIDS prevention. However, AIDS is only one STD, and not the only one that is either barely treatable or not treatable at all. The mortality rate may be more devastating, but for the individual woman who dies of preventable cervical cancer, the devastation is just as great. The only sure way to stop the spread of sexually transmitted diseases is to prevent them from occurring in the first place. By the time any individual's STD is diagnosed and treated, he or she can already have given it to others, unless the behavior that permitted the initial infection is changed. Better diagnostic and treatment protocols, after the fact, will not stop the spread of HIV, herpes, or human papilloma virus.

Better and more accessible provision of STD services might mean that more people would get examined and treated. Good STD services are those provided by a nonjudgmental and compassionate staff, at convenient locations and times (not in the morning, when prostitutes are likely to be asleep), at affordable cost, providing accurate diagnoses and effective treatments matched to the diagnoses. However, several observers have told me about visiting STD clinics where prostitutes are examined on a kind of assembly line, with the speculum merely swished around a bit in a pail of water, possibly containing some disinfectant, between examinations.

It is not that providing STD services for prostitutes is a bad idea in itself. In fact, most prostitutes prefer to be examined on a more or less regular basis, for their own peace of mind. One of the worst aspects of the current situation is that prostitutes, especially those who are women, are stigmatized, marginalized, and often denied adequate health care services through either neglect or hostility. It is important that a full range of health care services, including health care for their children and not just STD services, be made more accessible—and acceptable—to prostitutes.[32] However, if they are to be examined with unsterile speculums, or injected with reused and unsterile syringes, advising prostitutes to be examined regularly for STD could actually increase their risk of a variety of STDs, and HIV.[33] There is a need for good epidemiological research to investigate the implications of the possible use of unsterile injection equipment, either in STD clinics in poor countries, where electricity is often unreliable, or in the highly popular but informal injection sites that are common in many countries where seroprevalence is high.

If the only reason for providing prostitutes with STD services is to protect others from them, nothing will change. Sex workers will continue to get the message that their lives are valued less than those of the heterosexual men they serve or their future children, and they will be reluctant to trust or participate in AIDS prevention interventions.

ANOTHER OPTION, ANOTHER DISCOURSE: COMMUNITY-BASED EDUCATION AND ORGANIZING

A second response to AIDS and other STDs, and one which is relatively new, emphasizes education and community organizing rather than medical examinations. In the context of prostitution, it means involving both sex workers and clients in efforts to change the community behavior norms in such a way as to reduce their vulnerability to HIV infection and other STD.

Some countries have been wary of establishing prostitutes' projects because of the legal status of prostitution. However, the reality is that, regardless of the laws, commercial sex occurs in every country and culture, its extent determined largely by economic forces, not by laws. No effort to eliminate prostitution has ever been successful, although the more repressive the system, the less safe are the working conditions and the more difficult it is to reach the workers or support their efforts to change their behavior. However, it is possible to establish sex workers' projects no matter what the legal structure, and effective interventions have been established even where police harassment is extensive, as it is in the United States.

Despite the often-hostile legal situation, a number of community-based projects were developed in both industrial and developing countries in the mid-1980s, some by existing prostitutes' organizations, others by new organizations formed for that purpose. As a result of the success of some of the early projects, governments, international donor organizations, and private foundations are increasingly providing support to similar projects around the world, facilitating the diffusion of a new approach. Many countries have now established voluntary interventions targeting sex workers which focus on helping the prostitutes protect themselves from HIV infection. Some of the best-received intervention projects were developed by sex workers' organizations, and others have employed current and former sex workers to both participate in the design of the projects and provide the outreach and education.

Sex workers' involvement is crucial because, in any country, they know more about the industry than any outsider.[34] Moreover, they can take advantage of their knowledge of human, and especially male, sexuality to overcome resistance to condom use, whether by other sex workers, by managers, or by clients. As workers on the front lines, prostitutes know best the obstacles to behavioral change, whether it is the frequency with which police confiscate or damage condoms; sex workers' belief that ingesting semen keeps one young, healthy, and attractive[35]; managers' fear of lost business; or clients' belief that health certificates guarantee noninfection.

Prostitutes Respond: In the United States

As soon as it became clear that AIDS might be sexually transmitted, COYOTE,[36] the prostitutes' rights organization based in San Francisco, began to advise prostitutes to use condoms to protect themselves. At its 1985 national convention, COYOTE adopted several resolutions dealing with AIDS. At the same time, the organization began providing technical assistance to Project AWARE, a research project looking at women's risk for AIDS. This study charted new territory by involving prostitutes in the development and implementation of the study, including hiring prostitutes as interviewers and as participants in analyzing the results. As the study got underway, it became clear that police often confiscated condoms when arresting prostitutes, or punctured holes in them and gave them back. In 1986, COYOTE, AWARE, and several other community agencies met with police representatives and convinced them to stop confiscating condoms and bleach containers as evidence of intent to commit prostitution.[37]

In 1987, members of COYOTE formed the California Prostitutes' Education Project (CAL-PEP), in order to accept a government grant to do outreach and education to street prostitutes. CAL-PEP's basic premise was that, as experts on sex work, prostitutes are the best people to serve as educators and role models for other prostitutes and to begin the process of changing the norms of sex work practices to ensure safety for both prostitutes and clients. As a result, a majority of both the staff and the governing board were current or former sex workers. The project used a combination of face-to-face street outreach and education, during which peer educators distributed both condoms and small bottles of bleach, and more-or-less-monthly workshops which permitted more in-depth discussions. In 1989, with its first private foundation grant, CAL-PEP purchased a large camping van to use as a mobile unit, to bring peer educators, condoms, and a private space for counseling (and health care provided by Project AWARE) to women on the stroll.[38]

During that same period, the Whitman-Walker Clinic, in Washington, D.C., a gay men's health organization, initiated the AORTA Project to do outreach to female and male injection drug users, including those who were prostitutes. Most of the outreach workers were former (and sometimes current) prostitutes or injection drug users, or both. The project developed some innovative approaches to ongoing training and support for street outreach workers in order to reduce the high turnover common to such projects.

By 1989, the strategy of prostitutes' serving as peer educators was well established in the United States, and similar projects operated often with government funds, in a number of cities, including Boston, Denver, Honolulu, Los Angeles,[39] New York, and Phoenix.

Prostitutes Respond: Around the World

By October 1986, when the International Committee for Prostitutes' Rights (ICPR) organized the Second World Whores' Congress, in Brussels, Belgium,[40] prostitutes and prostitutes' rights organizations in many countries were heavily involved in the fight against AIDS.

As early as 1985, the already-existing Australian Prostitutes Collective (APC), in Sydney, and the Prostitutes Collective of Victoria (PCV), both of which had been formed and coordinated by a coalition of current and former prostitutes and nonsex-worker allies, received government funding to establish sex workers' AIDS prevention projects. They provided a range of services, including legal assistance, referrals to decent health care providers and drug treatment agencies, and distribution of sterile injection equipment, as well as emotional and sometimes practical support.

An innovative and widely imitated component of the Australian strategy was what they called a "Safe House Endorsement" scheme. The collectives held meetings with owners and managers of brothels and other sex establishments, to convince them it was in their self-interest to support the routine use of condoms in their establishments. To reward those businesses that both agreed to an all-condom policy and had relatively decent working conditions, they issued Safe House Endorsement stickers and camera-ready logos that the businesses could use in their advertisements. Although this strategy became unnecessary as condom use became the norm in Australia, it has been adapted by a number of projects in other countries, because it was so effective in reducing the pressure on individual sex workers and businesses to forgo condoms in order to remain competitive.

Both collectives publish a magazine or newsletter containing articles by and about prostitutes, updated information about AIDS, and information about dangerous clients through an "Ugly Mug" list that enables prostitutes to inform their colleagues about uncooperative or dangerous clients. After the list was in existence for a while, the police began to take crimes reported by prostitutes more seriously and to step up prosecution efforts. This component has also been adopted by sex worker projects in a number of other countries.

By 1988, every state in Australia had at least one prostitutes' collective, funded by the government to do AIDS prevention work, with similar organizations in each state of New Zealand. At a national conference that year, the collectives founded the Scarlet Alliance to act as an umbrella organization. The alliance has played an important role in law reform efforts, as well as in facilitating communication between the state organizations, and has also begun collaborating with projects in Thailand, the Philippines, and Indonesia to exchange information and explore ways to help Southeast Asian women who migrate to work in Australia's sex industry to work safely.[41]

While COYOTE (funded by individual donations and volunteer labor) and CAL-PEP (with government and foundation funding) divided up the political and AIDS service tasks, the Australian organizations took the position that it is impossible to separate AIDS prevention from efforts to change the prostitution laws. In fact, most states in Australia are reviewing and modifying their laws in rational ways. At the time of this writing, the Australian Capital Territory is considering legislation that would decriminalize all aspects of prostitution and extend standard occupational safety and health and other workplace regulations to cover sex work businesses. This stands in sharp contrast with the United States, which continues to use draconian methods.

In 1986, members of the Canadian Organization for the Rights of Prostitutes (CORP), in Toronto, formed the Prostitutes' Safe Sex Project (PSSP) and received funding to do a street outreach project. PSSP's policy was that it was important that most, if not all, outreach workers and educators be currently working prostitutes, to demonstrate that it was actually possible to change one's practices and continue working. They developed a variety of educational materials, including buttons that prostitutes (and their friends) could wear with pride, bearing such slogans as "I'm a Safe Sex Pro." These have become popular with sex worker projects (and allies) in many countries. They also developed the first wallet-sized card that prostitutes could give to clients to convince them to use condoms, another approach that has been used by many projects.

Meanwhile, in Europe, prostitutes were actively involved in both research and interventions. For example, members of the Comitato per i Diritti Civili delle Prostitute collaborated with a number of research projects in northern Italy, and in 1986 the organization began publishing articles about AIDS and AIDS prevention in its newsletter. More recently, they have begun collaborating with a Dutch allies' organization, de Graaf Stichting, to study the impact of migration on sex workers' safety in both countries and to develop strategies to reach and involve the migrant workers, who are often the most vulnerable to arrest.

De Rode Draad,[42] in the Netherlands, received funding from the government to work on a variety of issues affecting prostitutes, including AIDS prevention. As the most visible form of prostitution in the Netherlands is that involving storefronts, or windows, in red-light districts, the project developed a sticker promoting condom use, that women put on their windows to let clients know of the requirement to use condoms before negotiations begin. More recently, as the AIDS prevention work done by government agencies has proved to be appropriate and well accepted, De Rode Draad has shifted its focus back to the more overarching issue of prostitutes' rights and law reform.[43]

A group of current and former prostitutes who worked on the design, implementation, and analysis of a university-based research project in Edinburgh,[44] eventually left the university to form Scot-PEP, an AIDS prevention and community support project, In addition to the traditional outreach, education, and condom and needle distribution, the project offers a part-time STD clinic and drop-in center. The coordinator of the project is also actively involved on the board of the International Coalition of AIDS Service Organizations (ICASO).

Aspasie,[45] in Geneva, Switzerland, opened a clinic for prostitutes in the primary sex work district, organized outreach, and published AIDS education materials, including a comic book and a magazine, *Mots de Passe.* Like De Rode Draad, they devised a condom promotion sticker whose design prostitutes have used in their ads, again to let clients know of the condom requirement before any contact is made.

One of the first projects in Africa to involve peer educators was started in Yaoundé, the capital city of Cameroon. Two physicians were approached by the health ministry and asked to start "something." As neither had any experience working with prostitutes, they were rather daunted at the prospect. However, when one began spending time talking to women working in the bars and hotels, he soon realized that they were ordinary people and that he rather liked them. He identified a number of women who seemed to be natural leaders in the community, some of whom were already members of an informal network, and trained 20 of them to serve as peer educators. At first they met with their colleagues in bars and clubs, talking with them about AIDS prevention and teaching them how to use condoms properly. When the original grant for the project ran out, the women kept meeting, kept organizing, and eventually formed a theater group. The group, Les Amies de Douglas et Rose, developed and performs a play about women working in a bar, their relationships with clients and bar owners, and how they negotiate condom use with clients. The play is enormously popular, and the project has since expanded to several other cities in Cameroon.[46]

In Calabar, Nigeria, a study of sex work–related behavior grew into a peer education project and has been organizing women who work in small hotels in Calabar and in larger hotels in the neighboring city of Ikom. Recognizing that AIDS is only one issue that affects sex workers, the project staff has also met with the police department to discuss problematic incidents between prostitutes and police, with a resulting decrease in the level of police harassment. In addition, they have worked to get better STD services for prostitutes.

When the project first began, many of the women expressed serious concerns about the potential loss of income if they rejected clients who refused to use a condom. As it was, they were earning relatively little money, and many of the women felt quite trapped. After some discussion, they decided, as a group, to raise their prices in order to make up for lost business, raising them again some months later. The project staff was able to convince the owners of the bars and hotels not to raise the room charges commensurately, thereby enabling the women to realize a greater share of the income from their work. As a result, many women began to feel much more in control and less helpless about their situations, and in some cases began to like their work. This kind of change is important if sex workers are to be able to protect themselves from AIDS. Because of the high rate of migration between Calabar and cities across the border in Cameroon, the projects in these two countries are hoping to work jointly to ensure that women in either country will be able to protect themselves and their partners from HIV infection.[47]

In Bulawayo, Zimbabwe, what began as a study of both prostitutes and clients became a peer education project (with 48 trained peer educators, 38 women and 10 men). By mid-1992 it had expanded to four additional sites, and by the beginning of 1993, nine projects using the same model had been initiated in Zimbabwe, Namibia, and other countries in the same region. Using dance, drama, and music, like the Cameroon project, they have provided education, motivation, and condoms to some 15,000 sex workers in bars and hotels, as well as to clients in bars and at work sites that employ large numbers of men. This addition of a client focus has been in response to the consistent complaint of prostitutes, in virtually every country in the world, that too many clients refuse to use condoms. Both the Nigerian and the Zimbabwean projects have focused on strengthening the skills of some of the peer educators, to enable them to take over control of the projects.[48]

In Ethiopia, after the Department of AIDS Control discovered alarmingly high rates of HIV infection in a number of cities among groups of women who worked in bars and sometimes engaged in prostitution, they assigned two women to develop a community-organizing intervention. At that time, each city in Ethiopia had a formal network of neighborhood organizations (*kebeles*) that were involved in community development and health care projects. In a pilot project in Nazareth, about 60 miles from Addis Ababa, the neighborhood organizations in districts with large numbers of bars held meetings with women from each bar. They identified and trained women with leadership potential in each neighborhood to act as peer educators and to sell condoms to their coworkers at a low, subsidized price. During a preliminary evaluation of the project's impact, 81 percent of the prostitutes interviewed said that they used condoms with their clients. What was striking about the women's reports was the reasons they cited for using condoms: they felt cleaner, they noticed that they had fewer episodes of STD, and the condoms meant they could stop taking birth control pills, which had made them feel ill.[49] The project is being expanded to some 23 cities in other parts of the country. Since the change in government has resulted in the disbanding of the kebele structure, the coordinators of the project have encouraged cities to identify particularly effective peer educators and hire them to take on some of the local coordination of the projects.

In Latin America, the prostitutes' rights organization Prostitution and Civil Rights,[50] in Rio de Janeiro, Brazil, developed educational materials, including one of the first *fotonovelas* for female prostitutes and two comic books aimed at male hustlers and transvestite prostitutes, respectively, before they had identified a reliable source of funding. The organization also developed guidelines for physicians on how to provide good health care for sex workers. By 1990, they had received sufficient funds to launch an educational outreach and condom distribution in several districts in Rio. In Uruguay, the Asociacion Meretrices Publicas del Uruguay (AMEPU), which has more than 300 members, operates a residence for prostitutes with AIDS and other life-threatening illnesses and publishes a newsletter containing writings on a variety of issues, including information about AIDS and AIDS prevention.[51]

In Nicaragua, a community-based AIDS organization, Fundacion Nimehuatzin, involved prostitutes in the development of locally relevant strategies. These include pressuring sex work hotels to provide condoms in guest rooms and providing prostitute-sensitive STD services in several cities. When the project staff realized that the closing of the brothels several years earlier had increased the danger and isolation of prostitutes' work, they began helping women to develop *cooperativas* to increase their control over their working conditions, including keeping a larger share of the income.[52]

One of the oldest projects in Asia is EMPOWER, in Thailand. EMPOWER is a community development organization that was originally formed to help female prostitutes find other occupations. However, they soon realized that not all prostitutes wanted to change occupations, and that even for those who did, it was not always possible to find other ways to make a living. Therefore, they felt it was important to improve prostitutes' living conditions even while they continued to work in the sex industry. As a result, EMPOWER began providing English lessons for the women who worked in the bars and nightclubs of the Pattpong district of Bangkok, so that they could negotiate more effectively with their clients. When the first cases of AIDS were diagnosed in Thailand, EMPOWER recognized the importance of adding AIDS prevention activities to its agenda.

EMPOWER, which now has four branch offices in different parts of the country, supports women who work in the sex tourism sectors and who have Thai clients. It is staffed by a combination of prostitutes and nonprostitutes and is becoming increasingly involved in representing the full range of prostitutes' concerns. For example, the organization has begun providing information to women who are thinking of migrating to other countries— about working conditions, immigration laws, and strategies for getting help if problems arise, such as from organizations like Australia's Scarlet Alliance, which can provide legal assistance to migrant prostitutes.[53]

Many organizations that originally were formed to fight "trafficking in women" quickly recognized that the problems they faced were not simply those of women victimized by "traffickers." Often women migrate with the conscious intent to work as prostitutes in the host country, as a way to improve their own economic status or to help their families at home. However, the laws against prostitution, as well as limits on legal immigration, leave them extremely vulnerable to serious economic exploitation, unsafe working conditions, and physical abuse. Thus, such organizations as Vrouwenhandel Stichting in the Netherlands and Amnesty for Women in Germany are increasingly focusing on the same work-related issues as do prostitutes' rights organizations.[54]

Talikala,[55] a sex worker–initiated project in Davao City, Philippines, has been providing AIDS seminars to hospitality workers, both male and female, in the context of a broader range of services, such as financial assistance to women who are unable to work because they have an STD. Among other things, they publish a journal with articles by and about the lives of the women affected by their project. There are two other projects in the Philippines, both of which have focused on finding ways to strengthen sex workers' ability to control their working conditions, Kabalikat ng Pamilyang Pilipino Foundation, in Metro Manila, and a project based in the City Health

Department in Olangapo/Angeles City. Although most of the international spotlight on prostitution in the Philippines and Thailand has focused on sex tourism, most prostitution in fact involves local men, who are much less willing to use condoms than tourists. Although HIV prevalence remains quite low in the Philippines, some groups of prostitutes have a high rate of other STD, which means that they are vulnerable to HIV infection.[56]

In India, some of the first projects that worked with prostitutes did little more than test them for HIV infection. Unfortunately, in some cases, the spokespersons for these projects felt it necessary to publicly announce when they found someone who tested positive and, in at least one case, to identify a brothel as an "AIDS house." Thus, when other projects tried to arrange to offer AIDS education sessions in brothels, they were initially met with distrust. At least two projects, one in Madras and another in New Delhi, were able to overcome this distrust and to begin organizing the women in working-class brothels to adopt the practice of using condoms on a communitywide basis. However, the Madras project found that working with the women was not sufficient, because of client resistance. Therefore, they began holding educational sessions at truck stops and other gathering places for groups of men.[57]

In all of these projects, prostitutes have played a central role. Most projects have found themselves focusing on more than just the promotion of condom use and other safe-sex practices. They have dealt with police problems, put pressure on the health care system to provide better services and to treat prostitutes with more respect, and helped the women to establish community-based self-help and self-advocacy organizations. In 1991, representatives of sex work projects decided to form a Network of Sex Work–related HIV/AIDS Projects, in order to facilitate the sharing of information, strategies, and other ideas between projects around the world, especially in developing countries. In conjunction with the 8th International Conference on AIDS in Amsterdam in July 1992, the network organized a one-day meeting of representatives of sex work projects from around the world, as well as a three-session minicourse on sex work–related issues; both were well attended. At the time of this writing, they are working on the first issue of a newsletter and collaborating with local sex work projects to organize similar satellite meetings in conjunction with regional AIDS conferences.[58] They also plan to develop ethical guidelines for research involving prostitutes and to review the ethics of existing research.

TARGETING CLIENTS: THE NEXT STEP

All over the world, the most consistent obstacle to the use of condoms in sex work is client resistance, and it is clear that condom promotion efforts that target only sex workers, and not clients, will be only partially successful.[59] That is, if only the prostitute half of the prostitution dyad is educated, some clients will continue to offer more money not to use condoms or to boycott sex workers who insist on safer sex practices. By 1989, only a small number of projects reported singling out clients for education efforts,[60] and even then, the first instinct for some was to say to clients, "Don't have sex with prostitutes."[61] The result of such an approach is equivocal, at best, if it depresses the market and leaves sex workers increasingly vulnerable to clients who offer extra money to engage in unprotected sex. A more positive approach is that of a Dutch project, Men in Prostitution, started by a small group of men who were sex work clients. Essentially, their strategy is to have clients approach other clients in the legal red-light districts, handing them condoms and providing them with safe-sex information.[62]

The number of sex work projects that recognize the need to educate clients is slowly increasing, particularly in developing countries, and more of them have begun to do outreach to and hold workshops for clients in bars, at truck stops, and at companies that employ large numbers of men, such as factories and trucking companies. In Ethiopia, the Department of AIDS Control developed a client project after prostitutes complained about client resistance. They identified and trained men to serve as peer educators and motivators in their workplaces, as well as to sell condoms at a low, subsidized cost. They also held major condom promotion events at sports stadiums and other public locations.[63] In Kenya, Tanzania,[64] Nigeria, and India, intervention projects are focusing on both truckdrivers and the people who provide a variety of services at truck stops. In some cases, as the project staff spends informal time with the target audiences, they are learning that there is more variety to the transactions involved in sex work than traditional KABB studies have identified (not everyone does only vaginal sex, and in some sites, homosexual as well as heterosexual prostitution takes place).[65]

Projects that have targeted clients and men likely to be clients, have found that such targeting makes a difference. For example, prostitutes in Benin reported that client resistance to condom use declined after a condom promotion campaign began to be aired on the radio.[66] In Ethiopia, when the project approached prostitutes first, the women complained about client resistance. However, when the project started out by targeting men in their workplaces and then later approached prostitutes, the women were happy to take the condoms, saying that their clients had been asking for them and sometimes bringing their own.[67] Although the evidence is still somewhat spotty, it suggests that it is not as difficult to convince heterosexual men to modify their behavior as it once seemed. For example, in Switzerland, which has had a continuous, highly visible, and entertaining condom promotion involving billboards, commercials in movie houses, and television, more than 60 percent of 17- to 30-year-olds in 1990 reported using condoms some or all of the time with casual partners, compared with less than 35 percent in 1987.[68]

CONCLUSION: WHAT DOES IT ALL MEAN?

An important result of sex work–related projects and of the active role prostitutes have been playing in AIDS prevention campaigns on every continent, is the beginning of changes in the discourse around the issue of prostitution and disease. Whereas the first reports of interventions were framed in the context of protecting clients, now the focus is increasingly on the need to organize prostitutes in their own interest. Similarly, whereas the early viewpoints tended to focus only on the prostitutes' role, most projects today are increasingly stressing the importance of educating clients and men likely to be clients. Increasing attention is also being paid to the owners and managers of sex work–related businesses, so that the task of preventing the spread of this disease can be shared by all the players.

Perhaps the most important result is that, as governments have begun funding prostitutes' organizations and other organizations that give voice to prostitutes, the sex workers' point of view is gaining prominence. In other words, the concept that prostitutes have the right to be protected from disease—by routine condom use, by safe and clean working conditions—is beginning to supplant the age-old idea that it is only the health of clients (and their "innocent" wives and girlfriends) that matters.

However, prostitution remains almost universally illegal and tightly regulated, even if the enforcement of the laws varies considerably from place to place. The result of regulation, which is particularly severe in the United States, is a perpetuation of the stigma and intimidation of those prostitutes who want to work for change but are threatened with arrest if they go public. In addition, the stigma of being a "whore" compounds the already existing stigma of being female and conflicts with the need for the approval of men, on whom most women depend for survival. AIDS and the money that has been available for projects for prostitutes have created an opportunity for change.

Major modifications of sexual behavior require profound changes in the way we think about sex, about women, about men, about ourselves. Peer education projects, in which working prostitutes are seen as sex *workers*, professionals in a recognized field, with knowledge worth sharing among their colleagues and clients and with other people, are part of a long process that will change all of our thinking. These community-based projects are based in the perspective that women have a right to engage in sex and to do so safely.

The prostitutes' rights struggle, born before AIDS but strengthened as a result of AIDS, is part of a global struggle to change the terms of female sexuality. Until a woman who suggests using a condom is not distrusted as a whore, and until a whore is not considered expendable, how can we hope to stop HIV and other STD? Until we stop seeing AIDS, or herpes, or even pregnancy,[69] as women's (or gay men's, or injection drug users') just punishment for wayward behavior, these diseases will continue to plague us, the "innocent," along with the "guilty." The destigmatization of prostitutes and those on the margins of sex work is essential.

As the number of projects focusing on sex work increases, community organizing must become integrated into the AIDS prevention model. If interventions are done in the traditional, paternalistic ways of the past, the demand for behavior change will seem to be one more face of the almost universal oppression of prostitutes. But, if prostitutes are organized in their own interest, as both workers and members of a sexually active community, the behavior that makes them vulnerable will change.

Those of us who are prostitutes have the central role in all this. But those of us who are not prostitutes also have an important role to play. As allies, we can and must work together to convince police not to confiscate condoms or to use them as evidence, to get public health officials to dismantle forced testing programs, to pressure health care providers to change their attitudes toward sex workers who come to them for help, to ensure that funders allocate money to support the efforts of sex workers to organize, and to support sex workers' efforts to get the laws changed. In the end, those of us who are not prostitutes must recognize that our own sexuality is affected as much by the condemnation of prostitution as by the fact that prostitution exists, and that all women will benefit from the empowerment of prostitutes, whether in the fight against AIDS, the fight against brutal or exploitative pimps, or the fight against the laws that control women's sexuality.

NOTES

[1] I have used both terms, *sex worker* and prostitute, throughout this paper, in order to make it clear that prostitution is work, not a sexual characterization. I am indebted to Carol Leigh, also known as Scarlet Harlot, for the term *sex work*, which also includes performers in pornography, another form of sexual activity for income.

[2] Throughout history, male prostitution has functioned alongside female prostitution, whether in religious or in secular sites. However, as the history of efforts to regulate, control, and abolish prostitution make clear, prostitution is identified in most minds as a strictly female phenomenon. Nonetheless, some of these same arguments apply to male prostitution.

[3] For example, Japanese soldiers "recruited" Korean women during World War II to act as "comfort women" for Japanese soldiers occupying Korea or to work in brothels in Japan (David E. Sanger, "Tokyo Cringes as a Japanese Says He Seized Korean Women," *International Herald Tribune*, 10 August 1992; George Hicks, "A 'Comfort Women' Screen Hides the Enduring Shame," *International Herald Tribune*, 14 April 1993). Lest anyone think this is a situation unique to Japan and its conquered territories,one has only to look at the role of the U.S. military, which organized prostitution near U.S. bases during the Civil War and the westward expansion [Anne M. Butler, *Daughters of Joy, Sisters of Misery: Prostitutes in the American West* (Cham-

paign, IL: University of Illinois Press, 1985); the U.S. occupation of Japan after World War II , and Vietnam and Thailand during the Vietnam War [Thanh-Dam Truong, *Sex, Money and Morality: Prostitution and Tourism in South-east Asia* (London: Zed Books, 1990)]; Cynthia Enloe, *Bananas, Beaches & Bases: Making Feminist Sense of International Politics* (London: Pandora Press, 1989); the Philippines until the eruption of Mt. Pinatubo in 1991 (personal communications with representatives of AIDS prevention projects in the Philippines, numerous newspaper articles over the years); and Honduras during the counterrevolutionary actions in Nicaragua (an article in the *San Francisco Chronicle* about the sudden appearance of AIDS among female prostitutes working near an American base in Honduras, probably in 1984 or 1985).

[4]Luise White, *The Comforts of Home: Prostitution in Colonial Nairobi* (Chicago: University of Chicago Press, 1990).

[5]The term *core group of high-frequency transmitters* was first used in a paper on the control of gonorrhea in 1978. It has gained wide usage only with AIDS, for example, in the writings of Frank Plummer's group at the University of Nairobi and King Holmes, of the University of Washington in Seattle. Until very recently, it was used almost exclusively to refer to female prostitutes, despite the well-documented greater efficacy of male-to-female transmission of all STD, including HIV, over female-to-male transmission. More recent articles have used it to refer to 'truckdrivers," but the problem of viewing people as vectors who need to be controlled, rather than people who may be at increased risk of STD and therefore in need of good health care services, is the same.

[6]The terms *reservoir* and *pool of contagion*, which have been applied almost exclusively to women, are interesting in that they appear to view women as passive bodies, waiting to endanger he who invades them, I suppose. Perhaps it is a reincarnation of the mythic vagina dentata. The linguistic shifts from passive to aggressive are fascinating.

[7]Steffen Johncke, "Prostitutes and the Precariousness of Policy: AIDS and the Stigmatization of Prostitutes/Sex Workers" (Paper presented at the AIDS and Anthropology Group Conference on Culture, Sexual Behaviour and AIDS, 24–26 July 1992, Amsterdam). See also Gail Pheterson, "The Social Consequences of Unchastity," in *Sex Work: Writings by Women in the Sex Industry*, ed. Frederique Delacoste and Priscilla Alexander (San Francisco: Cleis Press, 1987).

[8]Judith R. Walkowitz, *Prostitution and Victorian Society: Women, Class, and the State* (Cambridge: Cambridge University Press, 1980). Feminists who organized to repeal the Contagious Diseases Acts were concerned that female prostitutes were being falsely blamed, inasmuch as many of their clients spent long months at sea, isolated from women, and might very well be engaging in homosexual activity and infecting each other, only to infect the prostitutes when they were on shore leave (p. 130). It is possible that a similar dynamic may be at work in regions now said to represent exclusively heterosexual transmission (Randall M. Packard and Paul Epstein, "Medical Research on AIDS in Africa; A Historical Perspective," in *AIDS: The Making of a Chronic Disease*, ed. Elizabeth Fee and Daniel M. Fox (Berkeley: University of California Press, 1992, p. 353).

[9]Jill Harsin, *Policing Prostitution in Nineteenth Century Paris* (Princeton, N.J.: Princeton University Press, 1985).

[10]Ruth Rosen, *The Lost Sisterhood: Prostitution in America, 1900–1918* (Baltimore: Johns Hopkins University Press, 1982) 10. See also Mark Thomas Connelly, *The Response to Prostitution in the Progressive Era* (Chapel Hill: Princeton University Press, 1980), 81.

[11]Nell Kimball and Stephen Longstreet, *Nell Kimball: Her Life as an American Madam* (New York: Macmillan, 1970). See also *Madeleine: An Autobiography 1919* (New York: Persea Books, 1986).

[12]Allan M. Brandt, *No Magic Bullet: A Social History of Veneral Disease in the United States since 1880* (New York: Oxford University Press, 1985); "A Historical Perspective," in *AIDS and the Law: A Guide for the Public*, ed. Harlon L. Dalton and Scott Burris (New Haven: Yale University Press, 1987); and "AIDS: From Social History to Social Policy," in *AIDS: The Burdens of History*, ed. Elizabeth Fee and Daniel M. Fox (Berkeley: University of California Press, 1988). See also Thomas Connelly; Rosen.

[13]S. Moses, F. A. Plummer, E. N. Ngugi, et al., "Controlling HIV in Africa: Effectiveness and Cost of an Intervention in a High-Frequency STD Transmitter Core Group," *AIDS*, April 5, 1991, 407–411. In this article, the authors report that one man became infected with HIV after a single contact with a prostitute. After a number of people who had visited the University of Nairobi projects told me they had reservations about that conclusion (one person said that men with STD in Nairobi always say they had sex with a prostitute; another said that this particular man didn't even say that, it was enough that he lived in the same district with prostitutes), I questioned Plummer, whom I met in Amsterdam, about the conclusion. His response was, "It's probability."

[14]Kenneth Castro et al., "Investigations of AIDS Patients with No Previously Identified Risk Factors," *Journal of the American Medical Association* 259 (March 1988):1338–1342. See also Joyce I. Wallace et al., "HIV-1 Exposure Among Clients of Prostitutes" (Paper presented at IVth International Conference on AIDS, June 1988, Stockholm, no. 4055).

[15]Prostitution arrests are almost always for the offense of soliciting, not for actually engaging in any sex act or for receiving (especially not for paying) any money. Many laws now carry fairly stiff penalties for an arrest subsequent to testing positive for HIV—up to 20 years in Nevada, regardless of whether the accused ever engaged in an actual risk behavior (such as unprotected vaginal intercourse).

[16]In 1991, the California Supreme Court upheld that state's law, finding that the public health interest in identifying HIV-positive prostitutes, and permitting the disclosure of test results to prosecuting attorneys and others in the law enforcement system, outweighed the accused's right to confidentiality. The same court upheld confidentiality protections in another case, in which survivors of people who died of AIDS contracted through blood transfusions tried to identify the donors as part of their lawsuit against a California blood bank. Thus, blood donors' confidentiality was protected even though a death had resulted, while the prostitutes' confidentiality was violated in the absence of evidence of either exposure or transmission, let alone death.

[17]Numerous studies have found that substantial majorities of prostitutes in Western countries use condoms for vaginal and anal sex, and often for fellatio as well, most or all of the time, and that a substantial proportion of the sex negotiated on the street involves only hand and blow jobs. Male prostitutes are not generally targeted by

registration systems; they also are less likely to be arrested when prostitution is illegal.

[18]Diane Smith, "Green Cards for Sex Workers," *World AIDS,* July 1990, no. 10, Panos, London.

[19]Deanna Hodgin, "Activists Sound Alarm over Fate of Prostitutes in Thailand," *The Advocate,* 16 June 1992, p. 30. At the VIIIth International Conference on AIDS, in Amsterdam, members of the International Committee for Prostitutes Rights (ICPR) organized a demonstration to protest these and other brutal violations of prostitutes' human rights. Unfortunately, press coverage credited ACT-UP, instead of the ICPR, effectively silencing prostitutes from speaking out on their own behalf.

[20]Privileged communication with representatives of AIDS prevention projects in the Philippines.

[21]Privileged communication with a representative of Singapore's medical scheme.

[22]Meurig Horton, World Health Organization, Global Program on AIDS, personal communication.

[23]Shyamala Nataraj, "Indian Prostitutes Highlight AIDS Dilemmas," *Development Forum,* November–December 1990, pp. 1, 16.

[24]Patricia Uribe et al., "Analysis of Factors Related with HIV Infection in 961 Female Sexual Workers" (Paper presented at VIth International Conference on AIDS, San Francisco, June 1990, Th.D.777).

[25]See papers presented at VIth International Conference on AIDS, San Francisco, June 1990, dealing with registration systems: Hans W. Doerr et al., "Prevalence of HIV Infection in Prostitutes from Frankfurt/W. Germany," FC626; I. N'Doye et al., "Sentinel Surveillance of STD: Its Implications for AIDS Control in Senegal," 3178; Russell Reade, Gary Richwald, and Nancy Williams, "The Nevada Legal Brothel System as a Model for AIDS Prevention Among Female Sex Industry Workers," SC715; and Anastasia Roumeliotou et al., "Prevention of HIV Infection in Greek Registered Prostitutes, a Five Year Study."

[26]Privileged communication with an AIDS prevention specialist who visited Indonesia to provide technical assistance to the government.

[27]Privileged communication with a representative of Singapore's prostitution medical scheme.

[28]Russell Reade, Gary Richwald, and Nancy Williams, "The Nevada Legal Brothel System as a Model for AIDS Prevention Among Female Sex Industry Workers" (Paper presented at VIth International Conference on AIDS, San Francisco, 1990, SC715). Also, the author's analysis of arrest statistics in the United States between 1973 and 1987, and estimates by police and prostitutes in a number of cities concerning the proportion of prostitutes who work in different parts of the industry. See my article "Prostitution: A Difficult Issue for Feminists," in *Sex Work: Writings by Women in the Sex Industry,* ed. Frederique Delacoste and Priscilla Alexander (San Francisco: Cleis Press, 1987) for a more extensive discussion.

[29]G. Papaevangelou et al, "Education in Preventing HIV Infection in Greek Registered Prostitutes," *AIDS* 1(1988): 386–389.

[30]Edwige Bienvenue, formerly of the STD service, in Dakar, Senegal, and King Holmes, University of Washington, Seattle, personal communications.

[31]The historic record suggests that the ratio of "registered" or "official" prostitutes to "clandestine" workers is fairly consistent over time and geographic distance. See, for example, Brandt; Harsin; Frank Mort, *Dangerous Sexualities: Medico-moral Politics in England since 1830* (London: Routledge & Kegan Paul, 1987); and Walkowitz.

[32]Some specialists in occupational health and safety issues have begun to look at other aspects of prostitutes' health related to their work, including back and foot problems related to standing and walking for long hours, particularly while wearing high heels, and working on bad beds, as well as respiratory problems due to being out in inclement weather.

[33]Packard and Epstein.

[34]There are a number of books containing first-person accounts of sex work, including Frederique Delacoste and Priscilla Alexander; Roberta Perkins and Garry Bennet, *Being a Prostitute* (Winchester, Mass.: Allen & Unwin, 1985); and Claude Jaget, ed., *Prostitutes—Our Life* (Bristol, England: Falling Wall Press, 1980). However, even reading the first-hand accounts cannot substitute for the knowledge that comes from direct experience. In addition, these books are difficult to obtain in many countries.

[35]This belief was reported to me by a consultant working for the World Health Organization who had interviewed women working in a number of African countries. In addition, a number of African studies have found that both women and men complain that using condoms changes the meaning of sex, which doesn't seem "real" to them unless there is skin contact and ejaculation within the woman's body.

[36]COYOTE is an acronym for "Call Off Your Old Tired Ethics." Margo St. James told me that the reason she chose an organization name without the word *prostitute* in it was that, in 1973, it was controversial to even say the word on television. In addition, the term *coyote* has a certain resonance for prostitutes. The coyote, in American Indian belief systems, is a trickster, often seeming to be something different than it is, so that the name fits the aspects of prostitution that are related to illusion. In addition, it echoes the slang term for client, *trick,* and the practice of "turning a trick." In addition, the coyote and the prostitute are both endangered species. Finally, the person who smuggles people from Mexico into the United States is called a "coyote." For a history of COYOTE, see "COYOTE/National Task Force on Prostitution," in Frederique Delacoste and Priscilla Alexander; and Margo St. James, "Preface," in *A Vindication of the Rights of Whores*, ed. Gail Pheterson (Seattle: Seal Press, 1989). For an account of how COYOTE became aware of and responded to the early AIDS epidemic, see Priscilla Alexander, "A Chronology, of Sorts," in *AIDS: The Women*, ed. Ines Rieder and Patricia Ruppelt (San Francisco: Cleis Press, 1988).

[37]San Francisco Police Department, Department Special Order 87-13, W/06140, "Seizure of Condoms and Bleach Containers Pursuant to Vice Arrests," 10 April 1987.

[38]Priscilla Alexander, *Prostitutes Prevent AIDS: A Manual for Health Educators* (San Francisco: CAL-PEP, 1988). This manual, which was distributed by the San Francisco AIDS Foundation, as well as by CAL-PEP, was purchased by more than 200 agencies in the United States, Europe, Asia, and Africa by the Fall 1989.

[39]See Reback article, elsewhere in this volume.

[40]Gail Pheterson.

[41]The problems of migrant prostitutes are generally more severe than those of local sex workers, in part because of language, but also because of immigration laws which

deny them the right to work legally, even when some or all aspects of prostitution are legal for citizens of the host or receiving country. As a result, the businesses that hire them are likely to be farther underground and have worse working conditions.

[42]Hansje Verbeek and Terry van der Zijden, "The Red Thread: Whores' Movement in Holland," and Marjan Sax, "The Pink Thread," in Frederique Delacoste and Priscilla Alexander.

[43]The negotiations with the government that appeared to be leading to a rational change in the law to permit prostitutes to organize for more control over their working conditions broke down following the appointment of a conservative minister of justice. Instead of giving more control to the prostitutes, the minister, in trying to appease right and left, has proposed keeping the laws against prostitution businesses on the books but permitting cities to carve licensing exceptions in a system that gives more control to the owners and denies women from non-EC countries the right to work legally. This leaves them even more vulnerable to abuse than in the current blind-eye approach.

[44]Ruth Morgan Thomas, "AIDS Risks, Alcohol, Drugs, and the Sex Industry: A Scottish Study," in *AIDS, Drugs, and Prostitution*, ed. Martin Plant (London: Tavistock/Routledge, 1990).

[45]Aspasie was organized by a group of prostitutes and health care and social workers to provide both services for and advocacy on behalf of the women who work in the main sex work street in Geneva. The organization is named after Aspasia, "perhaps the most famous prostitute of classical Athens," according to Nickie Roberts, in her groundbreaking book, *Whores in History: Prostitution in Western Society* (London: Harper Collins Publishers, 1992), the first major survey of the history of prostitution written by and from the point of view of a sex worker.

[46]Marcel Monny-Lobé et al., "Prostitutes as Health Educators for their Peers in Yaoundé: Changes in Knowledge, Attitudes and Practices," WGO21, and "The Use of Condoms by Prostitutes in Yaoundé-Cameroon," WDP87 (Papers presented at the Vth International Conference on AIDS, Montreal, June 1989), and personal communication, October and November 1989; Lisa Mbele-Mbong, personal communication, April 1992.

[47]Many conversations with Eka Esu-Williams, founder of the Cross River State Commercial Sex Work Project and President of the Society for Women and AIDS in Africa (SWAA). Cf. Eka Esu-Williams et al., "Sexual Practices and HIV Infection of Female Prostitutes in Nigera" (Paper presented at the Vth International Conference on AIDS, Montreal, June 1989, WGO24); Eka Esu-Williams et al., "Nigeria: Empowering Commercial Sex Workers for HIV Prevention" (Paper presented at the VIIth International AIDS Conference, Florence, 1991, WD4041).

[48]Many conversations with David Wilson, Department of Psychology, University of Zimbabwe, Bulawayo. Cf. David Wilson et al., "A Pilot Study for an HIV Prevention Programme Among Commercial Sex Workers in Bulawayo, Zimbabwe," *Soc. Sci. Med.* 31 (1990): 609–618.

[49]Fekerte Belete et al., "Social Mobilization and Condom Promotion Among Sex Workers in Nazareth, Ethiopia," *The Ethiopian Journal of Health Development* 4(1990):219–224. Also, personal communications with Fekerte Belete, Almaz G/Kidan, and Carol Larivee.

[50]Gabriela Silva Leite, "Women of the Life, We Must Speak," in Pheterson.

[51]Several issues of AMEPU's newsletter, as well as privileged communications with a representative of Montevideo's STD service.

[52]Many conversations with Rita Arauz, coordinator of Fundacion Nimhuatzin.

[53]Many conversations with Chantipwa Apisuk, founder of EMPOWER; Andrew Hunter, coordinator of the Scarlet Alliance; and Cheryl Overs, coordinator of the Network of Sex Work HIV/AIDS Projects.

[54]This change in focus is reflected in such publications as the *VENA Newsletter* issue on "Traffic in Women" (vol. 1, no. 2, November 1989) and ISIS' *Women's World* devoted to "Poverty and Prostitution" (no. 24, Winter 1990/91).

[55]*Talikala* is an old Cebuano word for "bonding" or "chain."

[56]Conversations with Elizabeth O'Brien, coordinator of Talikala. Cf. Marvic R. Desquitado, *Behind the Shadows* (Davao City: Talikala, Inc., 1992), and articles published in Talikala's newsletter.

[57]Many conversations with Sundararaman Swaminathan, coordinator of the project. Cf. Sundararaman Swaminathan and G. Kumaresan, "Shifting Needs: Prostitute Intervention to Client Intervention" (Paper presented at VIIth International Conference on AIDS, 1991, WD58).

[58]Cheryl Overs, Network of Sex Work HIV/AIDS Projects, personal communications.

[59]Tidiane Siby et al., "Surveillance Education Sanitaire des Prostituées au Senegal" (Paper presented at Vth International Conference on AIDS, Montreal, June 1989, WDP91); Nzila Nzilambi et al., "Evaluation of Condom Utilization and Acceptability of Spermicides Among Prostitutes in Kinshasa, Zaire" (Paper presented at Vth International Conference on AIDS, Montreal, June 1989, WAP96); Marcel Monny-Lobe, "The Use of Condoms by Prostitutes in Yaounde-Cameroon" (Paper presented at Vth International Conference on AIDS, Montreal, June 1989, WDP87); Christ'l Praats et al., "Female Prostitutes in Antwerp: A Risk Group for Infection" (Paper presented at the Vth International Conference on AIDS, Montreal, June 1989, MAP49); Stephen T. Green et al., "Glasgow Street Prostitutes: A Study of Sexual Behavior and Injected Drug Use" (Paper presented at the Vth International Conference on AIDS, Montreal, June 1989, ThDP3).

[60]Hilary Kinnell et al., "Male Clients of Female Prostitutes in Birgmingham, England: A Bridge for Transmission of HIV?" (Paper presented at the Vth International Conference on AIDS, Montreal, June 1989, WDP41); Arletty Pinel, "Sexual Behavior Survey of Brazilian Men That are Clients of Transvestite Prostitutes (Paper presented at the Vth International Conference on AIDS, Montreal, June 1989, TDP78).

[61]Elizabeth Petterson et al., " 'Twilight Phenomena'—A Project Concerning Men as Buyers of the Services of Prostitutes as a Risk Factor" (Paper presented at the Vth International Conference on AIDS, Montreal, June 1989, ThDP21).

[62]Privileged communications with representatives of Men in Prostitution at a Dutch STD Foundation conference in 1989 and the European Prostitutes Congress in 1991.

[63]Fekerte Belete et al.

[64]George K. Lwihula, "AIDS and the Trucking Industry in Tanzania: Long Distance Truck Drivers, Their Sex Partners and HIV Transmission in Tanzanian Truck Stops" (Paper presented at the Conference on AIDS & Anthropology: Culture, Sexual Behavior and AIDS, Amsterdam, 24–26 July 1992); Christopher L. Mwaijonga et al.,

"HIV/AIDS Education and Condom Promotion for Truck Drivers, Their Assistants and Sex Partners in Tanzania" (Paper presented at VIth International Conference on AIDS in Africa, Dakar, Senegal, 16–19 December 1991).

[65]The denial of homosexual activity in Sub-Saharan Africa (by epidemiologists, modelers, Africans, and Europeans) is phenomenal. However, one East African researcher told me that, after listening to me, he had asked some of the women in his project if they knew of any male homosexuals, and they said, "Oh yes, over there." In another East African country where officials deny any homosexual activity, visiting Western gay men are propositioned frequently by local men. Whether either anecdote reflects "homosexuality" in the American sense, with a fully delineated identity, is unlikely, but there is clearly some homosexual activity, the epidemiological weight of which remains unknown. There is also documented homosexual behavior in Kenya and Nigeria, some of which involves crossing genders, and a multiracial gay rights organization is active in South Africa. Some Africans more or less dismiss the homosexuality by ascribing it to Arab influence, while the North African countries, where Arab influence is greatest, also deny that homosexual activity occurs. Cf. T. D. Moodie, "Migrancy and Male Sexuality on the South African Gold Mines," in *Hidden from History; Reclaiming the Gay and Lesbian Past*, ed. M. Duberman et al. (New York: New American Library, 1989); S. Nanda, *Neither Man nor Woman: The Hijras of India* (Belmont, CA: Wadsworth, 1990); A. Schmitt and J. Sofer, eds., *Sexuality and Eroticism Among Males in Moslem Societies* (Binghamton, NY: Harrington Park Press, 1992); G. Shepherd, "Rank, Gender, and Homosexuality: Mombasa as a key to understanding sexual options," in *The Cultural Construction of Sexuality*, ed. P. Caplan (London: Tavistock Publications, 1987).

[66]Privileged communication from an anthropologist who has worked with the sex work project in Benin.

[67]Personal communications with Fekerte Belete and Almaz G/Kidan.

[68]D. Hausser, F. Dubois-Arber, and E. Zimmerman, "Assessing AIDS Prevention in Switzerland," in *Assessing AIDS Prevention*, ed. F. Paccaud, J. P. Vader, and F. Gutzwiller (Basel: Birkhäuser, 1992).

[69]In my reading of the discourse within the anti-abortion movement, I have seen many references to women's needing to accept unwanted pregnancy as the consequence of or punishment for their waywardness, if they have been so unwise as to engage in sex outside of marriage or without using effective contraceptives. Thus, although pregnancy is quite different from disease, much right-wing discourse equates them as punishments for "bad" women.

Cathy Stein Greenblat

Women in Families with Hemophilia and HIV: Improving Communication about Sensitive Issues

WOMEN, HEMOPHILIA, AND HIV

Beginning in the early 1970s, major advances were made in the treatment of hemophilia. Before that time, men with hemophilia[1] who suffered from unpredictable bleeding episodes were regular visitors to clinics and emergency rooms, where they required immediate medical attention and blood transfusions. The consequences of their bleeding were cumulative, often resulting in joint deformity and a subsequent need for bracing, physical rehabilitation, and joint repair surgery. Lowered life expectancy and a range of psychosocial problems also resulted. For those who triumphed over the disease's worse effects, a sense of invulnerability ("I can beat anything") sometimes emerged. For others came a sense of lack of control over their lives. Their family lives were heavily shaped by the disease. Many of those affected by hemophilia found information and support not only from the health professionals from whom they obtained treatment, but also from fellow members of the chapters of the National Hemophilia Foundation which were in operation around the country.

In the decade and a half since the mid-1970s, the development of concentrated factor VIII and factor IX and the availability of home care has had several consequences for people living with hemophilia. Medically, the men were able to gain significant control over the course of the illness, infusing at home as hemorrhaging occurred. Numbers of clinic visits were significantly reduced, and a much more normal lifestyle, both socially and psychologically, became possible. The life expectancy of hemophiliac men increased to close to the national average, and the experiences of their wives and mothers became much more normal. Though the men with hemophilia and their family members were surely affected by the presence of a chronic illness, it was no longer an ever-present, life-threatening force. The need for and use of support groups to deal with hemophilia subsided, and many chapters remained alive in name only. Talking as a way of coping—either among the men themselves or among their intimates—also subsided.

The new procedures that made this freedom possible involved the creation of coagulation factor concentrates from the blood of multiple donors. From 1978 until 1985, when processes for testing blood for HIV antibodies were developed, many of these concentrates were contaminated with HIV. As a result, in 1991 it was estimated that 60 to 70 percent of the approximately 20,000 hemophiliacs over age six in the United States were HIV infected and had the potential to develop AIDS (this is not a latent viral infection).[2] Approximately 15 to 20 percent of the wives of married men with hemophilia were estimated to be seropositive.

In February 1991, a National Hemophilia Foundation publication reported that, as of November 30, 1990, there had been 1,589 cases of AIDS in the United States among those with hemophilia and related bleeding disorders; 1,071 (67 percent) of them had died.[3] Hemophilia existed in all racial groups: 83 percent of these AIDS cases were white, 7.4 percent were black, 8.4 percent were Hispanic, and the remaining 1.7 percent were Asian/Pacific islanders, American Indians, or unknown. The report also indicated that 72 cases of AIDS had been found in the heterosexual partners of people with hemophilia, and that 9 perinatal transmission cases were on the records. The April 1991 figures provided by the CDC raised the hemophilia case numbers to 1,608, while the number of heterosexual partners with AIDS climbed to 86.[4] Given the long latency period and the high percentages of males with hemophilia known to be HIV positive, the number of cases of AIDS from this community can be expected to rise significantly in the next few years.

HIV has created an enormous set of personal and family problems among those with hemophilia at the same time that coping skills and support resources in the hemophilia community have grown rusty or are not fully developed. A high proportion of adult men with hemophilia are between the ages of 20 and 49 and are living in intact families; their HIV problems and the ripple effects on other family members are thus somewhat different from those of gay men or injection drug users. Others are children or young adults, who enter puberty saddled with HIV infection that is sexually transmitted; they face an added serious burden, with new problems for them, for their parents, and for counselors who wish to assist them. There are often multiple effects, as in families like one in which a woman's seven hemophiliac brothers as well as her sons are infected.

In light of this situation, educational and counseling needs are high. Among the many problems is the need to talk with others about new and significant issues. At a number of clinics and chapters around the country, social workers found that the women intimates of these men—mothers, grandmothers, sisters, daughters, friends—also need assistance in coping with the burdens HIV places on their loved ones and themselves. Indeed, it was often found that, while the men were in denial or ready to engage in one-on-one discussions only with their physicians or health educators, the women were ready to join in collective efforts at understanding the psychosocial burdens and the physical risks presented by HIV.[5] People running day-long or two-day conferences for women affected by hemophilia and HIV sought materials that would assist these women in addressing sensitive issues and in developing the communication skills needed to deal with their problems, including the risk of HIV transmission through sexual activity. To this end, the ENCOUNTERS simulations approach was developed.

THE ENCOUNTERS APPROACH

Much current AIDS education involves information about the transmission of HIV. This can be useful in dispelling myths and reducing misconceptions: regular updating of the information for women affected by hemophilia and HIV is an important responsibility of health educators and physicians. The provision of information is not enough, however. If attitudes are to be examined and behavior is to be changed, AIDS education and counseling efforts cannot be limited to pamphlets, posters, and lectures. Participants in education, training, and counseling efforts that aim to develop more compassionate responses to people with HIV infection and AIDS and to ameliorate the psychosocial difficulties brought on by HIV need to be more actively engaged in the learning enterprise, rather than passive recipients of information provided by others.

One focus of these expanded efforts is the communication difficulties faced by almost all people involved with the epidemic: those who are HIV infected or have been diagnosed with AIDS, their family members, and health care workers. As Figure 1 indicates, the person with HIV infection or AIDS must communicate with people from the medical world, from his or her own personal social world, and from the larger social world. Members of these realms, too, must talk with others. For instance, the wife of an HIV-positive man must address the concerns of other family members and often must discuss issues with medical professionals and representatives of the larger community. The topics that people need to address are sensitive ones—death, sex, fear, and discrimination. Historic social taboos have impeded some discussions of these topics. Even where it has been considered acceptable to address such topics, few people will have had much practice discussing them with others. Education and counseling programs, then, must make such conversations plausible and make participants more comfortable in potentially awkward situations, or people will continue to avoid such interactions. The ENCOUNTERS family of simulations does this through offering participants a safe opportunity to practice telling others about the ways in which HIV affects them and their intimates. The ENCOUNTERS simulations also give them a chance to experiment with ways of handling these new situations and provides them with practice in doing so more assertively.

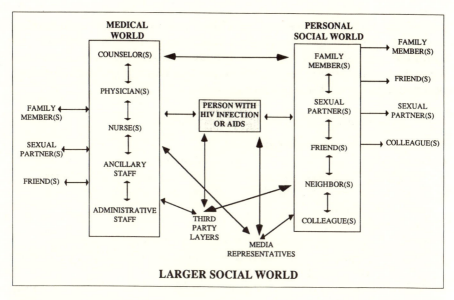

FIGURE 6-1. HIV and communication Needs

The structure of the ENCOUNTERS simulations was created by this author, John Gagnon, and Diana Shannon in the design of the original set, CRITICAL ENCOUNTERS, a simulation sponsored by the World Health Organization for training health professionals to deal with HIV issues.[6] Following demonstration of this simulation at the Mt. Sinai Medical Center, Region II Hemophilia Diagnostic and Treatment Centers (New York City), the center director and several members of the social work staff became enthusiastic about adopting the approach for use in counseling and training their clientele. With assistance from one of the social workers, Susan Katz, a small preliminary set of encounters, dealing with the issues faced by wives and mothers of hemophiliac men and boys, was designed and employed with considerable success at a women's workshop in New York City.[7] Subsequent funding from the U.S. Office of Public Health, Division of Child and Maternal Health, Hemophilia Program, permitted a collaboration with the Mt. Sinai Hemophilia Center staff to expand that early effort into the current form of ENCOUNTERS WITH AIDS: WOMEN, HEMOPHILIA, AND HIV.[8]

Creation of the full set of encounter issues initially involved interviews with women who had family members with hemophilia and HIV, as well as with experts on this population. These efforts focused on identifying current attitudes and behaviors of women confronted by the dilemmas of HIV disease, specific HIV issues confronted by these women, and changes they desired in attitudes and behaviors. A partial list of the major psychosocial communication issues for women in different relationships to the hemophiliac male included the following (there is more overlap in issues from one population to the next than is reflected in the list):

Communication issues for sexual partners and wives

- Fear that she may be infected
- Decision whether to marry a seropositive man
- Countering neighbors' and friends' fear of transmission of the virus
- Desire to reverse a decline in sexual activity within the couple and to practice safer sex
- Eroticizing safer sex
- Need to inform other family members of partner's AIDS diagnosis
- Desire for pregnancy, coupled with fears and worries about HIV transmission while conceiving
- Dealing with heavy denial of the seriousness of a father's AIDS diagnosis by an adult child
- Decision making about life changes (job changes, vacations, spending patterns) in the face of uncertainty
- Coping with his denial, anger, depression, or preoccupation with AIDS
- Family objection to her taking an active public role regarding AIDS
- Decision making about separation or divorce in a troubled relationship or marriage
- Discussing his wishes about "death with dignity," last resorts
- Dealing with the anticipated death of a spouse/partner
- Need to acknowledge and understand the stress and pressure she is experiencing and to seek help
- Decline in her ability to participate in outside activities as HIV-related concerns consume more of her time

Communication issues for mothers of children with hemophilia

- When to tell a child he is seropositive
- Talking to a child about not taking risks
- How to inform school authorities about his seropositive status
- Dealing with the anticipated death of a child after repeated infections, hospitalizations
- Experiencing guilt as the transmitter of hemophilia
- Gaining increased assistance from her husband (or ex-husband) as the child's illness progresses
- Need to acknowledge and understand the stress and pressure she is experiencing and to seek help

- Decline in her ability to participate in outside activities as HIV-related concerns consume more of her time

Communication issues for mothers of adolescents with hemophilia

- Obtaining information from doctors
- How to tell him he is seropositive
- Helping with his problems in romantic relationships
- Talking with him about safer sex
- Control versus independence of late adolescent
- Experiencing guilt as the transmitter of hemophilia
- Gaining increased assistance from her husband (or ex-husband) as their adolescent's illness progresses
- Need to acknowledge and understand the stress and pressure she is experiencing and to seek help
- Decline in her ability to participate in outside activities as HIV-related concerns consume more of her time

Communication issues for other relatives (or for wives or mothers)

- Helping sons, fathers, siblings cope with HIV
- Helping daughters, mothers, siblings cope with HIV stresses
- Finding information about treatments
- Making decisions about what drugs and when to use them; use of underground market
- Need to explain to friends the importance of their support and continued friendship during crisis period
- Reconnecting with other family members who have been distant
- Making decisions about responsibility to self versus responsibility to family

This list was narrowed to yield a balanced set of 20 items, which included problems with other family members, problems with friends, and problems with health care professionals. The issues selected include communicating with doctors about HIV anxieties, talking with a spouse about eroticizing safer sex, and exploring conflicting thoughts about parenthood plans in light of the dangers of transmission (see summary in Figure 2). These issues were then worked into the ENCOUNTERS format.

The simulation has five individuals working together in one long session of approximately three hours or in shorter sessions spread over two or three days. Several groups can participate simultaneously. Within a session, each participant rotates through the five roles, having an opportunity to play each one: speaker A, a woman with a hemophiliac family member who must deal with an HIV or AIDS issue with another person; speaker B; one of two advisers who offer suggestions and moral support; and the group leader,

1   A NEIGHBORLY DISCUSSION
Speaker A is the wife of a man with hemophilia who is HIV positive. She will confront Speaker B, a neighbor and close friend, about the cold treatment A and her husband have received lately from neighbors and friends.

2   HIV AND A MARRIAGE PROPOSAL
Speaker A is a 25-year-old woman who has been involved in a serious relationship with a man with hemophilia and HIV infection. They are talking about marriage, and she is not sure what to do. She consults Speaker B, her best friend, to obtain advice.

3   HIV ANXIETIES Speaker A is a woman who will talk to her doctor, Speaker B, about her fears that she has become infected through sexual relations with her lover, who has hemophilia and is HIV+.

4   EROTICIZING SAFER SEX Speaker A is the wife of a man with hemophilia who is HIV+. She has decided to ask Speaker B, who is also married to a man who is HIV+, about eroticizing safer sex.

5   A TALK ABOUT SEXUAL INTIMACY Speaker A is the wife of Speaker B. She will discuss with him some problems she senses in their recent sex life, and some possible solutions to these problems.

6   HIV AND PARENTHOOD PLANS
Speaker A is the wife of a man with hemophilia. A and her husband have been trying to conceive, but they just learned that he is HIV+. A will talk with her mother, Speaker B, about her confusion about what to do.

7   AIDS AND YOUR MOTHER-IN-LAW
Speaker A is the wife of John, a man with hemophilia and HIV infection. He has just been diagnosed with AIDS.

He never told his mother he was HIV+; A has decided to tell her mother-in-law about John's health.

8   PLANNING AHEAD Speaker A is the wife of a man with hemophilia who was recently diagnosed with AIDS. She will talk with him about some of the plans she feels they need to make for the future.

9   GOING PUBLIC Speaker A is the wife of a man with hemophilia who is HIV+. She will talk to her husband, Speaker B, about his objection to her taking a public role about the problems of families coping with hemophilia and HIV.

10   HIV AND YOUR CHILD Speaker A is the mother of a 12-year-old HIV+ boy with hemophilia. She will discuss with Speaker B, the father, how to talk to their son about his health condition.

11   REACHING OUT TO DAD Speaker A's 9-year-old son has hemophilia and is HIV+. A wants more participation in the child's medical care from her husband, Speaker B, who spends most of his limited family time with their older, healthy son.

12   YOUR CHILD AND THE SCHOOL
Speaker A's son has hemophilia, is HIV+, and has been developing infections. She will confront Speaker B, the principal of his junior high school, with the need for help and support if her son is diagnosed with AIDS.

13   SOURCES OF SUPPORT Speaker A is the mother of a 17-year-old with hemophilia and HIV infection. An HIV support group, sponsored by a local gay organization, has provided her and her husband with support and friendship. A has decided to confront a woman friend, Speaker B, who has made homophobic remarks about A's new friends.

FIGURE 6–2. Summary of the ENCOUNTER Issues

14 A TALK WITH THE DOCTOR
Speaker A is the mother of an 18-year-old with hemophilia. She is worried about his dropping T-cell count, and has decided to talk with his doctor, Speaker B, about her son's condition.

15 THE NEW FACTS OF LIFE
Speaker A is the mother of a 15-year-old with hemophilia who is HIV+. She has not spoken with him about sex since she told him the facts of life 4 years ago. Now she has decided she must talk with him about safer sex.

16 THE COLLEGE APPLICATION
Speaker A is the mother of Speaker B, an 18-year-old with hemophilia and HIV infection. B wants to attend a college 100 miles away. A will discuss with B why she and her husband would like him closer to home.

17 HIV, YOUR SON, AND OTHERS' FEARS Speaker A's son Andy has been dating Susan for the past two years. Last night Susan told him her parents won't let her see him anymore, and A is sure it is because of his HIV infection. She will try to talk Susan's mother out of this position.

18 MY BROTHER'S KEEPER?
Speaker A is the 21-year-old sister of a 17-year-old who has hemophilia and is HIV+. Both live at home with their parents. A has planned to move into an apartment with B, a close friend, but is torn about whether to stay and help her brother or to move in with B.

19 THE REALITY CHECK Speaker A's father has hemophilia and has recently been diagnosed with AIDS. A feels that her mother has been denying the seriousness of the illness, and needs more assistance and a greater acceptance of reality.

20 THE MINDFUL MOTHER-IN-LAW
Speaker A is the paternal grandmother of 10-year-old Raymond, who has hemophilia and is HIV+. She feels that her daughter-in-law, Speaker B, is preoccupied with AIDS issues, and talks to her about putting the illness in better perspective.

FIGURE 6–2. (Continued)

who keeps the simulation going and leads a postencounter discussion. By taking these different roles, participants will gain differing perspectives on a set of issues.

Those who have evaluated AIDS education programs have concluded that role-playing is one of the most effective techniques.[9] Standard role-playing is likely to be more effective in bringing about attitude examination and behavior change than is lecturing or asking participants to "pretend" they are in a situation. The ENCOUNTERS designers believe, however, that standard role-playing is considerably less effective than the structured role-playing approach in these simulations. Much traditional role-playing takes place in one of two modes: the performance mode or the dyad mode. In the more common, performance mode, two or more participants are selected to enact a situation for the larger group. If they have poor thespian talent, others will be bored; if they act well, the group may be entertained, but their involvement will be limited and their skills will not be honed. The performance mode does not maximize learning. In the other mode of traditional role-playing, a large group is divided into dyads. Dyad members are instructed to alternate playing the roles and then comment to each other about the strengths and weaknesses of their partner's handling of the roles. There are several potential problems that can limit the effectiveness of these exercises. A weak partner limits the learning for a strong one. The dynamics of the process are too unstructured for many participants, for there is usually little information to guide them and no social support. Finally, feedback mechanisms are weak; one's feedback comes from the same person to whom she or he needs to give feedback, and norms of politeness and fear of retribution may hinder honest assessments.

The structured role-play approach in the ENCOUNTERS simulations provides experiences more in accordance with basic learning principles. It creates wider involvement, as all group members are active participants in the process. In their groups, participants must plan, execute, and assess five sets of interaction strategies, and later discuss each strategy and alternatives to it. In their individual roles, participants are given sufficient information to provide structure and to identify the problems, but not so much information that they cannot bring personal values, experiences, and interpretations to the exercise.

The provision of five basic roles is designed to satisfy the recommendations of O. K. Moore and A. R. Anderson,[10] who argue that learning is most effective when participants can look at issues from a variety of perspectives. Thus, participants sometimes act, sometimes react, sometimes advise, and sometimes observe and give feedback. The simulation also requires that participants not simply anticipate what they might do or strategize about what they should do, but, in addition, practice putting their plan into action. This rehearsal takes place in the supportive context of a small group structured around principles of helping. It is emphasized that there is not a single "right" way to solve any of the problems and that these are difficult situations that may not lead to immediate successful plans of action.

The simulation thus provides participation, involvement, and problem-solving tasks; it promotes diverse perspectives through the learning exercise; and it offers opportunities to practice in sensitive encounters. In addition, the simulation has a self-sustaining character, as each five-person group has a group leader to keep the action going. This allows the operator to circulate through the room, to observe the different interactions and solutions to the same issues, and later to act as the overall discussion leader and coach. These advantages are summarized in Figure 3.

Figure 4 presents a page from the operator's manual. It reproduces the role information given to the two speakers (who also receive instructions on the process) for one of the encounters. Speaker B also is given four potential "stances" for each encounter; the operator can assign one of these or can permit the participant taking the role of speaker B to select one. In all cases, the first stance allows the participant to play as her values and responses dictate; the second leads her to be cooperative; and the third and fourth lead her to be more difficult, presenting a greater challenge to speaker A. In the side panel the issue is elaborated upon, and potential discussion topics are suggested to the operator.

THE SIMULATIONS IN USE: COUNSELING AND TRAINING

As a result of demonstrations, training programs, and distribution procedures developed by both Mt. Sinai Medical Center's Hemophilia Center and the Women's Outreach Network of the National Hemophilia Foundation

DIMINISH RELIANCE ON	AUGMENT PROVISION OF
Preaching and pontificating as in the lecture mode. It assumes all the wisdom resides in the one who lectures to others. It does not tape the expertise or experience of those in the "audience."	*Participation and involvement* In simulations all group or class members are participants and none are passive observers. Hence everyone is engaged in an active learning experience.
"Pretend" situations without interaction as in "what would you do if . . ." challenges on paper or in oral presentations. The absence of interactive cues and of any negative consequences of poor decisions, divorce this hypothesizing from reality.	*Problem-solving tasks* Participants should be in situations in which they are given enough information about the problem to act reasonably, but not so much information that they cannot bring their own values, experiences, and interpretations into play.
"Performance" demands as in standard role plays where two people act out a situation for the remainder of the participants. It may be dull or entertaining, depending upon the thespian talents of those selected to perform. Either way, others will be uninvolved and will not develop their skills.	*Perspectives vary during different phases of the learning activity* The most effective learning environments put learners in different perspectives over the course of the lesson. Perspectives make different demands of the learning, such as acting, reacting, observing, giving feedback.
Paired role plays as when the group is divided into pairs, and each pair performs the role play twice, alternating roles. This may work well for some participants, but weak partners limit the gains for the others. In addition, poor dynamics and weak feedback hinder the overall effectiveness of this technique.	*Practice* Participants learn not only to anticipate doing something, but to practice in safe environments. Small supportive groups can be helpful. It is important to limit expectations of immediate "success"—if these were not difficult tasks, the practice wouldn't be needed.

FIGURE 6–3. Underlying Philosophy of the Simulation Approach (to foster questioning of attitudes and to promote behavioral change)

ENCOUNTER ISSUES

All too often, safer sex is reduced to one phrase: "use condoms." Aside from being incomplete and uninformative, this advice fails to address the rather complex emotional issues that practicing safer sex, particularly with an HIV positive partner, presents. Most of us experience some discomfort when discussing sexual matters. The fact that one partner is HIV positive confounds the situation and makes it more precarious. The first step in eroticizing safer sex may involve helping the person feel "safe" enough to communicate openly about his or her fears and anxieties. This may take time and effort and may not be accomplished in one session or trial. Perhaps there are ways that women can be helpful to each other in exchanging information, experiences and new techniques. Learning the language and technology of sexual behaviors that are safe and erotic can be a playful and enjoyable process if handled with competence and respect.

Encounter 4 provides the opportunity for a wife of an HIV positive man with hemophilia to courageously ask another woman about her experience with safer sex. It can be played with a respondent who is appreciative of this woman's courage and wants to help, with one who incessantly questions the woman, or with one who feels that no answers can be given unless both parties are present and willing to talk.

DISCUSSION TOPICS

- What makes it difficult to talk about sex? What makes it easier?
- What is your understanding of safer sex? What sexual behaviors put one at risk?
- How have you and your partner (your patients/clients) handled your (their) concerns about HIV transmission?

SPEAKER A

You are the wife of David, a man with hemophilia. You and David have had problems with your sex life since you learned that David is HIV positive about two years ago. Both of you understand the importance of practicing safer sex, and you use condoms whenever you make love. The problem is that you make love less frequently and less satisfactorily these days because of the condoms. David has a difficult time maintaining an erection, and you feel very anxious. You have only vaguely talked about the problem; although both of you are unhappy about the situation, neither of you has known what to do.

SPEAKER B

You are the wife of Sam, an HIV+ man with hemophilia. In the first few months after you and Sam learned he was HIV+, there were serious problems with your sex life. Condoms were a definite turn-off for both of you, and as a result, you each found ways to avoid making love. Fortunately, you heard about a safer sex workshop, and both you and Sam attended a few months ago. The workshop emphasized three main themes:

- that sex consists of more than intercourse—it is also fondling, foreplay, intimacy, friendship, communication;
- that familiarity with condoms can help overcome many of the initial problems couples face. Putting them on a partner can be very erotic;
- that couples can learn to obtain pleasure from related activities such as choosing lubricants, or using erotic videos.

Since you put these principles into practice, you and Sam have found that your emotional relationship improved as well as your sexual relationship. This may be due to better communication.

Last week at a support group meeting sponsored by your treatment center, you met Speaker B. She stated that she and her husband, Sam had some sexual problems when they first found out he was HIV positive. Thanks to their participation in a week-end workshop, their sex life is now better than ever. You couldn't ask her more in public, and you can't imagine attending a large workshop on the topic of sex. But today you arranged to meet with B privately to ask for advice on how to eroticize safer sex.

At a hemophilia center support group meeting last week you mentioned that you and Sam have succeeded in overcoming these problems. Last night, Speaker A, a member of that support group, called to ask if you would meet with her. You suspect she wants to ask you about your comments.

Stances for B:

1. How you respond should depend on your reaction to what Speaker A says and how she says it.
2. You are pleased that she had the courage to ask. Praise her and talk about some things that might be helpful.
3. You feel that you need data before giving advice. Ask A a lot of questions about her intimate life and personal marital relationship.
4. You would like to help, but you feel that A is only one half of the problem or the solution. You think her husband should also be present. Suggest that she try to get him involved.

FIGURE 6–4. Sample Page from the Operator's Manual

(WONN), the simulations are now used around the country and in Canada for both counseling and training professionals.

The first stage of the expansion was timed to provide a subset of encounters for use in WONN's first national skill-building workshop, held in Minneapolis in September 1989. WONN had just been created as a consumer-driven initiative to empower women within the hemophilia community to take a leadership role in helping cope with the many stresses imposed by the AIDS/HIV crisis. More than 80 women were brought together from 32 states and Canada for this three-day workshop. They ranged in age from 22 to 65 and were wives, sexual partners, mothers, grandmothers, sisters, and daughters of people with hemophilia. The simulations were nested in the middle of a rich program that included focus groups, panels of psychosocial professionals, panels of women whose husbands or children were very ill with or had died from AIDS, and workshops on mobilizing community support, accessing and disseminating information, and creating local and regional peer programs. The simulations allowed many women to share their feelings and strategies for coping with issues, without having to discuss their personal situations. As indicated in Table 1, their feedback suggested that they found the encounters successful in representing the issues they face. The proportion of "Excellent" ratings increased further when women's actual position corresponded to the relationship described in the encounter (for instance, wives rating Encounter 1, mothers rating Encounter 10).

The women also reported that their participation in the simulations was worthwhile, as shown in Table 2, although several of them were apologetic on their evaluation forms ("I thought the simulation was wonderful, but I could only indicate that it improved my knowledge 'somewhat' because I already had a great deal of knowledge."). By 1991, the network had expanded to 317 women, who brought peer HIV risk-reduction education and support into their communities through a range of activities.[11] All WONN members are

TABLE 6–1. Encounter Ratings, WONN Workshop, September 1989 ("Please rate each of the encounters in terms of its representation of issues faced by women in families with a member who has hemophilia.")

	Poor 1	Fair 2	Good 3	Excellent 4	Total	N	Mean Score (1–4)
Encounter 1	0%	3	36	61	100%	75	3.59
Encounter 9	1%	4	28	67	100%	75	3.60
Encounter 10	0%	0	21	79	100%	29	3.79
Encounter 12	0%	4	37	59	100%	49	3.55
Encounter 15	0%	4	33	63	100%	73	3.59

TABLE 6-2. Evaluations of Participation in ENCOUNTERS WITH AIDS, WONN Workshop, September 1989

	Not at all	A little	Some- what	A great deal	Total	N	Mean Score
Participation in ENCOUNTERS WITH AIDS:							
improved my *knowledge of the range of problems faced* by women in families with hemophilia and HIV	8%	10	41	41	100%	78	3.15
increased my *empathy* for women coping with problems of hemophilia and HIV in their families	1%	13	27	58	99%	78	3.44
increased my *skills* in talking about problems of hemophilia and HIV	3%	18	45	34	100%	76	3.11
increased my *confidence in talking about my own problems* of hemophilia and HIV	3%	17	47	34	101%	77	3.12
increased my *confidence in talking with other women* about their problems concerning hemophilia and HIV	3%	9	36	53	101%	76	3.38
I found participation in ENCOUNTERS WITH AIDS was:							
a *valuable* experience	0%	9	18	72	99%	76	3.63
an *enjoyable* experience	1%	9	29	61	100%	76	3.49

provided with a large resource kit including educational tools, videos, books, directories, and ENCOUNTERS WITH AIDS. A number of local and regional chapters have employed the simulations in their programs, and anecdotal reports indicate that they, too, have found it to be of great use in opening discussion and practicing strategies for difficult conversations.

The simulations have been made available and utilized through the national network of treatment centers, thanks to a training program run by the Mount Sinai Medical Center, funded by the U.S. Office of Public Health, Bureau of Maternal and Child Health. (The training program also included use of a parallel set, CLOSE ENCOUNTERS: ADOLESCENTS, HEMO-PHILIA AND HIV.) This effort involved workshops in 1989 and 1990 at which over 300 professionals from the United States and 25 from several provinces in Canada participated. The program assessment concluded that the project was very beneficial and that the workshop participants were enthusiastic about their own gains in insight and about the potential of the tool for training other professionals and for direct counseling efforts with their clientele. Participants were provided with sets of materials, and many put them to use in their clinics.

An indirect measure of the success of the simulations is that, as men with hemophilia and HIV became more interested in the support group approach, a parallel set of ENCOUNTERS WITH AIDS for men was commissioned by the Canadian Hemophilia Society in cooperation with the National Hemophilia Foundation, both of which now use it in their programs of training and counseling.[12]

NOTES

[1]Hemophilia is a sex-linked genetic disorder. It is carried by women but appears almost exclusively in men. Those with hemophilia lack a clotting factor and hence are subject to considerable damage through bleeding episodes, most of which are internal.

[2]The proportion was estimated to be higher (about 80 percent) a few years earlier, but dropped because of deaths and new births.

[3]National Hemophilia Foundation. "Aids cases and surveillance as of Nov. 30, 1990." *Hemophilia Information Exchange: AIDS Update.* Chapter Advisory No. 134, Medical Bulletin No. 125, 15 February 1991.

[4]Centers for Disease Control (CDC). *HIV/AIDS Surveillance: May 1991.* Atlanta: Centers for Disease Control, 1991.

[5]See Mason, Patrick, Roberta A. Olson, and Kathy L. Parish. "AIDS, Hemophilia and Prevention Efforts Within a Comprehensive Care Program." *American Psychologist* 43 (November 1988): 971–976.

[6]Greenblat, Cathy Stein. *Critical Encounters: Health Professionals and HIV.* Geneva: World Health Organization, 1988.

[7]Greenblat, Cathy S., Susan Katz, John H. Gagnon, and Diana Shannon. "An Innovative Program of Counseling Family Members and Friends of Seropositive Haemophiliacs." *AIDS Care* 1 (1989): 67–75.

[8]Greenblat, Cathy Stein, and Susan Katz. *Encounters with AIDS: Women, Hemophilia, and HIV.* Washington, D.C.: U.S. Office of Public Health, Division of Child and Maternal Health, Hemophilia Division, 1990.

[9]Office of Technology Assessment (OTA). *Effectiveness of AIDS Education.* Washington, D.C.: Office of Technology Assessment, 1988.

[10]Moore, O. K. and A. R. Anderson. "Some Principles for the Design of Clarifying Educational Environments." In *Principles and Practices of Gaming Simulation,* edited by Cathy Greenblat and Richard Duke. Newbury Park: Sage, 1975.

[11]Gerus, Kathy. "Women's Outreach Network of NHF." *Hemophilia Newsnotes* (May 1991): 10–11, 21. 1991.

[12]Greenblat, Cathy Stein. *Encounters with AIDS: Men and HIV* (in English and in French). Montreal: Canadian Hemophilia Society, 1991.

Barbara G. Sosnowitz

AIDS Prevention, Minority Women and Gender Assertiveness

D isease is a matter of cultural definition[1]—like beauty, it is in the eye of the beholder.[2] Opinions about causes and risks as well as preventive behavior are based in the social world. The social meanings attributed to AIDS and its consequences are in part responsible for several groups' marked tendency to deny its presence in their midst. AIDS was first publicized as being related to membership in certain "risk groups" (such as gay white males and, later, Haitians) rather than involvement in certain "risk behaviors" (such as sharing infected needles or having penetrative sex without a condom). Consequently in its short but virulent history, AIDS has been seen as a gay disease by nongay people, as an affliction of outcasts by those in the mainstream, as a problem for whites by ethnic communities, and as a dilemma for the damned by the virtuous. These constructs have continued to characterize the AIDS epidemic and prevention initiatives. The result has been a form of social paranoia in which members of some communities and ethnic groups have taken actions opposed to AIDS prevention initiatives.[3]

People understand social reality according to how the groups to which they belong shape and guide members' experiences. What is deemed "real" comes from whatever beliefs are held by a group about any particular subject. Groups' worldviews are formed by the actions people take toward one another and the social meanings given to those actions. It is only by paying attention to the ideas groups hold about AIDS that culturally sensitive prevention programs can be developed.

AIDS prevention programs have also been affected by the political atmosphere when the disease was first recognized. The dominance of a particular type of conservatism in the 1980s, which strongly promoted abstinence, contributed to the lack of sexually explicit prevention initiatives. Furthermore, boundaries between medical and social factors were blurred, creating considerable stigmatization of those contracting HIV and influencing the environment in which prevention education would be allowed for the public. AIDS was also used to express social fears involving differences of class, race, and ethnicity. All the negative social and political constructs of the epidemic have served to increase racial/ethnic group suspicion over

AIDS prevention initiatives.[4] The past experiences of these communities with health care directed by the dominant society furthered their desire to distance themselves from the disease and from the system's management of it.[5]

This chapter recognizes these factors—broad social meanings, cultural beliefs, and political climate—as crucial to the outcome of AIDS prevention programs. It reports on an interactive, participatory approach with women from a variety of racial/ethnic groups which took place on an urban university campus. The intervention was unique in that it was not the one-shot, two- or three-hour program typically given to late adolescents and college students, but a full 14-week semester.

Since the intervention project was based in an effort to understand the problems of earlier prevention initiatives and to take account of the specific concerns of a number of overlapping constituencies, a discussion of the complex responses of the black and Latino communities and that of adolescents as a group is presented before turning to a description of the intervention: the AIDS Discovery class.

BLACK RESPONSES

While there have been and are AIDS prevention efforts in the black community, the construction of AIDS among blacks has typically led to denial of the devastation this disease has inflicted in the African-American community and a reluctance to take steps to prevent further devastation. According to a variety of sources, this denial stems from at least four sources. First, black Americans see the larger society as trying to place blame for the origin and spread of AIDS on their race. Second, blacks have a deep-seated mistrust when whites take an interest in their health.[6] Negative experiences in the past, such as the infamous Tuskegee experiment, in which the government intentionally failed to treat black men infected with syphilis,[7] and government efforts to forcibly sterilize women on welfare, many of whom were black, have helped perpetuate these feelings.[8] Some blacks have even speculated that AIDS was invented by whites and allowed to spread as long as it was confined to minority populations.[9]

Third, homophobia in the black community inhibits responses to counter AIDS. As Dalton[10] puts it,

> My suspicion is that openly gay men and lesbians evoke hostility in part because they have come to symbolize the strong female and the weak male that slavery and Jim Crow produced. . . . Thus, in the black community homosexuality carries more baggage than in the larger society.

Fourth, the particular relationship between the black community and drugs complicates its dealings with AIDS. Drug use is so closely linked in the popular imagination with inner-city black neighborhoods that blacks fear that an acknowledgment of the relationship between HIV and injection drug use in their community will further stereotype all blacks as "junkies" and black culture as pathological.[11] A belief also exists in the black community that white America's commitment to solving drug problems is episodic, increasing only when suburban populations are affected. White America, it seems to blacks, is largely unconcerned with the crime and violence that has assaulted the black community.[12]

LATINO RESPONSES

Some similarities also appear to exist between the black and Latino subcultures in their construction of AIDS. First, deep anxieties about homosexuality are present in both subcultures. Sexism, too, makes AIDS prevention more difficult. By suggesting that women should be assertive in protecting themselves against disease and pregnancy by discussing sexual histories with their partners, prevention initiatives are asking for gender behavior that is discouraged in Latino cultures.[13]

Third, strong religious ties in the Latino community, primarily to the Catholic church but also to several fundamentalist religious groups, inhibit responses to the AIDS threat. These churches' stands against contraception, including condoms, create personal conflicts for those using protection against the disease. AIDS precaution messages that encourage condom use place Latinos and others in a position of being safe during this lifetime but, in their view, damned in the next. Furthermore, some believe that supernatural forces inflict punishments for unacceptable behaviors and that retribution is to be accepted passively.[14]

Finally, like blacks, Latinos have good historical reasons for fearing the dominant medical establishment. For example, by 1970, numerous U.S.-sponsored population control projects in Puerto Rico had surgically sterilized 35 percent of women able to bear children, contributing to a pervasive mistrust of government-sponsored health initiatives.[15] Such mistrust has led to questioning any allegedly altruistic effort of the larger society.

As minority children grow and are socialized in the black and Latino communities, they attend to and internalize the beliefs and prejudices of those around them.[16]

ADOLESCENT RESPONSES

Teenagers have not traditionally been considered different from adults with regard to health issues. Yet many risky health behaviors, such as excessive use of cigarettes, alcohol, and drugs and unprotected sex, are statistically normative behavior among young people.[17] Strategies to prevent such behaviors have not been overly successful. Young people do not absorb interventions and certainly do not change risk behaviors after one educational session.[18]

The path from childhood to adulthood involves choices that are influenced by community, family, and peers. As adolescents move toward adulthood in their communities, they must separate from their family of origin and, in many cultures, begin a family of their own. Young people seek emotional support from their peers. By participating in peer groups, adolescents are able to satisfy their needs for acceptance and yet be different from the adults in their life, from whom they must separate. The peer group has a major influence in directing adolescent experimentation,[19] which can lead both to health risks and to the development of appropriate strategies to avoid dangers. For this reason it is important to understand the social interactions that take place among adolescents.[20]

Minority youth who internalize cultural and ethnic interpretations of AIDS and indulge in typical teenage experimentation with drugs or sex are particularly vulnerable to disease. Many of these youth lack sexual information, live in poverty, face racism, and contend with other social problems which increase their risk of contracting the AIDS virus.

The number of adolescents with AIDS is difficult to determine and may be severely underestimated.[21] In 1990, the CDC reported 1,000 cases of adolescents with AIDS, a 40 percent increase over the previous two years. The latest estimates are that 20 percent of men and 25 percent of women diagnosed with AIDS are in their twenties. Since the incubation period for the disease is from seven to ten years, this statistic indicates that young people are becoming infected with HIV during adolescence. Several studies indicate that 50 to 70 percent of teenagers report being sexually active by the age of 19.[22] Of those who report being sexually active, only 47 percent of the females and 25 percent of the males use condoms.[23] Demographic comparisons indicate that black and Latino teenagers have earlier sexual experiences than whites and that those living in poverty have sex earlier than the more economically advantaged.[24] Teenagers from these groups are also less able to share sexual decisions than white youth from a more advantaged situations[25] and do not use contraception consistently.[26] In addition, poor, black, and Latino youth are more likely to live in an environment where injection drug use is common.[27]

Sexual responsibility falls to the female in both the black and the Latino groups, responsibility particularly difficult for some given these groups lack of openness surrounding the subject. Furthermore, females who feel guilty about having sex are less likely to take precautions against pregnancy or disease.[28] There is also evidence that young women of racial/ethnic groups, like young white women, frequently are unable to insist on methods that could protect them from sexually transmitted diseases.[29] They feel pressured to show trust in their partners, as demonstrated in such statements from black women as "We don't need no condom because he says he loves me," and "Even if he was screwing around nothing would happen because he says he'll never do anything that would mess me up, and I believe him."[30]

The combination of denial and the inability to discuss sex increases the likelihood of minority young women contacting a sexually transmitted disease, including AIDS.[31]

The risk of contracting a sexually transmitted disease and AIDS is rapidly increasing in the teenage population.[32] Ten years after the disease was first identified, the social stigma of AIDS has persisted, fostering a reluctance to recognize or even discuss transmission among this vulnerable population. Adolescents acquire AIDS for the most part heterosexually, are asymptomatic, and are predominantly from minority populations.[33] In late 1992, black and Latina females under 19 diagnosed with AIDS reached 199, while reported cases of white females under 19 were 73. Cases of black and Latino men under 19 totaled 349, with white males reaching 309. Cases of AIDS in the 20 to 24 age group were even greater. Black females totaled 892, Latina women 419, and white females 433. Males with AIDS in this same age group totaled 2,434 blacks, 1,510 Latinos, and 3,797 whites.[34] While some appear to be quite knowledgeable about AIDS and STD,[35] many young people, including the sexually experienced, continue to determine who might be infectious based on whether a person "looks" sick.[36]

Cultural imperatives, economic situations, and age and maturity levels influence teenagers' attitudes toward, understanding of, and meanings attributed to health initiatives. Past AIDS prevention efforts proceeded with little sensitivity to different subcultural concerns that might override fears about the AIDS epidemic, particularly in groups suspicious of the motives behind messages delivered by the predominantly white media, education, and public health establishments. Ignoring such differences led to the failure of many prevention efforts.[37] To mount successful prevention initiatives, it is important to understand the worldview of a targeted population, and key to this understanding is knowledge of the social meaning of AIDS in each group.[38]

While studies have found that college students have a good understanding of the AIDS virus and its transmission,[39] this has not dramatically changed at-risk behaviors. There is a high level of sexual activity with multiple partners among college students,[40] and most college students who are engaging in sexual relationships think of contracting AIDS as only a remote risk.[41] Minority youth, even those attending college, influenced by the constructs of AIDS in their ethnic backgrounds, are put at exceptionally high risk for both pregnancy and disease. Like their white peers, they use selective denial to overpower fear and achieve a sense of invincibility.[42]

However, several studies published recently have demonstrated that, when blacks and Latinos are college students, away from their home environment for short periods of time, there is an opportunity to persuade them to change their construction of AIDS and to personalize risk.[43] The rapid increase of AIDS in minority populations and the belief that young people can be induced to change their behaviors inspired this project.

METHODOLOGY

The overall goals of the part of the project described here were: (1) to change behaviors that could expose U.S. racial/ethnic minority students to AIDS, and (2) to personalize their risk for AIDS. The hope was to alter the norms of public discourse to include sex and to teach skills in negotiating interpersonal relationships.

A pretest, to establish a baseline of AIDS knowledge, was given in 1990 to 35 first-year college students from a variety of ethnic backgrounds at a university in the northeastern United States. The results of the pretest indicated that these students had not benefited from past AIDS prevention messages. They did not understand the language used. Neither the men nor the women understood the terms *vaginal, oral,* or *anal.* Furthermore, some did not understand the term *intravenous.* It was obvious that a more personal, understandable method was needed to discuss these terms, so that safe sex could be practiced.

While both quantitative and qualitative methods of inquiry offer important information on AIDS and related conditions, neither is intended to provide direct intervention. The interactive approach used in this project is intended to result in the development of interventions. It insists that reality cannot be measured, tested, and objectively verified, and seeks to understand the worlds of different groups by "knowing" in the same terms that group members themselves use. This participatory-action research approach sought to weld the ideas of social science to a more humanistic version of social research.[44] Its purpose was to increase understanding and simultaneously to take action. This project took a triangulated approach to clarifying how a particular group was personalizing AIDS prevention information. Surveys, direct observations, participation, and planned activities promoting AIDS prevention relevant to the lives of the participants were combined in a socially sensitive, nonjudgmental, informative environment, an environment engineered to facilitate the disclosure of personal beliefs and intimate behaviors.

Forty minority students from an educational opportunity program that brings inner-city youth to the university mentioned above were scheduled into one of two sections of a Fall 1991 AIDS Discovery class. Although students did not elect this class, they were given the opportunity to drop it. Each class contained 20 students and met once a week. The following sections will discuss 20 women who participated in the project. The group of women consisted of 5 Latinas predominantly from Puerto Rico, 11 blacks, 1 Asian woman, two women who considered themselves both black and white, and 1 white, all from inner-city high schools and ranging in age from 17 to 20. Sixteen of the women stated they had had sexual intercourse, and all with more than one partner. The STD epidemic was also reflected in these women; 6 had already had an STD and 4 were mothers.

Outwardly, the women resembled typical college students. They had resilience, intellectual as well as street knowledge, and a desire to be successful. However, after I had immersed myself in their world for 14 weeks, I began to understand that they were more like the youth Garbarino et al. describe, young women coping with the consequences of their community life and cultural imperatives.[45] Like many urban youths, they had experienced poverty, family disruption, racial discrimination, and violence. Although all the women claimed that they did not use drugs, they were familiar with drug use by their friends and families and had had experience with law enforcement, public schools, clinics, and welfare services.

The women were told little about the class before their advisor enrolled them. The project itself was described to them during the first class session. I told them that we would be working together to design a prevention initiative to reach other young people like them. To encourage cooperation, the grading procedure was reversed. Each student would start off with an A. The instructor assumed that those who chose to continue their participation in the research would be highly motivated to keep their A grade.

A survey was administered during the first and last class sessions. The language used in the survey was designed to optimize reading comprehension. Attention was paid to the ordering of questions, putting the most sensitive material at the end in the hope that participants' comfort level would increase as they worked through the survey.

The class met once a week, for one and one-quarter hours per session, for 11 weeks. Because each class period followed a set agenda, members of both sections were exposed to the same events. In addition, the women met for 3 weeks, once a week, two hours per session, in small focus groups.

The AIDS Discovery class was designed to include both didactic information as well as skill building. Student behaviors were observed, and their accounts were obtained as they organized, interpreted, and responded to the AIDS information provided in class and small groups. The underlying philosophy was that learning had to be fun if it was going to last. A variety of educational tools were used to begin the building of skills needed to negotiate behaviors that prevent contacting AIDS. The least sensitive and explicit topics surrounding sexually transmitted diseases were dealt with first, with information tailored to students' comfort levels, which allowed students time to familiarize themselves with the expectations of the class. Videos about AIDS were used to provide information in a nonthreatening way.[46] Discussion of personal beliefs, as well as questions surrounding sexual activity and drug use, were encouraged following the themes used in the videos. I used games, assignments, and role-playing to get students to explore the seriousness of AIDS.[47]

One assignment consisted of two activities, called "Finding Information About STDs" and "Pricing 'Preventive' Products," both taken from the book *Entering Adulthood: Preventing Sexually Related Diseases*, edited by Betty

Hubbard.[48] The purpose of these assignments was to encourage the participants to think about their own risk for STD. The assignments asked students to obtain information about STD from local agencies and to price preventive products, such as condoms and vaginal creams, mobilizing them into stores and helping them to recognize and purchase products effective against STD. Participants were advised to think about prices, brands, dates of expiration, and types of stores where STD-prevention products could be purchased. Groups of students played out different scenarios. First, a boy insisted on the use of condoms with the girl refusing.[49] Explained one young woman, "If a guy tells a girl to use a condom, some girls think the guys are 'dissing' [disrespectful of] them." Another scenario involved a young woman insisting on condoms and a boy refusing, causing the women to reflect on the need to carry condoms themselves and prompting concerns such as "If I carry a condom, they [men] automatically think I'm sleeping around."

Three different focus groups were formed for the women. The more mature, several of whom were single parents, were placed in a mixed-gender group; the remaining students were divided between those who seemed to have a strong ethnic identity, which would predispose them to work better with a minority leader, and those who seemed able to work with me, a white woman, as their leader.

REVELATIONS FROM WOMEN IN THE AIDS DISCOVERY CLASS AND FOCUS GROUPS

Despite the fact that most participants were sexually experienced, they revealed wide variation in sexual knowledge. Like other minority youth, these women seldom discussed sex within their families.[50] As one woman recounted, "My mother didn't discuss it because she just didn't want me to do it." It was also evident that participants misunderstood terms used in sex education classes. One women explained:

> If I'd known about all that stuff that I know now, I wouldn't have gotten pregnant. I was too scared to go to my parents. My parents weren't telling me anything. Everybody in school was talking about "it" [sex]. Wasn't nobody talking about using contraception or protection. Everybody was just talking about they was just doing "it." We didn't get [information] in school until it was too late for me.

The women engaging in sexual activity described doing it in the dark. If they used condoms, they were put on by the male, in private, hidden from the women's view. As in other studies of adolescents, many of the women were willing to have sex but not to *see* themselves having sex.

At the end of the third class session, students were handed an assignment to make something creative out of condoms. The assignment read as follows:

> You have received a handful of condoms. Use your creative imagination and make something usable. In the past, students have made bracelets, key holders, etc. I want you to be as creative as possible. You will be showing your creations to the class and will be marked on the completion of this assignment. THERE MAY EVEN BE A PRIZE FOR THE MOST ORIGINAL CREATION.

The purpose of this assignment was to force students to handle condoms without embarrassment. The women students made bracelets, earrings, anklets, ponytail holders, key rings, flower holders, and pins. All of these were worn to the next class. Students were having fun, opening, unfolding, and comfortably using something that many of them had never seen, touched, or admitted to using before. This assignment was the source of much discussion among their friends and roommates as well. The norms of public conversation were being changed. Without self-consciousness, the students were discussing condoms openly.

In the fourth class, a series of outdoor relay races involved cucumbers and condoms. Participants were divided into several teams. Each team was given one cucumber and each student a lubricated condom. The object of the relays was to rip open the condom package, place the condom on the cucumber *correctly* (leaving room at the end), and then remove it. The first team to finish was the winner. Several versions of the condom relays were played, including "hot" cucumber. Students were asked to stand in a circle, passing the cucumber from participant to participant until the leader yelled, "Stop!" The participant holding the cucumber at that moment had to demonstrate for the group the correct way to put on and take off a condom. The skill-building objective was not only to have fun, but to publicly display the activity, continuing to demystify condoms by openly discussing, touching, and using them. The laughter and relaxation of these exercises, out in public, with many of their friends cheering them on, only furthered the students' confidence and comfort in handling and talking about condoms.

Once the norms of public conversation changed, including discussion of sensitive subjects, the women visibly relaxed. They appeared to sense that this was a class full of surprises and information, as well as a place where questions about sexuality would be treated seriously. The next step was to divide the class into small groups. These focus groups met three consecutive times over a three-week period, during which time the AIDS class was suspended. These groups were formed to work specifically on skills in negotiating intimate behaviors. The discussion within the security of a small group was more intense. The group agenda with its interaction encouraged women to think about new ideas and to look at different perspectives by listening to the ideas and experiences of their peers.[51] Responses to the question "What did you like/dislike about the small groups?" were all positive. Some examples of comments are:

The most important things that I think we discussed in these group meetings were about the different kinds of sex, the different issues about condoms, and that we as a group got to know each other in a personal way.

I felt that we learned a lot from these group discussions because we got a chance to say just what we felt, how we felt about it, and even if we thought about it or not without someone looking at us funny or anyone saying something negative. We covered topics that we as teenagers go through every day and I think that was good. I think that we should have had more of these classes, instead of the big classroom.

Working with friends of students with whom they interacted outside of class also served to strengthen what took place in class. Halfway through the semester, students were encouraged to include their boyfriends or girlfriends in conversations about AIDS. The intent was to snowball the AIDS prevention messages and to create additional peer support for responsible and safe sex behavior outside the classroom.

DISCUSSION

When these women first entered the class, they were concerned primarily with occurrences in their day-to-day world. They worried about being able to handle a college workload, their finances, being a minority on a predominately white campus, and missing friends and family at home. Life-threatening diseases were associated with their parents' generation. Although most of them had been sexually active, they thought of AIDS as a remote risk and exhibited cultural paranoia similar to what Dalton[52] describes. As one women said:

Why just talk to minorities? It's not like we're the only ones in the world who get AIDS. It makes me feel mad. Educate everybody. Why just talk to minorities, like we're the ones giving it around? Everybody's giving it around, not just the blacks and Puerto Ricans.

But soon, other concerns surfaced. Another women said:

I worry about being protected from AIDS and leading a normal life without worrying about having a husband who will abuse my children sexually because of alcohol and drugs.

A third commented:

I don't feel that I should go to a party and have to carry my mace with me. I'm scared something's going to happen.

Participants' trust in their own personal abilities became the dominant component in dealing with risk, creating the illusion of protection from harm. Speaking of drugs, one women said, "If they respect you, they don't ask you to do it." Regarding sex another said:

I live in the projects. All these girls we hang together. We used to go to school together—and some of them aren't virgins. They're messing with every guy and stuff. My best friend used to say, "I'll never, I'd rather die. I'm going to marry the right way," and now she's pregnant and she wanted to go to community college and now she can't because she had to get her own place and everything.

However, the imperative to trust the men with whom they were having relations was enormous:

We made love. It hurt me because I have not done it for a real long time. We did not use a condom because neither of us have had other sex partners and we trusted each other.

You have to trust that person a lot. . . . Like I talk to him a lot and I ask him a lot of personal questions and stuff. Sometimes he gets stuck, sometimes he answers the questions that I ask him. That way I get to know some background. If a guy is able to tell you a lot about himself, then he's showing that there's not much to hide or whatever he has he wants you to know about.

The need to have trust in their male friends, combined with a need to deal with the racial prejudice and violence in their lives by living in the present, caused several of the women to focus only on the immediate consequences of their behaviors. This skill of surviving appeared similar to those of concentration camp prisoners: an orientation toward living in the here-and-now, psychologically as well as physically distanced from their home communities. The expressions "You do what you got to do" and "Take it day by day" were repeated often. AIDS was particularly easy to ignore because effects of infection would not be immediately apparent.[53] Pregnancy appeared to be the predominant concern. As one woman said, "Even though I already have a daughter, I worry about getting pregnant again." Most of the women had friends who had dropped out of school, were lonely and isolated, stuck at home with small infants. As one of the women said,

My best friend, she was a virgin. She "gave it" [virginity] up. Now, she's pregnant and she really loved this guy. This guy thought he loved her and now he's left her. If I make love to a guy, I want him to stay with me. . . . I've got to see the world really out there. These are dreams, we have but we have to face some guys will say "I love you" just to take your virginity and then walk off.

The women described their friends as having very little sexual knowledge. "I have friends that are pregnant now, they didn't know they were having sex. Things were coming out so quickly, they didn't know." Abstinence appeared to place extra pressure on some women. One young black woman who was willing to admit publicly that she was a virgin found herself lonely and isolated most of the semester. She stated, "I've been with a lot of guys I've been crazy about, but I realized my virginity. I love it a lot and I want to keep it so they [men] leave me."

Another young Latina woman listened intently during class discussions about sex. Halfway through the semester, she engaged in sex for the first time. The free discussion among her peers in some way made sex less threatening and seemingly more acceptable to her. The classroom interactions among the women constituted a kind of permission giving that contradicted the beliefs of this woman's culture. The change in her behavior may or may not have been the best decision for her, but it clearly marked an instance of the ways in which intensive sex education and AIDS education programs of the sort that are *not* available virtually anywhere in the United States might indeed undermine the traditional religious or cultural values of a church or culture, even when they are not directly intended to do so.

Though the women in the study became increasingly sensitive to their risk of contracting HIV, they remained even more concerned about the enormous gender barriers they would have to cross if they sought to protect themselves. "If I were to tell them [to use a condom], they would probably be, like, 'Why what you think I got something?' " Another said, "If you have a condom, it's automatically sleeping around." The women in the present study feared rejection.[54] Much discussion centered around "good girls" and "whores," their desirability, and status:

> I was really thinking about this. If I were in love with someone, it's hard to tell him to get checked for AIDS if I was going to marry him. It's hard because you don't know if he'll get offended or whatever.

> A lot of time like certain guys, he have a lot of things I look for in a guy. But, I had to give him up. It was very hard and painful. But a girl has to realize she has to set her standards and keep them. She can't give "it" [virginity] up.

> If you give "it" [virginity] up easy, they just tend to play with you.

> Boys don't get a bad reputation like girls do. Boys exaggerate more. Girls get a bad reputation because of it [sex]. Boys don't.

> I can't have a male friend. I live in the projects, and if I'm seen talking to one guy, I gotta be going with him. I have a boyfriend but if I get caught talking to somebody else, they'll go back and tell my boyfriend, I was doing this and I was doing that.

The women appeared to gain a great deal of confidence from the preventive exercises and information provided. The pre- and post-intervention surveys indicated improvement in several areas specifically with regard to increased knowledge about the spread of AIDS and use of protection against the disease. Of the 20 women participants, an increase from 9 to 15 indicated that they had a good understanding from the class of how AIDS was transmitted. The number of women who considered themselves more knowledgeable about how to use a condom correctly increased from 11 to 17. In addition, there was an increase from 15 to 17 of the women who felt capable of insisting on the use of condoms.

The number of women who felt able to stop the sex act completely if they didn't want to engage in it increased from 10 to 14. This newfound strength seemed to arise from the support of their female peers; however, there still seemed to be concern for how they would act when alone with a male. Initially, 2 of the women stated that they would be insulted if their partner were to insist on using a condom during sex. However, at the end of the 14 weeks, none of the women felt this way. When asked to describe their feelings about the study's action interventions, such as practicing with condoms, one woman summed up others' as well as her own response as follows:

> I got a lot out of the class. Now, I am using condoms like my name should be on them. I even did an eight-minute speech in my public speaking class. Every time I see the word *AIDS* or *condom*, I am turning my head to read about it.

In response to their gendered imperative to remain virgins until marriage, to marry early, and to have children, the women exclaimed:

> Anybody can get a man. It's like they're gonna always be out there. Once they strip everything else from you, you still got your education. That's one thing they can't take from you. You know what I mean? That's why I'm staying in school.

> I said this is my only chance to go to college cause I'm a ward of the state and that's the only way I'm going to college. I can't screw it up now. If I screw it up, that's the end of my life!

Based on the women's comments in class and in the focus groups, two learning activities appeared to be most effective with study participants. These were the class activities (condom games and homework assignments) and, above all, focus groups. With regard to condoms, for example, participants said:

> I've never even read how they have the dates on the boxes until I like heard you say that. I had to look in my bag and see if mine had dates on them.

> I feel I no longer have to be embarrassed about condoms or talking about them. Thanks to this class, my boyfriend and I are very open to each other and talk about anything and everything. I have definitely learned that "safe sex" is the only way to go.

> I was already familiar with condoms, but I never thought there was a specific way of putting it on, I didn't really think that the way you put it on could have a lot of importance. This was very helpful to me. Now, I know the correct way of putting it on. Also I didn't know one had to be so careful with it. This class made me realize I have been doing it wrong.

Initially, all 20 women in the study agreed that they were afraid of getting AIDS, but only 5 agreed that AIDS could easily happen to them. By the end of the study, 3 additional women felt that they could easily contract AIDS, and the women appeared to align their actions with their increased understanding of their risk for AIDS. In addition, they seemed to have gained a sense of control over pressure to be sexual. At the study's outset, half (10) of the women strongly agreed that they could "stop things before we had intercourse." This number had increased to 14 by the study's end. Initially, 5 women stated that they would be too embarrassed to buy condoms, a number reduced to just 1 by the end of the study. On the first survey, 13 women said that they would carry condoms with them when they anticipated having sex, a number that increased to 16 on the final survey.

The researcher noted that, as the group of women spent more time together, they became more open to discussing intimate relations with one another. They appeared to have overcome cultural barriers to identify with one another as women. The women expressed their opinions "honestly," as it was clear that their opinions and feelings were not much different than those they offered anonymously—though they were clearly different from the men taking part in the project. The men gave more intimate accounts of their behaviors anonymously, when they offered them at all. The interventions did not work as well for male participants. Environmental pressures may weigh so heavily on inner-city racial/ethnic minority men that they need more time, more interventions, and more social support to change their behaviors than their female peers require. The support provided for the women in this study appeared to be enough to encourage them to be more assertive in protecting their lives.

IMPLICATIONS FOR THE FUTURE

This report should be seen as providing information preliminary to a more intensive study, one which would encourage researchers and health promoters to consider the "lived" experiences of their subjects. The findings in this study poignantly suggest that the women "tuned in" closely to information that they recognized as directly relevant to their personal lives. Culture appears to frame the issues that women paid attention to, suggesting that messages, be they political or altruistic, must be delivered in a way that is culturally congruent with and personally pertinent to peoples' lives.[55] Comments about experiences with racial prejudice, neighborhood drugs, and violence corroborated Dalton's thesis that minorities are suspicious of the white majority's defining their problems and proposing solutions for them. For the women, private problems are located in historical events and social structures; their lives clearly demonstrated the impact of white domination and made more understandable their resistance to AIDS prevention efforts, which they perceived to be directed by an alien, predominantly white power structure. Even so, the women appeared to benefit from the intervention strategies, gaining an increased knowledge about how AIDS is spread; a better understanding of how to protect themselves against pregnancy, STD, and AIDS; and enough self-confidence to take protective actions.

Clarification of safe sex practices appeared to be a paramount need. The women confirmed that adolescents, particularly from minority cultures, are not understanding AIDS prevention messages as they are written. Since sexual discussions rarely take place in their cultures, sex education must take place elsewhere. However, if STD-prevention messages are produced using language adolescents can recognize, the public might find these distasteful. The most sensible solution would be to create small personalized prevention initiatives that can be organized in a variety of settings. In addition, these initiatives must take into account the youthful appetite for sex. STD preventions must include ways of conducting safe sex while engaging in multiple sexual encounters within a short time span. Since pregnancy is still a pervasive concern for many young women, it might be useful for education programs to continue to focus on pregnancy as the most likely outcome of unprotected sex.[56] Furthermore, these initiatives should provide information about how alcohol and drugs pose a threat to responsible sexual behavior.

Trust is an important issue with young people in general and with urban minority young people in particular. If they are willing to try behavioral change based on information and skills promoted by teachers, researchers, and health professionals, relying on them and accepting their information, professional ethics demand offering help in dealing with the personal and cultural difficulties that arise for these groups. The responsibility of professionals becomes even greater with inner city adolescents, who must expend so much energy to avoid any form of anxiety. Once a bond is formed, people will return to authority figures for support and advice. A strong relationship can be used to further the acceptance and continued practice of safe behavior, as well as to make leaders out of some of the youth themselves. As the cognitive and social skills of young people increase and mature over the course of an intervention effort, it is important to allow time for messages to sink in and to offer periodic "boosters" of health information and emotional support.

Small groups are a powerful means for handling increased anxiety and a vehicle for integrating problem-solving and personal coping techniques into women's everyday lives. Small groups can be used to empower women by providing a setting in which they can express inner fears and gain acceptance and encouragement from others. The social interaction in a group can serve to develop standards of behavior different from previous behavior patterns.[57] Peer acceptance in this project seemed to be enough to help women fend for themselves and demand safe sex practices. It appears that other women's approval is important and can strengthen womens' resolve to protect themselves and deal with the men in their lives.

The means for preventing STD must be accessible. Recommending behaviors that are difficult to carry out or financially costly are useless and can cause more distress than comfort and cure. For example, telling young women to use condoms to avoid AIDS or other STD and/or pregnancy is fine if condoms are readily available. The fact that some of the women in the present study were inconsistent in using protection despite the information they were receiving weekly could be attributed at least in part to the inconsistent availability of condoms combined with the spontaneity and frequency with which young people participate in sexual activity. At college, condom accessibility may make their use easier. At home in their inner-city neighborhoods, however, young women may have difficulty obtaining protection, not only because they are reluctant to violate local norms, but also because their finances are limited. Condoms are not cheap. Young women on limited incomes must decide how to spend these few resources. Given the choice of condoms, a sweater, or even a movie, some women will not choose condoms. Since AIDS is a public health problem, its prevention should be a public health issue. Condoms need to be free and readily available.

SKILL DEVELOPMENT

AIDS prevention programs must go beyond providing information and take a comprehensive approach, offering young people a full range of skills tailored to their specific age group and cultural needs, as well as to environmental settings that will enable them to make behavioral changes.[58] Decreased embarrassment in talking about personal matters and help in developing confidence to demand safe-sex behaviors must be taught, especially to young women. Providing skills for behavioral change improves self-efficacy and helps increase the likelihood that these behaviors will be continued. Self-confidence and knowledge come from concrete information, but every age group needs learning in which they feel comfortable discussing, carrying, touching, buying, and using condoms. Finally, help in anticipating events is important. Role-playing and consideration of "what if" questions are useful techniques. However, use of peer modeling to increase the acceptability of specific behaviors appears to be the most valuable approach.

NOTES

[1]R. Veatch, "Voluntary Risks to Health: The Ethical Issues," In *Moral Problems in Medicine*, 2nd. ed., ed. S. Gorovitz, R. Macklin, A. Jameton, J. O'Connor, and S. Sherwin (Englewood Cliffs, N.J.: Prentice-Hall, 1980), 578–586.

[2]P. Conrad, and J. Schneider, *Deviance and Medicalization: From Badness to Sickness* (St. Louis: Mosby, 1980).

[3]H. Dalton, "AIDS in Blackface," *Daedalus* 118(1989):205–227.

[4]Ibid.

[5]E. Brandt, "Implications of the Acquired Immunodeficiency Syndrome for Health Policy," *Annals of Internal Medicine* 103(1985):771–773.

[6]V. De La Cancela, "Minority AIDS Prevention: Moving Beyond Cultural Perspectives Towards Sociopolitical Empowerment," *AIDS Education and Prevention* 1(1989):141–153.

[7]S. Thomas, and S. Quinn, "The Tuskegee Syphilis Study, 1932 to 1972: Implications for HIV Education and AIDS Risk Education Programs in the Black Community," *American Journal of Public Health* 81(1991):1498–1504.

[8]A. Davis, *Women, Race and Class* (New York: Vintage Books, 1981); (N. Freudenberg, "AIDS Prevention in the United States: Lessons from the First Decade," *International Journal of Health Services* 20 (1990):589–599; S. Thomas, A. Gilliam, and C. Iwrey, "Knowledge About AIDS and Reported Risk Behaviors Among Black College Students," *Journal of American College Health* 38(1989):61–66.

[9]See De La Cancela; Thomas, Gilliam, and Iwrey.

[10]Dalton, 217.

[11]Ibid.

[12]S. Friedman, D. DesJarlais, and C. Sterk, "AIDS and The Social Relations of Intravenous Drug Users," *The Milbank Quarterly* 68(1990):85–110.

[13]J. Peterson and G. Marin, "Issues in the Prevention of AIDS Among Black and Hispanic Men," *American Psychologist* 43(1988):871–877.

[14]Stenger-Castro, E. "The Mexican American: How Culture Affects His Mental Health," in *Hispanic Culture and Health Care*, ed. P. Martinez, (St. Louis: Mosby, 1978), 19–32.

[15]See Davis; also R. Valdiserri, V. Arena, D. Proctor, and F. Bonati, "The Relationship Between Women's Attitudes About Condoms and Their Use: Implications for Condom Promotion Programs," *American Journal of Public Health* 79(1989):499–501.

[16]N. Weinstein, "The Precaution Adoption Process," *Health Psychology* 7(1988):355–386.

[17]W. Kane, and E. Duryea, "The Role of Education and Extracurricular Activities," in *The Health of Adolescents*, ed., W. Hendee, (San Francisco: Jossey-Bass, 1991), 139–161.

[18]D. Haffner, "The AIDS Epidemic Implications for the Sexuality Education of Our Youth," *Siecus* 16(1988):1–5.

[19]R. Lau, M. Quadrel, and K. Hartman, "Development and Change of Young Adults' Preventive Health Beliefs and Behavior: Influence from Parents and Peers," *Journal of Health and Social Behavior* 31(1990):240–259.

[20]P. Evans, "Minorities and AIDS," *Health Education Research* 3(1988):113–115.

[21]J. Curran, W. Morgan, A. Hardy, H. Jaffe, W. Darrow, and W. Dowdle, "The Epidemiology of AIDS: Current Status and Future Prospects," *Science* 27 September 1985, p. 1352.

[22]R. DiClemente, "Adolescents: An Emerging AIDS Risk Group," *MIRA* 4(1990):3; also, S., Hofferth, J. Kahn, and W. Baldwin, "Premarital Sexual Activity Among U.S. Teenage Women over the Past Three Decades," *Family Planning Perspectives* 19(1987):46–49.

[23]DiClemente.

[24]D. Gibbs, D. Hamill, and K. Magruder-Habib, "Populations at Increased Risk of HIV Infection: Current Knowledge and Limitations," *Journal of Acquired Immune Deficiency Syndromes* 4(1991):881–889.

[25]R. Schilling, F. Schinke, S. Nichols, S. Zayas, L. Miller, S. Orlandi, and G. Botvin,"Developing Strategies for AIDS Prevention Research with Black and Hispanic Drug Users," *Public Health Report* 104(1989):2–11.

[26]Alan Guttmacher Institute, *Teenage Pregnancy: The Problem That Hasn't Gone Away* (New York: Alan Guttmacher Institute, 1981).

[27]D. Thompson, "A Losing Battle with AIDS," *Time*, 2 July 1990, pp. 42–44.

[28]L. Winter, "The Role of Sexual Self-Concept in the Use of Contraceptions," *Family Planning Perspective* 20(1988):123–127.

[29]R. Schilling, N. El-Bassel, S. Schinke, S. Nichols, G. Botvin, and M. Orlandi, "Sexual Behavior, Attitudes Towards Safer Sex, and Gender Among a Cohort of 244 Recovering IV Drug Users," *International Journal of the Addictions* 26(1991):859–877.

[30]J. Adler, L. Wright, J. McGormick, P. Annin, A. Cohen, M. Talbot, M. Hager, and E. Yoffe, "Safer Sex," *Newsweek*, 9 December 1991, p. 56.

[31]W. Cates, and J. Rauh, "Adolescents and Sexually Transmitted Diseases: An Expanding Problem," *Journal of Adolescent Health Care* 6(1985):257–261.

[32]R. DiClemente, C. Boyer, and S. Mills, "Prevention of AIDS Among Adolescents: Strategies for the Development of Comprehensive Risk-Reduction Health Education Programs," *Health Education Research* 2(1987):287–291.

[33]K. Hein, "Commentary on Adolescent Acquired Immunodeficiency Syndrome: The Next Wave of the Human Immunodeficiency Virus Epidemic," *Journal of Pediatrics* 114(1989):144–149.

[34]Centers for Disease Control (CDC), Division of STD/HIV Prevention, *Annual Report* (Atlanta: U.S. Department of Health and Human Services, Public Health Service, 1992).

[35]L. Dusenbury, G. Botvin, E. Baker, and J. Laurence, "AIDS Risk Knowledge, Attitudes, and Behavioral Intentions Among Multi-Ethnic Adolescents," *AIDS Education and Prevention* 3(1991):367–375.

[36]J. Fisher, "Possible Effects of Reference Group–Based Social Influence on AIDS-Risk Behavior and AIDS Prevention," *American Psychologist* 43(1988):914–920.

[37]M. Singer, "Confronting the AIDS Epidemic Among IV Drug Users: Does Ethnic Culture Matter?" *AIDS Education and Prevention* 3(1991):258–283.

[38]P. Conrad, "The Social Meaning of AIDS," *Social Policy* 17(1986):51–56.

[39]See W. Atkinson, V. Kitsanes, and S. Hassig, "Knowledge and Attitudes About AIDS Among College Freshman in Louisiana" (Paper presented at the 3rd International Conference on AIDS, Washington, D.C., June 1987) J. D. Baldwin and J. I. Baldwin, "AIDS Information and Sexual Behavior on a University Campus," *Journal of Sex Education and Therapy* 14(1988):24–28; D. Chervin and A. Martinez, *Survey on the Health of Stanford Students* (Stanford: Cowell Student Health Center, Stanford University, 1987); V. Freimuth, T. Edgar, and S. Hammond, "College Students; Awareness and Interpretation of the AIDS Risk," *Science Technology and Human Values* 12(1987):37–44; R. McDermott, M. Hawkins, J. Moore, and S. Cittadino, "AIDS Awareness and Information Sources Among Selected University Students," *Journal of*

American College Health 35(1987):222–226. See also, H. Fineberg, "Education to Prevent AIDS: Prospects and Obstacles," *Science* 239(1988):592–596, for a discussion of this lack of change.

[40]Baldwin and Baldwin; McDermott et al.

[41]Hayes, 1987.

[42]T. Edgar, V. Freimuth, and S. Hammond, "Communicating the AIDS Risk to College Students: The Problem of Motivating Change," *Health Education Research* 3(1988):59–65.

[43]R. DiClemente, "Predictors of HIV-Preventive Sexual Behavior in a High-Risk Adolescent Population: The Influence of Perceived Peer Norms and Sexual Communication on Incarcerated Adolescents' Consistent Use of Condoms," *Society for Adolescent Medicine* 12(1991):385–390.

[44]A. Strauss, *Qualitative Analysis for Social Scientists* (Cambridge, Mass.: Harvard University Press, 1987).

[45]J. Garbarino, N. Dubrow, K. Kostelny, and C. Pardo, *Children in Danger: Coping with the Consequence of Community Violence* (San Francisco: Jossey-Bass, 1992).

[46]F. Rhodes, and R. Wolitski, "Effect of Instructional Videotapes on AIDS Knowledge and Attitudes," *Journal of American College Health* 37(1989):266–271.

[47]This variety of activities is similar to ones described by A. Lareau, and L. Hendrix, "The Spread of AIDS Among Heterosexuals: A Classroom Simulation," *Teaching Sociology* 15(1987):316–319.

[48]B. Hubbard, *Entering Adulthood: Preventing Sexually Related Diseases*, in Contemporary Health Series, ed. K. Middleton (Santa Cruz, Calif.: Network Publications, 1989).

[49]Schilling et al.

[50]Ibid.

[51]D. Morgan, *Focus Groups as Qualitative Research* (Newbury Park, Calif.: Sage, 1988).

[52]See Dalton.

[53]W. Gardner, and J. Herman, "Adolescents' AIDS Risk Taking: A Rational Choice Perspective," *New Directions for Child Development* 50(1990):17–34.

[54]These findings are similar to those discussed by C. Weisman, S. Plichta, C. Nathanson, G. Chase, M. Ensminger, and J. Robinson, "Adolescent Women's Contraceptive Decision Making," *Journal of Health and Social Behavior* 32(1991):130–144; and C. Woodard, "Smart Women, Foolish Choices," *In View*, May/June 1991.

[55]W. Gamson, "A Constructionist Approach to Mass Media and Public Opinion," *Symbolic Interaction* 11(1988):161–174.

[56]M. Eisen, and G. Zellman, "The Role of Health Belief Attitudes, Sex Education, and Demographics in Predicting Adolescent Sexual Knowledge," *Health Education Quarterly* 13(1986):9–22.

[57]R. Merton, M. Fiske, and P. Kendall, *The Focused Interview: A Manual of Problems and Procedures*, 2nd ed. (New York: Free Press, 1990).

[58]F. Sy, D. Richter, and G. Copello, "Innovative Educational Strategies and Recommendations for AIDS Prevention and Control," *AIDS Education and Prevention* 1(1989):53–56.

REFERENCES

Adler, J., L. Wright, J. McGormick, P. Annin, A. Cohen, M. Talbot, M. Hager, and E. Yoffe, "Safer Sex," *Newsweek,* 9 December, 1991, 52–56.

Alan Guttmacher Institute. *Teenage Pregnancy: The Problem That Hasn't Gone Away.* New York: Alan Guttmacher Institute, 1981.

Atkinson W., V. Kitsanes, and S. Hassig. "Knowledge and Attitudes About AIDS Among College Freshmen in Louisiana." Paper presented at the 3rd International Conference on AIDS, Washington, D.C., June 1987.

Baldwin, J. D., and J. I. Baldwin. "AIDS Information and Sexual Behavior on a University Campus." *Journal of Sex Education and Therapy* 14(1988):24–28.

Brandt, E. "Implications of the Acquired Immunodeficiency Syndrome for Health Policy." *Annals of Internal Medicine* 103(1985):771–773.

Cates, W., and J. Rauh. "Adolescents and Sexually Transmitted Diseases: An Expanding Problem." *Journal of Adolescent Health Care*, 6(1985):257–261.

Centers for Disease Control (CDC), Division of STD/HIV Prevention. *Annual Report.* Atlanta: U.S. Department of Health and Human Services, Public Health Service, 1992.

Chervin, D., and A. Martinez. *Survey on the Health of Stanford Students.* Stanford: Cowell Student Health Center, Stanford University, 1987.

Conrad, P. "The Social Meaning of AIDS." *Social Policy* 17(1986):51–56.

Conrad, P., and J. Schneider. *Deviance and Medicalization: From Badness to Sickness.* St. Louis: Mosby, 1980.

Curran, J., W. Morgan, A. Hardy, H. Jaffe, W. Darrow, and W. Dowdle. "The Epidemiology of AIDS: Current Status and Future Prospects." *Science,* 27 September 1985, 1352.

Dalton, H., "AIDS in Blackface." *Daedalus* 118(1989):205–227.

Davis, A. *Women, Race and Class.* New York: Vintage Books, 1981.

De La Cancela, V. "Minority AIDS Prevention: Moving Beyond Cultural Perspectives Towards Sociopolitical Empowerment." *AIDS Education and Prevention* 1(1989):141–153.

DiClemente, R. "Adolescents: An Emerging AIDS Risk Group." *MIRA* 4(1990):3.

DiClemente, R. "Predictors of HIV–Preventive Sexual Behavior in a High-Risk Adolescent Population: The Influence of Perceived Peer Norms and Sexual Communication on Incarcerated Adolescents' Consistent Use of Condoms." *Society for Adolescent Medicine* 12(1991):385–390.

DiClemente, R., C. Boyer, and S. Mills, "Prevention of AIDS Among Adolescents: Strategies for the Development of Comprehensive Risk-Reduction Health Education Programs." *Health Education Research* 2(1987):287–291.

Dusenbury, L., G. Botvin, E. Baker, and J. Laurence. "AIDS Risk Knowledge, Attitudes, and Behavioral Intentions Among Multi-Ethnic Adolescents." *AIDS Education and Prevention* 3(1991):367–375.

Edgar, T., V. Freimuth, and S. Hammond. "Communicating the AIDS Risk to College Students: The Problem of Motivating Change." *Health Education Research* 3(1988):59–65.

Eisen, M., and G. Zellman. "The Role of Health Belief Attitudes, Sex Education, and Demographics in Predicting Adolescent Sexual Knowledge." *Health Education Quarterly* 13(1986):9–22.

Evans, P. "Minorities and AIDS." *Health Education Research* 3(1988):113–115.

Fineberg, H. "Education to Prevent AIDS: Prospects and Obstacles." *Science* 239(1988):592–596.

Fisher, J. "Possible Effects of Reference Group-Based Social Influence on AIDS-Risk Behavior and AIDS Prevention." *American Psychologist* 43(1988):914–920.

Freimuth V., T. Edgar, and S. Hammond. "College Students; Awareness and Interpretation of The AIDS Risk." *Science Technology and Human Values* 12(1987): 37–4.

Friedman, S., D. DesJarlais, and C. Sterk. "AIDS and The Social Relations of Intravenous Drug Users." *The Milbank Quarterly* 68(1990):85–110.

Freudenberg, N. "AIDS Prevention in the United States: Lessons from the First Decade." *International Journal of Health Services* 20(1990):589–599.

Gamson, W. "A Constructionist Approach to Mass Media and Public Opinion." *Symbolic Interaction* 11(1988):161–174.

Garbarino, J., N. Dubrow, K. Kostelny, and C. Pardo. *Children in Danger: Coping with the Consequence of Community Violence.* San Francisco: Jossey-Bass, 1992.

Gardner, W., and J. Herman. "Adolescents' AIDS Risk Taking: A Rational Choice Perspective." *New Directions for Child Development* 50 (1990):17–34.

Gibbs, D., D. Hamill, and K. Magruder-Habib. "Populations at Increased Risk of HIV Infection: Current Knowledge and Limitations." *Journal of Acquired Immune Deficiency Syndromes* 4(1991):881–889.

Haffner, D. "The AIDS Epidemic Implications for the Sexuality Education of Our Youth." *Siecus* 16(1988):1–5.

Hein, K. "Commentary on Adolescent Acquired Immunodeficiency Syndrome: The Next Wave of the Human Immunodeficiency Virus Epidemic." *Journal of Pediatrics* 114(1989):144–149.

Hofferth, S., J. Kahn, and W. Baldwin. "Premarital Sexual Activity Among U.S. Teenage Women over the Past Three Decades." *Family Planning Perspectives* 19(1987):46–49.

Hubbard, B. *Preventing Sexually Related Diseases.* In Contemporary Health Series, edited by K. Middleton. Santa Cruz, Calif.: Network Publications, 1989.

Kane, W., and E. Duryea. "The Role of Education and Extracurricular Activities." In *The Health of Adolescents*, edited by W. Hendree. San Francisco: Jossey-Bass, 1991.

Lareau, A., and L. Hendrix. "The Spread of AIDS Among Heterosexuals: A Classroom Simulation." *Teaching Sociology* 15(1987):316–319.

Lau, R., M. Quadrel, and K. Hartman. "Development and Change of Young Adults' Preventive Health Beliefs and Behavior: Influence from Parents and Peers." *Journal of Health and Social Behavior* 31(1990):240–259.

Mackenzie, R. "Substance Abuse." In *The Health of Adolescents*, edited by W. Hendree. San Francisco: Jossey-Bass, 1991.

McDermott, R., M. Hawkins, J. Moore, and S. Cittadino. "AIDS Awareness and Information Sources Among Selected University Students." *Journal of American College Health* 35(1987):222–226.

Merton, R., M. Fiske, and P. Kendall. *The Focused Interview: A Manual of Problems and Procedures.* 2nd ed. New York: Free Press, 1990.

Morgan, D. *Focus Groups as Qualitative Research.* Newbury Park, Calif.: Sage, 1988.

Peterson, J., and G. Marin. "Issues in the Prevention of AIDS Among Black and Hispanic Men." *American Psychologist* 43(1988):871–877.

Rhodes, F., and R. Wolitski. "Effect of Instructional Videotapes on AIDS Knowledge and Attitudes." *Journal of American College Health* 37(1989):266–271.

Schilling, R., N. El-Bassel, S. Schinke, S. Nichols, G. Botvin, and M. Orlandi. "Sexual Behavior, Attitudes Towards Safer Sex, and Gender Among a Cohort of 244 Recovering IV Drug Users." *International Journal of the Addictions* 26(1991):859–877.

Schilling, R., F. Schinke, S. Nichols, S. Zayas, L. Miller, S. Orlandi, and G. Botvin. "Developing Strategies for AIDS Prevention Research with Black and Hispanic Drug Users." *Public Health Report* 104(1989):2–11.

Simkins, L., and M. Eberhage. "Attitudes Towards AIDS, Herpes II, and Toxic Shock Syndrome." *Psychological Reports* 55(1984):779–786.

Singer, M. "Confronting the AIDS Epidemic Among IV Drug Users: Does Ethnic Culture Matter?" *AIDS Education and Prevention* 3(1991):258–283.

Stenger-Castro, E. "The Mexican American: How Culture Affects His Mental Health." In *Hispanic Culture and Health Care,* edited by R. Martinez. St. Louis: Mosby, 1978.

Strauss, A. *Qualitative Analysis for Social Scientists.* Cambridge, Mass.: Harvard University Press, 1987.

Sy, F., D. Richter, and G. Copello. "Innovative Educational Strategies and Recommendations for AIDS Prevention and Control." *AIDS Education and Prevention* 1(1989):53–56.

Thomas, S., A. Gilliam, and C. Iwrey. "Knowledge About AIDS and Reported Risk Behaviors Among Black College Students." *Journal of American College Health* 38(1989):61–66.

Thomas, S., and S. Quinn. "The Tuskegee Syphilis Study, 1932 to 1972: Implications for HIV Education and AIDS Risk Education Programs in the Black Community." *American Journal of Public Health* 81(1991):1498–1504.

Thompson, D. "A Losing Battle with AIDS." *Time,* 2 July 1990, 42–44.

Valdiserri, R., V. Arena, D. Proctor, and F. Bonati. "The Relationship Between Women's Attitudes About Condoms and Their Use: Implications for Condom Promotion Programs." *American Journal of Public Health* 79(1989):499–501.

Veatch, R. "Voluntary Risks to Health: The Ethical Issues." In *Moral Problems in Medicine,* edited by S. Gorovitz, R. Macklin, A. Jameton, J. O'Connor, and S. Sherwin. 2nd ed. Englewood Cliffs, N.J.: Prentice-Hall, 1980.

Weinstein, N. "The Precaution Adoption Process." *Health Psychology* 7(1988):355–386.

Weisman, C., S. Plichta, C. Nathanson, G. Chase, M. Ensminger, and J. Robinson.

"Adolescent Women's Contraceptive Decision Making." *Journal of Health and Social Behavior* 32(1991):130–144.

Widen, H. "The Risk of AIDS and the Defense of Disapproval: Dilemmas for the College Psychotherapist. *College Health* 35(1987):268–273.

Winter, L. "The Role of Sexual Self-Concept in the Use of Contraceptions." *Family Planning Perspective* 20(1988):123–127.

Woodard, C. "Smart Women, Foolish Choices." *In View*, May/June 1991.

Ntombifuthi Agnes Mtshali

Transferability of American AIDS Prevention Models to South African Youth

Since the early 1980s, AIDS has been spoken about in many countries. It became a household word in South Africa in the late eighties. And today an average ten-year-old who has been exposed to some form of health education knows about AIDS.

Most people still talk about AIDS as a remote threat that is somehow unlikely to harm them. Still others are quite concerned about, even afraid of, what might happen to them and their families should they get AIDS. Listen to the voices of a group of women discussing the effects of AIDS on their lives:

> You are asking me about AIDS? Hey! I don't even want to think about it. It scares the living daylights out of me. I don't think I can live another day after hearing that I have AIDS. How can I look my children in the eye and tell them that I am dying any day any time?

> What? My husband coming back from the city with this AIDS? He had better stay there because I am not having my family going through the pain of watching him die. After all, it wouldn't be me that gave it to him. I know I am clean.

> Don't say that. You don't know what you are talking about. Your husband has been coming home once a month, yet you think that if he had AIDS today, you would be clean. Forget it. We really do have a problem. Us women have to stay at home while these men are messing around the city, and they bring home more pain and suffering than money.

> This actually scares me. My husband works in a big city and comes home every three months. Who knows what he is doing there? You really make me want to run away from my own life. To think that, even as I am talking to you, I might be a walking time bomb.

> All I see is a future where there are no young adults. The way these children carry on with sex, it's like it is going out of fashion. How many of them ever think about AIDS? How many of them see it as a reality? You know, some of these teenagers think they are untouchable. They think they cannot get AIDS because they have sex only during school holidays and even then only once.

> Well, sometimes I think we adults are responsible. How often do we talk about the virus? People talk about the sickness, yet teenagers never get to see somebody with AIDS. After all, how long does it take before somebody is really

sick? They have never seen a teenager with AIDS, yet there are hundreds of them with the virus and are positive. Do they even know what it means to be HIV-positive?

No! Stop! You are reminding me of that ad on television and posters that had a coffin and a handful of people around it paying their last respects. You know what? People started looking at the whole picture critically. Blacks saw the funeral as a big joke, because when they bury, it is an occasion. There are usually hundreds of people accompanying the bereaved family. This made them doubt the reality of AIDS.

This is the general conversation you pick up when women discuss AIDS. In rural areas, the media, in particular the radio, have been instrumental in developing AIDS awareness. Women there may not be very clear about what AIDS really is or what a person with AIDS looks like, because they have never seen one; however, they do talk about it. While they go on with their lives believing that they are safe, they still worry about their husbands and sons who are in the city and are likely to be caught in the grip of city life and its loose morals.

In and beyond the rural areas, South Africa has four distinct racial groups—whites, coloreds, Asians, and blacks. The blacks are African people. The African people are further divided into ethnic groups which have been geographically and politically segregated into homelands, while others have remained in the Republic of South Africa. In 1993 the republic itself was still divided into four groups of department and parliamentary houses. The whites fell into the House of Assembly, Asians fell under the House of Delegates, the coloreds fell under the House of Representatives, and Africans fell under the House of General Affairs, administered by whites for the Africans. There were 10 homelands which, along with the republic's 4 groups, made up 14 departments of health education.

Any form of health education therefore ends up having 14 variations, all prioritized differently depending on the department and house. The distribution of funds is also based on the "superiority of races," with whites first, followed by Asians, coloreds, and finally Africans. The Africans, who are in the majority, receive very little.

This article will look at how we may learn from the traditional African way of life in preventing AIDS, how that way of life can be blended with modern trends in health education. Although tradition seems to be a thing of the past, it continues to affect the lives of its people. I will also touch on African patterns of social control and order, to see how they, too, could help save lives today.

EXTENDED FAMILIES AND GRANDMOTHERS

Traditionally, the family is key to Africans. Extended families in particular were the expected form of domestic life. Grandparents lived with their siblings and with the grandchildren in one homestead. One family could be as large as 30 or 40 members. While the parents were busy in the fields and with other chores, the grandparents would spend most of their time talking to the younger ones. This was not just idle talk. This was how children learned about the family, the clan, and the community, as well as about right and wrong. Children always listened to their grannies. Sex education was also the granny's task.

Today, the grannies are a thing of the past, with Africans having been forced by circumstances to adopt nuclear family forms. It is still common today to find grannies in rural areas and nuclear families in the city. Parents have never before been responsible for sex education and this is where tradition holds them back. They know what to say but do not know when and how to say it.

Prevention models thus might take parenting as a good starting point. Parents need to be well informed on sexuality, especially adolescent sexuality. They need to be trained to communicate with their own children in general, as well as about sexuality. After all, sex talk has been taboo for ages—only grannies could talk to their grandchildren about sex. With improved parenting skills, the parents will be equipped with the necessary tools to tackle the subject of sexuality with confidence. They will also be able to address the most feared topic of all: HIV/AIDS. When parents get to the point where they can openly discuss such topics with their own children, then one may say that health workers have begun making a mark.

DECISION-MAKING MODELS

In African families, decision making is done by the adults, usually the father. In the absence of the father, the mother takes over, but only if she has strong ties to older family members, like her husband's brothers or uncles, if the grandparents are already dead. Children never contribute to decisions. They are expected to do as they are told. In the past, there were minimal problems with this kind of setup, because there was always an adult at hand to support the younger ones.

Today, a teenage girl must make decisions on a daily basis—a new task for her. She must decide what she wants to study at school, what friends to choose, how to spend her pocket money, what to wear for various occasions, which boyfriend to choose, and how far to go with him. She finds herself in a dilemma, which is compounded by the fact that females are expected to defer to males when it comes to decision making. Over the generations, young girls have been told that males are superior, know everything, and must be heeded. Female young adults are easily talked out of the choices they have made because they lack strong support.

The decision-making models that health workers typically teach teenagers would have a tremendous impact on South African youth—especially in the African ethnic groups. It is very easy for a teenager to make a mistake and simply say, "I didn't think." She needs to be educated to realize that "not thinking" is not an option; rather, she must admit that she has made a wrong choice and learn from it. Once her decision-making processes are strong and well applied, then she will be able to make the right choices, even on issues like when to have sex, with whom, and how. She will be able to make a choice concerning abstinence, safer sex, and so on.

THE CONTINUITY OF PEER EDUCATION

In the past, African sex education was done by grannies and peers. With the grannies it was informal, but with peers it was a more formal schooling that took place away from the main family residence. Older adolescents were responsible for educating younger ones—starting at puberty. They told females how their bodies functioned and what foods to avoid, lest their blood run so hot that they would fail to resist sexual pressure from males. They taught girls about courting and what to do during the process. Bigger sisters told them what to do, so they did not make their own decisions. Virginity was upheld as the highest value in a girl's life. Girls had to avoid all sexual advances until given permission by their sisters to accept petting— but not penile penetration. Any girl who lost her virginity was a disgrace to herself, her family, and the girls of her village. She was ostracized and suffered much shame.

Such schooling was very strong and passed on down the generations. It slowly disappeared with colonization, urbanization, Christianity, and civilization. The adolescents found themselves in a situation in which the church told them that the body was the temple of the Lord and that, as such, it must be respected. It did not tell them how to cope with sexual desires and advances. At this point, the grannies were no longer available to tell them what to do, and peer education fell off, as it was seen to be un-Christian. Parents knew what to say but not when or how to say it. They also felt strongly that it was not their responsibility.

Today, peer counseling once again seems to be the best solution, because teenagers listen better to their peers. The old and the new can be married. With more relevant information added to traditional values regarding teenage sexuality, a more acceptable, tradition-based model of sexuality can be born. This would then —eventually—allow teenagers to accept information and topics covered as their own.

The various curricula that have been used in sex education need to be adapted for South African youth. Information and knowledge, decision making and values clarification, abstinence programs and risk reduction would all be part of the core curriculum for South African youth. They need the information and knowledge about their sexuality. They need to know how and when to make decisions. Their values are confused, so they need to have them clarified so that they can make sense of them and learn to cherish them. They need to be taught assertiveness—especially females, who are regarded as minors. They need to be taught about safe-sex methods, such as the advantages and disadvantages of abstinence. Finally, they need to be taught the skills and strategies to resist peer and partner pressure. Mothers would also need to be well equipped with sex education information and skills, to serve as a source of reference and reinforcement. Mothers in particular are important because they are usually readily available, approachable, and sensitive to teenagers' needs and problems. They will usually try to work toward finding solutions rather than casting blame.

The youth have already structured themselves into social clubs, such as drama groups, singing groups (especially gospel music), sports like soccer and netball, and many more. They engage in these activities after school and on weekends. Such groups would provide a ready-made structure in which trained peer educators could provide information on HIV/AIDS and influence youth groups to think positively about HIV protection. The peer educators, of course, would have to be good role models. They, in turn, would need constant support from centers like the AIDS Training and Information Center (ATIC), where they could be updated on the latest developments. They should also be able to attend seminars organized to impart information on HIV/AIDS, from prevention to coping skills.

In formal schools there should be peer educators as well. In African schools, sex education is only now getting started, most often taught by health personnel. Where possible, all teachers are trained to address the topic at every available moment—over and above its own time slot in the curriculum. In most African schools, however, sex education has not even reached the classroom. It may take a long time before HIV/AIDS is discussed openly in class. AIDS educators may be invited into the schools, but there is need for even more of them, to be able to cover all schools, churches, clubs, and homes.

School-based youth centers where teenagers can get all the necessary counseling are not available. Contraceptive services for teenagers are not yet looked upon favorably. Most parents are opposed to contraception, stating that teenagers should have strong enough willpower to abstain. Even the ever-escalating numbers of teenagers becoming pregnant every year has not taught them otherwise. Sadder still, the adolescent age of pregnancy is dropping, now occurring between the ages of 12 and 15 years. Most of these teenagers simply do not understand the relationship between sexual intercourse and pregnancy. All they know is that they are or were playing a "game." This is the language boys use when they approach the girls: they say they will play a special game just for the two of them. It therefore becomes important to reach out to teenagers at a very early age. A large group of children are falling prey to ignorance.

One should not be deceived that this is an easy task. South Africans are still in a world of their own concerning AIDS. Most of them are still caught up in debating the origins of HIV/AIDS: Is it American or is it African? For them this is an easier battle to fight; it gives them the chance to escape through blaming someone else rather than dealing with the problem. African people have often found themselves being blamed for the spread of the disease. Because our large population lacks funds, accessible health services, and basic health services like clean water and sanitation, Africans have been blamed for the outbreak of cholera, gastroenteritis, scabies, TB, and other diseases.

So, even with AIDS they feel the government is just applying another strategy to fight against the large numbers of Africans. The older generations want to know where this AIDS was before and during their time. Why must it come now, just when they need all people alive to effect a change in the government? Is it yet another government strategy to cut down the number of African people? Since there is no cure it becomes very difficult to convince them otherwise.

Teenagers have labeled it "AIDS—America's Idea to Discourage Sex." It is not surprising to have them thinking it is American because, for them, anything new has been said to be American. Thus, when addressing youth, it is important to break through these barriers before talking about HIV/AIDS. Peer education will facilitate a wider outreach to teenagers, and I strongly believe that it is one curriculum that should be vigorously exploited and utilized.

THE ROLE OF TRADITIONAL HEALERS

The popularity of traditional healers has never faded; African people will almost always apply traditional measures to cope with any illness before resorting to Western medicine. Even when someone is admitted to the hospital, family and friends do not stop bringing concoctions prepared to fight the disease. This is also true of the Asians who use the temple to seek various cures and to ward off bad spirits.

Traditional healers are highly trusted, the supernatural aspect of the relationship produces confidence. Traditional healers spiritually call upon the sick person's or family ancestors to be present to help the healers sort out the problems. Indeed, the healers communicate their findings as directed by these particular ancestors. At the end of the session, the client or patient feels he or she has been treated as a unique individual.

Because traditional healers are so vitally linked to the people, they could have an early and crucial place in AIDS education. For example, education on using personal razor blades and cleaning equipment thoroughly is gaining momentum. People have started carrying their own razor blades when they visit traditional healers. This could provide a natural transition to discussing other hygiene measures.

For a long time, traditional healing has been dismissed by Western medicine, yet people never stopped going to the healers. Now we need to incorporate them into health teams, especially when we speak of comprehensive primary health care. Their role can be very significant when it comes to HIV/AIDS, because people believe in them and are more willing to do what the healers say.

USE OF SUPPORT SYSTEMS

The traditional extended family system allowed for communal living without ignoring respect for person or personal property. Traditionally, all adults were parents. They were able to correct, discipline, scold, protect, and even punish any child, not only their own. Today the African people are in transition—culturally, socially, politically, religiously. Parents can discipline only their own children; if they go further they are likely to face an offended, angry parent who feels he or she is being undermined. But even though traditions are changing, the support system is still strong. The African people still do away with formalities both in need and abundance. Time means nothing when a brother is in need; they may even lose their jobs if necessary, as long as they have satisfied a brother's need.

Support systems for people with AIDS could be set up along the same traditional lines with variations and adaptations here and there to fit in with the needs of these special people. Traditionally, African people take care of their own. Applying the same principle to people with AIDS, they can be trained to look after their own instead of setting up cold, remote homes. The American model has the advantage of support among people with AIDS themselves. This should be adopted in South Africa as well, as it reduces loneliness. The adults will need to set an example for the teenagers. HIV/AIDS is still very much in the closet and there is a strong need for people with AIDS to come out. It took South African homosexuals a long time but they are coming out; now they can even hold marches. The communities will need to be more accepting, understanding, supportive, and caring so that AIDS sufferers may feel that they still belong. This will teach children to love their fellows regardless of their plight.

People will need to learn to talk about AIDS as openly as possible. They need to be encouraged through seminars, workshops, and media exposure. African people are usually able to talk about things, especially those that touch their feelings. When they fail to talk, they act as though they are angry and start a fight. To encourage them to talk will also help ease the tension that surrounds AIDS. In opening up, they will get more support from family and friends, and even beyond those two circles.

Dramatization of the disease, so that people can see as well as listen, is also essential. Acting reaches out to people. Drama groups could send the message, and although this has already started, we need more of these groups to reach out to the various communities with presentations adapted to suit various target groups. The youth social groups would fit well in this strategy. The youth like music and singing, and using rap music to reach them could be very effective. There are, of course, other styles of traditionally African music that could also be used.

In conclusion, a great deal can be adopted from American prevention and management models, but if the models are to succeed, they must adapt through links with African tradition. This grafting of models would allow the African people to design strategies that would truly be their own. Internally, some issues would need to be addressed immediately:

- The illegal polygamy of extramarital affairs that may bring home not only misery and pain, but also sexually transmitted diseases like HIV/AIDS.
- The practice of keeping the menfolk away from home working in the mines, visiting their families only monthly, every three months, or even once a year. This causes smaller "families" to develop in the city when men are not allowed to bring their wives to the working place.
- The undermining of the role played by traditional healers in the general health of an African person. They will have to share the same platform with Western doctors if the health needs of Africans are to be met fully.
- The availability and accessibility of health services for all people, especially in rural communities. Health plans that make care available but are too costly for most people will not work. In the provision of services, need should be the criterion, not color or racial "superiority."
- Equal educational opportunities for all people of South Africa. With the appropriate education and with basic needs met, health education will fall on fertile ground, and HIV/AIDS prevention will not sound like some distant warning signal.

Peer education will be well meshed into the traditional educational strategies. If the old yet familiar is married with the new and foreign, a divorce is not likely. Drawing a similarity between modern prevention methods and the traditional ones allows for freer acceptance and compliance with the modern trends of disease prevention and treatment. The traditional support systems will need to be widely exploited in order to get support for HIV/AIDS patients and sufferers. Safer sex and condom use education need to reach out to all youth at home, schools, churches, clubs, centers, and gatherings, both modern urban and rural traditional.

The road ahead is long and rough; however, constant sharing with other countries and accepting AIDS as a reality will serve as a springboard for prevention education. The youth is at the top of the priority list, without them, there will be no adult population. If they are given tools to prevent and avoid contact with the virus, then there is hope that one day a cure or vaccine will be found, and that HIV/AIDS can be counted with the likes of tuberculosis, leprosy, and smallpox.

Constructing the Outreach Moment: Street Interventions to Women at Risk

I n successful intervention programs to reach women at high risk for HIV infection, trust is the most essential component; in outreach work trust is established when women from the community identify with the outreach worker and claim her as "one of their own." The paraprofessional outreach workers come from the communities they now work in, so they are culturally sensitive and have personal knowledge of high-risk sex and drug behavior. This chapter explores strategies that were found to be effective in a Los Angeles–based program.

In 1987, the National Institute on Drug Abuse funded a three-year, multisite study of women at high risk of HIV infection. This project, known as the Women and AIDS Risk Network (WARN), was conducted in Los Angeles, Phoenix, and Boston. When funding for Los Angeles WARN began to diminish, new monies were sought on county, state, and federal levels to allow for continued outreach to women in the Los Angeles area. As funding for the national WARN project ended, a private, nonprofit Los Angeles agency, called PROTOTYPES: A Center for Innovation in Health, Mental Health and Social Service, sought new funding to continue the work. In 1990, as new grants and contracts were funded, WARN became the AIDS prevention division of the umbrella agency PROTOTYPES.[1]

Although funding sources and organizational structure have changed, outreach to women in Los Angeles continued despite changes in funding sources and organizational structure. Throughout the past five years, WARN has conducted outreach to thousands of women in several communities within Los Angeles County. Outreach techniques have been modified and strengthened as they have grown from trial-and-error discovery to a field-tested strategy. The material for this chapter relies on in-depth interviews with six members of the WARN staff, all of whom either currently are or have been community outreach workers, and on participant observations conducted in the field.

THE WOMEN AND THE PROGRAM

Although particular funding sources determine the specific target populations and geographic locations of outreach, WARN generally conducts

Many thanks to Dr. Vivian Brown and Ruth Slaughter for their comments, and to all the women at WARN, especially Lori, Marina, Mary, Nicole, Nina, and Olivia.

outreach to women with one or more of the following risk behaviors: injection drug use, noninjection drug use, exchange of sex for drugs or money, sexual contact with one or more injection drug users, and/or former drug use. When fully staffed, WARN employs approximately 20 full-time community outreach workers, who conduct outreach to the following communities on a daily basis: South-Central Los Angeles, Watts, downtown Los Angeles, Hollywood, the Wilshire district, Silverlake, Boyle Heights, East Los Angeles, City Terrace, Santa Monica, Venice, and Mar Vista. All of the neighborhoods visited within these communities are low income and predominantly African American and Latino.

WARN outreach workers are indigenous to the communities they serve. This is not to say that every outreach worker must have engaged in sex work or injection drug use to be hired at WARN; however, all outreach workers must identify on *some* level with the target population. Throughout the article, Lori, Marina, Mary, Nicole, Nina, and Olivia (introduced alphabetically), will share their knowledge of the field as well as their feelings about and strategies for outreach.

Lori   is a 30-year-old African American who has been working for WARN for two years. She started as a prevention specialist worker and currently holds a supervisory and administrative position. Lori does not have a history of drug or alcohol addiction; however, she identifies herself as a woman who has been in abusive relationships. Lori holds a B.S. degree in health administration from a midwestern university.

Marina is a 22-year-old Latina. She is currently pregnant with her first child. Marina was a teenage alcoholic/addict who survived incest, molestation, rape, and two lockups in an institution for the mentally ill. Despite drug and alcohol addiction, Marina graduated from high school and was awarded a full scholarship at a prestigious East Coast university. However, she used her scholarship money to buy drugs. Marina has been working for WARN for more than two years, starting as the teenage outreach worker and gradually moving up to her present supervisory and administrative position.

Mary   is a 37-year-old African American who identifies as lesbian and has one child. Mary has been working for WARN as a community outreach worker for nine months. She spent several years on the streets as a noninjection drug user and alcoholic. For years, Mary exchanged sex for money and drugs and, as a result, temporarily lost her child to the system. She has also survived incest and battering relationships. Clean and sober for five years, Mary now lives with her son and often shares with women on the street the pain of losing her child and the process of getting him back.

Nicole is a 39-year-old African American. She has three children. Her oldest, born when Nicole was 12 years old, was conceived when

Nicole was raped by her stepfather. She had her third and last child at 18. Nicole began drinking and using drugs at the age of 16 and continued for 20 years. Her favorite injection drug was heroin, and her noninjection drug of choice was crack cocaine. Nicole exchanged sex for drugs on occasion but never became prolific at it and now laughs at her few unsuccessful attempts at sex work. She has survived incest, molestation, rape, and battering relationships. Nicole has been clean and sober for three years; she has been working at WARN for ten months.

Nina   is a 38-year-old Latina and mother of five children. She had her first child at the age of fourteen, and her youngest is nine months old. Nina spent over 20 years as an injection and noninjection drug user, alcoholic, and sex partner of drug users. While drinking and using, she was arrested more than 40 times and has been incarcerated for several years. In the last two years, Nina has regained custody of two of her children. She currently lives with her nine-month-old baby, two older children, and the father of her youngest, a man she met the last time she was in jail.

Olivia   is a 49-year-old Latina. She used drugs on the streets of Los Angeles for over 35 years and identifies as a user of injection and noninjection drugs, an alcoholic, and a sex worker. At the end of Olivia's drinking and using, she lived in an alley in downtown Los Angeles. She worked the streets in the mornings and evenings, giving businessmen blow jobs for three to five dollars, trading sex for barely enough money for drugs and survival. In the afternoons, Olivia shot drugs with the guys in the "cardboard condo" at the other end of the alley. She has survived several physically abusive relationships. Through her many hospitalizations and incarcerations, Olivia has become "institutionalized"; she knows how to work the system.

The construction of a successful outreach program begins long before the outreach worker enters the field. Theoretically, the construction of the outreach "moment" begins during the job interview. At WARN, senior outreach workers, rather than managerial staff, interview and recommend candidates for outreach positions. The outreach workers know the field, and they know what qualities make for a strong interventionist.

Although many members of the WARN staff are women in recovery from drug and/or alcohol addiction, recovery is not necessarily a prerequisite for outreach. Furthermore, many women enter their personal recovery program with apprehension, anger, and mistrust. This is often a reasonable response to a life of abuse and misuse; nevertheless, these emotions are disruptive in the field. Because WARN conducts street outreach to women, the agency must hire women who trust other women and consequently can place their trust in other women.

Once the staff have been hired, it is incumbent on the managerial team to model the work principles that will be taken out into the field. The ultimate goal of outreach is to empower women at risk and, to work with women to achieve their self-defined goals. However, outreach workers cannot empower women on the streets if they themselves have not been empowered; empowerment must therefore be an integral part of the work environment. At weekly staff meetings, for example, outreach workers are called upon to contribute to program planning and development. Neither counselors nor advisors, members of the managerial team, are there to support the outreach team. When an outreach worker enters the field, she has been trained to be confident that each woman she will meet has her own inner strength.[2] This philosophy must be modeled in the work environment before it can be taken out onto the streets.

Staff meetings and in-service training focus on a variety of topics, ranging from ethnography and crisis intervention to understanding homelessness, domestic violence, and cultural sensitivity. In addition to participating in regularly scheduled training, each outreach worker is encouraged to "follow her own dream." Whether an outreach worker's desire is to run a recovery home or go back to school, the managerial team works with her to attain her goal, just as the outreach worker works with the women at risk to reach their dreams.

THE THEORY BEHIND THE PRACTICE

Successful outreach efforts are interdependent, reaching several different levels of interaction simultaneously. Figure 1 illustrates the model of interaction between actor and action.[3] The outreach workers foster the development of trust through interaction, by sharing their personal histories; by exhibiting knowledge of gatekeepers and culturally appropriate referrals to treatment centers, shelters, and agencies; and by gift-giving in the field. As trust grows, through a process of interaction and intervention, a woman will sometimes change her high-risk behavior to low risk, thus empowering herself and others. Therefore, the key to successful interventions are the codes and symbols that lead to the development of trust, social interaction, and empowerment in the outreach relationship.

Trust: Creating the Moment

WARN, like many other outreach programs, has found it essential to the success of the program to hire indigenous community outreach workers. If she comes from the community, the outreach worker enters the field with a sense of identification. Even when the indigenous outreach worker did not live in the specific community, she is familiar with the structure, language, rules, and roles of the streets. In some situations, she knows the markets and

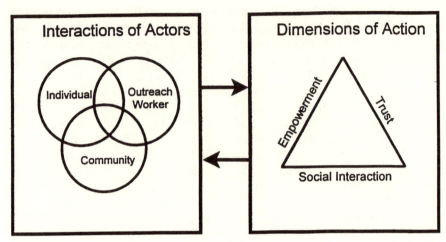

FIGURE 9-1. Model of Interaction Between Actor and Action

restaurants, the shop owners and merchants, the social service agencies and clinics. And, in still other situations, as Nina describes, the outreach worker knows the women.

> When I'm out doing outreach, there are a lot of women [on the streets] that have gone to jails, and a lot of times I'm recognized. I hear my name, "Nina," and I've got to turn because she knows that name. So basically they know where I've come from. They know that I've come from the prison system, and it's just amazing to them that I'm clean.

Identity runs deep. When a woman on the streets recognizes an outreach worker as a former "running" partner, she not only recognizes her face, she recognizes her lifestyle as well. This immediate acknowledgment sets the stage for the intervention. As Nina states, "I've got to turn." The connection is quick. Additionally, the indigenous outreach worker remembers her years on the streets and knows how she would have liked to be approached when she was living there.

Understanding the psychology of the target population also helps the outreach worker pace herself and maintain balance. Nicole discusses how insights from her own drug addiction contribute to understanding the women with whom she now works:

> I feel that what makes outreach effective for me is that the people we reach out to are people that are addicted. They're into their disease, and having a background of addiction is a plus. I don't get burnt out because when [you're] doing interventions, you got a woman that says she's interested in drug treatment, and after a whole day of work and making the arrangements you go to pick this woman up. You go pick her up and she's not there. I'm not

disappointed in this woman, I'm not frustrated, I'm not angry at her. I don't experience those feelings 'cause I know what it's like. For me it's like chopping down a mountain with a toothpick.

Knowing the community and identifying with the target population is a fundamental first step; however, it is very different from developing the trust of the women. Trust is not automatic just because an outreach worker is recognized from prison or as someone who used to shoot drugs on the streets. In fact, at times that identification can produce hostility and mistrust. Establishing trust takes work, and the onus of this work rests on the outreach worker.

Outreach begins before outreach starts, so to speak. Weeks before a new outreach worker hands out her first bottle of bleach or her first condom pack, she begins mapping out the community—defining boundaries, identifying high-risk areas, walking the streets, talking to members of the community, and introducing the AIDS prevention program to the women. Therefore, continuity in the field is established even before the actual outreach process starts.

Trust is contingent on continuity. Outreach must take place at the same park, the same street corners, the same housing project, week after week after week. And, insofar as possible, the same outreach workers must go to the same sites. Marina discusses the importance of continuity: "Being there. Because the women start to know you, they know when to expect you. Just seeing your face on a regular basis makes a big difference." WARN outreach workers show up at MacArthur Park every Friday afternoon. The women in the park know when to expect WARN, and they await the arrival of condoms and bleach. Consistency is the prerequisite for establishing trust. As Nicole explains, without continuity little else can be accomplished:

I think effective outreach is repetition. . . . You have to be consistent. It's like, if you want to become a part of the community, you gotta be there, you have to be there. In order for the women over in South-Central to know me, I can't come like once a month and give out gifts. Then they think I'm the one that comes once a month and gives out gifts. If I'm there every week and I have gifts, I have conversation, I have some information, then I'm part of that community. When they see me standing on the corner I'm as much identified with that corner as they are.

Continuity—just showing up week after week—signifies to the women that the outreach workers are committed to being there. Consistency in the field demonstrates commitment, which, to the women, translates into a reason to talk about risk behavior. The outreach worker proves she is trustworthy.

Soon after the outreach worker has become recognized in the community, she will begin talking with women about high-risk activities. Again, how-ever, a woman will not open up to someone she does not feel safe with. It is the job of the outreach worker to earn the trust of the women and the community. As Olivia states, "they've been lied to and jived to and connived to, and the last thing they need. . . . You know, if I see there's a little trust in their reaching out, the last thing I want to do is break that trust . . . lie to them once, and you'll break it." Being inconsistent, not showing up when you say you will, is lying to the women and the community. Olivia continues, "Anybody can go once and never go again."

Trust is an essential component, not only in working with individual women, but also in working with the entire community. Outreach is conducted in areas where there is high density of high-risk drug and/or sex behavior. In Los Angeles, these are typically economically depressed communities. Many have a large homeless population, and all are predominantly African American or Latino. Many neighborhoods have seen social service programs come and go; therefore, the community members respond to the appearance of yet another agency with extreme trepidation. Continuity addresses this community apprehension.

Similarly, if an outreach worker fails to show up for a scheduled appointment, the trust is broken, not only with the woman but with the community. Lori explains:

> [I]f you're not there when you're saying you'll be there, then you've failed. You've let the community down, and you've let the woman down. You can lose it, and it takes a long time to build that back up again. It can be done, but it just takes a little bit of hard work, and you really don't want to go that route. It would take you from other things that you need to get done. Not showing up can truly break that, but it can be brought back, depending on what you've done in that community. Whether you can get [the trust] back and how quickly you get it back depends on what your efforts have been in the past, how active you've been in that community.

In a world with so little funding and so much work to do, it is a waste of time, money, and energy to rebuild trust. It is far more effective to maintain trust.

When trust is established between the women and the outreach worker, the intervention relationship begins. As in any interpersonal relationship, people begin to open up once they sense trust. By tracing the development of the outreach relationship, one can observe the central role played by trust when HIV information is being delivered. In the following example, Olivia poignantly describes the interdependency among continuity, trust, and AIDS education:

> I remember one of the most significant things that's happened to me working for WARN. And [it happened] because I showed up on a continual basis and showed them. The consistency says we care, that we're able to be there. A woman chased me down the street yelling, "Olivia! Olivia!" And I said, "What? What's the matter?" She said, "Nonoxynol-9. How do I use it?" *I was so touched* because I had been there often enough for her to have enough trust to be able to do that. I guess what I'm saying about continuity is if I had just seen her once she might not have felt comfortable in asking that.

Another time I remember a woman that I met and worked with, a lesbian woman I met in Boyle Heights [a predominantly Latino neighborhood adjacent to East Los Angeles]. My partner and I talked to her about sexual practice. At first when I met her she was very closed, and then I saw her again and she began to ask some questions about sexual activity. We were able to do some intervention and teach her how to use a dental dam, and we were able to talk to her about having a lover that is an injection drug user. We told her she was putting herself at risk. And she was real amazed to hear this but, you see, she opened up like a flower. In the beginning she was very closed. The next time she was glad to see us, and then the third time she really opened up. Women might not be willing to talk on the first meeting, maybe not even the second, but eventually the consistency . . . , by seeing it, they begin to see that we're not there to intimidate them. We're really not there as sidekicks from the cops. We're really not there to do any harm. It's easy to see a woman and say, "We really care about you and we're concerned about your health issues," and then never see them again. Then it's six months later and they're gonna say, "Yeah, bullshit."

In the field, trust requires an interactive relationship. The outreach worker demonstrates that she is trustworthy by showing up week after week. The women display their trust by opening up, reaching out, and being willing to ask personal questions regarding high-risk behavior.

Of equal significance in the development of trust is honesty. A guideline in WARN's code of ethics reads: "Do not make promises that you cannot keep." The WARN lingo refers to these as empty or false promises; they negatively impact both the outreach worker and the women. An empty promise is immediately recognized, and trust is broken. The tenuous relationship between the outreach worker and the woman is quickly severed. As Olivia stated earlier, "lie to them once and you'll break it." With regard to the outreach worker, empty promises lead to frustration, a sense of failure, and low morale. Marina explains:

Empty promises, promising something that you really can't keep such as, "Whenever you call me I can get you in." That's bullshit because you're not in control of the system. You lose trust and you lose yourself. I think for me what has happened the most is my own sense of failure, sense of guilt. And you have the chance of turning into just one of those other agencies, cause there are a lot of places that give people empty promises. Just like the broken promises that they have in their past, we all do. Just becoming part of that group of people who aren't really trustworthy who don't do what they say they're gonna do. Losing that trust.

Empty promises, therefore, not only sever the trust between the outreach worker and the woman, but can also lead to a sense of failure in the outreach worker. Mary discusses the helplessness an outreach worker feels if she is not familiar with current referrals:

The whole goal is to be able to help this woman when she is ready to be helped. My job is not to just go out and hand out condoms and bleach; it's to help that woman who you tell, "Give me a call if you need anything." And then she calls me and says, "Hey, I'm ready." And I don't have anything available for her, or I keep working with the system where I'm beating my head against the wall. I feel helpless, I feel hopeless. It's like, what am I doing? Then, too, when I go back into that community I'm gonna see this woman again. And, that's her community, and she'll put the word out. She'll put the word out on me that WARN's full of shit.

The importance of not making empty promises is twofold: first, as in Marina's example of the woman who is promised entry into a detoxification program whenever she is ready, the empty promise gives the woman expectations that prove unrealistic, thereby violating her trust. Second, when promises are continually met with defeat, the work environment becomes one of disappointment and failure rather than of success and empowerment.

It is impossible to predict the moment a woman on the street will ask an outreach worker for help in entering a detoxification program or shelter or taking an HIV test. The moment is immediate and unpredictable. At that moment, it is essential that the outreach worker have up-to-date referrals. Gatekeepers are the intermediary between an agency and a detoxification unit. It is the gatekeeper who opens the doors to detoxification. Nicole notes that the same "law of the streets" that applies to the connection also applies to the gatekeeper. If an outreach worker knows the right gatekeeper, it is equivalent to knowing the right connection.

It's just like buying drugs. If you come in there and so-and-so brought you in, that makes you cool. That makes you okay. It's the same thing with the gatekeeper. If you know the gatekeeper then you're okay because she's okay. . . . There's a very crucial time on this seesaw, I say seesaw because it's that emotional. And it's that time when she's at her bottom that, if you can get a person right in that time, then you may be able to work with her. If you provide this woman with enough adequate and up-to-date resources at this time, then you may be able to help her.

A knowledge of gatekeepers and referrals is symbolic to the woman at risk. This information translates into a code that says, "I can trust her, she knows what she is talking about, she has done this before, she is one of us." Marina elaborates, "That means you really know your shit, that you *really* have done this before. The fact that you know the gatekeeper makes it more than just an agency out there, it make it more human." Knowledge of gatekeepers, access to appropriate programs, and up-to-date referrals are all symbolic. This information represents to the woman at risk that the outreach worker identifies with her lifestyle, respects her life, and has the ability to work the system. Olivia shares her experience in this area:

I can't put these women on hold. "Olivia, is there any place I can get into, I need some help, I think I'm dying." [If I answer] "Yeah well, check this out, I'll be back in half an hour, let me go make some calls and see what's up," she's gone.

I could lose her; the cops could bust her, she could go with the connection, or I could lose her to her own fear. "Yeah, I want help," and then the fear kicks in because it's a giant step to step out of that lifestyle into a new lifestyle. But if I tell her, "Hey, I happen to have a couple of phone numbers here, would you like to go to the phone and we can call?" I've had women walk with me to the nearest phone and I'm real grateful I had those referrals right there. I've had others who say, "Well, I can't right now." "Well, then good. Let me give you these phone numbers and when you can, call." She might not call that day, but the next day she might look at those numbers and call. She has an option. Now, she has been given an option.

The social service system is structured according to funding sources, target populations, and numbers. For the women, this translates into money, intake interviews, and waiting lists. Therefore, as Nina explains, at any moment she is prepared to offer a woman a set of alternatives:

> I'm a walking referral system. I need to have the knowledge because of the way the system is set up. I need to have Plan A, Plan B, and Plan C. And even Plan D to go that extra mile for the woman.

When a referral is finally made and a woman is placed, it is important that that referral be appropriate. An inappropriate referral is like an empty promise; it does not help the woman, and it breaks the bond of trust. Mary discusses appropriate referrals as they relate to cultural sensitivity:

> You don't want to send a woman to anywhere that's insensitive. You want to actually help the woman. And it's important to know where you're sending her because it could do more damage to her, as opposed to helping her. So I think it's really important that you understand the sensitivity of the treatment centers, recovery homes. You have to do some homework on it. For example, if you send a Latina woman somewhere they don't speak Spanish, it's like, what are you doing for her? So it's really important that you have a history or some knowledge of where you send these women. And it's really important that you have a list of referrals that work. Because otherwise, I think as an outreach worker you'll get burnt out. You won't feel like you're accomplishing anything.

Therefore, several components play an interdependent role in the development of trust: identifying with the community, consistency in the field, honesty, and current and culturally appropriate referrals.

Interaction: The Outreach Moment

Outreach is quick. Often before the outreach worker realizes it, the interaction is over and the woman she was talking with a moment ago is now walking over to a friend. Maybe she left with the outreach worker's name, maybe she left with her card, maybe she left with a condom pack or a dental dam or a bleach bottle—or maybe not. With any luck, the outreach worker got her name and was able to tell her a little about WARN; or the outreach worker may have had the opportunity to tell her a little about HIV and risk behaviors. However, if this is the first time the outreach worker and the woman have met, and there is no mutual friend (a woman WARN has been working with) present to serve as a contact, the outreach worker may only get the chance to give the woman a nod and a quick hello and hope the woman will remember who she is. In the ideal scenario, the woman is left with a connection that can eventually lead to a bond of trust.

Nicole: In outreach work you may have about three minutes to talk with a woman. Three minutes. Especially if she's in a hurry, she may give you three minutes of her time. In that three minutes you've got to introduce yourself, get her name, tell her about your program, assess her knowledge of HIV, give her condoms, and find out where she lives. That's all in three minutes. Then the next week you come back, you might be able to go through that whole thing again and find out if she has any children living with her. Then the next week you come back, you find out where she's from originally. The information about her living situation gives you a better understanding of the woman that you're working with.

Many AIDS prevention programs agree that hiring outreach workers who are indigenous to the community and the target population fosters the identification that can create the outreach moment. The key moment of identification often comes when the outreach worker shares her personal experiences. At that moment, the woman at risk realizes that the outreach worker does, in fact, understand her lifestyle. Once the moment of identification takes place and a connection has been established, there is a potential for building trust. The goal is for the outreach worker and the woman on the street to share information on risk behaviors; however, unless there is trust, the woman will be unwilling to discuss intimate or illegal activities. Trust begins when the woman at risk marks the outreach worker as "one of our own." Outreach work is urgent, so the outreach worker looks for the easiest, fastest way to connect with the woman. Often that is by saying, "I know, I've been there."

Olivia: I just don't blurt it out just to say it, but if the opportunity permits I'll say, "You know what, I've shot drugs on these streets and I really understand what you're saying to me. I really do understand." And it's almost like it'll help form a bond of trust, and that's what I initially want to establish. So when I'm able to do that with these women, I'm telling them who I am. That's what they want to know. They don't care what I do. They want to know who I am. . . . Because so much outreach is that quick, that might be the only time you have with them. What I try to do in that brief moment or five minutes I have with them is give them as much as I can. As much information about things that will help them as I can.

Mary: I think [sharing personal experiences] has been most effective in my outreach. Because it's brought on the language of the heart. Meaning we're talking the same language. I understand because I was there. I haven't just walked up to a woman and said, "Hi, I'm an alcoholic and a dope fiend, so you can trust me." It's those days when they come to you crying, and, for me, a woman that says, "My children were taken away from me." I get to tell her, "My son was taken away from me, and I have him back now; here are the steps I took." And they still might not be ready. But sometimes they may sit and listen to me and call me back a month later. So I think it's very important.

However, there is a fine line between the sharing of a personal story, which is effective, and the creation of false hopes, which is destructive. Outreach workers are careful not to create a false impression by making statements such as, "If I can do it, you can." The outreach worker does not know which women can effect which changes in their lives. For one woman, asking her battering partner to use a condom—or leaving him—might appear unrealistic; however, it might be within the realm of possibility for that woman to clean her needles with bleach and water or to use a condom on dates. Because every set of circumstances is different, it is unrealistic to assume that all women on the streets can modify the same high-risk activities simply because they interact with an outreach worker who has done so.

WARN strives to deliver empowerment and hope. WARN outreach workers want to maintain relationships with the women they meet. However, when the outreach worker says, "If I can do it, you can," and the woman *can't*, she may walk in the other direction the next time she sees that outreach worker approaching. It takes delicate balance to create identification without setting up a situation that could fail.

Lori: One thing we have to remember is not to say, "If I can do it, you can do it. Because I've been there and I know." Because what you're setting up is if the woman doesn't follow through we don't want to label her as being a failure. She doesn't want to label herself as being a failure because in her head she was saying, "Well, gosh, she said that if she can do it I can do it, then why am I not doing it?" And so in her head you don't want to give her room for defeat, because that's what that's doing. . . . [It's] a real sticky situation because you want to give her something to feed on, [and] telling your story is important, but saying if I can you can . . . 'cause maybe she can't.

Nina: A lot of times I'm asked, "How did you do it," and I let them know how I did it. But I've never used the term, "If I did it you can do it." Because it might seem unrealistic for them to get to where I'm at, and I don't want that projected. I always emphasize the baby steps.

In addition, sharing personal experiences does not work for all outreach workers. Some may not feel comfortable, others may not have had the same experiences as those of the women they are working with. For example, not all outreach workers have been to prison, used injection drugs, or engaged in alcoholic drinking. Some outreach workers were raised in the community but never practiced high-risk behaviors. Experiences and personalities vary. Outreach workers are not seeking an exact match; rather, they are looking for a connection. If sharing personal experiences helps foster a connection, an outreach worker may opt to tell her story. However, if that is inappropriate, she looks for another way in—another way to construct an immediate interaction that catches the woman's attention.

The Indirect Approach, or "Gifts"

Another effective outreach strategy is approaching the woman indirectly: "Hi, I'm Olivia. I work for the women's organization, WARN. Can I give you a gift?" The gifts WARN offers at the first moment of intervention are personal cosmetic and bath items such as perfume, lipstick, body lotion, earrings, powder, or nail polish. The gifts are fun, and they are a luxury[4]; they excite the woman's interest and hold a specific meaning for her. Because they are luxury items rather than necessities, the gifts really are gifts, not handouts. Consequently, the giver is coded as a friend, not a patron. Nicole elaborates:

> But when you bring someone something and you open the gift and you show them that it's something pretty and it's just for them, it brings on a different meaning. It's like, "That's really great, you want to do something just for me." It's not like giving me a sandwich, a handout; this *is* a gift.

Olivia continues, explaining why talcum powder is her favorite gift to give to women on the streets:

> I think [a gift] is a real good icebreaker. . . . [J]ust having information on HIV can be offensive to some. But if you're able to give them something, like some powder or something like that, it signifies something, all of a sudden you become a friend . . . I like the talcum because I think it also works for lesbian women as well as heterosexual women. It doesn't have a connotation. You know, some of the women that are lesbian—for example, one woman that I worked with for a long time doesn't wear the earrings. That's not her style of dress, so for her that's an inappropriate gift. The powder she can use. Some of these women don't get to bathe on a daily basis, so they get to feel fresh [when they] put a little powder on. Some of these women do get to bathe . . . I like to put powder on after a bath, so I can only guess that they do too.

If the woman accepts the gift, the outreach moment may last up to five minutes. As the woman applies the lipstick, smells the fragrance of the cologne, or puts on the earrings, the outreach worker talks to her about risk behaviors and offers her condoms, a dental dam, bleach, and, ideally, makes a connection that develops into trust.

Nina: It's their time, it's not our time. It's their lives we're talking about. . . . Of course we deal with our own personal life, but it's like it's on their time. They're in the progression of their disease and they're practicing it, and they have the attitude that their time is precious. When they say that they are not responsible people, they are very responsible as far as having to do the upkeep on getting their drugs; they got better and bigger things to do than to stop and talk to us. That's the attitude of the addict, and we cannot deny that attitude—the attitude that we're up against. So giving them a gift is an incentive to . . . catch that moment that we might be able to get a chance to listen to the woman or get a chance to speak to the woman. And that moment is very, very important.

For some, the gift is the hook. For others, sharing personal experiences is the hook. However, as Lori notes, the real gift is the information.

What I'm finding with the gift-giving, people need incentives in every avenue; I mean, I would want it. Especially if you're trying to get to know me for the first time. She doesn't know that once she's talking to you and she's sharing with you things in her life, that she's releasing something within her. She doesn't understand yet, because at this point she may not trust you. So the gift-giving, in the beginning, is really good because all she wants, maybe, is what you have to give. She doesn't understand the communication, the interaction that's really happening that's deeper. So in the beginning, the gift-giving is good, and then I think it gets to a point where she understands that it isn't about the gift; it's about what I'm actually saying. I think the gifts are powerful, and I think they work. And I think they work so powerfully because the woman doesn't really understand what happened during that whole dynamic of gift-giving and how this conversation just happened. And then she walks away happy about this gift, and in the back of her head something just jelled about the conversation. "No one has ever rapped to me that way, no one has ever told me this is how I could handle this situation. Or yes, there are things you can do so this doesn't happen and you can get out of this situation." These things are just starting to jell in her mind, and then when you see her that second and third time, that gift starts to be put aside. She's seeing more of the meat and potatoes of the conversation. She's starting to get the real gift.

A cosmetic gift may capture the woman's attention, but it is the connection, the interaction, that will sustain her interest. Through the process of interaction, the outreach worker assess the woman's risk behaviors.

WARN outreach workers do not enter the field with one outreach strategy for sex workers and another for injection drug users. A woman may have one primary high-risk behavior, with other risk behaviors directly or indirectly resulting from the one primary behavior. For example, a woman may smoke crack or inject drugs (or both) and occasionally exchange sex for money or drugs. However, she may not identify as a sex worker. Furthermore, she may use condoms when working but still have difficulty negotiating condom use with her boyfriend or husband. Additionally, she may also be the sex partner of a drug user, and she may or may not be aware of her partner's drug use. A variety of profiles can be imagined. For this reason, WARN adopts an open outreach strategy that does not assume one or all risk behaviors.

As shown in Figure 2, a woman can have multiple risk statuses. An injection drug user may also be a sex worker and/or a "partner of." A "partner of" may also be a noninjection drug user (such as a woman who smokes crack or drinks alcohol) and/or an injection drug user. Therefore, risk behaviors are assessed rather than assumed. Nicole discusses a problem that can arise when a risk behavior is assumed:

> You're on the street, don't go approaching a sex worker with bleach. [If that were me] I'm not going to accept it from you because, first of all, I don't want you to know my behavior. I feel like a piece of shit. I'm very ashamed of what I do, and you come and you represent an authority figure to me. I'm not going to acknowledge to you that I need this bleach, no matter how badly I need it. For me to acknowledge that I need it is for me to acknowledge that I use drugs, is for me to acknowledge that I'm a little bit lower than you, because this is the way I feel.

In the above scenario, the woman would be immediately alienated. She does not trust the outreach worker; she feels defensive and judged. Consequently, she is left unprotected against possible HIV transmission. In addition, Nicole notes how, in the field, outreach workers can represent an authority figure. Although outreach workers are hired because they are "from the community," they return to the community playing a different role. An outreach worker presents herself as a peer, yet she is a peer with information. Therefore, as Nicole states, women look to her as someone with knowledge: someone who has been there but is no longer there. This subtle distinction transforms the outreach worker from a peer to a peer advocate.

In the following exchange, Olivia and Nicole role-play a common response they have received when they have assumed a risk behavior:

Olivia: I don't walk up to a woman I don't know on the streets and say, "You want some information about AIDS? Would you like some bleach?"

Nicole: "Do you think I'm a drug addict?"

Olivia: That's the first reaction that I've always gotten, "What do you think, that I shoot up?" Or else the woman will come in with something like, "What's that for?" and she could be all marked up (i.e., needle marks) and I haven't been effective.

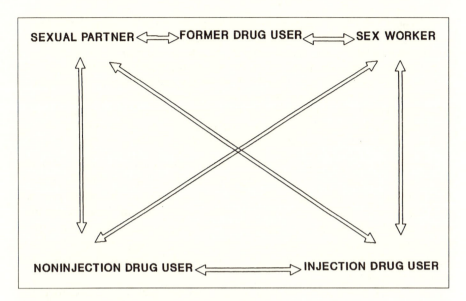

FIGURE 9–2. Outreach Strategy for Women at Risk

Olivia continues by stating that she has found the same to be true when an outreach worker assumes a woman is a sex worker or has multiple sex partners. If one approaches a woman for the first time with condoms but without an introduction, Olivia explains, it is not uncommon to hear the following reaction: "What do you think I am, loose?" Lori tells of an experience she had when handing a woman a condom packet:

> I extended my arm and I gave her a packet and I said, "Just some information for you today." And she took it, which was a plus, and then she looked at it, and she threw it on the sidewalk and said, "AIDS? I don't have AIDS!" I didn't give her much more conversation than that, and I think when we give women those kind of things . . . there needs to be some type of rap first. But what's the easy door? The easy door is to hand someone something. But I think when you're handing someone something, it's what you say when you're handing them that information that makes it jell.

Just giving a woman condoms and bleach is only doing half the job. As outreach workers, it is easy to get into the trap of thinking, "Well, we did our job okay, she has the packet." However, as Lori explains, you're not really doing your job if there isn't valid information to accompany the condoms. In addition, simply handing a woman a condom could be offensive. It is important to be culturally sensitive, but one may not know the cultural or religious background of the individual. Through trial and error, Lori discusses what works for her:

She could have been religious, and this kind of thing just doesn't jive in her world, we don't know that. What I would recommend is . . . "I have some information here today about women's health, would you be interested in having something like that?" [I try to make] sure that she has that option, because sometimes we just hand it out, and it happens all the time. But I think what I have learned through the years is that we let them know what's up. We let them know what's in this packet, and we make [them] real concerned [by saying], "Hey, this is about saving your life, this is about you saving other women's lives and letting other women know that this is what we are about."

. The commonality among Nicole's, Olivia's, and Lori's approaches lies in the fact that all three outreach workers find a way to give women information without appearing aggressive. The outreach moment is turned around, and the woman decides whether or not to accept the gift, be it a cosmetic, condoms, bleach, or an AIDS pamphlet. The woman does not feel trapped; she is not forced into a situation in which she must explain or defend her behavior. She is given a choice, an option. The moment is hers, the empowerment begins.

After a risk assessment has been made, the outreach worker conducts the appropriate intervention. For example, Marina conducts groups for nonusing Latinas who are sex partners of drug users. She often finds it better to approach the topics of sex, drugs, and HIV slowly and indirectly. When working with women in this population, their children and community can be the "hook." According to Marina, discussions of their own empowerment, or their children, are most effective:

If they are housewives [sic], then, with them it's talking about their own empowerment. If they have children, their children. Talk about protecting themselves. Latinas will be talking about our protection. Like we're women, we have children, we have to take care of our children and of ourselves, too. We may not have control over our partner, but there is something we can do to protect ourselves. That type of thing.

Similarly, Nina discusses her strategy for working with female sex partners of drug users. Like Marina, Nina also focuses on children, family, and community:

I will bring up her children, talk about [all] children, not in particular her children. Then I talk about my children, I will disclose. The importance of her being a mother and giving the information to her children. And maybe not necessarily her children, if she has younger sisters or younger brothers or aunts or uncles. I talk about how a woman is a mother, and she takes the lead, she makes dinner and she cooks and she cleans; and how we need to take the lead and take the information back to our family. I use this in the Latina and African-American culture.

Female sex partners, to me it's a slower process because, for one, you've got that denial, and you've got to be very careful because they're very fragile. They can run at any point. So I use a slower process with the "partner of." I try to share the importance of learning the prevention modes and being able to share that with her partner, she might be saving his life. I direct it to the partner because her whole world is surrounded by her partner. It's not her life she's concerned with, she's concerned with her partner's life. So before I can reach her, I've got to reach her through her partner and then bring it back to her. That's how I work with the "partner of."

Like Marina and Nina, Olivia uses the indirect approach when working with the female sex partner. Again, she captures the woman's attention by focusing on her children:

The thing that I think works for the Latina woman is to come in through the back door and talk about her children. "This is some information you might want to know about the risk of the virus in the community, 'cause I'm sure you have children or brothers or sisters or friends, you might even know people that are injecting drugs." Or, "here's a gift for your children." It's like all of a sudden you've captured her, there's a little trust now. So you have to be culturally sensitive.

Outreach workers are skilled at strategies for capturing "the outreach moment." In that moment, in a three minute conversation on health issues, an interaction that can lead to empowerment begins.

Empowerment: Maintaining the Moment

Establishing trust and interacting with the woman and the community are both mechanisms for conducting effective outreach. As trust develops and the outreach worker listens to a woman's needs, she determines how to help the woman accomplish her goals. All of these factors are centered around the philosophy of empowerment. Empowerment is the hub of WARN. At WARN, empowerment means assisting and supporting a woman to realize her self-defined goals; be that leaving an abusive relationship or going back to school. Empowerment is realized through (1) listening to the women; (2) entering the field with a value-free attitude; (3) working with a woman according to her own agenda; and (4) giving her the tools to achieve her goals. As Marina states, "Her life is still in her hands, we can just kinda help her get over the bumps."

One avenue to empowerment is providing a woman with knowledge of her options. Therefore, a prerequisite to empowerment is listening. Outreach workers must listen to what a woman is saying. We have learned from our own experiences and from the women we meet that women have a good sense of what their needs are, although many do not have the resources or knowledge to meet these needs. For example, a woman may feel that she is ready to enter a detoxification program, but she may not know how to work the system. She may know that eventually she will leave her battering relationship, although today she cannot imagine how that will happen. She may know that she is at high risk for HIV infection and would like to be tested for HIV antibodies, but today she doesn't have money or transportation, or she doesn't know which agency provides free and anonymous testing. Some women are not clear about their needs. However, it has been our experience that, when given an opportunity to talk and explore options, women become more focused—perhaps not immediately, but eventually. As Mary states, "The whole goal is to be able to help this woman when she is ready to be helped." Consequently, as Nina elaborates, much of outreach is listening:

> Being able to listen and being real patient. Being able to just be yourself and not going in with any attitudes whatsoever. If that woman is approachable, you approach her. If that woman is not approachable, you do not approach her. Respecting, first of all, the disease of addiction and respecting the woman for whatever she may be has worked for me. Just showing them, maybe sitting close to them if they allow you to, if they let you, or letting them sit next to you.

Conversely, Marina explains that an inappropriate form of outreach is to enter the field with answers before there are questions:

> Coming off as someone that you're not, not listening to the woman. The outreach worker doing all the talking. Not asking her what she needs, rather telling her what she needs. Sounding judgmental. Or even putting across that you're uncomfortable talking to her.

Implicit in this strategy is the philosophy that listening is important, because each woman knows her own life situation and needs. She knows the answers that are right for her, although she has not been afforded the opportunity for these answers to materialize. Each woman has her own inner strengths. However, through years of living on the streets, in housing projects, or in abusive relationships, her inner strengths may have been buried. Outreach workers are skilled human archaeologists who enter the field and unearth valuable shards.

Olivia: I believe that most of the women that we work with have many, many fears. I believe that they're survivors. I believe that they are real creative. They don't know these things about themselves; they feel like they are a big hole in the doughnut, as I felt at one time in my life. And [I try to allow] them to see that they have these things and . . . that they have survived this and they have made decisions. Probably more crucial decisions than maybe they'll ever make again, and allowing them to know that.

Empowering women starts with listening to women—talking *with* women and not *at* them. Nicole notes that many of the women she works with are accustomed to a form of communication in which they are talked to and talked at. She understands being placed in a submissive and powerless role, particularly in relation to someone she perceives to be an authority.

> Although I'm out there to do the AIDS prevention and promote behavior change, often I can't do that right away because that's not first on her agenda. So I have to learn to listen to her and to talk with her and not talk at her. Talking at her is something that she's accustomed to having done to her. So what I'm doing is talking with her, and I'm listening and I'm able to listen to the feelings. And I listen to her whether she is minimizing her behavior or justifying her behavior. In order for me to do AIDS prevention effectively, I need to know . . . some of the issues that this woman is facing.

Talking with a woman and listening to her feelings, following her agenda—rather than imposing the agency's agenda on her—places her in the position of power. She is the authority on her life. WARN allows women to take responsibility for their lives. Outreach workers inform women of their options (up-to-date referrals to shelters, drug treatment programs, social service agencies); however, the decision is theirs. This sounds simple enough, but when a woman's goals do not match those of the outreach worker, it can be extremely difficult. Olivia addresses the conflict that arises when theory and practice clash:

> I had a woman that I did an intervention with. It was *her* choice to go into a detox, and there's a lot of controversy about detoxing a pregnant woman, but I allowed her to make that decision. She came out of detox, she was also offered a program. She chose not to go, and she fell back into her addiction. And a little while later she wanted to go on methadone maintenance, because they have various programs for pregnant women. That wasn't my agenda for her. That was *not* my agenda for her. *She was clean. She was free from drugs. She could have gone to a program.* That was *my* agenda, but I had to allow her. Do you know that this woman got on methadone maintenance, and I believe she either had the baby or she's due to have the baby. One of my coworkers ran into her, and she's so happy and grateful. She's so happy and grateful. And it was because I stood out of the way—when I say [that] I mean my agenda—and I allowed her to make her own decisions. This is working for her. I would have never thought it would. So one more time I learned that empowerment is very important, because it allows the women to make their own decisions.

The context in which WARN uses the word *empowerment* is exemplified when an outreach worker listens to a woman and works with her to turn dreams into reality. Realization of the dreams of a woman who has lived for years in the alleys of downtown Los Angeles can be an overwhelming challenge. Such a woman may hear of a detoxification program for which she qualifies, yet the barriers to reaching that program appear staggering. The outreach worker serves as a mediator, working with her to remove these barriers. WARN adheres to the "fish" philosophy: Give a woman a fish, and feed her for the day; teach a woman to fish, and feed her for life. By walking a woman through the barriers, rather than removing the barriers for her, WARN teaches women to fish.

When a woman chooses her options and begins the process of realizing them, she starts to create a sense of self-worth. The outreach worker stands by the sidelines as a witness to the woman's growing self-esteem. And, as an indigenous member of the community, the outreach worker identifies with the transformation. Olivia tells her story:

> When people allow me to make my own decisions and I make them and I walk through it and I choose an option and I utilize it, I feel so good inside. *I feel so good inside* and I would like to pass that on to the women. I would like to give them that same feeling inside. If I control their life I'm robbing them of those good feelings, and I feel it's important to allow them that. They have a right to that. That's theirs. It belongs to them. It's only my job to help show them that they can get there too.

Outreach workers walk the streets with HIV information. The tools of the trade are condoms, dental dams, bottles of bleach, and literature. Every outreach worker comes to HIV/AIDS work with her own personal history. She enters the field with strong ideas regarding what works and what does not work, all based on what has been effective for her. She has her own values. It is not requested or expected that an outreach worker abandon her personal philosophy of life. However, she is asked to become aware of that philosophy, thus allowing her to enter the field value-free. The "value-free" concept assumes that each individual has a worldview; however, her particular ideology is not a part of outreach. Olivia admits, "Before I came to work for WARN, I used to hate methadone maintenance, and I have my own personal beliefs about methadone maintenance, but I've seen that the best some of these women can do at that moment is methadone maintenance, and I have to allow them to make those decisions if that's what is best for them." If one is truly committed to working with women on *their* agendas, she must listen and hear what they are saying.

CONCLUSIONS

Effective outreach is cyclical. It begins with establishing trust, which is contingent on "showing up" and acting consistently in the field. When the outreach worker and a woman meet, they engage in a responsive interaction rather than a unilateral conversation. The mutuality of the interaction—listening, suggesting options, and looking at a woman's inner strengths—leads to empowerment.

Outreach workers personify empowerment. They go into the streets equipped with condoms, dental dams, bottles of bleach, AIDS literature, and their personal histories. The empowerment that outreach workers model every day when they walk the streets is not hard to recognize. As Mary states, "I walk in my own brand of dignity."

NOTES

[1]This article does not address the findings of research conducted during the national WARN project, which was funded by the National Institute on Drug Abuse through the California School of Professional Psychology. Rather, the focus of this article is on the outreach strategies that are a structural component of PROTOTYPES/WARN. Throughtout this article, the name WARN refers only to PROTOTYPES/WARN.

[2]I would like to thank Ruth Slaughter for her contribution to developing this analysis of empowerment in the office environment and in the field. The phase "Each woman has her own inner strength" is all Ruth's.

[3]Many thanks to George Huba and Lisa Melchior for their creative input in developing this figure.

[4]Through the campaign efforts of the outreach workers, these gifts have been donated to WARN by cosmetic companies.

PART III

Women Organize AIDS Care and Foster Social Change

Rebecca Denison

Call Us Survivors! Women Organized to Respond to Life-threatening Diseases (WORLD)

To explain how and why I started WORLD,[1] you need to understand what it was like before.

In June of 1990 my best friend (whose sister had AIDS) told me she'd made an appointment to get tested. I decided, what the hell, I'd take the test too. I told myself she needed the support.

Her test came back negative. Mine was positive. I didn't really expect it—I'd been in a monogamous relationship with Daniel for five years, and I definitely wasn't prepared for it. When the counselor told me my test had come back positive, life number one ended, forever.

Two days later, I called my husband in Guatemala, where he was studying Spanish. He flew home and took the test. The next day, while we were waiting for his results, the 6th International Conference on AIDS started in San Francisco. ACT-UP was there, demonstrating in front of the building where I worked. They were chanting, "Women die faster," and I believed it. I thought I had six months to live, so I started thinking about my funeral.

Daniel's test came back negative—the first good news I'd heard since I got my diagnosis. I tried to call an old boyfriend from 1983. We hadn't spoken to each other in over six years. A relative informed me that my friend had died of AIDS.

I was lucky. My extended family and friends were very supportive. But that didn't change the fact that I felt I'd been handed an automatic death sentence. And no matter how much they loved me, they couldn't reach through the glass wall that had come between me and the rest of the world.

I realized I needed to find some other women living with this disease. I didn't know whether to plan for life or for death. I needed proof that my life could go on.

One of the biggest disappointments of my life was when I realized that the women's movement that I had been a part of for years couldn't help me. I had been involved in International Women's Day marches, Take Back the Night marches, and others. But I realized that, in the six years since my first women's studies class at UC Santa Cruz, no one had ever addressed AIDS as a women's issue. Never. Furthermore, of all the women I had met as an activist, only a few called me after word got out that I was HIV-positive. They weren't avoiding me. They just didn't know what to say. I thought to myself, "Where the hell have we been?"

I learned a lot from my friend Pam, a woman with chronic fatigue. I had watched her lose the ability to walk over time, watched her come to terms with needing a wheelchair. We talked a lot, and she helped me realize people with HIV aren't the only ones who feel isolated. People with *any* disability or illness are invisible in this society. I just hadn't noticed before. As a healthy person, I didn't have to. Now I did.

I realized that I needed a women's HIV support group. I called one agency, then another, then another. Each one told me they didn't have services for women, but were sure *someone* out there did, and they would give me another number to call. After five months, I figured out that, even in the San Francisco Bay Area, I didn't qualify for a single group. There was one for women, but you had to have an AIDS diagnosis (I was only HIV-positive). There was another one for lesbians. I remember trying to figure out, "How would I be most convincing: as someone with full-blown AIDS, or as a lesbian?" I vowed then that, if I ever had the opportunity to keep another woman from going through the isolation I felt then, I would do it.

I was afraid to turn to Becky (my friend's sister) for help. She was so sick I didn't want to cause her any more trouble than she already had. I'll always be grateful for the fact that she reached out to me. She sent over a packet of information and talked to me on the phone. I remember her telling me, "It's too late for me, but there might actually be some hope for you. Keep fighting this thing. Remember that it's the 'problem patients' who return home from the hospital."

I went to an AIDS march in Palo Alto, and there a woman with two young children spoke about what it had been like to test positive. I followed her around, trying to get the guts to talk to her. I didn't know what to say, I just wanted someone to teach me how to "live" with HIV. The only part I had ever heard about was the death part. Finally my husband went up to her and said, "My wife over there just tested positive. She's having a really hard time." And Suzin came right over and gave me a big hug. She told me I'd be okay, that AIDS was a very good teacher, and she reassured me that I'd make lots of new friends. We marched together, and when she saw a friend way up ahead, she said, "Come on, let's run so you can meet my friend." Run? I had forgotten that I could.

I did finally find a support group. I did it by standing up in a conference of 250 nurses and saying (OK, really I was crying), "You all know how to find each other, but I'm HIV-positive and I can't find anyone else who knows how I feel. What am I supposed to do?" There were women with AIDS on a panel, and they said, "Come to our group!" But the facilitator stepped forward and said it was only for women with AIDS. Being HIV-positive wasn't enough.

Fortunately, one of the nurses came over and told me about a group her friend was starting. The women in that group saved my life. It was a place where we could speak the same language. Still, I kept thinking about all the women that would follow me. Where would they go? I didn't want any woman to have to go through what I went through to find support.

In December 1990, I went to a national conference on women and AIDS in Washington, D.C. I learned a lot, both from the workshops and from the women in ACT-UP who were there, yelling a lot. But for me, the best part was a lounge for HIV-positive women that had been arranged by Michelle Wilson from the Positive Woman in Washington, D.C. I met women with HIV from all over the country, and I met more positive women from San Francisco there than I had met at home in the Bay Area. It was wonderful.

I came home wondering how best to keep up communication among those of us living in the Bay Area. I thought it would be nice to have a local newsletter by and for HIV-positive women. I suggested it to some folks in the AIDS community, but most people said, "HIV-positive women don't really get involved." One person said, "Please don't. My organization's applying for a grant to do one, and if they see you doing it for free, the funders won't give us the money." Others said women should just join the AIDS groups that already existed. Well, maybe they should have (or maybe not), but the fact was, they weren't joining.

My friends in ACT-UP supported my dream of forming an organization for women with HIV. Brenda Lein, of ACT-UP Golden Gate, even came up with a name: WORLD (Women Organized to Respond to Life-threatening Diseases). One night at a meeting, with ten minutes' warning, Brenda announced: "There's a new organization for HIV-positive women called WORLD. WORLD has an appointment to talk to the surgeon general this weekend. If you want to go, talk to Rebecca." Just like that, WORLD was formed. There were six of us in the original delegation to see the surgeon general: an Asian woman in her early twenties, a white lesbian activist, an African-American mother of two, a white wife of a hemophiliac, an African-American grandmother, and me, a white woman with no idea how to start or lead an organization, but the willingness to try anyway. Of that initial group of five, there are two of us left.

In March of 1991, I went to Washington, D.C., for the AIDS Clinical Trials Group (ACTG) meeting, to learn more about federally funded clinical trials. The night before the meeting started, I got a call in my hotel room. My friend told me that Becky had died. I was devastated. I wanted to go home, but I stayed. I thought, "Becky would want me to stick around and learn all I can," so I did.

The next day I talked to a researcher who was doing a study of a massive antibiotic. I said, "What impact will this have on women? I know HIV-positive women already have problems with yeast infections, and that antibiotics can often cause yeast infections. Are you going to study this?" And he looked down on me and said, "I believe a woman is supposed to have a pap smear once a year. That ought to take care of it." He was clueless; I was furious.

I came home still livid. My friend was dead, and research on women was going absolutely nowhere. My friends in ACT-UP were supportive, but they were either men or HIV-negative women. Where were the HIV-positive women?

I was mad at myself, too. Mad that I hadn't done more for Becky. Mad that women with HIV weren't organized and visible and strong like the gay men were. We needed to have some kind of community, and I realized that I didn't have the patience to wait for somebody else to do it.

I still wanted to do a women's newsletter, to create a place where we could share information, where women in the closet could have a way to connect with others. What held me back? Professionals in the AIDS industry were still telling me that "women don't get involved." How could I start anything with no money and no organization to back me up? Fortunately, my friends from ACT-UP said, "Just do it!" Then one day Daniel called me over to his computer, where he had set up the first page of the WORLD newsletter. He said, "Here's your newsletter. Now go write it." So I did.

The first issue—"A Bay Area Newsletter by, for, and About Women Facing HIV Disease"—came out on May 1, 1991, containing information about the gynecological manifestations of HIV in women, two observational studies that women could join, and a list of support groups. It also had a Latina grandmother's testimonial about her experience of testing positive:

> The test turned out positive. I couldn't believe it. I was sure that it had to be a mistake. I took the test three more times before I could accept it. . . . My boyfriend went crazy, yelling and blaming me for everything. I blamed him, too, because I believed he had infected me. He didn't want to accept it, saying that if he really had AIDS he would kill himself. In the end, he abandoned me. Who knows how many women he has infected since then. . . . I feel like I want to do something, to educate people and to reach out to other women who are living with this disease. . . .   —Alba

A friend at ACT-UP made copies for me at her job after hours. Other friends helped stuff envelopes. Our original mailing list had 200 people, mainly activists, agencies, and some HIV-positive women I had met from the Bay Area. I remember feeling insecure: "Everyone says this won't work. Who do I think I am, thinking that it will?" I decided that, if no one was interested, that would be OK too. It had been a lot of work to put together. I was really tired.

A week after it came out, the *San Francisco Examiner* ran an article about it in the weekly AIDSWEEK column. The next day I got over 30 calls from all over the state. The next issue—"A Northern California Newsletter . . ."—went out to 300 subscribers. Since then, the WORLD newsletter has gotten about 100 new subscribers each month and is now sent to over 3,000 women in every state and around the world.

One of the women who called lived in Nevada City, a small town in rural northern California. She wanted to tell her story for the next issue:

> My boyfriend [at the time I tested positive] was a "religious" person. Eventually, he came out with this statement: "AIDS is the wrath of God sent down to destroy the sinners." Our relationship was not good to begin with, but when he said that I realized that I'd had enough. I broke up with him. It wasn't easy after that. I was lonely and depressed. I was certain that no one else would ever want me. I went back to him. I was willing to put up with almost anything in order to not be alone.   —Debra

Eventually Debra broke up with her boyfriend. Later she met an HIV-positive man in her support group. They fell in love, and in December 1990, they were married:

> My experience of HIV has not been what I expected; it has been all about healing and love. The final outcome may not necessarily be about survival. Yes, I have lost dear friends, but this, too, has opened my heart. I don't know what the future will bring, but I do know that I don't have to face anything alone.
>   —Debra

The testimonial became the signature of the newsletter, and Debra became a lifeline to WORLD for positive women living in rural northern California.

The newsletter has given few statistics. We can talk about x number of children who will become orphans in the epidemic. But women like Bonnie, who told her story in the third issue of the WORLD newsletter, bring it to life:

> When I was diagnosed with HIV, I denied the accuracy of such a diagnosis. I denied that it could happen to me; after all, I was married with a baby, for God's sake. I had been married for seven years! I was sure the tests were wrong. I got retested at least twice before I would believe the truth.
>
> I bargained. I bargained with myself, I bargained with God, I bargained with my boss, I bargained with death. If only I had a positive attitude, I could beat this thing. I would be the one to make the miracle happen. I knew I could. If I ate the right foods, exercised enough, took enough vitamins, I could make it go away. If I believed and visualized, and prayed, and meditated enough, then I would be whole again.
>
> Do I need to describe the bone-crushing disappointment when none of these things worked the way I wanted to? I mean, I expected that if I did all the right things that it would buy me a miracle—and it never came.   —Bonnie

She goes on to share her "good-byes" to her loved ones. This is for her four-year-old daughter, Shannon:

Shannon, I love you, my precious baby, forever and always. Of all the extraordinary people in my life, I believe I will miss you the most. If I could, I would be with you as you grow up, watching you, talking with you, loving you through the pain and delight that you will experience in your life. It won't be easy for you, I know, and I hope someday you will forgive me for leaving you.

I sit and wonder what you will look like when you grow up—my imagination strains at this when I look at your radiant still-developing face. I ache when I think of this, and I wonder, "what can I leave you that will comfort you when you think of me?" And it is this: Know that nothing destroys love. Not death, not war, not time. Love is forever and it endures. It is the spirit that binds us all, and that which enables us to rise above the pain and bitterness to realize our greatest and highest good. I will tell you now that I will love you always, wherever I am, and if you are ever in need of it, it will be there inside your own heart, where your memories reside.   —Bonnie

We started to have monthly meetings. We'd all bring food and invite a speaker to come teach us more about HIV, or about alternative therapies or treatments. Sometimes we'd just get together to talk. Someone came up with the idea for a retreat. Could we do one with no funding? Subscribers were sending in money for the newsletter, and there was enough that we thought we could help those women who couldn't pay their own registration fees.

We found a cheap but beautiful place, bunkhouses across the Golden Gate Bridge from San Francisco. It was right by the beach for $65 a weekend. Thirty women signed up. That first night, we sat in a circle and talked. It was awe inspiring. Women from all walks of life. For most it was a first chance to be around other positive women. One woman had tested positive only days before. With tears in her eyes, she looked around the room. "You all look so happy! How can that be? I'm so afraid. . . ."

We talked, painted, went for walks by the beach, gathered sage from the hill to do a healing ritual. It was an artificially created community of women, but a community all the same. On the last day, we came together to share our feelings and talk about the future. Thirty women came alone, feeling afraid; thirty women left feeling inspired. Things were beginning to happen.

For many women, the retreat was a springboard from feeling like victims to taking control over their lives. When the retreat ended, each one of us returned to our various communities and the work began. Positive women became speakers, joined organizations, got on decision-making boards of AIDS organizations, educated their communities, and reached out to other HIV-positive women living in isolation. For many of us, reaching out to educate and support others became part of our survival strategy.

One of these women was an African-American woman named Sharon. After returning home, she gave permission for her story to be printed in the newsletter:

For three months [after I tested positive] I did nothing but what I thought was essential to my minimal existence. For three months I cried and couldn't tell anyone why I was crying or what I was feeling. For three months I felt as if I had slipped into Hell. And because of that slip I had completely forgotten about the joy and beauty of life and what I had accomplished prior to that time.

I had completely forgotten that I had successfully raised a beautiful son (now 22), gone back to school at age 26, graduated from a prominent university with a Masters in Public Administration, and that I had successfully founded and implemented my own nonprofit organization. All I could see and feel was pain and darkness. . . . But guess what? I discovered there is a happy beginning connected with that HIV diagnosis. I reached out and found help . . . with the help of my support network I am able to freely live. . . . One day at a time!

—Sharon

Long before testing positive, Sharon had shared her life's dream of doing public policy work with her employer. This individual, a white woman, told her to give it up: "Forget it. You'll never make it." Sharon held on to the dream anyway. After the retreat, she began advocating for the needs of women and children affected by injection drugs. She became one of WORLD's first board members, joined the board of another local AIDS organization, became active on the county AIDS advisory board, and began facilitating a support group for HIV-positive women. Today, despite (and partly because of) her struggle with HIV, she is at last fulfilling her lifelong dream. Sharon recently began working as a public policy advocate at the local, county, and state levels with the Black Coalition on AIDS in San Francisco.

Since that first retreat, we've had three more. The last one had over 100 inquiries. Women come from all over California, as well as Arizona, Texas, Washington, Nevada, and Missouri. We talk, play, meditate, make masks, and walk on the beach. The retreats are a testimony to the need that women have to find motivation through shared experiences with others. The retreats are also a testimony to the fact that women need opportunities to get away from the kids, the partners, the jobs, the housework, and the city environment to a place where nature takes them in and lets them be who they are, HIV and all.

Perhaps the most powerful gathering at the retreats is the HIV-positive mothers' group. Some of their kids are infected, others are not. They are universally hard on themselves—feeling that, even when they give their last ounce of energy for their children, it is never enough. They grieve the children they have lost and share their fears that they might not be here to watch their children grow up. It is the place where women most readily transcend the barriers erected by centuries of racism and classism, to share their grief and support one another. In spite of all the "isms" that divide, a mother's love for her child is universal.

HOW WE'VE GROWN

Over the past two years, WORLD has grown, like a child that you love even when she grows so fast you can't keep up. We receive calls from HIV-positive women all over the country who are seeking information, resources, and, above all, someone to talk to. We hold social and educational activities, some open to the public and some for positive women only. Women from WORLD's speakers' bureau are courageously speaking out about HIV and AIDS in schools, universities, conferences, and churches. Every time a woman with HIV speaks out, another one learns she is not alone.

This past year we formed a board of directors. Unlike most boards, which are made up of professionals with a small or even token number of "consumers" or people of color, ours is made up primarily of the women we are trying to reach. Most are women living with HIV, representing many communities and life experiences: young and old; African American, Latina, and white; lesbian and straight; mothers and grandmothers; women in recovery from drug addiction and/or abuse; and women in recovery from law school. The level of commitment from this group of women is phenomenal. This work may sometimes be political, but it is always deeply personal.

The president of our board of directors is Doris Butler. Doris is an African-American woman who first went public in the video *Absolutely Positive*. In that video, she spoke of her struggle as the mother of an infected child ("Jared"), as a woman living with HIV, and of her fears about how her church would react when the video came out. She also told her story in WORLD:

> I had been strong for a long time. But after Jared died I couldn't sleep, I had absolutely no appetite, and I didn't want to talk to anyone. This went on for about three weeks. I lost 21 pounds, and my T-cells dropped 200 points.
>
> Finally, I came out of my fog. . . . After Jared died, I realized I had to pull myself together for [my 17-year old daughter, Kelli]. For the first time I stopped to really look at my health and get serious about taking care of myself, because I'm all she has left. I have to be healthy for her . . .
>
> People often ask me, "How do you keep going?" It's an important question. Everybody has their beliefs and strengths. All my strength comes from the Lord. I believe if it had not been for Him I could not make it day to day. Sure I question why he has allowed sickness to come upon us and all these things to happen to me. I'm scared every day, scared I'll get sick, scared I'll lose my home. But then I calm down and remember a verse in the Bible (2 Timothy 1:7): "God has not given us the spirit of fear, but of love and of a sound mind."
> —Doris

Today Doris is employed as project consultant for the World Institute on Disability (WID), where she is working to bring disability awareness to the AIDS community and AIDS awareness to the disabled community.

Ours is a working board, and each member belongs to or chairs one of our committees. For example, the publications committee was started by Barbara Garcia, a white grandmother who wanted to create a Survival Guide for newly diagnosed women. The role that HIV-positive women will play in producing the book, and the visibility of positive women and their voices ringing through it will make the survival guide unique. We all remember how isolated and afraid we felt when we were first diagnosed. We want a beautiful book full of pictures of HIV-positive women living, climbing mountains, talking with friends, holding their children, laughing—a book that conveys the message of hope in addition to practical information. We want women to see our motto—"You are not alone"—with every turn of a page.

Barbara knows why this project is so important. She tells this story about her first support group:

> I saw that these women were not ashamed of themselves. It didn't cause a miraculous awakening for me, but it planted a seed. . . . If they had HIV and were the good people I believed them to be, then maybe I wasn't so bad either. . . . When I think that I'm going to put my name on an article that identifies me as HIV-positive, I really have to smile. Seven years ago I couldn't tell a soul. Four years ago I was plotting how to remove my medical records from San Francisco General Hospital so there would be no record of my HIV status. Three years ago I had to have my therapist hold my hand so I could tell my daughter. And today? Well, I'm off methadone, I don't need antidepressants, and I have more friends than I would have ever thought possible.   —Barbara

Today Barbara works for Planned Parenthood, providing peer support to newly diagnosed women and helping them to access primary care. Often WORLD is the only resource she has to give women. She wants to give them more, and she wants something that can reach newly diagnosed women wherever they live.

SURVIVING

We dream of doing so much more than we can really do. On top of declining health, with trips to the doctor and hospital, our community has faced the loss of children, physical and emotional abuse, a husband beaten by police, rebellious teenagers, becoming homeless (again), relapse into drug abuse, poverty, child custody battles, and more. For many, AIDS is just one more problem added to an already-long list. And still we survive.

Diane K. Haas is a lesbian mom. Until last month, when her health forced her to resign, she was our vice president and coordinator of our speakers' bureau. In June of 1993, Diane spoke on a panel of long-term survivors at the 9th International Conference on AIDS in Berlin. Reflecting on that experience, she later wrote:

As a lesbian in recovery who has survived sexual abuse, heroin and cocaine addiction, prostitution, jails and homelessness, I consider AIDS to be yet another life-threatening disease. I believe that my past experiences have given me the tools with which to survive. . . . I am committed to living, one day at a time, as a survivor, and even after I die, I want to be known as a survivor!

—Diane

Gloria Martinez Little Moon, our president-elect, is active with the Clinica de la Raza in Oakland and the American Indian AIDS Institute in San Francisco. She is also involved with the WORLD's speakers' bureau. In September 1991, she wrote:

In 1986, I tested positive. I was pregnant at the time. I had a lot of stress in my life, I was homeless, and had poor prenatal care, mainly because I was poor. As a result of all that I miscarried and lost my baby.

Even though I was positive, I still really wanted to have a baby. I'm Hispanic, the oldest of five kids in a large, extended family. My husband (who is also positive) is Native American. In our cultures, the oldest kids are expected to be the first to start the next generation. I've always expected to have children, and even now, knowing that I'm positive. I want to have a baby.   —Gloria

Shortly after that, Gloria became pregnant again, and she and her husband celebrated that they would finally become parents. In Spring 1992, they were devastated by another miscarriage. This year she and her husband have both been sick a lot. But, despite poor health and economic hardship, she continues to survive:

When people ask me how I survive (and I have had to struggle just to survive a lot of the time), I tell them that being involved in a supportive community is the most important. In my case, I'm involved in several communities: the Latino community, the Native American community, the homeless community (even though we have an apartment now), the AIDS community, and WORLD.

My inner strength comes from my spirituality. My faith is based on several spiritual cultures: I get strength from the Native American community and spirituality; I am helped by elements of the Catholic culture in which I was raised; and I find strength through my NSA Buddhist religion, in which I chant: "Nam Myoho Renge Kyo."

Becoming an activist has helped me to get educated about AIDS and to reach out to women in communities that haven't been educated about AIDS yet. . . . I want other women to know, especially women who are in a difficult situation—whether it's living with HIV, fighting an addiction, trying to overcome being homeless, being in a relationship with a bisexual man, or some combination of these—you are not alone!   —Gloria

WHERE ARE WE NOW?

There are so many more stories, victories and defeats, hopes and dreams. We can say that WORLD has created a community that welcomes all women with this message: "You are somebody. Even though your life has been filled with pain, you have something to offer. What you think and feel is important."

The women in WORLD are like the ripples that form on a lake when you toss in a stone. Each one receives something from someone and in turn reaches out to someone else. WORLD is a family where no one cares "how you got it." Aspects of a person's life that were formerly liabilities (a history of drug addiction, prostitution, poverty, homelessness) become assets. No one can reach a community more effectively than someone who belongs to that community.

WORLD has created a space where it's OK to talk about the hard stuff. Our most recent issue, "So Let's Talk," included a story by a woman infected through incest. Her story prompted other incest survivors to open up and seek support. The newsletter also allows us to deliver valuable and timely information to the people who need it. Knowledge is power, so we try to give information to HIV-positive women directly, so they can control the decisions that will be made about their disease and how they live their lives.

One of our greatest challenges is our diversity. We come from so many walks of life that, at times, HIV appears to be our only common ground. For some women, HIV is the first major disaster in their lives. For many more, AIDS is just one more problem on top of many others. At times, diversity is our strength. AIDS gives us common ground where we can learn about each other, where we can learn about how racism, classism, and homophobia have affected us differently, and where we can identify the life experiences, values, and dreams that we hold in common. We share a desire to live, fear of illness and isolation, and concern for our loved ones. But the issues that make us different are very real. Although we may all have a nice time at a retreat, there is no getting around the fact that the woman who returns to public housing will not have the same experience as the woman who returns to a nice house and a well-paying job. The women in prison who read, share, and write for WORLD don't get to come to retreats, support groups, and events on the outside. Women who have children or partners to care for get involved in AIDS activism at great expense, sacrificing what little "free time" they may have. These differences mean that finding common ground won't "just happen." You have to work at it—and we do.

The joy of being an organization by, for, and about HIV-positive women is the sense of pride and accomplishment that women are gaining by being able to say, "We're learning to do this for ourselves." Low self-esteem is a significant "co-factor" that led many women to be at risk of acquiring HIV.

Many suffered years of abuse (physical, psychological, or sexual) that led to self-destructive behavior. Some used drugs to mask the pain. Others agreed to sex in the hope that it would bring love into our lives, though usually it didn't. Through hard work we are learning to replace victimization with self-reliance, and the hard work pays off. The response to AIDS is more effective when we, the "consumers" of health care, have a voice.

The problem with being a self-empowerment organization is that we have many limitations and difficulties to contend with: lack of funding, health problems, economic disaster, unsupportive or even abusive partners, children who need our attention, and our own fears that come up every time a new friend becomes ill. We are pulled in many directions, and sometimes a sign of true empowerment is knowing when you can't do it all, and saying "no."

Women who were well when we began are getting sick. Last week I held the hand of a friend during the final hours before she died. The next night we had an annual WORLD event. With so much work to be done, there was no time to grieve. Fortunately, the next night, when there was time, there were supportive friends to grieve with.

We are limited by our lack of funding. Before we could apply for grants, we had to learn how to make grant applications, how to develop programs, how to use the computer, how to incorporate and apply for nonprofit status, how to function as a board of directors, how to recruit and use volunteers. All of this takes time. Often it takes longer to learn it for ourselves than to bring in people who could easily do it for us, but the process is an important part of who we are. Women with HIV need food, help with the rent, money for child care—things we aren't in a position to provide. However, we are in a position to help women find a support network, to build their self-esteem, to secure their dignity, and to become part of a community of women fighting AIDS and supporting one another, where you are not judged by "how you got it."

Living with a life-threatening illness means we have a different sense of time than most people do. A volunteer facilitator recently suggested that we make a long-range plan. To her, that meant five years; to us, it meant one. Five years? Who among us will be here in five years? So as we write our plan we think not simply of what we want to accomplish in our own lifetimes, but of the legacy we want to leave for those who follow. I believe our legacy will not simply be what we did. Our legacy will be that, during a time of despair, a bunch of women came together to live and hope, squeeze the best we could out of life, and fight AIDS. I believe Diane spoke for all of us when, at the 9th International Conference on AIDS in Berlin, she said:

> Some of us have to survive, and like the Jews, Gypsies and Queers would whisper to one another in Nazi Germany, "some of us have to survive so that we can tell the story."

NOTE

[1]WORLD has a monthly newsletter in English, a quarterly newsletter (*Mujer Imagen de Vida*) in Spanish, and a fact sheet with statistics on women and AIDS. Subscriptions to the newsletter are determined by one's ability to pay ($0–20 for low-income and prisoners; $20–50 for individuals; $50–100 for organizations). We can be reached by writing to WORLD, P.O. Box 11535, Oakland, CA 94611, or call us at (510) 658–6930. Our fax number is (510) 601–9746. You are not alone!

Gloria Lockett

CAL-PEP: The Struggle to Survive

I joined the prostitutes' rights organization COYOTE in San Francisco back in 1982 because I was being prosecuted in a case that I thought was stupid, racist, sexist, and biased. I had heard of Margo St. James before; she was the only person I had ever heard talk positively about prostitution. In 1978, I was working with a group of eight women. We were busted for prostitution and conspiracy. The prostitution charges we could deal with, but conspiracy is a felony. We spent a year in court. It cost the taxpayers over a million dollars, and in the end they found us guilty of being in a house of prostitution, but not of conspiracy. That's six months' probation, which I could deal with. In fact, we had offered to plead guilty to that charge in the beginning.

The police were very mad, to say the least. They had spent a lot of the taxpayers' money and a bunch of their time trying to bust us. And they needed to justify it. They were also mad because they knew we were working together. And they were right, we were working and living and being a part of each other. So they stayed after us.

For at least 12 years, there was a group of about seven of us. We always supported each other, we always helped each other. We put the money in a bag, and whatever we wanted, we got. You know, food we bought together, the house we took care of together. We actually had a couple of businesses that we ran together. One was a boutique shop, and the other was a wig shop. We also raised five kids together. Doing all that really taught me how to work with other women. But the police didn't like any of this. To them we were just a "prostitution ring."

The next bust, they only went after me, my lover (who was black), and one other woman (who was black). They tried to get all of the white women and the Mexicans to testify against us! It was a huge case, and they charged us with every felony there was. My bail was $500,000. My old man's was $1,000,000. When I got the first case, I had tried to call Margo St. James, but I didn't really follow up. But when I got the second case, we really needed some kind of help and support.

Margo St. James went to court with us every day. I won my case; the other woman pleaded guilty and did a year and a half. My old man got twenty years. He did two and a half and then won on appeal. Still, they took almost

This chapter is based on an interview conducted by Wendy Chapkis in 1993.

all our property, everything we had. None of that was easy, and all of it, I think, prepared me for what I am today. It prepared me to be able to do all the things that I do. When it gets difficult, I reach back and say, "I remember this." I'll relate it to something that used to happen, and it'll work out. I try to make people understand that, if it had not been for this devastating stuff, I would never be an advocate. I would never have taken my time and realized how important it is to have support out there.

When I got involved with COYOTE, we started doing conferences and rap groups. In 1984 we had a nationwide conference with about 50 people—prostitute supporters, advocates, working prostitutes, and ex-prostitutes, at Margo St. James's place in Mill Valley. The name "CAL-PEP: California Prostitutes Education Project" came out of that conference.

Already in 1984 we realized that, in the very near future, prostitutes were going to be scapegoated for AIDS. At that time, all the attention was on gay men. Well, anybody with any sense whatsoever knew that, if they were saying that it is sexually transmitted, if the way you got it was through your sexual behavior, the next group of people they were going to target would be prostitutes.

We didn't have any money, but we started meeting right after the conference and started talking. Our monthly meetings turned into rap groups about what we were going to do with this AIDS epidemic. Around the same time, I started working for the AIDS research and education project, Project AWARE, as an interviewer. It was clear to me that prevention didn't have enough of a focus, it was getting lost. All you had time to do was interview women and give them a condom. There just wasn't a lot of time for the interviewers to interact with the clients. That's not a putdown, it's just that it was a research project. But something more definite had to be done with prevention and education.

In 1985, a Request for Proposals came from the State Office of AIDS. We wrote a grant for $50,000 for CAL-PEP, being very conservative, hoping that they would fund me and Priscilla Alexander from COYOTE. They gave us only $30,000, which was not enough for both of us to get paid. Since there was only one salary, and I was the one who would be going out on the streets, I became the project director. We knew really soon that I couldn't do all the work by myself, I needed help. After that, whenever we saw any grants for prevention and education, we applied.

In the beginning, we wrote a couple of grants with Project AWARE, applying to do research, and with CAL-PEP, applying to do prevention and education. We received a CDC (Center for Disease Control) grant and one from NIDA (National Institute of Drug Abuse). At that time, *research* was a real nasty word to me. I really thought then that I would never be interested in research.

I had heard so much about the powers-that-be coming down researching people, doing their studies, and then walking off and leaving them holding basically nothing. People who sat down and gave powerful information didn't have a thing to show for it. And this information was sitting in a safe or somewhere, but nothing useful was being done with it. So, to me, research was just a waste of time. I changed my mind about research later on, but the need for prevention work was most important to me.

Once we got that first grant, we realized that we needed a board, but we didn't know anything about that kind of thing. At first there were basically just four of us—two ex-prostitutes and two advocates. We knew we had to have sex workers on the board, but it was very hard to have sex workers who were working. They wanted to know, "Am I going to get paid to sit there and spend three hours with you and spend this extra time?" And, of course, you can't pay boardmembers, so that was hard. So we changed a few of our bylaws, now the board is 40 percent people who have been in the sex industry in some way, with a goal of at least 60 percent people of color.

We've got nine members now. As I see it, the main function of the board is supposed to be raising money and making policies. What federal grants and other funders want you to do is to have a percentage of your own money that is not restricted. And "not restricted" means that the money comes either from private foundations or individually donated. That's very hard to get.

Our board used to be all women, with no men at all. We felt that we had to have men if we were going to be representative of the community, if we wanted them to donate their money. Now we're about 50 percent women and 50 percent men. Besides, it's very, very difficult to work with the woman without working with her man. In the beginning, people would say, "You mean you want to work with pimps?" Whoever her man is, we want to work with her man, because nine times out of ten, she's not going to get infected by herself!

For African Americans, it has always been important to look at the whole family. Even though some lesbians are prostitutes, for the most part we are trying to reach a heterosexual group. So if we look at the woman, we also have to look at her man, because she often won't talk to us otherwise. We have to bring her man into it or let her know that he's welcome in some kind of way. For one thing, it's not just her problem. It's his problem, too. They both have got to change.

Once a month we do workshops intended for the johns, the prostitutes, everybody. It's a three and a half–hour session where they learn AIDS 101, do some role-playing about condoms, and have food. Mostly it's the women and some of their regular customers, who the women make attend. Reaching her pimp, that's easy, because he's down there saying, "What about my woman? I want to take care of my woman. You bothering her, talking to her, she's supposed to be making my money." It's like, "Come on over here; we want to talk to you, too!" But partners that don't identify as being part of the sex industry are hard, because they don't want to identify as being the partner. It's real hard for straight people to realize that both of them have a problem and that both of them need to be sitting down in the same room talking, sometimes with other people. Keep in mind that I'm still talking basically about African Americans.

It's difficult breaching their privacy, and it's difficult for them to identify with other women partners. But some of the things we've been doing are working inside juvenile hall, working in the jails in Santa Rita, and working with work furlough programs. These are the women's partners, even when the partners are not directly there. This is where they are, you know: 80 percent of the men on the streets have either been in jail or are on their way to jail. And it really works out well, because the same people we see on the streets we see in the jail. And by then, you know, the trust is built up. "Oh, that's them. They ain't nothin'. You can talk to them, man." It's not like they're going to get intimidated by us. So partners are definitely our most difficult people to reach. But we keep trying to reach them.

I guess if I could say one overall thing that has made CAL-PEP work, it's the peer model. People looking at us, relating to us, saying, "Hmm, if they could do that, man, I can do that." "Man, I can remember when she was down at such and such . . ." "Yeah, Man, if she could do that. . . ." That's really what we want people to see, that's been our overriding strategy. If we have another peer to talk with them, then they can get the word out better than any other way.

I think in 1985 it was very important as a straight woman that I be involved in the AIDS epidemic. Many gay men let me know the importance of being a heterosexual African American woman involved in AIDS. I was asked to be a part of the Third World AIDS Task Force because they needed people to look at them as more than just a gay male group. For a long time, AIDS had been a gay field, made up of gay men and lesbian women, with lesbian women as the caretakers of gay men who were dying. I felt as if I had to be around, because otherwise they would say, "Oh, it's just those gay men," or "That's just some lesbians." At one time, though, it was real hard for me because I didn't want to identify as anything. What is "straight"? Give me a break! And it's none of your business, whatever I am. But after a while I realized that it was important so that other people would know that this is everybody's problem.

About 1988, the San Francisco AIDS Foundation wanted to become more culturally sensitive, to reach a wide spectrum of people including sex workers and other women, and to do a whole bunch of other things that they just weren't good at doing. So they came to me and asked how we could help each other. Priscilla and I had put together a quiz called the "Hot and Sexy Safe Sex Quiz." But we didn't have any money to offer as a prize. It was 25 questions that were real graphic; it was really fun going through it. We wanted to give the winner of this contest $100.

Well, we didn't have $100. So when the AIDS Foundation said, "What can we do?" we told them, "You can pay this $100 for us." They helped us with the first one, and then we were giving contests every three months. It made us real popular on the streets. Later, when we had less money for the quiz, we had to drop the prize to $25. I didn't really want to do it. But you know what? It works just as well. People still get the money and go, "Oh, my goodness, I've got $25 cash." So it still works. The CDC didn't want to pay for it; I had to be creative, and they finally paid for it.

All our materials are really explicit. You can't educate people if they don't understand what you're saying. We don't want people to have to write down the word and look it up later. What we have to do is be real clear, whatever we write, whatever we develop. Now we're developing role model stories that we are going to put out in our newsletter. We've decided to have three different versions—one for straight people, one for fast people, and one for juveniles. Because even though straight people have multiple, multiple, multiple sex partners, they still don't want to hear about injection drug users and crack users. People that are on the streets want you to talk straight to them, they want you to say "suck dick," they want you to say "fuck." It's really important to me that any materials we develop be short, to the point, and as graphic as possible without being offensive.

You've got to talk to people in a language they understand and treat them with respect. One of the things that CAL-PEP does is help teach outreach workers to work with prostitutes. Whenever the AIDS Training Center in San Francisco does CHOW (community health outreach worker) training, they invite somebody over from CAL-PEP to talk about prostitutes and how to talk to them. People just have to learn to look at prostitutes like they're real people. For some reason, people want to act like they don't know any prostitutes, those foreign creatures out there with horns on their heads. If you treat them like people, there's nothing extra you have to do. That's it, you know.

We just want to make sure that people are sensitive enough to reach the people they're trying to reach. If they're working with prostitutes, they have to know how to approach them, how to talk to them, and when to talk to them. Like if a prostitute is on the street talking to a customer, that's not the time to approach her. If you walk up to her and she's talking to the customer, she's probably going to cut you off even if she really needs and wants the information.

When I started working with women on the stroll, with prostitutes, this one woman came up to me and said, "I'm positive. What does that mean? I don't know if that means I have it or not. What does it mean?" It was devastating; she didn't even know what "positive" meant. I sat down with her for a long time, trying to help her see what it all meant. At that time, I was furious because I thought nobody told her; later I realized that people told her, but she didn't hear. It was devastating news, and she just didn't want to hear it. It took a lot more than the one shot interaction people were given at that time to understand HIV and AIDS.

That's why I knew that it was real important that CAL-PEP talk with people in a way that they could hear. They knew that they could trust what I said, without thinking that I had some hidden motive, like I wanted to research them for my own benefit.

We realized pretty early that it was very hard to get prostitutes to come to our office. We needed to go to them. There were three types of prostitutes that we were really working with at that time: injection drug users, crack-using prostitutes, and career prostitutes. The biggest scare was injection drug–using prostitutes, and they were the hardest to reach. Those were the women who would not go far from their friends and their connections. They were not going to go far from where they bought their drugs or wherever their friends could find them.

And so we got the idea, "Let's find somebody to buy an RV so we can go down and give them a safe place to talk." With an RV, they can look out the window and see if their connection is out there and not be so worried about losing out on something. We got a grant in 1989 from the Robert Wood Johnson Foundation for the van. It was very popular from the moment we got it, and it's just as popular now. We're still trying to get money for another one, but that's not easy. Most federal agencies don't want to fund something like that, even though they know it's valuable and they want to use it. Still they don't want to fund it. It's real crazy.

We took the van to Mission Street and 16th and down to the Tenderloin. At that time, we were basically reaching just female prostitutes. Then we realized that there were a lot of transgender people who needed our assistance; they were really isolated in a world by themselves.

I had been an interviewer for a while for another research project. I interviewed probably about 300 male prostitutes, and my specialty was interviewing transgender people. What we realized from that study is that there was a lot of drug use and high-risk behavior. CAL-PEP wrote a proposal to organize a support group and work with transgender people. We wanted to make sure that we hired transgenders to do the outreach. That was a problem because they had a lot of drug and alcohol problems. We've had several transgenders who've worked for us over time and whenever we did, it made it much easier to reach the transgender population.

One of their hangouts is the Ambassador Hotel. So we would set up shop at the hotel, bring in food, cook, have a safer-sex workshop, and just invite everybody. When we didn't have money to rent a room, the manager of the hotel would let us use his room for the workshops. The magic part of all of this is going to where the people are.

Over the years, we realized that we had to hire people who were comfortable going inside projects, who felt comfortable going inside crack houses, who were comfortable going out late at night—you know, working. And the most comfortable ones were the people who had been there. I just recently realized how valuable it is that I've never been afraid to go inside crack houses. That's because I was raised in the housing projects. I mean, that's home to me. I can go inside a project, and it won't intimidate me whatsoever—I don't care how bad they say it is. It's like these are my people I was raised with, so what's the fear?

When I was raised, I was raised with everybody—poor whites and poor blacks and poor Mexicans, just poor everybody. So it's made me be pretty flexible, and, of course, I never would say that I'm not racist at all, but I think I know how to work with all types of people, without expecting too much of them. People are just people, and they're not going to give you more than they can, and sometimes no more than what the situation calls for. I mean, if you've got six white guys and they're all assholes, even if one of them doesn't want to be an asshole, he's going to be an asshole because he's with the others, you know. And that's the way I've always thought, is that people are really good, but it depends on what the environment is and how easy you make it for them. I mean, it's a difficult world.

But I think that prostitution itself has helped me look at things differently, so that things just don't faze me like they do a lot of other people. I just don't get upset. I learned a long time ago that I can't let my feelings be so easily hurt. People can tell me "no" and it's okay. And if I keep asking, they're going to tell me "yes." I guess that's one of the biggest things, not being afraid to ask, not being afraid to take chances, and knowing how to relate to everybody—well, most people.

I was the oldest sister, so I was always taking care of other people. The whole time I was a prostitute, my mother never said the word *prostitute*, never said it, ever. But she always supported me. It was like, "You don't have to do that, do you, have to go out there, do you?" "Yeah, Mom, I do." "Alright, come on back and try and get some rest," you know. "You can get some rest here."

My parents always supported me, and they never looked down on me. My grandmother was also very supportive of what I did, though I wasn't sure how much she knew about what I was doing, and I wasn't going to tell her. But one time I was on the "Donahue Show," and don't ask me why I didn't think that my grandmother would see me on television. I called back home, and she said, "Honey, I seen you on television." I said, "Whoops." I said, "Really! What did you think?" "Well, honey, I was so proud of you."

They've been supportive, and I think that's what made me feel that I am what I am and I don't have to hide anything. If I didn't have to hide anything from my parents and my people and my family, I'm definitely not going to hide anything from anybody else. It's made me be able to be more forward than a lot of other people, because I don't have anything to hide. Though sometimes I'm sure I should.

Being who I am has definitely been an advantage in a lot of ways for this work. I would say that women on the streets are basically 75 percent people of color, mostly black and Latina. And they are the biggest percentage of the women jailed for prostitution, too. One of the things that CAL-PEP has done since it started was to work in the jails. It's just ridiculous how many women of color go to jail.

One of the problems I have with other organizations, like COYOTE, is that they're just too white for me. Most of those people don't go to jail, mainly because they're white and they're call girls. I mean, it's not their fault. The police want to bust people who are easier for them to bust, and that's the women who are on the streets. It's that simple. People of color, especially blacks and Latinas, are the ones who are in jail most, and that's not because they commit more crimes. They're just easier to get, and people can believe that they committed a crime easier than they can believe that blondes commit crimes.

Women working indoors are a little less likely to get busted. CAL-PEP has done some outreach work with those women, too. We went around carrying flyers, talking to them about support groups, trying to pass out condoms. The women in those places usually are wise enough to know how to take care of themselves; they know that they have to use condoms. We've done some support groups with them, and they're usually very, very knowledgeable. When we first started, people weren't letting them use condoms. They definitely were not. But, you know, since then, a lot of things have happened. Even at most of the places in Nevada, you have to use condoms; otherwise, you can't come into the house. So things have changed a lot.

Most career prostitutes know that they have to use condoms all the time, they know how to use their hand, they know how to use their mouth instead of their vagina. They know all these tricks to make the guys think that they're not using condoms when they really are! And they're sharp enough because they're not addicted, they're not hooked on anything. So they can be sharp enough to fool most men. And some of them just say, "Forget it, you have to use a condom, period. If you don't, you won't be able to date me. Here's your money back." Well, only rarely will they offer to give the money back. But if you're addicted, it's harder for you to insist, you know.

Some of the addicted prostitutes live from day to day. They'll pay their room for one day, and then they have to go out and turn a date before they can get another room. And so, for instance, if it's 2:00 and they haven't had a date, and a guy comes along and says, "Here, I want to date you, but you can't use a condom," they're not going to use a condom. And they've told us that over and over again.

So what CAL-PEP tried to do is work with them by telling them the games that they can play, what they can do to protect themselves and still get the money. We also try to make them understand what the risks are, because some of them really, really don't know or haven't paid enough attention. They haven't stopped long enough to find out exactly how bad the risk is.

That's why we've been concentrating on addicted prostitutes because the other prostitutes, I mean the career prostitutes, don't need us to tell them much. In fact, they can teach all of us a lot, serious. I started using condoms way, way back in the early seventies. Me and people that hung around with me used condoms all the time. We were buying cases of condoms. Almost every time that I got arrested, there were so many condoms they would talk about them.

What used to happen was the policemen used to take the condoms and say either, "You shouldn't be working," or "We know that you're working because you have these condoms, so, you know, if you don't have any condoms, that means you have to go home." Or they'd say, "Go ahead and try to date now without the condoms; we really don't care." Or they would take condoms and poke holes in them. A few years ago, we got a police order in San Francisco that said that they could not confiscate the condoms, and they could not charge prostitutes with having paraphernalia on them if they were carrying bleach or water. Sometimes women used to get charged just for carrying water! That's harassment. They got away with it for so long because nobody challenged them. I mean, one of the worst things about prostitution is that it doesn't have a loud voice. There's not a lot of people who will speak up for it. Fortunately, I put myself around people who will speak up, so I can feel proud.

The fact is, we are ex-prostitutes; we go on television, and we tell everybody about it, and we make them deal with it. You either deal with it or you don't. Somebody made a statement not too long ago calling us "Cal Whores" instead of CAL-PEP. It gives me headaches to make sure that I do things right all the time because of my background. I know people are watching me. I know people want us to mess up. I've always felt like they wanted to say, "Oh, we gave it to them. See what they did? They fucked it up." I mean, either for being black or for being a prostitute or for being a woman, or for all three of those. I always feel like people are going to come back and say that, so I have to make sure that I do things as right as possible. And I feel like if I do things as right as possible, if they don't come out right, fuck it. I did them as right as possible. I mean, I can't worry about it then.

We have had some funders who have said things like, "Those prostitutes are going to teach other prostitutes how to be prostitutes," or something stupid like that. I think that sometimes people don't put as much confidence in us as they do in groups that are not started by prostitutes. I mean, I think sometimes they don't look at us as being a real group. "CAL-PEP? They don't know any better!" A couple of times large organizations have said things like, "Well, we're real leery of giving anything to a group of people that has the word *prostitutes* in its name."

That's one of the reasons why we've got a couple of different names now. We wrote one grant under the name "CAL-PEP: the California *Prevention Education Project*," because when some people heard the word *prostitutes*, they just backed off. So there are times when I use *prostitutes*, and there are times when I use *prevention*.

And, in fact, our category is much broader. Even though we're also always going to work with prostitutes, we're always going to work with people in jail, and we're always going to do things that other people don't do, like go inside crack houses.

Still, CAL-PEP has grown tremendously from the beginning. Because, at first, it was just for female prostitutes, then it was also male prostitutes, then it was transgenders, and it was crack addicts, and all their sexual partners. And now it's basically people on the streets.

I think about 40 percent of the people we target now are prostitutes, but about 60 percent are not. We've basically become a minority organization, because we have chosen to work the cities that are mostly African American. For instance, Oakland is like 55 percent African American, but the people on the street are more like 85 percent African American.

So we've become this outreach program with a reputation of going in places other people may call risky and dealing with all kinds of people who are on the streets. There were just too many types of people who were coming up saying, "Hey, Sister, I want some condoms. What do you mean, you're only talking to her? What do you mean you only want to talk to this prostitute? What about me; you don't care about my life?" We realized after a while that that can't work, so now we're working with just plain people on the streets.

Most of our outreach is still about AIDS and sexually transmitted disease. But we also have quite a large research program now. Last September, we were approached by Dr. Lum who worked for the Health Department. He asked if I wanted him to write a grant for us. I didn't know at the time that it was a research grant. He just said, "The CDC has this pot of money; it's for prevention for women and infants." I knew that it had a pretty rigorous evaluation component, but I didn't know it was research.

So come to find out, when we received the grant, it was indeed a research project. I thought "Oh my God, what are we doing? I'm not sure this is where I want to go." But I fell in love with it. I think now it's something that is real important to Oakland, but also real important to African Americans. I mean, for years it's always been the white people coming in researching us, instead of us researching each other. I think the answers are going to be a lot different than they would be if the work were being done by some people from the University of California.

For years, black people have been researched, for years it's been where we are savvy enough to know how to work it. If you give me $25 for me to do this questionnaire, then I'm going to tell you what I think you want to hear. And basically I think the research has been wrong because we've been telling them what we wanted them to hear, and what we thought they wanted to hear.

But I think with us, meaning black people basically, doing the research, with us down there asking the questions, us coming from the community, there's already trust there. There's already an attitude of "Hey, maybe there's something to this research. Maybe it may mean something if you guys are doing it." There's a tremendous feeling about being able to help my people not only by helping them with AIDS and STD, but also by educating them to be researchers.

We've got four research assistants. Not all of them are black, but my goal is to train as many African-American people in what I'm learning, because I'm learning how to be a researcher. It's gotten to be something that I'm real proud of. But I'm protective, too, because the same branch of government that's funding us funded the Tuskegee Project. It's not the same people, of course, but it is the same branch. My director of research is this wonderful black woman. Still, I feel like we have to make sure that we are not using people in any way whatsoever. All this work feels like it's sort of a mission. It's definitely something that I could do and I felt like I have to do.

Amber Hollibaugh

Lesbian Denial and Lesbian Leadership in the AIDS Epidemic: Bravery and Fear in the Construction of a Lesbian Geography of Risk

WANTED: ATTRACTIVE FEMININE WOMAN FOR ROMANCE, PLEA-SURE AND POSSIBLE LONG-TERM RELATIONSHIP, NO HIV+'S NEED APPLY.

LOOKING FOR SERIOUS RELATIONSHIP WITH WOMYN-LOVING-WOMYN—NO BUTCHES, DRUGGIES, DRINKERS OR HIV'S.

LESBIAN LOOKING FOR LESBIAN LOVE, HOT SEX, GOOD TIMES, GREAT PARTNER . . . COULD BE PERMANENT! FEMMES, FATTIES, HIV+'S, DON'T BOTHER.

These are examples of personal ads running in lesbian newspapers around the country. I found them in lesbian papers published in San Francisco, Los Angeles, New York, Illinois, and Michigan. These magazines ran the gamut from lesbian-separatist newspapers to sex-positive lesbian magazines like *On Our Backs*. And while they contain many descriptions that are awful, each contains one identical and terrifying disqualifier: no HIV-positive lesbians wanted here.

I spend an incredible amount of my time as the director of a lesbian AIDS project disagreeing with other lesbians who are still repeating the dyke mantra, "Real lesbians don't get AIDS," while listening to the numerically spiraling voices of lesbians who are HIV-positive or have AIDS, or while talking to their friends and lovers. Between these two groups of women is a third chorus of female voices full of panicky questions about risk, about whom to believe and how to think when they look at their own behaviors as lesbians. How can lesbians' risk for HIV/AIDS still be debatable 13 years into the epidemic? How can some lesbians still not know any lesbians with HIV?

MY OWN HISTORY, COMING HOME

I have been organizing and writing about sexuality for 15 or 20 years, and doing work around HIV for nearly 10. I have been part of the large contingent of lesbians who, from the earliest days of the epidemic, began to do AIDS work and became . AIDS activists. And, through those years, I have talked to lesbians about what compelled us to get involved. For some of us, it was the shared *gay* identity we felt with gay men which brought us forward early in the epidemic; for some of us, it was the dramatic increase in the already-devastating daily occurrences of homophobia and gay bashing which occurred because of the government's misrepresentation of AIDS (or GRID—gay-related immune deficiency disease, as it was known then) as a gay disease. In that increased violence, "all gay people, both gay men and lesbian, looked alike." For many gay women and men of color, the devastation in their communities and the need for their engagement and activism was urgent and obvious to them. For many progressive lesbians, the communities most under siege were exactly the communities they were committed to working within (women in prisons, poor women, women of color, young women). And many of us were losing friends every week, every month, more each year. Our reasons as lesbians were numerous, varied, and passionate.

All these reasons applied to me—and one other I have only seen clearly in the last year or so, of which I speak much less openly. I was deeply disillusioned and bitter at the horrific fights about sex that erupted so viciously 12 years ago in the feminist, lesbian-feminist, and antipornography movements of the early eighties, the fights that have now been called "the sex wars" in the feminist movement. I come from a poor-white-trash, working-class background, and I am a high-femme dyke passionately committed to butch and femme lives. The sexualities that I defended in those bitter fights and the sexualities I wanted to continue to explore were drawn from all the ways women (and men) feel desire. But I was particularly driven to explore a woman-identified sexuality which was risky, smart, dangerous, often secretive, and capable of encompassing great variation of erotic need between women who sleep with women. And I wanted sex to have a right to its own history without forcing some women to hide or reinterpret their past (or ongoing) desires through a constantly shifting lesbian ideology. I was also tired of trying to say that the political lesbian community was only the smallest tip of the lesbian iceberg, with the vast majority of lesbians still an uncharted, vastly different set of groupings of desires, identities, contradictions and sexual dynamics. Many brave feminist women spoke against the right wing drift of the sex wars and the porn fights, but we were a minority in a feminist and lesbian movement already beleaguered by Reaganomics, Christian fundamentalism, and the fight to keep open women's ability to control our own reproduction. Times were hard.

THE WOMEN I COME FROM

Finally, I wanted to return, to go home again to the women I came from. I longed to build a *new* revolution, made up of lesbians who had mostly been left out of the current feminist explosion: working-class women; women in prisons, reform schools, and juvenile halls; women locked in mental institutions for being too queer; women of color; women in the military and in the bars; women surviving in "straight" marriages and dead-end jobs who longed each day to touch another woman; women who were peep show girls; sex workers; carnival strippers; women who shot drugs and women in recovery from those drugs and the streets; women in trailers, small towns, and cities across America, women who filled the floors of the factories, fast-food restaurants, and auto plants of this country; women whose lives were centered in PTAs, shopping malls, and teamster's unions. These were the women I came from, and they were the women with whom I longed to build a movement. It was here, with these women, that I hoped for the possibility of a new political dialogue about sex and desire and power. They were also, I quickly realized, the women most immediately at risk for HIV.

The struggle against AIDS brought (and continues to bring) all my worlds together, instead of being barely tolerated because of my sex politics and my sense of urgency about the meaning and power of erotic desires. (Was that really political?) Here, in this movement, I was welcomed. In those early years, when the government refused to take on the leadership of this battle (we still have to wait and see about Clinton), it forced us to create a movement based on grassroots organizing, word of mouth, and long-range goals. Each day we had to bite back our urgency and despair at how to get the messages out quickly enough. It was a movement that understood the critical need to talk about the uncomfortable or ragged edges of our sexualities and desires and wasn't fooled by what each of us called ourselves—as though those identity words would explain what we did in bed (or who we do it with), or who we were on the streets or in our jobs.

My first paid job doing AIDS work was with the AIDS Discrimination Division of the New York City Human Rights Committee. The work was to intercede against the fear and stigma that had arisen so violently around HIV. The work relied on and demanded a sharp understanding of class and race in this country, in order to know where to look for those most vulnerable to HIV. And, as an educator and filmmaker organizing at a community level, my passion was fed by the desire to bring forward the voices and stories of the women (and men) who lived in long-overlooked communities, letting them and their stories finally stand center stage where they belong. In spite of the struggles over sexism and racism, and a refusal to understand or support women and men whose risks were different than those generally understood as gay, it was still work where everything remained to be done and anyone willing to confront those obstacles could join. And my heart was breaking from the deaths of those I loved. Life and death among my friends and in my communities, the urgency of people struggling to live with HIV, the need to integrate sex issues through the grid of race, class, and gender, my love as a filmmaker for working-class peoples' stories, each of these pieces added up in ways that compelled me forward.

As I was doing the work, I began to confront my own history in a way I had never before seen it. At some time in my life (and into the present), I had engaged in every one of the behaviors that I knew put lesbians at risk. I heard my own personal and often secret, unspoken narrative in the stories and histories of the lesbians I met who had AIDS or were at risk for HIV. I was a lesbian and had been one for 27 years. Through those years, I had engaged in all the risky activities associated with AIDS, regardless of what I called myself at the time I was doing them. If that was true for me as a lesbian political organizer and activist, what was really happening for the vast majority of lesbians, bisexual women, young lesbians, transgendered lesbians, lesbians who were "coming out," passing women, and women-who-partnered-with-other-women? What about the hundreds and thousands of women who used none of these words as they loved and desired another woman? What was happening to them? And what about the huge unseen numbers who reside primarily outside the confines of our political networks; that vast geography of women building their lives against or with their desire for another woman, which runs like an underground river beneath the "straight" female landscape of America?

Creating the Lesbian AIDS Project at Gay Men's Health Crisis has been a major part of that answer for me; it is my own history coming home. And because I see the issues of HIV for lesbians totally intertwined with the issues of sexuality, class, race, gender, and erotic desires on which I have been working much of my political life, it has thrust me back into a level of organizing I haven't been involved in since the early civil rights and antiwar movements of the 1960s and 1970s. I went back to this work with my history and as an organizer committed to a politics of inclusion. Returning as a 46-year-old lesbian who has been doing this political work since she was 17 allows the richness of my own life history to illuminate the gigantic map of our actual lesbian world, a map that I see as needing to comprehend and chart the wildly disparate universes of queer female lives and communities in order to win our survival.

A PROJECT FOR WOMEN-WHO-PARTNER-WITH-WOMEN

The Lesbian AIDS Project at the Gay Men's Health Crisis (GMHC) in New York is a year old and only one of two funded projects in the world. The other project is at Lyon-Martin Women's Health Clinic in San Francisco. The project has two major missions. The first is to break the silence and denial about HIV in lesbian communities. The other is to demand that lesbians be counted as an essential component in the larger HIV/AIDS communities, as well as in the health, youth, people-of-color, and women's organizations, where we are in danger of struggling to survive with HIV.

In fulfilling these tasks, our job is to specifically identify our vulnerability to HIV and to identify the lack of services, visibility, and inclusion for HIV-positive women-who-partner-with-women. The Lesbian AIDS Project is dedicated to enlarging our understanding of who is affected by the epidemic and to educating about our risk for HIV among the distinct and varied lesbian and female bisexual communities to which lesbians belong.

We have not been seen or counted. The Lesbian AIDS Project is dramatically changing that. In our first year, we conducted a sex survey of women-who-have-sex-with-women. We set up support groups for lesbians at GMHC and other sites, and beginning in the summer of 1993, internships for young lesbians at risk were available in our research and documentation project. Already, we have created an information packet and the first lesbian HIV newsletter, *LAP Notes;* we are working on a safer-sex brochure and kit. Plans in 1993 also included setting up a lesbian mothers' HIV group, a lesbian couples' group, and an HIV-positive lesbian substance users recovery group. We will begin to offer safer sex workshops for HIV-positive lesbians and their partners, led by HIV-positive lesbians and their partners.

We are talking with other concerned groups in various communities to lobby for a lesbian prison discharge planner who will work with women to support their lives outside prison as lesbians living with HIV. In the winter of 1994, LAP will begin an HIV lesbian leadership training group and will be working inside GMHC to guarantee that our own house (its organization and services) are lesbian-specific or lesbian-sensitive. In 1994, we will hire two more staff members to continue and deepen our community organizing and outreach efforts and to develop models and manuals that can be used to train the other communities about women-who-partner-with-women and HIV.

The Lesbian AIDS Project is about community, visibility, and resource sharing. We do a great deal of work around general sexuality and lesbian health issues and are committed to guaranteeing that no lesbian will have to hide her identity or have others automatically assume she is heterosexual.

Doing this work has been incredible and has called on all my experience and intelligence. It is a project about making visible hidden women and communities, while protecting any woman's right not to identify if she doesn't choose to. Because of the complexities of our communities and of HIV work itself, it remains constantly challenging and demanding.

LESBIANS' LEADERSHIP IN THE AIDS MOVEMENT

Lesbians have been leaders in the AIDS movement since its beginning. We have influenced and shaped the discussions, outreach programs, demonstrations, services, and prevention drives since the first moments of this crisis. Working early on with gay men, we were often the first women to see how broadly different communities were being affected by HIV and to use our political histories as organizers and health, feminist, civil rights, and left-wing activists to inform the creation and responses of this new movement. In the broad leadership by so many varied men and women fighting against HIV, lesbians' role has been consistent and powerful.

Many of us doing this work, together with the HIV-positive lesbians we are beginning to meet, first began to talk among ourselves about the risks lesbians were facing in the epidemic. But for many years it was a quiet discussion between lesbians doing AIDS work and HIV-positive lesbians, all of whom kept coming up against the growing numbers of HIV-positive dykes we were meeting every day. This was at the same time we were being told by the AIDS service organizations and by government agencies in charge of the epidemic that "lesbians are not at risk for HIV." We would meet in small groups together to repair ourselves from the sexism or racism of this new movement but quite quickly move into talking about how many lesbians, how many women-who-sleep-with-other-women, we were seeing who were HIV-positive. We would compare notes and shake our heads. It just didn't add up, and we would speak of it late into the night, trying to unravel the keys to our risk at the same time that we remained completely invisible as a community at risk for AIDS.

WHO IS THE "WE" IN OUR SISTERHOOD?

The lines on the map linking our communities of women-who-partner-with-women are very faint. The terrain through which most lesbians can openly travel is very restricted. It is a geography rigorously determined by our backgrounds, our class and color, by rural landscape or city street, by whether we are politically active or spiritually inclined, by the narrow confines of age and health and physical ability, by the marks on the map that identify us as lesbians from the bars, the trade unions, the military, from gay studies programs or as art history majors, by how we each came out and with whom, by the shape of our desires and our willingness (or ability) to risk it all on our love for a woman, by our status as mothers or our decision not to have kids, by the nature of our dreams and aspirations, by our very ability to nurture and sustain hope for our future.

As lesbians in this culture, we suffer from the same lack of power and resources common to all women. Within that oppression we must also navigate our health, sexuality, and social existence in an environment committed to imagining all women are heterosexual. In a universe without voice or presence, lesbians and our particular risks for HIV have remained submerged inside a "straight" female landscape, keeping us ignorant and uninformed about our own risks for HIV. We are a specific population of women with high numbers of HIV-positive members but no official recognition or accounting.

The "secret" of lesbian risk continues, and lesbian deaths increase. There is confusion among us, leading the entire community into doubt and anger.

Some lesbians deny all vulnerability to HIV, making the question of risky behaviors, from shooting drugs and sex with men to safe sex between women appear negligible or unrealistic and unknowable. This guarantees that lesbians who are HIV-positive or have AIDS will come up against a wall of silence and denial and be marked outside the status of "real" lesbians. Our histories as women engaged in these activities and behaviors has worked to disown us as an integral part of the larger lesbian landscape.

And it is here that race and class background become particularly vicious components of our risks and our understanding about HIV. For middle-class lesbians, the margins from birth can slip quickly away when (or if) it becomes known that we are sleeping with other women. For working-class women without any buffers, the picture is immediately more fragile, yet our need for our communities of birth is accentuated if we are women of color, women whose first language is not English, or poor or working-class women who are responsible for and committed to the survival of our extended families. In this already contested setting, HIV/AIDS is often devastating, while our resources remain scarce. We are often forced to lie and hide our sexual desire for other women so that we can access the health care or social services we need. We also hide in order to guarantee the commitment and support of our biological families, our jobs, our neighborhoods, our children, our language, and our access to valued cultural institutions. Medically, socially, and economically, the less room we have to turn around, the more problematic our crisis becomes as we balance precariously between the women we desire and the help and support we need.

The process of "coming out," one of the most celebrated aspects of lesbian writing and storytelling, is often a high risk activity. Think of it. This is often the time when confusion and silence about desire for another woman is the most terrifying to come to terms with. It is often a time of lots of sexual experimentation, often combined with drug use and drinking. It is a period when we feel between communities and identities, and it can often be a time of isolation and shame from former friends, our families, and the authority figures in our lives. At whatever age, "coming out" is a highly charged and often dangerous path each of us walks. HIV magnifies that risk a thousand times over.

HIV makes a mockery of pretend unity and sisterhood. Though the women now affected cross all classes and races, they are predominantly lesbians of color or poor white women, usually struggling with long histories of shooting drugs or fucking men for the money to get those drugs. These are not the women usually identified as the women the feminist movement or the lesbian movement most value and try to organize to create a progressive political agenda. The HIV-positive lesbians who continue to come forward as leaders in the lesbian AIDS movement have histories and lives lived in neighborhoods most gay studies courses rarely describe, let alone use as the bases of understanding queer females' lives.

The question of HIV, of race and class, becomes a question of whose lesbian movement and whose leadership. Will lesbians who shoot drugs or are in recovery be the women turned to to speak for our movement? Will categories that depend on the construction of a "real" lesbian disappear and reveal instead the incredible numbers of women who hold another woman in their arms, regardless of what each woman calls herself or who else she may be fucking? Will histories of low-paying jobs; the revolving door of prisons, the military, and bar life; the sounds of kids playing while the lesbian consciousness-raising group convenes begin to be common and ordinary? Will the power of being butch or femme, the stories of life as a lesbian mom or as a runaway teenage street dyke predominate? When will femmes with long nails and sharp-assed attitude be the voice heard leading gay pride day marches? Whose movement, whose voice, whose stories, whose hope for transformation and change? Whose? These are the questions I see in front of me every day.

SOME COMPLICATIONS ON THE WAY TO UNDERSTANDING LESBIAN HIV

The crisis for lesbians struggling to understand the impact of HIV in our communities is compounded by the general lack of decent, nonjudgmental information about lesbian sexuality. Because it remains unacceptable to love and desire other women sexually, we are also left with little substantial information about what we do in bed with each other, including what might put us at risk sexually. STD (sexually transmitted diseases) of all kinds are little understood or discussed between women partners, and the fear and ignorance surrounding HIV compounds the already existing blank space silencing this discussion in our communities. And, like all silences and prejudices, homophobia hurts us profoundly, leaving us unarmed and unprotected, as though forbidding the word *lesbian* in our existence can stop the act of our love. It doesn't of course, it just leaves us vulnerable and uninformed. Our confusion about whether AIDS is really a lesbian issue reflects this oppression.

The denial of our risk for HIV is often supported by a circumscribed lesbian sexual border that some lesbian-feminists have constructed, which refuses to acknowledge or accept that we sleep with each other in many, many different ways. We are butch/femme women, we are queer or androgynous, we are lesbian-feminist, we don't believe in labels; we practice s/m, we use our hands, our mouths, our bodies, sex toys, to pleasure and please each other; and we may also sleep with men, whether we call that "bisexuality," "coming out," "economic necessity," or we don't dare talk about it.

For a small, though growing number of HIV-positive lesbians, the only (or primary) risk for HIV is their sexual relationship with a female partner who was HIV-positive when they became lovers. When these lesbian couples looked for good information about female-to-female transmission, they were rarely successful. And when they went to other lesbians to try to discuss it (if they dared), few other lesbians could help. Like all the other risks in our communities, female-to-female sexual transmission remains scientifically undocumented and unreliably researched. This lack of knowledge combines dangerously with continuing drug and alcohol use throughout our communities which has always been an unrecognized crisis. This crisis is compounded by our invisibility and our lack of political clout. And suicide, especially among young lesbians, is another epidemic in a population of women who love each other.

These activities and identities are components of our communities' sexual and social lives. While women-who-partner-with-other-women have taken an extraordinary risk daring to love another woman, this has not guaranteed that our judgments against each other's erotic or drug choices won't be as cruel as the general culture's judgments against us. Our understanding of the reasons many of us shoot or snort drugs, drink till it harms us, experiment with substances that can kill us are stories that we have not let surface enough inside our community, hoping that, by not telling aloud those pieces of our lives, we will not be hit any harder by social condemnation than we already are. It's as though we think that, by disavowing a set of activities (and the women we stereotype as doing them), we can protect ourselves from even more homophobia.

We also carry those historical silences into our sexual judgments as well, thinking that, if we don't enjoy a particular sexual activity ourselves, no other lesbian could either. If another woman *wants* differently, she is in danger of having her credibility as a "real" lesbian questioned. Yet we are women who are sexual originators and social inventors, leaping across the sexual and emotional silences surrounding women's desires for other women, daring to touch and possess each other sexually, daring to claim our right to be sexual, to love and want another woman.

SO AMBER, WHAT'S YOUR PROBLEM ANYWAY?

The Lesbian AIDS Project sex survey is very explicit and was done to try to determine how we are really having sex with each other, how often, in what combinations and with who else, and what we think of ourselves as we do it. This was not a survey primarily about relationships. It appeared in the 1992 *Lesbian and Gay Pride Guide,* of which 60,000 copies are printed for the June Gay/Lesbian March and which is picked up and used as a resource book by a wide variety of lesbians, including women who don't necessarily hook into the gay bookstores and lesbian political organizations in New York City. When the survey appeared, my answering machine was suddenly full of "anonymous" messages from "normal dykes" suggesting that what I really needed was to go "fuck a man." Sometimes the messages were from "regular" lesbians telling me how sick they considered some of the categories and activities that I had included on the survey. Usually those messages ended with a free-wheeling interpretation of what they imagined "I was into." These anonymous messages always hurt. It was clear to me how problematic the real world of female sexuality is for all of us and what an added minefield being a lesbian could be when it was thrown into the mix. Sex in our community remains our smoking gun, and the fight for whose hand is on the trigger counts.

Still, many women were thrilled by the survey; over 1,600 women filled them out and sent them back. The results of the survey were available from LAP in Fall 1993. Women wrote their opinions in the margins and on Post-its stuck over the sections they loved or despised. Lesbians said, "Congratulations. I've waited a long time for someone to care enough about our survival to finally ask us what we do sexually." Women who answered used exclamation marks and red pens to write their ideas and express their opinions. "I didn't even know lesbians could do this!" "I love these questions. My girlfriend and I are going to try them all before we finish this survey." "Hot survey! Getting steamy just answering it." But other women wrote, "I didn't even know that lesbians could get AIDS."

In one of the surveys, I found this note attached. It said, "I am glad you're doing this survey for those lesbians that can use it, but my lover and I don't really have any use for these questions. *We are both women and because of that we understand each other's bodies and desires.* Maybe women that are more fucked up don't understand this, but for us it's really just natural. Thanks anyway."

In anthropology, this is called magical thinking, and this magical thinking is rife throughout the communities I have to speak with every day. It is the most central idea I hear wherever I travel among lesbians. The notion that, because we are women touching women, we automatically understand and empathize so completely that we know intrinsically how to touch or caress each other, how much pressure to use when we suck or lick each other's bodies, how to stroke or fuck each other to climax is very dangerous and very widespread. It is hard to imagine, then, how to begin discussing safer sex, negotiating with a lover, HIV and STD protection methods, talking openly about our drug or sex histories. In this context, magical thinking leads most women to assert that they don't think we can transmit sexual diseases to each other. And it leads to dangerous and incorrect sexual notions that I also hear too often, like if STD are transmitted between women partners, it's probably due to a "bisexual" woman. In this lesbian worldview, men are dirty, women who sleep with them are contaminated, only real lesbians remain pure. Yeast infections are spread between us sexually, and high rates of STD are increasingly prevalent among lesbians at risk of HIV infection,[1] and still this is rarely discussed. How can safer sex ever be a regular part of our lives, when we are literally forced to risk our right to community to tell the truth about what we do and who we do it with? The legacy of being women in this culture, of being denied decent nonjudgmental information about our bodies and our desires is multiplied for us as lesbian women.

HIV-POSITIVE LESBIANS AND YOUNG LESBIANS LEAD THE WAY

Still, in the face of this culturally imposed ignorance, I see women who love other women trying to carve out an erotic terrain of their own which claims and encourages all of us to explore and reckon with our desires for each other. It assumes that there are thousands of complex ways each of us feels desire and passion. Especially in younger lesbians I have seen a much more matter-of-fact acceptance of HIV risk for lesbians. These are women who have grown up sexually in the first decade of AIDS, and they are much less resistant to the idea of lesbian risk and HIV safety. And in lesbian communities already hard hit by HIV, the question of safer sex, regardless of presumed mode of transmission, is also different and more open. It is there, in working-class lesbian political and social organizations, that I see the most innovative and least judgmental struggle to integrate HIV knowledge into daily lesbian life. These are often communities of lesbians that have had the tragic example of numbers and the powerful voices of HIV-positive lesbians to reckon with and lead the discussion. For example, Bronx Lesbians United in Sisterhood (BLUeS), a membership group of 1,000 estimates that 10 percent of their members are HIV-positive. There, HIV is no stranger. In these communities, HIV-positive lesbians are lovers, mothers, sisters, best friends.

Growing numbers of HIV-positive lesbians are speaking out more and more often. More than anything else, it has been their bravery and their insistence to tell the truth of their own lives (and histories) that have cracked the silence and denial in the larger lesbian communities. Like the role that HIV has played in other settings, AIDS transmission always exposes the gap between who we want to believe ourselves to be and what we really do in our regular lives. The leadership of lesbians who are infected or affected by HIV is a powerful and original model for the building of a new, more inclusive movement of women-who-partner-with-other-women. It brings into one dialogue the lives of all of us throughout our evolution as lesbians. These are often lesbians who become activists and HIV workers when they are told their own antibody status. The work being done by these lesbians in AIDS organizations, women's outpatient health clinics, detox centers, youth programs for runaway lesbians, prisons, recovery programs, and neighborhood organizations is rarely documented, but it is some of the most powerful lesbian activism happening. And it is building a new foundation and a different class base for a larger lesbian political movement.

CLAIMING THE POWER OF OUR LIVES

Our right to be sexual with each other and to struggle with the issues of our daily lives, like our drug use and the sex we have with men, are all pieces of the lesbian puzzle. Whether or not the larger culture acknowledges us, we must recognize each other and our different struggles. The lesbian map is very large, our numbers are significant, and we must pick up this fight to protect ourselves and each other while we fight to be seen and respected. We can't wait for other people to see what is right in front of our noses; that we are an integral part of this world, not outside it—and so is a potentially life-threatening virus, HIV. Our community is not immune, and lesbianism is not a condom for AIDS. Like everyone else, we are vulnerable and must take the steps necessary to learn how to protect each other's lives. No one else will do it for us, and no one will do it as well. For millennia, we have been taking risks to love each other. Now we need to expand our understanding of who we are and what we do in order to understand the many ways we need to go forward. Our communities are fabulously sexual and inventive, our lives and histories varied and full of meaning. We can support each other in taking the steps each of us needs to be safe, erotic, and powerful. And we can build a movement, starting here, which refuses to privilege rigid ideological categories over the truths of our lives and which bases its theories on a more complicated map of lesbian desire and lesbian voice.

NOTE

[1]Surveillance Branch, AIDS Office, San Francisco Department of Public Health, "HIV Seroprevalence and Risk Behaviors Among Lesbians and Bisexual Women: The 1993 San Francisco/Berkeley Women's Survey," 19 October, 1993.

Some Comments on the Beginnings of AIDS Outreach to Women Drug Users in San Francisco

Everything has a beginning. AIDS has a beginning. AIDS and men. AIDS and women. AIDS and injection drug users (IDUs). AIDS and prevention has a beginning. AIDS and outreach has a beginning. Scores of epidemiologists, medical historians, anthropologists, journalists, social scientists, and other armies of commentators will author their versions of the beginning. This is one such comment on the history and the beginning of AIDS prevention for women IDUs. It is not epidemiological. It is not social science, and it will not pretend to be objective. It is simply one woman's localized view of how the powerful forces of politics, racism, sexism, classism, and traditional scientific inquiry shaped the delivery of AIDS prevention messages to women at highest risk for HIV—injection drug users.

It feels strange to be framing events that happened only nine years ago as "the old days" or "ancient history," but that is what AIDS has done to history and to our sense of time. For those with HIV/AIDS and for those struggling beside them, AIDS has compressed time and irrevocably altered our sense of history. Now there is only AIDS, and then there was simply that time somewhere, far back in our distant memories, when the word did not exist. Nine years is a lifespan for someone infected with HIV.

I welcome your comments on my story and all opportunities to set the record straight. Is it ever possible to get people to agree on what really happened? I take responsibility for these views. They are solely mine and not those of the editors of this book.

ONE BEGINNING AND ONE STORY: JEANNETTE'S STORY

On June 11, 1986, I turned 40 years old. That day I found myself sitting in the room of woman called "Jeannette." She had participated in an AIDS research study several months earlier, and I was there to give her her HIV-antibody test results. Jeannette lived in an inner city hotel, in the center of the sex and

The author of this chapter wishes to thank the women in the Tenderloin for their willingness to share their lives and to Karen Vernon for her fine editorial assistance.

drug trade zone. She rented her destitute room a few days at a time, depending on her cash flow, which meant that she was often without a room unless she could crash with someone else in the hotel. Jeannette was at the end of a three-day stay and was facing imminent eviction. Nothing new here. Well, not quite nothing new. Jeannette was in the throes of a profound psychotic state with no one to help her. I was turning 40 years old and knew very little about how to handle someone in a profound psychotic state.

Jeannette was a speed user, and she was "tweaking." This meant that she had been up for three days straight and hadn't eaten, bathed, or performed any of those other basic human functions that help us get through each day. Jeannette was definitely not in any shape to make decisions about her predicament. She was too busy trying to decide whether she should kill herself or the man who had supposedly stolen her knife.

I knew something about tweaking. I had just spent the previous year interviewing people who put needles in their arms to alter their view of the world or block it out completely. My colleague, Rose Dietrich, and I had just completed 413 lengthy one-on-one interviews that asked these folks the most intimate questions about their medical, drug, and sex histories, and about their knowledge and attitudes about AIDS. Today, this kind of interviewing is commonplace, but back in "the dark ages," New York and San Francisco were the only places in the country where people were conducting research with injection drug users. At the drug treatment clinics where we asked these incredibly personal questions of their clients, the staff hadn't a clue as to why we were there. We had a nurse with us, Bonnie Fergusson, who poked the clients for two tubes of blood and paid them $15 for their time. Now these drug treatment clinics depend on AIDS research money in order to provide other kinds of services that were cut in the Reagan/Bush years. But in 1985, this kind of AIDS research was in its infancy, and Rose, Bonnie, and I were perceived as weirdos with a prurient interest in the drug use and sexual habits of their clients. We didn't have our own private offices where we could ask these questions confidentially, and we had to rely on whatever clinic space the staff could allot us each day. Often we would begin an interview and have to move when the occupant of the office came back from lunch or a meeting. One drug treatment counselor always referred to us as "those people who like to ask all those weird questions about AIDS." He informed me that "there's no AIDS in this clinic because gay men don't like to come here."

Fortunately, Bonnie had been a nurse at the Haight-Ashbury Detox Clinic for many years and was very knowledgeable about drug users. We learned a lot from Bonnie, but we learned everything else from those clients during the hour or so we were ensconced together. My master's degree was useless here—I learned much of what I know today about drugs, drug use, and drug users from talking with these folks. Rose and I particularly liked to interview women, and we went out of our way to recruit women into the study. They were generally more responsive and forthcoming with their answers, and we sensed intuitively that once all the facts were in, women would be just as much at risk for AIDS as men. The rumors were already circulating about Africa and New York City. We committed ourselves to recruiting 33 percent women, which is the generally accepted percentage of female to male injectors.

I should tell you about the early days of this research project, and how I ended up spending my birthday in a hotel room with Jeannette almost a year after I began interviewing injection drug users in clinics.

BACKGROUND AND SOME HISTORY: QUANTITATIVE AND QUALITATIVE METHODS

In 1985, the National Institute on Drug Abuse (NIDA) had funded a two-part research project. The first component was an ethnographic or qualitative study of high risk neighborhoods in San Francisco. The second component collected quantitative risk behavior information and HIV seroprevalence data from injection drug users. For this second quantitative component, approximately 300 interviews and blood serologies were collected at drug detoxification programs. "Quantitative" refers to traditional research methods of collecting and interpreting data. We administered a standard interview to all our clients which was designed to elicit "yes/no" or multiple-choice answers. These answers can be coded and turned into numbers or "quantitative data" (for instance, "When asked if they always used condoms with their main sexual partners, 11 percent of IDUs responded, 'Yes.' "). Quantitative research can easily analyze specific information from very large groups of people.

For the most part, only the traditional quantitative Western scientific research model is funded by the federal government. This research model is based on the methods of scientific inquiry originally developed to test physical and chemical properties. These methods generally require the researcher to enter the "experiment" with a hypothesis or question and collect data that will prove or disprove this hypothesis. This laboratory model is rigid and controlled because it is tightly focused on proving or disproving a single hypothesis or answering very specific questions.

The NIDA-funded research project adhered to this model. The principal investigators—that is, the people who were given the money—had the credentials to conduct the research in this mode. I learned this model in graduate school, but I also learned about the importance of ethnography, which I was told was nothing more than "systematized gossip"—the very heart of peoples' lives.

Ethnography requires observing social interactions, keeping field notes, and interviewing "informants" who reveal important information about the beliefs, values, attitudes, behaviors, social relationships, daily happenings, and gossip of their world. This requires a high degree of trust and acceptance between the observer/ethnographer and the informant. Good ethnography that results in a true picture of a social group is difficult to carry out and, when skillfully conducted, is an art. Whether or not it is science and the information can be called scientific data will always be debated.

The first component of our project was conducting ethnography of San Francisco's high risk neighborhoods. Ethnography results in qualitative data, which usually takes the form of words rather than numbers. Its difficult to put qualitative data into a computer in order to analyze it, "crunch" it, or reduce it to numbers without losing its richness and its ability to portray peoples' lives accurately. The information generally applies to smaller groups of people but gives us a broader, more holistic understanding of those groups. Both kinds of data have their place in research, prevention/ education, and evaluation. Well-conceived projects use both tools to get meaningful answers to the questions. Theoretically, both approaches complement each other. Unfortunately, this rarely happens. Numbers are considered "hard science" when compared to the "soft words" that are required to explain qualitative data. When both methods are used in a project, the power of hard data usually takes fiscal and design precedent over the soft data.

The qualitative project directors, both sociologists, used this ethnographic approach to learn about drug users' attitudes about AIDS and their drug and sexual behaviors. They "hung out" in hotels like Jeannette's, leaned against parking meters, and generally tried to look as if they belonged in an inner city neighborhood. They were often mistaken for narcotic police or "narcs."

While Rose and I were busy doing interviews in the clinics, meeting the hundreds of drug users who would become part of this story, the ethnographers were making contact with small needle-sharing circles, building trust, and gaining entry into the lives of injection drug users. Hundreds would be affected by the information, ideas, and intervention strategies that were beginning to percolate from both approaches. NIDA was thrilled—the data were rolling in.

Then, about six months into the study, the director of the quantitative study, Dr. John Watters, had the foresight to move that component out of drug programs and concentrate on the out-of-treatment drug users. Simultaneously, a University of California research project was beginning which would concentrate on the in-treatment population. Watters's project would generate a broader picture of the problem and let us know if the out-of-treatment folks had the same or different attitudes and practices. The move was a wise allocation of resources, and ultimately responsible for the positive shape of subsequent events in the HIV-testing arena.

Anyway, NIDA never got so much for their money. These seroprevalence studies established a "baseline" HIV seroprevalence rate for in-treatment and out-of-treatment injection drug users that would be the foundation for evaluating the effectiveness and impact of all future prevention programs in San Francisco. The window of opportunity for collecting meaningful clinical and behavioral data was closing fast as the HIV virus passed from one syringe to the next in San Francisco's sharing circles. Seroprevalence rates were also rising in Oakland, Los Angeles, San Jose, San Mateo, San Diego, Sacramento, and other large urban areas of California with a concentration of injectors.

THE BEGINNING OF COMMUNITY AIDS WORK

In March of 1986, Rose, Bonnie, and I entered Jeannette's hotel to do our first interviews outside of a drug treatment program. I'll never forget it. (We're not at Jeannette's story yet. That's not for a few more months.) I wasn't scared. I was thrilled that we were finally getting the opportunity to bring AIDS consciousness to this very high risk neighborhood. Rose and I had come to realize that we were not conducting pure research but were giving people the opportunity to think about their possible exposure to AIDS (we didn't call AIDS "HIV" in those days) during the course of the interview and maybe later, when they were alone at night or shooting up with friends or strangers. The research was not designed to educate but that's what was happening. People who put needles in their arms taught us over and over again that they did not want to get AIDS. They only wanted to get high. They were not on a "death trip." People believe that now because there is a ton of research data to support it, not because needle users said it back then. Rose and I, like a few other people in New York, Baltimore, Washington, D.C., and San Francisco, believed it then. We were excited about being there.

On that first day, the sociologists introduced us to their informants, who had agreed to be the first people in the hotel to be interviewed and tested. Each person would be paid for their time answering our interview questions and giving us their blood samples. The informants promised to tell their friends about the study, to spread the word about the test and the money, and to vouch for us. They trusted that we would not use their names, that they would be assigned ID numbers, and that no one else would see their test results. We carefully explained what the AIDS antibody test was and was not. Today, we call this standardized pre- and post-test counseling. But at that point, a specific protocol for explaining this to drug users had not been invented, and we made up our own guidelines along the way.

"Joe," my first research subject, and I rode the elevator up to his sixth-floor room. Rose left with his partner, "Karen," a transsexual, and went to a friend's room. Joe's hotel room was his house. For him, this room was not an eight-by-ten, cockroach-infested transient or SRO (single rate occupancy) hotel room. He invited me in, was the perfect host, and extended the hospitality of his home. I liked Joe immediately, and we both felt at ease with each other. I didn't feel like my anthropological heroine, Margaret Mead, when she first arrived in Samoa in 1928. Joe was a person whose culture I could relate to and understand. The only difference between him and me was that he used drugs and put needles into his arm. I smoked cigarettes while he stepped into the curtained alcove to fix. He didn't seem any different when he came out. He talked the same. He walked the same. We began the interview.

For me and Rose, Joe and Karen were the beginning of street-based outreach in San Francisco. Joe and Karen kept their word about telling their friends. We were able to interview four more people that day, and when we arrived at the hotel the next day with the sociologists, there was a riot waiting for us. Word had spread like wildfire. There was a huge crowd clamoring to talk to us, to get tested, and to get their money. That day and the rest of that week, Rose and I interviewed and drew blood on 113 people. We knew we had hit on the right method, but we had to work hard to get the women to participate. For the most part, the men were the dealers and the buyers. They were more visible and accessible. Early on, we knew we had to give priority to women. Any women who showed up got to go before the men who were already waiting. The men didn't like that, but they were encouraged to bring their girlfriends, their wives, their women friends, their cousins. Special recruitment policies for hard-to-reach women were the only way I was ever going to get to women like Jeannette, but I didn't know that yet.

Exuberant and exhausted on our second day, we finished our "draw" and left the hotel, left Joe and Karen, the people they shared with, the people they bought and sold drugs from, the people we hadn't met yet, the people already infected, the people yet to be infected, the wonderful and supportive manager, Hank Wilson, who understood why we were there, and the women. I couldn't forget the women I saw hanging out in the lobby giving their babies bottles of orange soda and candy for breakfast. I couldn't forget the 17-year-old prostitutes or the older prostitutes. I couldn't forget the ones that I knew were not "Rg's" (real girls). The transgender folks we met were often sexually indeterminate. When I think about women drug users and AIDS, I also include transgender people, who want the life of a woman. They face the same world as the other women in this hotel and in this neighborhood, and then so much more. I knew I wanted to spend a lot of time at that hotel and get to know everybody at risk, especially the women. My interest in women's issues was fueled partly by my feminism and my degrees, but mostly it was because women were barely being discussed in reference to AIDS.

I'd like to spend some time here talking about the positive forces in the community. Aggressive lobbying from African-American community leaders, such as Calu Lestor, Shirley Gross, Pat Evans, and Sala Udin; the NIDA-funded research project; community activists like Hank Wilson; and others whose names have gone unrecorded resulted in the city and county of San Francisco slowly awakening to the need to respond to the spread of AIDS among IDUs. Early in 1986, a minuscule amount of funds was designated from the health department to be "sole sourced" (this means that there was no request for proposals, or RFP, issued to the service providers in the community) to several key agencies to conduct various AIDS prevention activities. The Youth Environment Study (YES) and the Haight-Ashbury Detox Clinic were contracted to provide approximately $55,000 worth of these activities. These funds were tacked onto the remaining funds from our NIDA grant and provided the seed money to hire the city's first community health outreach workers (CHOWs). It was not clear how long the money would last or if there would be any additional funds in the future. In other words, the outreach program was started with no guaranteed funding beyond the first six months. It took courage and faith to start such an ambitious undertaking on so little. The newly hired outreach staff knew about the funding picture and were willing to accept their positions under those circumstances. Everyone knew that the possibility to affect the HIV seroprevalence rate of drug users would be lost without aggressive intervention now. Otherwise, San Francisco would look like New York, where early seroprevalence rates for injection drug users were already estimated to be around 50 to 60 percent. Other funding ideas were identified from federal and state sources, and the tedious process of responding to RFPs began.

The original players in this story had applied for separate funding from NIDA, and by late summer of 1986, I was working half-time on each project, coordinating the street-based seroprevalence study and supervising the CHOWs. Line staff on both projects were diverse, multicultural, and committed to doing great work at an impressive level. They worked long hours, were grossly underpaid, and developed prevention and research strategies that are still in existence today and have been copied all over the country. The "teach and bleach" strategy was tested and launched. We never asked for permission or approval from funders or the local health department. We just started putting those little plastic bottles in the hands of the people who needed them. Jennifer Lorvick, at age 22, figured out, with feedback from us, how they should look and what they should say. I wonder how many bleach bottles have been distributed in the United States since 1986. We loaded backpacks with condoms, bleach, and "How to Clean Your Works" cartons, and saturated the neighborhoods where we were sanctioned to work.

Every six months like clockwork, we went back to the three neighborhoods where we could do "draws" and retested everyone and sent CHOWs out to recruit new folks. One month later, the research staff and the CHOWs would go back to that neighborhood and pay people to come back to get more information about AIDS and their test results if they wanted them. HIV-positive folks would be hooked up with a CHOW and helped through the ensuing emotional roller coaster, then connected to what few services there were that knew how to work with injection drug users and could respond to their special needs. HIV-positive folks were paid to come back in two weeks to be offered more support and help, besides what the CHOWs could provide.

The CHOWs ended up wearing many hats—they were health educators, counselors, lay ethnographers, social workers, legal experts, chauffeurs, baby sitters, bankers, barefoot doctors, community organizers, and advocates for people already infected. The problems and the lack of resources for drug users overwhelmed the CHOWs so much that they had a difficult time fulfilling their prevention duties. It's only in the last few years that new agencies have been established to help specific populations and that old agencies have learned how to handle special populations beyond gay white men. "CHOWs" became synonymous with AIDS prevention and drug users. Street-based outreach was the only way to stop the second wave of the AIDS epidemic, and bleach bottles were the primary weapon.

The women infected early in the epidemic were still treated as anomalies. No one knew that by 1990, AIDS would be the leading cause of death for women of childbearing age in the New York metropolitan area and the fifth leading cause nationally. For most people, AIDS was still thought of as a "gay disease," and the new consciousness in targeting injection drug users for prevention efforts focused mainly on men.

The San Francisco Women's AIDS Network (WAN), however, held the first Bay Area Research Conference on Women, Children, and AIDS in March 1987. Surgeon General C. Everett Koop even came and spoke to a standing-room-only crowd at the Health Commission Hearing Room at the San Francisco Department of Health.

Those of us committed to working with women attempted to learn everything there was to know about women and HIV. Sadly, that didn't take long, and we quickly became "the experts for doing outreach with women in the streets." We joined the ranks of the early pioneers in the Bay Area, like Dr. Nancy Stoller (Shaw), Dr. Judith Cohen, Dr. Connie Wofsy, Shirley Gross, Cheri Pies, Priscilla Alexander, Gloria Lockett, Ruth Schwartz, and Laurie Hauer.

Dr. Cohen and Dr. Wofsy began the AWARE (Association of Women's AIDS Research and Education) Project by hiring and training prostitutes from the prostitutes' rights organization, COYOTE (Call Off Your Old Tired Ethics), to interview and draw blood from women drug users in detox clinics and out in the streets. COYOTE then entered the vanguard of AIDS prevention for women at highest risk for HIV. They went on to form their own AIDS education organization called CAL-PEP (California Prostitutes Education Project). Today, AWARE and CAL-PEP are recognized internationally for their groundbreaking work with women. Dr. Stoller organized the Women's and Children's Program at the San Francisco AIDS Foundation and provided psychosocial support for the first women in the Bay Area who had AIDS or who were infected with HIV. Their program today, led by Catherine Meier, serves hundreds of women a year and can barely meet the demand for their services. Laurie Hauer, a nurse at San Francisco General Hospital, was caring for pregnant women with HIV at a time when little was known about perinatal transmission and the effects of pregnancy on the immune system. Dr. Peggy

Weintraub clinically followed the infants and babies born to these women, and gathered some of the earliest data on pediatric AIDS.

"ISMS" AND EMPIRE BUILDING: THE SAME OLD STORY

The researchers who had started the traditional research and outreach projects made half-hearted attempts to build coalitions with some of these women's projects. The coalition building failed because of both perceived and real sexism, racism, and classism. Some of the researchers showed a lack of understanding and respect for the work that these women had already accomplished. There was a lot of talk about providing prevention and education materials for high-risk women, but there was not the necessary impetus from program administrators or the dollars to support it. This is where female drug users and the female sexual partners of male drug users were shortchanged on prevention services.

I also began to wonder where the African-American and Latino researchers were. The few minority researchers who attempted to collaborate on our NIDA-funded project were viewed as inexperienced in research methodology. The concerns and issues they raised about minority research subjects' participation in the project were not taken seriously. Seroprevalence rates were beginning to skyrocket in these ethnic groups.

The research heads failed in their attempts to subsume the leaders from the African-American and the women's community, and individuals from within our agency were often left to develop their own relationships with these communities. Our CHOWs were not able to enter all high-risk neighborhoods in San Francisco because local neighborhood leaders and service providers would not allow the white researchers to work on their turf because of these politics and problems. The inability of projects to form and maintain coalitions resulted in competition for funding resources and political back-stabbing that carved deep wounds in the AIDS service-provider community and left women and minorities at increased risk for HIV.

The agency's reputation suffered so much that the project and their outreach program were not refunded by NIDA. However, the early pioneering efforts of our original program, formulated by an enthusiastic, committed, and imaginative staff, were duplicated all over the country when NIDA funded 68 demonstration outreach and research sites. The new funds were given to the only key player from the beginning who had demonstrated a willingness and a commitment to work with everyone: Dr. John Watters.

BACK TO JEANNETTE'S STORY

And so there was Jeannette, still in danger and at risk for HIV, and no place to send her. Her needs were overwhelming, so I put on my social worker hat in an attempt to prioritize those needs. She was a danger to herself and needed to be "5150'd," a legal definition for people who are a danger to themselves or others. Turning her over to the system would take care of her immediate housing needs, and she would then be in the hands of people who knew a lot more about this than I did. AIDS prevention was low on her priority list. Fortunately, there was a drop-in mental health clinic in her neighborhood that was able to do this, so I asked her if we could go there and get her 5150'd. She knew all about this and readily agreed. She was as anxious as I was to take care of herself.

We walked up the street to the clinic, and she talked to herself the whole way. I tried to bring her back to reality, but she was engrossed in a conversation in her head with the knife thief and was talking to him as we walked along as if he were right next to her. Then she was engaged in planning her attack on him, but she did not speak to me. For her, I sensed that I was not there, and she did not know that her inner dialogue was coming out of her mouth. The clinic did a lengthy intake interview with her and then admitted that there wasn't really anything they could do with her except take her to the Psychiatric Ward at San Francisco General Hospital if she was willing to go. However, they were not allowed to take her; we could call an ambulance. We called a cab instead. When we got to the hospital, they all knew her and welcomed her back. She knew exactly what to do and did it cheerfully. She dumped her purse out on the counter, and about twenty blackened, bent hypodermic syringes fell out. She didn't bat an eye and seemed unconcerned about any possible legal ramifications for possession. There wasn't much else in her purse.

When she was settled, I left. I gave her my work number and told her to call me when she got out. Remember, I had gone to Jeanette's room to give her her HIV antibody test results. Here it was eight hours later, and I had never given them to her. What did AIDS mean to her at that point in her life? Luckily her results were negative! What if they had been positive? Would the psychiatric unit of the hospital have taken her in those days? Did the hospital have protocols and procedures for people with HIV who could not take care of themselves?

Three days later, I was back at her hotel, and so was she. When I saw her, it was as if those events had not taken place. She greeted me warmly and told me she was staying with a friend in the hotel but had to be out by tomorrow. Did I know anyplace she could go? I referred her to two shelters in the area and then reminded her that our study still owed her money. I could give her more information about AIDS and her test results, but only if she wanted them. Would I have said that if she were positive? Today, early diagnosis and treatment are state-of-the-art, but in "the old days," we were still debating about the pros and cons of testing because there were no resources for drug users. *Culturally appropriate* were still just words. Drug users were not comfortable utilizing the services for gay men. Women with HIV got great psychological support services at the Women's Program at the AIDS

Foundation, but medical, gynecological, housing, and drug treatment programs that were specific to their needs had not been developed. Women could be referred to Project AWARE for some services, but our agency had not geared up to provide all the other services that women needed. I believed strongly that people should be given all the information they needed in order to decide for themselves about testing and test results. I couldn't decide for Jeanette. I could only give her information to help her decide. I couldn't diagnose her ability to make an informed decision. In Jeanette's case, I could gently hint that I had good news for her. (I wasn't always able to do that later on.) Like many others, I began to question what I was doing asking women to deal with AIDS, when they didn't even know where they were going to sleep. She wasn't a prostitute. She was a chronically mentally impaired, homeless drug addict who wasn't always capable of taking care of herself. I remembered from our interview several months ago that she had told me she had been raped so many times she had lost count. She had had four miscarriages and four babies taken away from her at birth whom she had never seen, but she had never had an abortion. The Jeanettes of this world had these problems long before AIDS came along and will still have them if they survive the epidemic or even if there is an AIDS vaccine. What were we doing bringing the AIDS education and prevention message into their lives when they couldn't even give us an address to deliver it to? Rape, sexually transmitted diseases, violence, homelessness, hunger, cold, mental health problems, unemployment, addiction, unwanted pregnancies, sick kids, kids taken away, life-threatening diseases, the criminal justice system, the welfare system, child protective services—were more real than trying to convince some guy to put a condom on it or to bleach an old blood-encrusted, bent spike that had just enough dope in it to make them forget everything for a little while. Antibody test results, five dollars, and a couple of condoms seemed like a pretty pathetic arsenal to deal with all of that.

SOME BAD NEWS AND SOME GOOD NEWS

By 1989 AIDS had become the only money game in town. Virtually every community-based organization (CBO) and health and human service agency applied for every AIDS education and prevention dollar that was put out to bid. The Jeanettes of the world and their male counterparts were going to be bombarded with AIDS information no matter what else was happening with their lives. As we know, the Reagan years had left their fiscal mark on health and human services. But, thanks to aggressive lobbying and organizing by AIDS activists and people who knew about AIDS and where it was headed, AIDS prevention money was available at a time when services for all those other problems were being massacred. So what happens? Jeanette can't get the mental health services or a medical detox for her amphetamine addiction, but I'm paid to tell her how she can protect herself from AIDS. She hadn't had an STD screening, family planning services, a pelvic or any physical exam for years, but I can give her her AIDS antibody test results. And after me, an army of service providers was funded to send AIDS educators and outreach workers to her inner city neighborhood to do the same thing for her year after year. This happened all across America, not just in San Francisco. And, of course, a lot of the people who work in these neighborhoods know the score and try to bridge the gap between the reality of these folks' world and AIDS prevention. Community AIDS educators and other providers help people get food, or food stamps if they're lucky enough to be eligible, temporary shelter, clothes for their kids, and other basics of survival.

Of course, there weren't enough AIDS dollars for treatment, prevention, or research. It just seemed like a lot compared to what was happening to all other services. In California, successive governors cut budgets that provided women-specific health services, such as family planning and women's clinics, up and down the state. Again, in the middle of the 1980s, we asked ourselves what good is it to provide a woman at risk for HIV with risk reduction programs if we can't get her to a clinic to treat her latest episode of pelvic inflammatory disease (PID) or give her a pregnancy test in her first trimester so that she can get into early prenatal care or even consider an abortion?

After Jeanette, I met Holly. She was an 18-year-old prostitute who still had baby fat on her rosy cheeks and long blond hair that was her pride and joy. She had been one of the first women tested at the hotel, and we developed a friendly and trusting relationship. I knew from her interview how many tricks she turned a day and how costly her dope habit was. She had an old man who protected her when he wasn't in jail. I never tried to get her off the streets or into detox. We mostly talked about the neighborhood and how hard her life was. After I had been hanging around her neighborhood for several months and meeting her almost every day on the same street corner, she started talking about getting into a residential detox program and quitting "the life." I told her about the prostitutes' rap group and offered to take her any time she wanted to go. She asked me to help her get into a drug program, which I did. After a few days, though, there she was back on the same corner. She told me it was too hard to quit cold turkey and then asked me to help her get into an outpatient program, which I did. When she got into that program, however, she didn't stop working the corner. Her beautiful hair started to look greasy and matted. Her rosy complexion turned pale and haggard. She looked tired and unkempt standing on the corner. Whenever I tried to talk to her, she would ignore me and look down at the sidewalk. A few days later, I was at the detox clinic where she was a client. The clinic director asked me if I had seen Holly. They were worried about her because she hadn't been in for her methadone in four days, and they would have to drop her from the program. I promised to tell Holly what she said. I wrote Holly a note and passed it to her when I walked by her the next day.

She ran after me and asked if we could talk. She told me that she hadn't been able to stop using and was "on a run." She was afraid I would be disappointed in her, disgusted with her, and ashamed of her because I had gone to all that trouble to get her into detox twice, and she had failed me. I quickly explained that I was not here to judge her and that I would never hassle her about her drug use. But even after that, our relationship was never the same. It made me wary of helping women get into drug programs. They weren't used to someone being nonjudgmental and still saw AIDS educators and outreach workers as drug counselors, that is, people whose job it was to nag them about their drug use.

AIDS has made drug treatment programs more compassionate, humane, and accepting of relapse as part of recovery and has increased the number of available drug treatment slots, especially for people with HIV. In San Francisco now there are residential programs for pregnant and postpartum addicts, lesbian and bisexual women, specific ethnic groups, and a variety of 12-step programs. Some day, we may even have drug treatment "on demand" and a legal needle exchange program. Needle exchange volunteers wouldn't have to break the law every week in order to get dirty needles off the street and clean ones into the hands of people who aren't ready or able to get into drug treatment.

I don't know whatever happened to Jeanette or Holly or all those other women I met in the old days of 1986. I think about them. I wonder if they got infected by a dirty needle or the semen of a guy who wouldn't wear a condom. I still look for them when I am in their neighborhood doing needle exchange or working with the women's outreach and research project where I now work. Jeannette and Holly have been "replaced" by other women with similar stories. I like to believe that these women have a better chance of avoiding AIDS because we now have programs here that offer them more sensitive and caring services, that they will have a little better shot at avoiding AIDS than Holly or Jeannette.

This history has a positive ending. I can't say it's completely happy because women got infected who shouldn't have. If all the ugly, tired old "isms" hadn't been operating so effectively in the old days, the appropriate AIDS prevention message might have gotten to them in time. HIV rates among women and minorities might not still be the fastest rising. But today, in San Francisco, women, whether HIV-positive or still only at-risk, are served by a variety of culturally diverse programs that operate in a community spirit of mutual cooperation, collaboration, and caring. Reproductive health care, family planning services, screening and treatment of sexually transmitted diseases, pregnancy testing, and other clinical "luxuries" are sometimes funded as a necessary component of comprehensive HIV prevention services for women. True, there are not enough resources for underserved women, and there may not be for a long time, given the destruction from the political climate of the Reagan/Bush era and the healing and building that Clinton will have to achieve. But we've come a long way, women!

In October 1991, San Francisco opened the doors of the first early intervention and resource center—the Center for Positive Care. This city-funded center provided one stop shopping for HIV-positive people in search of support agencies. The center was a collaborative effort of 18 community-based AIDS service organizations and had a specific women's component designed to find HIV-positive women and get them linked up with a variety of services for primary care, clinical drug trials, psychosocial and emotional support, financial, and gynecological/family planning services. Three experienced women's programs worked together to provide this new state-of-the-art care. One year later, the center closed, the victim of severe state and city budget cuts and probably some competing political agendas. Whether or not a decentralized AIDS service delivery system can still be consolidated and simplified for consumers remains to be seen.

AIDS clinical drug trials can no longer exclude women and drug users from their experimental studies unless they are pregnant. The federal government has even begun an AIDS clinical drug trial for pregnant women. The protocol is very controversial, but the point is that the National Institute of Health (NIH) has finally "bitten the bullet" and is testing the use of AZT in pregnant women to prevent perinatal transmission. NIH has also begun a women-specific clinical drug trial to treat the gynecological problems that plague HIV-positive women. That there has been any attention focused on the exclusion of women, minorities, and drug users from AIDS clinical drug trials is due to the relentless organizing activities of groups like ACT-UP (AIDS Coalition to Unleash Power). ACT-UP is also responsible for focusing attention on the limitations of the Center for Disease Control (CDC) definition of AIDS. Preliminary clinical and anecdotal data indicated that women and minorities with HIV were not always manifesting the same diseases that the CDC had originally defined as AIDS. Gynecological diseases were not included as one of the AIDS-defining criteria. Many HIV-positive people died without getting an AIDS diagnosis. Without an AIDS diagnosis, people are ineligible for most benefits. ACT-UP waged a national campaign to get the CDC to change their definition of AIDS. The CDC announced that, as of January 1, 1993, in addition to existing diagnostic criteria, anyone with a T-cell count below 200 or who was HIV-postitive and had cervical cancer would receive an AIDS diagnosis. (A T-cell count in healthy or uninfected people is about 1,000.)

ACT-UP also pressured NIH to hold the First National Conference on Women and HIV Infection. The conference was held in Washington, D.C., in December 1990, to coincide with the World Health Organization's International World AIDS Day, which was dedicated to Women and AIDS. The conference brought researchers, providers, activists, health educators, and women with HIV together to establish a national research priority agenda for women and HIV.

Our city and our history are not unique. We know that the struggle to stop HIV among women is repeated all over the country. Only the names, the dates, and the particular circumstances are different—the racism, sexism, and classism are the same. But then AIDS is only one example of how "isms" have always affected women. There are many versions of the beginning of these systems, but I hope we can use this AIDS history lesson as a catalyst to unite all of us who are struggling to create a world without "isms."

Brooke Grundfest Schoepf

Action-Research and Empowerment in Africa

T he future impact of AIDS will be felt most sharply in the Third World. In Africa, where inadequate health and social infrastructures have been further weakened by prolonged economic crisis and structural adjustment policies, AIDS prevention is a crucial development issue.[1] It is imperative to understand the social causes of this epidemic of what is, in the main, a sexually transmitted disease and to employ effective methods to limit its spread. The latter include education for personal and social empowerment, and policies and resources to make sustainable development more than a slogan.[2] Research to aid effective AIDS prevention has become an imperative of conscience for some sociomedical scientists and, arguably, of professional ethics as well.[3]

AIDS prevention is particularly complex, for the disease syndrome and its transmission are subject to polysemic cultural interpretation.[4] Wasting disease is profoundly threatening to many; it may be interpreted as deeply polluting, a sign of spiritual affliction or moral transgression. Transmission is related to blood, semen, and vaginal secretions, body substances heavily freighted with symbolic significance.[5] Infection occurs primarily as a result of heterosexual intercourse. As in most cultures, sexual relations and

First presented at the annual meeting of the American Anthropological Association, Chicago, 22 November 1987; an earlier version was tabled at the Social Science and Medicine Conference, July 1989. It will appear in *Social Science and Medicine*, 1993. A much-abridged version appears as B. G. Schoepf, E. Walu, wN. Rukarangira, N. Payanzo, and C. Schoepf, "Gender, Power and Risk of AIDS," in *Zaire, Women and Health in Africa*, ed., M. Turshen (Trenton, N.J.: Africa World Press, 1991), 187–203. This chapter has been substantially updated. Grateful acknowledgment is made to CONNAISSIDA colleagues, including my coauthors and our research assistants, particularly Abbé Latchung Amen, Eke Tukumbe, Makyla Hatayana, Ngirabakunzi N'mukulira, Evoloko Eyenga, Mironko Kamatali, Mivumbi N., Muyayalo Varya Vati, and Pika Nianga.

Gratitude is expressed to the Rockefeller Foundation, the Wenner Gren Foundation for Anthropological Research, OXFAM/UK, and the Bunting Institute, Radcliffe College, for support of CONNAISSIDA; and to the IDRC, NORAD, SAREC, SIDA, OXFAM/America, Wenner-Gren, UNICEF, UNIFEM, and Pathfinder International for support of the Pan-African Action-Research Network (PAARN). None of these institutions or individuals is responsible for the author's interpretations.

procreation are central to the personal identity and self-concepts of women and men. They are hedged about with rules for discourse and performance, and with rules for breaking rules. Because it is chiefly sexually transmitted, AIDS is frequently attributed to supernatural sanctions, particularly to sanctions intended to control women's sexuality. Discourse about the body often is a metaphor for the body politic.[6]

The sexual cultures of modern African cities are pluralistic; diversity has increased in response to the tremendous socioeconomic changes of the past hundred years. Rules and practices are in flux throughout the region, propelled by rapid decline in living standards.[7] Although some epidemiologists point to prostitutes as "reservoirs of infection," there are no empirically bounded risk groups. Unprotected sex, rather than a particular type of relationship, however socially categorized and labeled, is what puts people at risk. Prevention involves convincing many among the general population to alter activities that are widely considered "normal," "natural," and "inevitable."[8] Due to social and economic constraints, many people cannot limit their sexual relations to a single, infection-free lifetime partner. Therefore, correct and regular condom use offers the best protection currently available for prevention of HIV and other sexually transmitted diseases. Condoms, however, have not been widely accepted, either for contraception or STD prevention. Thus, research on sociocultural contexts of sexual relations sought ways to overcome resistance to change.

From 1985 to 1990, CONNAISSIDA, a transdisciplinary medical anthropology project, used ethnographic methods to construct a social history of the unfolding epidemic. Participant observation, focused interviews, group discussions, depth interviews, and life histories provided data on sociocultural aspects of the spread of HIV infection, on changing popular and official representations, and on the social impact of AIDS in Zaïre's two largest cities. These are Kinshasa and Lubumbashi, with a combined population of more than 4 million. At the time, annual incidence of new infections in Kinshasa was estimated at 1 percent.[9] The project acronym combines *connaissance*, meaning "knowledge," with *SIDA*, "AIDS" in French. Knowledge of AIDS was conceived as an active process of exchange. Studying popular knowledge to enhance our own, we also studied the biomedical literature and transmitted that knowledge to informants.

We assumed that increased information would be necessary but not sufficient to change complexly motivated sexual behavior.[10] We also assumed that poverty and gender inequality are related to the spread of HIV; as a corollary, unequal power also creates the conditions within which prevention takes place. Economic crisis has driven many women to exchange sex for the means of subsistence for themselves and dependents; many are not in a position to refuse risky sex. These working hypotheses have been confirmed by our research and by other studies in Africa and elsewhere.[11]

Further, we proposed to use action-research, incorporating an empowerment methodology (described below), to enhance the capacity of existing community groups and networks to undertake risk assessment and generate social support for behavior change.[12] We hypothesized that the method could be adapted to integrate HIV/AIDS prevention into programs of community development organizations, informal voluntary associations, such as the popular *musiki* (a form of revolving credit association), clan gatherings, sports clubs, trade unions, youth groups, and market women's associations. Since Zaïre shares borders and cultures with nine other nations, we hypothesized that our results would be widely applicable in the region.

Cited work analyzes underlying conditions and contexts, changing representations and popular responses to AIDS in Kinshasa; some are presented next as background to the main theme. The following section sketches the theoretical basis of action-research. Then community-based risk reduction workshops conducted with two groups of women in Kinshasa in 1987 are described, and lessons for prevention policy are discussed.

ECONOMIC CRISIS, GENDER, AND AIDS

Disease epidemics generally erupt in times of economic crisis; AIDS is no exception. Since the mid-1970s, most sub-Saharan nations have experienced chronic economic stagnation, increased poverty, debt, and growing inequality between classes. Throughout the continent, remedies proposed by lending organizations have increased, rather than alleviated, distortions of economies dependent on exports of a limited number of products to unfavorable world markets. Together, crisis and policies of "structural adjustment" have redistributed wealth upward to local rulers and outward to international capital. Budget cuts have curtailed already-inadequate health services and education. In Zaïre, per capita incomes are ranked among the world's lowest[13]; average figures mask wide income disparities. Many urban families eat only once a day, and malnutrition is widespread.[14] Deepening crisis has been experienced most severely by poor women and children.[15]

Economic crisis and the structure of employment inherited from the colonial period contribute to the feminization of poverty and consequently to the spread of AIDS.[16] Currently, Zaïre's cities contain as many women as men. However, only 4 percent of formal sector workers are female. Few jobs provide a living wage; public sector workers often go for months without pay. An estimated 40 to 60 percent of urban men are without waged employment; many are too poor to start families. Without powerful patrons or special job qualifications, these men and the majority of women work in the informal economic sector, which may account for as much as half of all marketed goods and services. Women's activities include petty trade, food preparation, market gardening, sewing, domestic service, hairdressing, midwifery, brewing, smuggling, and prostitution. While a small number have succeeded in becoming substantial entrepreneurs, most operate on a very small scale. Moreover, the crisis has rendered the already-crowded informal sector increasingly less profitable.[17]

Another consequence of the crisis is that many women who formerly could rely on steady contributions from sexual partners or from their extended families report that assistance has dropped sharply, even ceased. Husbands, brothers, and lovers, too, are hard pressed to make ends meet. Many women seek occasional partners, *pneus de rechange* or "spare tires," to help meet immediate cash needs. Although no statistics exist, observers agree that multiple-partner situations, particularly those involving various forms of sexual patron-client relationships, have multiplied as economic conditions worsen.[18] As the market for sexual services turns against the providers, they must take on more partners. This situation provides conditions for the rapid spread of HIV throughout the region; it may help to explain an apparent increase in the virus's virulence.[19]

Not surprisingly, young urban women are at high risk for AIDS throughout the region. Commercial sex workers are at highest risk. More than 80 percent of poor prostitutes tested in 1986 were reported infected in several cities of Central and East Africa. However, they are not the only women at risk. Many other types of multiple-partner relationships, with varying degrees of social recognition and legitimacy, exist among people of all social classes and ethnic origins. Polygyny, whether or not sanctioned by bridewealth, is an affirmation of men's social status. Other types of multiple-partner relationships, while not positively sanctioned, are condoned by some and practiced by many. That there are also some exclusively monogamous couples should not need to be stressed, but even socially recognized relationships may be of relatively brief duration, leading to what, in the West, has been termed *serial polygamy.*

As in much of the world, adolescence is a time for sexual experimentation. Half of Kinois sampled have had sex by age 16.[20] Few young men have the resources to marry; late marriage encourages multiple partners. Yet not all sex is for pleasure. Young women are seldom able to resist pressure from older men. Some exchange sex for stylish clothes and accessories which neither their poor parents, low wages, nor petty trade provide. Some seek money to remain in school. Others support themselves or make remittances to their families. Sexual harassment is said to be quite common. Schoolgirls and students may be required to provide sex to teachers or see their grades suffer. Numerous women state that they are required to extend sexual services to employers as a condition of employment and promotion.[21] Stranger rape is rarely reported to the authorities or prosecuted. Nevertheless, deepening crisis appears to have brought an increase in attacks on women and girls.[22]

Our studies show that condoms are rarely used in stable relationships or in those in which partners have an emotional stake; they are commonly perceived to offer protection for men against women.The health consequences of sex with multiple partners unprotected by condoms, serious in the past, became much more dangerous with the spread of HIV. Young women's vulnerability is reflected in the seroprevalence rates, with teenage girls two to six times more likely to be infected than boys. Some may be infected during their first sexual experience when the hymen is ruptured.

ACTION-RESEARCH FOR HIV PREVENTION

CONNAISSIDA was initiated in 1985 when four sociomedical researchers began "talking about AIDS" in diverse social milieus.[23] In April 1987, a fieldwork grant enabled the group to add research assistants, who received training in medical anthropology and HIV/AIDS, a practicum in ethnographic team research, and training-of-trainer workshops on communication and sexuality.

By mid-1987, informants were even more eager than in previous years to discuss AIDS and more avid for information. Moreover, increased seroprevalence meant higher risk of infection. The group therefore reaffirmed our earlier decision that it would be unethical to collect data without giving knowledge in return. Weekly team meetings were held to share experiences. Fieldwork produced rich texts about resistance to change and how socioeconomic conditions contribute to the creation of risky situations. The results guided the experiential workshop design. Exercises were designed to address some of the constraints originating in psychodynamics and cultural expectations of sexual partners. Grounded in group dynamics, action-research in the original meaning of the term uses experiential, or "process," training to stimulate personal and social change.[24] It begins with the principle that people already know a great deal about their own situations. It builds on this knowledge, using structured exercises and social interaction to develop a "critical consciousness" about human behavior and the causes of social phenomena.[25]

Didactic presentations are kept to a minimum. Exercises such as role 'plays, case studies, and simulation games are used to illuminate real-life situations in a nonthreatening manner; they provide the group with a common experience to discuss. The variant adapted by the author uses an "experience cycle" to structure the process.[26] The trainer proposes an exercise, then invites the group to share observations about the experience. What did participants see and hear? How did they feel while doing or observing it? The trainer groups these responses together so that participants can transform them into more general insights. Finally, they are invited to apply what they have learned. Application is concretized by a new shared experience. This may be another structured exercise in the workshop or an activity planned, carried out, and evaluated by the group in the community.

Most groups are able to produce valid generalizations and apply them creatively. This needs to be emphasized because, although AIDS education is indeed difficult, the chief difficulty may reside in the teaching methods, rather than in cognitive deficiencies of the learners or their belief systems. Because the group is actively engaged, much technical information can be conveyed and misinformation corrected without exhausting participants' attention and causing them to "switch off." Exercises with emotional impact facilitate retention. Culturally contextualized, new information can be anchored by social reinforcement. Groups rapidly develop subcultures with norms and values that enhance learning of new concepts and skills. Positive social interaction enables both cognitive learning and behavior change to occur more rapidly and in different ways than in one-on-one encounters such as counseling.

Participants are empowered to make their own situational risk assessments and to decide on appropriate actions to take as individuals and as a group. In contrast to the directive methods of conventional public health education, workshop trainers do not give advice or transmit messages. Instead, they promote problem posing and the search for solutions. The training approach enhances participants' capacity to work in groups. It also builds experience of personal autonomy and power, thus increasing their capacity to control risky situations. Telling people who have experienced social stigma, powerlessness, and low self-worth how they "should" act is tantamount to blaming them for their predicament.

The need to increase feelings of personal competence and to minimize anxiety and guilt, with their resulting denial, blame casting, and avoidance, was identified from data contributed not only by sex workers but by many others who requested workshops. Instead of focusing on behavior that cannot be altered under present circumstances, experiential training helps people discover what they can do to make their situation somewhat better in the short term. Although the method concentrates on self-empowerment, it also can be used to initiate and sustain other, broader types of socially transformative change.

The approach rests on learning theories drawn from several sources.[27] These principles and the method have been adapted to diverse types of planned social and behavioral change in the West and in the Third World.

EMPOWERMENT WORKSHOPS

Community-based risk reduction workshops began in October 1987 with women residents of a low-income community, most of whom could not read. The sessions used active learning methods, including role plays, simple posters, small group discussions, and structured group "processing" to elicit reflection and demonstrate to participants their own ability to reduce their risk of AIDS.

The first workshop took place in a suburban neighborhood with a network of 15 sex workers. Locally they are called *mingando*, a disparaging term that refers to their ethnic origin, their poverty, and their virtually exclusive reliance on sex with multiple partners for a livelihood. The women reported receiving payments equivalent to 50 to 60 U.S. cents per encounter. Low fees and family responsibilities meant that they needed numerous partners: between 5 and 40 clients per working week. None used condoms; most reported recurrent bouts of sexually transmitted diseases. Given the high numbers of contacts, their risk was undoubtedly higher than that of their clients or of the stylish young women who work the downtown nightclubs and casinos. The latter reported fewer clients, more of whom were likely to accept condoms.

When the sex workers were contacted in June 1987, most knew that multiple sex partners could lead to AIDS. With no other way to support themselves and dependents, however, their attitudes included apathy, fatalism, and denial. By October 1987, awareness of personal risk had grown, and their existential dilemma could no longer be denied. The national mass media campaign stressed avoidance of prostitutes, and the women reported that neighbors had begun pointing hostilely at them as "disease distribu-tors." The network leader asked CONNAISSIDA to provide AIDS preven-tion information. Due to the experience of stigma, the women wanted the workshops to be held somewhere other than their open yard. When the deacons of a local church refused them space, sessions were held in a walled garden situated about 500 yards from their homes. Four morning-long workshops were held in late October and early November 1987.

A few examples will illustrate the method. An initial role play served as an ice breaker. A male visitor fails to recognize that the woman who welcomes him to her village is a chief. The scene was adapted from a passage in Dr. David Livingstone's diary relating his visit to a Lunda group in what is now southeastern Zaïre, where women chiefs were common a century ago.[28] The women immediately saw the visitor's problem and laughed at him.[29] Participants were asked to describe what they had seen, heard, and felt. The sketch provoked the insight that women's responsibilities often go unrecog-nized. Applied to AIDS, they concluded that they must take care not to become infected, because AIDS is fatal and others, including children, siblings, and elderly parents, depend on them for support. Used to demon-strate the experiential cycle of psychosocial process training, the initial exercise was followed by an exercise on expected workshop outcomes.

Exercises showed metaphorically how HIV progressively attacks the body's defenses against disease and can be transmitted by healthy-looking carriers. A dramatization of mother-infant transmission, during which mother and grandmother take a sick baby to the health center, elicited strong emotional reaction. One participant exclaimed, "Oh, the poor thing hasn't even begun to live and now he's dying of AIDS!"

An entire session was devoted to familiarization with condoms, demystifying what was to most an unfamiliar, uncongenial, unnatural, foreign technology, beset by frightening rumors and moral stigma.[30] The group consumed soft drinks together. A facilitator produced a box of condoms and displayed one, irreverently drawing it over her forearm. The condoms were passed around, and each participant rolled one over her empty soft drink bottle. Some broke, giving rise to jokes, which provided opportunities for further learning. In the ensuing role play, a sex worker showed a reluctant client how to use a condom, summoning her powers of seduction to eroticize the situation and overcome his resistance. Played to the hilt, the scene caused great mirth. Participants took condoms to try out with clients and shared their experiences in the next workshop.

When the Mothers' Club of the local Protestant church learned of the workshops for sex workers, they asked CONNAISSIDA to hold workshops in the church; 60 women attended. Since we felt we could not turn women away, we often divided participants into small groups for discussions. The wider family health context was explored first, since AIDS is only one of the health issues with which people must contend. An effort was made to remove some of the stigma and guilt associated with the link between sex and AIDS by enabling couples to speak of other possible transmission routes. For example, malaria prevention was included as one means to reduce the need for blood transfusions among anemic mothers and children. Steriliza-tion of needles and syringes also was addressed, since poor people cannot afford to purchase disposables for each injection. Although unsterilized instruments are probably not a major route of HIV transmission, this danger has been widely publicized. Following this role play, women decided to check on hygiene standards in neighborhood dispensaries. The experience was empowering because it gave women confidence in their ability to effect a change in their environment. It will help to reduce risk of other infections, such as hepatitis B, that may be acquired in the course of health care. Moreover, the community health focus provided support for the hypothesis that AIDS prevention can integrate safe motherhood, contraception, and legalization of abortion, since complications of pregnancy are major causes of transfusions in women of reproductive age.[31]

Nevertheless, sexual transmission was uppermost in the women's minds. Participants devised a role play to help wives persuade husbands to remain at home instead of accompanying their friends to bars where they spend money on beer and sexual adventures. The women showed through drama how male peer group pressures work to prevent behavior change. Partici-pants decided that, although married women are definitely subordinate within the household, the wife-and-mother role also provides some opportu-nities to cajole husbands into dialogue about the need for protecting parents and children. The workshops provided a forum in which to practice communication skills and to develop confidence in parrying male resistance, denial, and deception. This, too, was experienced as empowering.

In the churchwomen's group, the "condom seduction" was played as a wife-husband dialogue. The cajoling wife was played by a young sex worker who also took part in the other workshop. We later learned that the grandmother who acted the reluctant husband formerly had been a commercial sex worker. Their membership in the church mothers' group taught the research team that categorization of women in mutually exclusive social/sexual-status pigeonholes, such as "prostitutes," "mothers," or "church members," can be both misleading and counterproductive.

Several divorced, abandoned, or widowed women with children received alms from the congregation. The Mothers' Club president stressed that dire poverty and lack of economic alternatives made it likely that some would soon be obliged to resort to sex work, as would former sex workers who had attempted to find other means of support. Working with the two groups simultaneously sharpened the team's understanding that, for most poor women, prostitution is not a chosen profession; it is a last resort when other survival strategies have failed.

The experiences of women in this neighborhood confirmed those of informants in the budget study cited above.[32] Both sex workers and churchwomen identified income-generating activities as the most pressing need for themselves, and especially for their daughters. Most have tried with scant success to find other ways to enlarge family resources so as to survive without resort to sexual services. As noted above, deepening crisis has rendered poor women's survival in the overcrowded informal sector problematic, making fundamental economic change essential.

Although many sexual partnerships involve material exchanges, it is incorrect to assert that there is little difference between prostitutes and wives. Most of the churchwomen had married in early adolescence and said that they had never had another partner. Even in ethnic groups that value women's fidelity in marriage, however, relationships vary according to the circumstances in which women find themselves at different moments in their life careers. Negative value judgments and reluctance to be associated with stigmatized social categories hinders people from making realistic risk assessments. It also adds to the difficulty of introducing condom negotiation into relationships in which trust is an issue. AIDS programs that target prostitutes as "core transmitters" link condoms and sexually transmitted diseases to a moral discourse that renders them unacceptable to many who need protection. This association impedes condom use within partnerships based on social and emotional bonding, whether these be formally married couples, cohabiting partners, or lovers.[33]

EVALUATION

User-focused evaluation assessed responses to the interventions. At the end of the fourth week, participants in both groups demanded: "Teach us to do what you do so that we can inform our colleagues." Following a practice session, the sex workers demonstrated the method to friends in the presence of an international site visit team. The performances made clear that considerable new knowledge had been retained and some misinformation dispelled. This constituted an initial form of evaluation. Condoms were made available on a continuing basis, and workshop participants were encouraged to share their knowledge and supplies with others.

Twenty additional women attended the fifth session at the church. The first group of Mothers' Club members taught the newcomers to the workshop what they had learned. Role plays were enacted with great success. As before, the drama of the sickly infant aroused strong emotion. Two women testified that they had experienced this situation in their own families. Participants suggested that this and other family-centered scenarios would also be appropriate for men's groups. Participants contrasted the active learning experience with conventional health center education. There, mothers attending a monthly well-baby clinic sit in rows and receive a lecture on a different topic each month, sometimes participating by learning a song.

Additional meetings were held at three and eight months following the workshops to determine what changes, if any, were sustained. At the end of three months, all but one of the sex workers reported using condoms regularly. The nonuser reported that a genital ulcer made condom use painful, so we assisted her in obtaining hospital treatment.[34] Even without laboratory tests, which would have necessitated two revisits and doubled the cost, the fee was equivalent to 20 client encounters.

Client acceptance of condoms was reported high, despite wide publicity about a purported "cure." Two women said that they had turned away men who refused condom protection. Others agreed that this was wise, but that sometimes they needed immediate cash and had no other clients waiting. One woman who solicited in a popular entertainment district reported that she found it difficult to refuse the extra money clients offered for unprotected sex. The group urged that men in all social milieus be educated to the value of condom protection, since their clients are extremely diverse and since, in the final analysis, men control the decision.

Participants perceived the training as valuable. Knowledge of AIDS apparently raised their status among clients and community residents. Clients were surprised to discover that the sex workers knew about the value of condoms for AIDS prevention. The women felt somewhat less threatened by neighbors. They also had gained in status among rival networks of sex workers to whom they spread the word. They mentioned these immediate social and psychological benefits. Actual AIDS prevention was less tangible to them and, indeed, less certain.

At eight months post-intervention, in July 1988, however, sex worker participants reported that condom use had declined from "almost always" to "sometimes." Their confidence in condom protection had waned. Two women said that a medicine shop clerk (mistakenly) had told them that the condoms we supplied were outdated. They asked us to provide a more attractive product distributed by a contraceptive social marketing project which had achieved remarkable success in the interim.[35] By June 1988, "Prudence," the marketed product's brand name, had become synonymous with "condom" among university students.

Still more serious, the sex workers' recently developed felt need to use condoms with their multiple partners was undermined. The reasons for this undermining are complex; they indicate the permeability of the local social field to wider influences. The neighborhood in which the women live and work is situated near the university. Student clients are highly regarded by these poor women, who were born in the interior and have had little or no formal primary education. Studies of student knowledge, attitudes, and practices conducted in April through July 1987 discovered that, like others, they held numerous misconceptions about condoms and that, despite knowledge of AIDS as a fatal disease, few had begun to change their behavior. One year later, some students reported that they avoided prostitutes and used condoms with other women. Nevertheless, these students appear to have been a minority.

Like other members of the elite, many university students had read or heard about the April 7, 1988, issue of *Paris-Match*, quoting a sex researcher to the effect that condoms provide incomplete protection from HIV infection. In Kinshasa this was translated to mean that condoms are useless. The first televised promotion of condoms made the same week by the national AIDS coordinator failed to override the authority imputed to the international news media.

The sex workers, in turn, had been misinformed by the students. Like most poor and working-class inhabitants of Kinshasa, they do not own radios or have access to television on a regular basis.[36] The women could not remember having heard anything about AIDS from these sources during the three previous months. Nor can they read newspapers or handbills. Thus, apart from "SIDA," a record of advice set to music issued by a popular musician, the late Luambo Makadi (Franco) in May 1987, and the CONNAIS-SIDA workshops, the "sidewalk radio" (gossip network) was their principal source of AIDS information.

As members of the educated elite, students are a credible source of information. When they said, "No need to use those things!" the women accepted this incorrect advice. They feared losing these preferred clients, often steady customers to whom they gave cut rates. This collective denial occurred in a community where a bar owner and three of the sex workers who paid him in kind for the right to solicit clients in his establishment were said to have died of AIDS. It is testimony to the influence of social status as a determinant of popular knowledge. Communication systems are social systems. In hierarchical systems, the reception of information and the capacity to act on information received are differentially distributed. Consequently, differences in social power must be considered in designing prevention strategies.

Poor sex workers are at higher risk than their student clients. The women serve between 250 and 1,000 clients annually, whereas each student uses their services once or twice a month. The young men's rejection of condoms and the sex workers' acceptance of their authority increased the women's risk. It underscores the need for empowerment education that enhances the sex workers' sense of self-worth and for continuing outreach to clients.

In February and March 1990, a third evaluation found that two sex workers in the network had died, reportedly from AIDS. Survivors reported using condoms in all encounters. They all carried condoms, ready to supply them if the client did not have his own or if a second episode took place during the encounter. In the interval, more students and other clients learned from a variety of sources how to use condoms. The women expressed appreciation for the intervention that had enabled them to become aware of HIV risk earlier than most of their colleagues.

The experience suggests that the stage of the epidemic is an important factor in behavior change. Given time and the advice reaching the students from numerous channels, change probably would have occurred without the workshops. It also seems likely, however, that participatory learning can bring about earlier change, especially among marginal social groups, before the mounting death toll heightens general awareness.

Empowerment was an issue for the churchwomen as well. One-third of 60 participants reported that their husbands utterly refused to consider using condoms or even to discuss the risks the couple might face. Some of these were older men; their wives believed they no longer sought extramarital sex. Some husbands who were known or suspected to have multiple partners, however, responded with anger and threats. For example, one woman's spouse refused to give her the monthly housekeeping allowance, telling her to go out and hustle for it.

Another third of the participants reported that they had been able to open a dialogue, but that their husbands had persuaded them that their risks were negligible. In this subgroup, both partners affirmed either that they had had no other partners since marriage or had had none in the past several years. The final one-third of women said that dialogue had succeeded and their husbands agreed in principle to use condoms. They already had numerous children, and the AIDS danger triggered action on an already-perceived need to use condoms to limit births and protect the wife's health. Instead of addressing HIV risk head on, these women had suggested that condoms could be used to space births so that children could be provided with education necessary for the future. Their creativity in persuading husbands can be taught to others. Couples in both the second and third categories agreed that older children needed to be informed about AIDS. Several mothers requested boxes of condoms to take home for them. However, most said that they would have to maneuver their husbands into granting permission first. They also reiterated the need for neighborhood health services that treat STDs with free or low-cost antibiotics.[37]

During the third evaluation, women reported that husbands who had refused dialogue earlier continued to do so. However, women with older children had overcome their own reluctance to discuss the subject with these adolescents. The workshops and continuing discussions of AIDS among the group had provided social support which strengthened the mothers' resolve and their ability to negotiate with their husbands. As one woman said, "This is a question of my children's lives so I have to talk about it with them!" Presented with this extension of the maternal role, husbands did not object, although they might have preferred to avoid the issue. One mother, whose 14-year-old daughter traversed the vast, sprawling city daily to attend school, often returning at nightfall, said that she was relieved to discover a condom in her daughter's schoolbag: "At least that way I know that she is protected if she succumbs to temptation."

With older men seeking young schoolgirls, whom they assume to be free of HIV risk, poor mothers' fears are realistic. They have no way to provide their daughters with the clothes, cosmetics, treats, or even school fees that "sugar daddies" offer. The experience of having posed these problems in the group and analyzed their sources enhanced the participants' capacity to act within the channels open to them. Their solidarity as an already established group provided support for their efforts and was further reinforced by the workshops.

The participatory, process-learning method and structured exercises were new to the women. Nevertheless, they met with enthusiastic acceptance. "This is how learning should be done!" they said. The workshops were enjoyable; most participants returned for four or five sessions, despite heavy workloads. They provided a context for learning more about wider issues related to health, household economics, gender, and other social relationships. Although many women often discuss these topics, the group method enables people to probe for causes and determine possible solutions.

The churchwomen advised that workshops be organized for husbands, adolescents, and young adults living in their households. As noted above, some mothers found that they could talk to their sexually active older children about AIDS and actually began to supply them with condoms. Like other informants, however, prior to the workshops most had felt constrained by traditional taboos against sharing intimate knowledge between parents and children. This does not mean that there is a blanket taboo across generations. Teaching by aunts, uncles, and grandparents is considered appropriate by many, even where Christianity has done away with sexual joking relationships and initiation customs. But these relatives may not be present or if present, may not possess the necessary new information.

Moreover, some adults are uncomfortable with the knowledge that young people are sexually active. Men, especially, tend to deny their daughters' sexuality. These factors prompted wives of elite men to request workshops for adolescents and young adults living in their households.

One month following the demonstration workshop they staged to empower their peers, the church Mothers' Club organized a festive meal for participants and CONNAISSIDA. Closing the proceedings, the Baptist minister advised the assembly that, "since AIDS is divine retribution for sin of fornication, the righteous have nothing to fear." His advice followed similar comments broadcast by a Protestant bishop some days earlier. Although those present were too polite to contradict these authoritative voices, each knew women whose husbands' activities put them at risk. In subsequent visits they rejected the moralistic message. A deaconess commented: "Innocent or not, the wife, who has no control over her husband's moving around, gets painted with the same brush. She is his wife, so she is expected to suffer the consequences. That is unjust!"

Local officials (all men), informed of CONNAISSIDA's activities in an authorizing letter from the governor of Kinshasa, also requested workshops. They perceived that their own eagerness for interactive forms of AIDS prevention education was widely shared. They judged the method to be effective in raising awareness and helping people to pose the problem of AIDS in their own and their families' lives. As word spread, requests came from many churchwomen's and other women's groups, colleges, and labor organizations. Designs were adapted to suit these diverse needs. The role plays and picture codes developed with the women's groups proved useful in all-male and mixed-sex workshops, including with leaders of the Traditional Healers' Association.[38]

By themselves, women cannot effect widespread AIDS prevention. Nonetheless, many people perceive a need for AIDS information presented in an interactive setting. The method creates opportunities for critical reflection about the causes of the pandemic. Men who are concerned with family, community, and cultural survival can use this consciousness raising to act in concert with women to reduce sexual risk.[39] In the context of a social movement, the transformative method provides ways to change gender relations, demand new development strategies, and hold policy makers to account.

POLICY ISSUES

Local officials asked CONNAISSIDA to develop a communitywide mobilization outside the formal health care institutions. They considered these inadequate to the task of spearheading changes in sexual behavior. Although the central government, including the National Security Council, had authorized the initial research in 1986, this was prior to the creation of a new

WHO-funded AIDS bureaucracy. The National AIDS Control Committee refused to allow the participatory intervention method to become generalized to local communities.[40] As the Mobutu government's control came to be widely contested by a "prodemocracy" movement, we abandoned attempts to reactivate the project.

To date, most policy advice has come from a narrow biomedical perspective on AIDS control. Apart from mass media and school information campaigns featuring abstinence and marital fidelity, condoms and STD treatment are targeted to "core transmitters" with high rates of partner change. STD treatment, peer education, and social marketing of condoms certainly have their place in AIDS prevention.[41] Broad access to free services can protect many new recruits to commercial sex work, their clients, and their clients' partners. They must be available in market towns and peripheral urban neighborhoods, as well as in the central city. Free services are essential because payment requirements limit utilization, particularly among poor women. For people to use condoms regularly, however, their partners must accept them. Condoms, as noted above, are least likely to be used with habitual clients, lovers, and spouses. In 1992, between 10 and 35 percent of sexually active men and women in many cities and towns of Central and East Africa were seropositive. High levels of infection outside identifiable categories of "core transmitters" rule out attempts to find cheap solutions.[42] Moreover, because STD treatment is laden with cultural meanings, stigma, and misinformation, health workers need special training to provide sensitive, confidential, effective care.[43] The unmet reproductive health needs of women of all ages should be an urgent health priority.

The narrow public health perspective corresponds to a view of development in which messages promoted by the mass media bring enlightenment to the Dark Continent. In contrast, we viewed the communicative arena in the sociopolitical context of a continuing state-society struggle. Closely controlled by the state, the media provided channels through which the powerful speak to (talk down to) the disempowered. As vehicles of the dominant ideology, they aid in maintaining and reproducing hierarchical social relations. Because of this ideological role, messages met with skepticism and popular resistance, particularly since many high government officials failed to follow the advice.

We proposed a variety of alternative channels likely to enhance the diffusion of credible information. We further argued that the necessary next step toward behavior change would be interactive communication at the local level to enable people to make their own decisions and generate social support for change. We listed organizations that could take on this task. We suggested that AIDS prevention based on social and self-empowerment techniques could strengthen primary health care delivery systems as well as other special (or vertical) programs. Most still fail to incorporate vigorous community participation. Assessment of prevention methods ideally should be made by means of controlled comparisons that allow their effects to be determined. Though random assignment of a population to experimental and control groups is neither ethically justifiable nor methodologically feasible, CONNAISSIDA proposed to compare a matched sample in a distant neighborhood where network membership does not overlap. However, action-research to test empowerment methods was rejected by several funding agencies in favor of questionnaire surveys and limited interventions. Our approach was deemed "excessively academic" by one agency and "too political" by another. Funders may have agreed with Zaïrian health officials that it was not politically opportune to foster critical consciousness about the causes of the pandemic. They opted instead to support the status quo and added substantial resources to health department patronage networks. Even today, while the term *empowerment* is used, it does not seem to be understood as a process of experiential consciousness raising.

PERFORMANCE AND EMPOWERMENT

Action-research methods are widely applicable because they respond to conditions common throughout Africa. They can be adapted to integrate HIV/AIDS prevention into programs of existing community, workplace, health care, and youth organizations.[44] In addition to their value to the participants, the workshops provided data on the changing cultural constructions, social contexts, responses to, and impact of AIDS. Exercises using projective techniques enabled participants to give information in a general way without exposing their own behavior. They suggested areas of high anxiety and emotional resistance. Participants' questions indicated areas of misinformation and suggested new ideas about how to convey information effectively. Performances, discussions, and actions taken at home and in the community demonstrated the multiple dimensions of women's power and powerlessness. They also revealed opportunities for negotiations in various situations and thus illuminated relations between social structure and human agency.

At the same time that researchers had the benefit of informants' knowledge, they provided a service that helped informants to protect themselves and others. The women's performances and discussions helped them to display their knowledge of culture and society, thereby enhancing their sense of self-worth. In societies where women's knowledge has been silenced by a "double patriarchy" of colonial authorities and male elders, and further rejected in the postindependence periods by male elites, this affirmation is the first step to empowerment.

The workshops rapidly generated an atmosphere of confidence between people of markedly different social status. The relaxed yet structured process generated rapport that made it possible to conduct depth interviews with individuals and small groups on sensitive subjects such as sexuality. Ethnographers usually work for months to develop such relationships with key informants.

Action-research is a powerful tool for in-depth research. The researchers provide situations based on prior research, and informants create scenarios according to their own understanding and interests. Projective techniques, participatory learning and empowerment exercises make action-research distinctively different from focus groups and from group interviews used in rapid assessments. All are qualitative methods. However, with the latter, the interviewer—generally a member of the educated elite—controls the discussion. What emerges is mainly normative information: what people say should be done, or what they believe the interviewer wants to hear. Rarely do they generate in-depth insights into lived reality. Action-research, in contrast, requires researchers to listen attentively, to ask fewer direct questions, to observe interactions, and to register and acknowledge emotional responses—their own, as well as those of informants. Informants act as reflexive performers of their culture.

The relationship between performance and power has been theorized by Johannes Fabian for societies like Zaïre in which colonial domination was followed by quasi-totalitarian regimes, "where expression of opinion, social criticism, and the free play of the imagination are severely restricted." Fabian uses the term *performance* to describe both the ways people enact and become conscious of, or "realize," their culture and "the method by which an anthropologist produces knowledge about that culture." Involving people in changing their culture through performance and reflection, this type of gnosis aims "to discover more about the nature of cultural knowledge and the nature of knowing about cultural knowledge,"[45] and to make the fruits of this knowledge accessible to those who share in its production.[46] A similarly dialogic epistemology informed CONNAISSIDA's choice of methodology and is encapsulated in the project's name.

CONCLUSION

Like many other disease pandemics, AIDS is propelled by socioeconomic and political forces. The heaviest burdens of prolonged economic crisis and structural adjustment rest upon the shoulders of poor women. The disease syndrome expresses persistent inequalities in bodily form. AIDS embodies patriarchal gender and class relations—relations between sex, money, and power—in a new and particularly tragic way. With little economic independence or social autonomy, relatively few women can avoid sexual risk.

Action-research with women in Kinshasa shows how political economy, culturally constructed gender relations, internalized social prescriptions, and individual psychodynamics act together to block change. The experiment also shows that empowerment training with content based on ethnography can raise knowledge levels, correct misinformation, and foster personal risk assessment. Together with social support, these can generate and sustain significant behavior change.

However, sex is a social activity. Since effective prevention lies mainly beyond the scope of individual action, culturally appropriate education is a necessary, but not sufficient, part of AIDS prevention. Power relations and economic dependency, determined by the structure of the wider society, continue to limit the possibilities for many highly motivated women to alter their behavior. Because multiple, often competing discourses occupy the terrain, the changing representations of AIDS are a necessary point of departure for behavior change. Without widespread implementation of community-based prevention coupled with broad cultural change, we can expect differences in the incidence of new HIV infections to follow existing differences in power and access to information.

Empowerment training for AIDS risk assessment may be used to enhance the capacities of individuals and social groups to bring about redefinition of gendered identities and wider social change. As people evaluate their own risks and together reinforce awareness of their need for protection, they can become creatively engaged in solving the problems of AIDS prevention in their own lives. The participatory method can be used to encourage critical thinking, enabling people to probe for the causes of their situations and plan collective action. Community organizations and informal networks can use empowerment methods to help support members' efforts to bring about change.

The devastating pandemic raises fundamental questions about the development and health strategies of many African governments and international donors. It is unrealistic to expect African governments to sustain AIDS prevention programs given the prolonged economic crisis. Health "on the cheap" will not stop AIDS.

Since paradigms used to understand disease influence research and policy, it is essential to attend to wider issues of patriarchy, inequality, economic stagnation, and distorted development. Economic crisis, structural adjustment policies, and political uncertainty have exacerbated poverty, particularly among women. Political crisis has heightened physical insecurity and increased violence against women. Failing to grasp the significance of situations and meanings that frame AIDS prevention, the problem of relative social power—and powerlessness—has been neglected in global prevention policy. Linking macro-level political economy to micro-level sociocultural analysis shows how strategies adopted for survival contribute to sexual risk. Therefore, broader political and socioeconomic changes that reduce poverty and inequality are necessary to control the HIV/AIDS epidemic. Findings from Zaïre are widely applicable in the region. The devastating pandemic raises fundamental questions about the development and health strategies pursued by many African governments and international agencies during the 1980s.

NOTES

[1]B. G. Schoepf, wN. Rukarangira, C. Schoepf, N. Payanzo, and E. Walu, "AIDS and Society in Central Africa: A View from Zaire," in *AIDS in Africa: Social and Policy Impact* ed., N. Miller and R. Rockwell (Lewiston, N.Y.: Edwin Mellen, 1988), 211–235. Reprinted in D. Koch-Weser and H. Vanderschmidt, eds., *The Heterosexual Transmission of AIDS in Africa* (Boston: Abt, 1988), 265–280.

[2]B. G. Schoepf, "Gender Relations and Development: Political Economy and Culture," in *Twenty-First Century Africa: towards a New Vision of Self-Sustainable Development*, ed. A. Seidman and F. Anang (Trenton, N.J.: Africa World Press, 1992), 203–241.

[3]See Schoepf, "Gender Relations and Development" also B. G. Schoepf, "Ethical, Methodological and Political Issues of AIDS Research in Central Africa," *Soc. Sci. Med.* 33(1991):749–763; B. G. Schoepf, "Culture and AIDS Prevention in Africa: Issues of Ethics and Methodology" (Paper tabled at Workshop on Culture, Sexual Behaviour and AIDS, University of Amsterdam, 24–26, July 1992); B. G. Schoepf, wa N. Rukarangira, and M. M. Matumoma, "Etude des Réactions à une Nouvelle Maladie Transmissible (SIDA) et des Possibilités de Démarrage d'un Programme d'Education Populaire" (Research proposal submitted to Government of Zaire, Conseil Executif, WHO, USAID, IDRC, and other agencies, Kinshasa, 15 August 1986); B. G. Schoepf, N. Payanzo, wN. Rukarangira, E. Walu, and C. Schoepf, "AIDS, Women and Society in Central Africa," in *AIDS 1988: AAAS Symposium Papers*, ed. R. Kulstad (Washington, D.C.: AAAS, 1988), 175–181.

[4]See papers listed in note 3; also, B. G. Schoepf, "AIDS, Sex and Condoms: African Healers and the Reinvention of Tradition in Zaire," *Med. Anthropol.* 14(1992):225–242; B. G. Schoepf, "Women, AIDS and Economic Crisis in Central Africa," *Canadian Journal of African Studies* 22(1988):625–644; B. G. Schoepf, "CONNAISSIDA: AIDS Control Research and Interventions in Zaire" (Proposal submitted to The Rockefeller Foundation and others, 12 November 1986); B. G. Schoepf, "Représentations du SIDA et Pratiques Populaires à Kinshasa," *Anthropologie et Sociétés* 15 (1991):149–166.

[5]See Schoepf papers in note 4. Also M. Douglas, "Risk as a Forensic Resource," *Daedalus* 119 (1990):1–16; C. Taylor, "The Concept of Flow in Rwandan Popular Medicine," *Soc. Sci. Med.* 27(1988):1343–1348; M. Douglas, *Purity and Danger: An Analysis of the Concepts of Pollution and Taboo* (London: Routledge and Kegan Paul, 1966).

[6]Douglas.

[7]In addition to the Schoepf papers previously cited, see the following for a fuller understanding of the changing nature of sexual cultures in Africa: H. Standing, and M. N. Kisekka, *Sexual Behaviour in Sub-Saharan Africa: A Review and Annotated Bibliography* (London, Overseas Development Administration, September 1989); D. Pellow, "Sexuality in Africa," *Trends in History* 4(1990):71–96; B. M. Ahlberg, *Women, Sexuality and the Changing Social Order: The Impact of Government Policies on Reproductive Behaviour in Kenya* (Philadelphia: Gordon and Breach, 1991); B. G. Schoepf, "Women in the Informal Economy of Lubumbashi: The Case of the *Ndumba*" (Paper presented for the International Congress of the Anthropological and Ethnological Sciences, Delhi, December 1978. French version presented at 4th International Conference on African Studies, Kinshasa, December 1978. Revised version, "Women and Class Formation in Zaire," presented at the Annual Meeting of the U.S. African Studies Association, Bloomington, In., October 1981; B. G. Schoepf, "Sex, Gender and

Society in Zaire," in *Sexual Behavior and Networking: Anthropological and Socio-Cultural Studies on the Transmission of HIV*, ed. T. Dyson Derouaux-Ordina Liese: 353–374; I. Schuster, *New Women of Lusaka* (San Francisco: Mayfield, 1979); C. Obbo, *African Women, Their Struggle for Independence* (London: Zed Books, 1980); C. W. Hunt, "Migrant Labor and Sexually Transmitted Diseases: AIDS in Africa," *J. Hlth Soc. Behav.* 30(1989):353–373; M. T. Bassett, and M. Mhloyi, "Women and AIDS in Zimbabwe: The Making of an Epidemic," *Int. J. Hlth. Serv. Res.* 21(1991):143–156; K. Jochelson, M. Mothibeli, and J. P. Leger, "Human Immunodeficiency Virus and Migrant Labour in South Africa," *Int. J. Hlth. Serv. Res* 21(1991):157–173; C. Obbo, "Sexual Relations Before AIDS" (Paper prepared for IUSSP seminar on Anthropological Studies Relevant to the Sexual Transmission of HIV, Sonderborg, Denmark, 19–22 November 1990); B. G. Schoepf, "Women at Risk: Case Studies from Zaire," in *The Time of AIDS: Social Analysis, Theory and Method*, ed. G. Herdt and S. Lindenbaum, (Newbury Park, Calif.: Sage, 1992), 225–242; B. G. Schoepf, and E. Walu, "Women's Trade and Contributions to Household Budgets in Kinshasa," In *The Real Economy of Zaire*, ed. J. MacGaffey, (London: James Currey, and Philadelphia: University of Pennsylvania Press, 1991), 124–151; B. G. Schoepf, E. Walu, with D. Russell, and C. Schoepf, "Women and Structural Adjustment in Zaire," in *Structural Adjustment and African Women Farmers*, ed. C. Gladwin (Gainesville: University of Florida Press, 1991), 151–168; see also B. Verhaegen, *Femmes Zairoises de Kisangani: Combats pour la Survie* (Paris: L'Harmattan, 1990).

[8]See Schoepf, "AIDS, Women and Society in Central Africa"; Schoepf, "AIDS, Sex and Condoms"; Schoepf, "Women, AIDS and Economic Crisis in Central Africa"; Schoepf, "CONNAISSIDA."

[9]B. N'Galy, R. W. Ryder, B. Kapita et al., "Human Immunodeficiency Virus Infection Among Employees at an African Hospital," *New England Journal of Medicine*, 319(1988):1123–1127.

[10]See Schoepf, "CONNAISSIDA," and D. Nelkin, "AIDS and the Social Sciences: Review of Useful Knowledge and Research Needs," *Rev. Infect. Dis.* 9(1987):980–986; H. G. Miller, C. H. Turner, and L. E.Moses, eds., *AIDS: The Second Decade* (Washington, D.C.: National Academy Press, 1990).

[11]In addition to the Schoepf studies, see PANOS, *AIDS in the Third World* (London: The PANOS Institute, 1989); PANOS, *Triple Jeopardy: Women and AIDS* (London: The PANOS Institute, 1990); M. de Bruyn, "Women and AIDS in Developing Countries," *Soc. Sci. Med.* 34(1992):249–262; B. G. Schoepf, "Gender, Development and AIDS: A Political Economy and Culture Framework," in *Women in Internat. Devel. Annual*, ed. R. Gallin, A. Ferguson, and J. Harper, (Boulder, Colo.: Westview, 1993, vol. 3, 55–85; M. Berer, with S. Ray, eds., *Women and HIV/AIDS: An International Resource Book* (London: Pandora Press, 1993); E. Reed, "Gender, Knowledge and Responsibility," in *AIDS in the World*, ed. J. Mann, D. Tarantola, and T. Netter (Cambridge: Harvard University Press, 1992), 657–667.

[12]This methodology is described in Schoepf et al., "Etudes des Réactions à une Nouvelle Maladie Transmissible (SIDA)," and Schoepf, "CONNAISSIDA."

[13]World Bank, *World Development Report* (Washington, D.C.: World Bank, 1986, 1991).

[14]J. Houyoux, et al., *Budgets Ménagers à Kinshasa*, (Kinshasa, Zaire: Département du Plan, 1986); E. Walu, "Stratégies de Survie des Femmes à Kinshasa" (Colloquium at

Center for International Studies, Chapel Hill, University of North Carolina, 15 November 1987); E. Walu, "Women's Work in the Informal Sector: Some Lessons From Kinshasa, Zaire" (M. A. thesis, Institute for Social Studies, The Hague, 1991); see also Schoepf, "Women, AIDS and Economic Crisis in Central Africa."

[15]Studies reviewed in C. Gladwin, "Women and Structural Adjustment in a Global Economy," in *Women in International Development Annual* vol. 3, 87–112; see all Schoepf papers.

[16]See especially Schoepf, "Women, AIDS and Economic Crisis in Central Africa," and Schoepf, "Sex, Gender and Society in Zaire."

[17]See notes 8 and 15.

[18]Schoepf, "Women in the informal economy of Lubumbashi."

[19]P. W. Ewald, "Transmission Modes and the Evolution of Virulence," *Human Nature* 2(1991):1–30.

[20]J. T. Bertrand, M. Bakutuvwidi, L. M. Kinavwidi, and D. Balowa, "AIDS Related Knowledge, Sexual Behavior and Condom Use among Men and Women in Kinshasa, Zaire," *Amer. J. Pub Hlth.* 81(1991):53–58.

[21]Reported in Schoepf, studies and E. Walu, "Women's Work in the Informal Sector: Some Lessons from Kinshasa."

[22]Rape of women prisoners and those taken in demonstrations and rebel communities is reported to be commonplace. Moreover, HIV prevalence is believed to be especially high among the military, and rapists sometimes threaten their victims with infection. This vengeance, both personal and political, exercises a chilling effect. B. G. Schoepf,, "Human Rights and Gender Discourses in Eriaz" (Paper presented at annual meeting of the American Anthropological Association, New Orleans, 29 November–2 December 1990); also, E. Walu.

[23]See notes 1 and 2, as well as wN. Rukarangira and B. G. Schoepf, "Unrecorded Trade in Southeast Shaba and Across Zaire's Southern Borders," In *The Real Economy of Zaire*, ed. J. MacGaffey (London: James Currey, and Philadelphia: University of Pennsylvania Press, 1991), 72–96; wN. Rukarangira, K. Ngirabakunzi, Y. Bihini, and M. Kitembo, "Evaluation of the AIDS Information Program Using Mass Media Campaign in Lubumbashi, Zaire" (Abstract FD844. 6th International Conference on AIDS, San Francisco, 22 June 1990).

[24]K. Lewin, "Group Decision and Social Change," In *Readings in Social Psychology*, ed. T. Newcome, (New York: Henry Holt, 1947).

[25]P. Freire, *The Pedagogy of the Oppressed* (New York: Seabury Press, 1970); P. Freire, *Education for Critical Consciousness* (New York: Seabury Press, 1973); A. Hope, S. Timmel, and P. Hodzi, *Training for Transformation: A Handbook for Community Workers*, 3 vols. (Gweru, Zimbabwe: Mambo Press, 1984).

[26]Since 1971 I have used the method with agricultural researchers, officials, and community development workers in Zaire; women political leaders in Zimbabwe; community leaders and hospital managerial staff in the United States, and engineers in Mali.

[27]See note 1, note 26, and A. H. Maslow, *The Psychology of Science* (New York: Harper & Row, 1966), 46–47; Jean Piaget cited in R. P. Lynton and U. Pareek, *Training for Development* (Homewood, Ill.: R. D. Irwin, 1967), 175; J. Dewey, *The Child and the*

Curriculum and the School and Society (Chicago: University of Chicago Press, 1956). "Progressive" education was widely accepted among U.S. educators of young children by the 1950s, and processual learning modes gained acceptance in some innovative secondary schools during the 1980s. However, their application requires institutional support not found in most public school systems.

[28]D. Livingstone, *Missionary Travels and Researches in South Africa* (London: John Murray, 1857), 274–295; B. G. Schoepf, "Social Structure, Women's Status and Sex Differential Nutrition in the Zairian Copperbelt," *Urban Anthropology* 16(1987):73–102.

[29]Used in a mixed group of community development workers in 1989, this role play missed the mark. Despite her ways of sitting, moving, and speaking that convey power and authority in Central Africa, male participants failed to perceive that the woman portrayed was a chief. Their blindness opened the door to discussion about how gender constructs influence perception, role stereotypes, and the need for change in social relations.

[30]See Schoepf,, "Culture and AIDS Prevention in Africa" and "AIDS, Sex and Condoms."

[31]See B. G. Schoepf, Draft Strategy Proposal on HIV/AIDS for UNICEF's Collaboration with the Government of Tanzania, Dar-es-Salaam, UNICEF, 16 October 1991. The International Planned Parenthood Federation (IPPF) has developed a series of training manuals that integrate AIDS and reproductive health issues using active, participatory education methods. See G. Gordon and T. Klouda, *Preventing a Crisis: AIDS and Family Planning Work*, rev. ed., (London: IPPF, 1989). PO Box 759, Inner Circle, Regents Park, London NW1 4LQ, England.

[32]See Schoepf, and Walu, "Women's Trade and Contributions," and Schoepf, et al., "Women and Structural Adjustment in Zaire."

[33]Some biomedical researchers who focused on "core transmitters" to break the epidemic have recently acknowledged the need to address the issue of condom use among stable couples. See M. Temmerman, F. M. Ali, J. Ndinya-Achola et al., "Rapid increase of both HIV-1 infection and syphilis among pregnant women in Nairobi, Kenya," *AIDS* 6(1992):1181–1185. Seroprevalence in this sample rose from 6.5 percent in 1989 to 13 percent in 1991. In Kigali, by 1988, 32 percent of a sample of childbearing women were infected. Most were married and believed that they were in monogamous relationships; 68 percent had never had another sexual partner, and many thought that they were not at risk. C. Lindan, S. Allen, M. Carael et al., "Knowledge, attitudes and perceived risk of AIDS among urban Rwandan women: Relationship to HIV infection and behavior change," *AIDS* 5(1991):993–1002. These authors state that "obstacles to changing behavior in Africa are not well understood." Quite the contrary. Papers cited in this chapter point to the substantial literature on sociocultural, economic, and psychological constraints; also S. Moses, F. Manji, J. E. Bradley et al., "Impact of user fees on attendance at a referral centre for sexually transmitted diseases in Nairobi," *Lancet* 340(1992):463–466.

[34]This woman died in 1990, reportedly from AIDS, as did one of the network's youngest members (E. Walu, interview, March 1990).

[35]Background research was conducted by members of the CONNAISSIDA team. According to the former marketing director, a 1987 CONNAISSIDA research assis-

tant, sales in Kinshasa reached 300,000 per month after one year of operation. N. Mivumbi, "Le Marketing Social Comme un des Moyens de Lutte Contre le SIDA" (Presentation at N'Sélé Condom Conference, Kinshasa, October 1988). Nine million condoms were sold in 1991. See also wN. Rukarangira, and B. G. Schoepf, "Social Marketing of Condoms in Zaire," *WHO AIDS Health Promotion Exchange* 3(1989):2–4. At the same time, one should be skeptical of exaggerated and exclusive claims made for the method by contractors seeking new markets.

[36]The 1986 survey by Houyoux and colleagues found that only 36 percent of randomly sampled families in Kinshasa owned radios.

[37]See references in note 34.

[38]Schoepf, "AIDS, Sex and Condoms."

[39]See references in note 32.

[40]Acknowledging the pilot project's success in reducing sexual risk, the AIDS coordinator suggested that the author draw up a plan to use the method with high officials of government and industry (interview with Dr. N'Galy Bosenge, 6 June 1989).

[41]B. G. Schoepf, "Socioeconomic and Cultural Factors in the HIV/AIDS Pandemic: Constraints and Change" (Paper presented at UNICEF AIDS Strategy Retreat, New York, 1–3 December 1991. Revised version, Uganda ACP IEC Seminar, Entebbe, 1 April 1992). See also note 36.

[42]See note 34.

[43]B. G. Schoepf, "Pan-Africa Action Research Network: A Methodology for Community-Based HIV/AIDS Prevention" (Report of PAARN Workshop, Arusha, Tanzania, 15–29 August 1991, July 1992). See also note 32.

[44]See note 1 and numerous papers and articles presented in the last five years. C. Obbo, "Gender, Age and Class: Discourses on HIV Transmission and Control in Uganda" (Paper presented at the Workshop on Culture, Sexual Behaviour, and AIDS, University of Amsterdam, 24–26 July, 1992); B. G. Schoepf, "Political Economy and Culture in AIDS Control" (Paper prepared for International Union of Anthropological and Ethnological Sciences, Zagreb, 18 July 1988). Revised version, "Political Economy, Sex and Cultural Logics: A View from Zaire," *African Urban Quarterly* 6(1993):2–25; C. Obbo, "Sexuality and Economic Domination in Uganda," in *Women-Nation-State*, ed. N. Nyuval-Davis and F. Anthas (London: Macmillan, 1989), 79–91; C. Obbo, "HIV Transmission: Men are the Solution" *Population and Environment* 14(1993):211–243; M. N. Kisekka, "AIDS in Uganda as a Gender Issue," *Women and Therapy* 10(1990):35–53; Society for Women and AIDS in Africa (SWAA), Report of the 1st International Workshop on Women and AIDS in Africa, Harare, 10–12, May 1989; M. E. Ankrah, "AIDS and the Social Side of Health," *Social Science and Medicine* 32(1991):967–980; M. Vaughan, "Syphilis, AIDS and the Representation of Sexuality: The Historical Legacy," in *Action on AIDS in Southern Africa*, ed. Z. Stein, and A. B. Zwi (Report of Maputo Conference on Health, New York, Committee for Health in South Africa (April 1990, 1991), 119–125; A. B. Zwi, and A. J. Cabral, "Identifying 'High Risk Situations' for Preventing AIDS," *British Medical Journal* 303(1991):1527–1529. See the PAARN concept paper on adapting the methodology to other settings. K. Kalumba, B. G. Schoepf, B. M. Ahlberg, J. Nguma, and C. Obbo, Pan-African Action Research Network for Community-Based HIV/AIDS Prevention,

November 1990; also J. Fabian, *Power and Performance* (Madison: University of Wisconsin Press, 1990), 17–18; B. G. Schoepf, "Breaking Through the Looking Glass: The View From Below," in *The Politics of Anthropolgy: From Colonialism and Sexism toward a View from Below,* ed. G. Huizer and B. Mannheim (The Hague: Mouton, 1979), 325–342.

[45]Fabian.

[46]Schoepf, "Breaking Through the Looking Glass."

Nancy E. Stoller

Lesbian Involvement in the AIDS Epidemic: Changing Roles and Generational Differences

U nderstanding lesbian involvement in the AIDS epidemic requires analysis beyond the question of ethical choice. Participation in any social movement, including the response to AIDS, is highly determined both by internal movement factors such as recruitment and mobilization techniques,[1] and by external factors such as potential recruits' shared values, sympathy for political goals, and existing organizational memberships. Thus, the values, social location, and occupation of a lesbian significantly affect the possibilities of her involvement in AIDS work. To understand their complex relationship to AIDS, we need to know the dominant networks, cultures, and institutions of North American lesbians when AIDS was first identified in the United States.

FEMINISM

During the 1970s, the combination of the second wave of feminism with the emergence of the gay liberation movement led to a complex flowering of culture and social organization by women. Many of the leadership roles in the women's movement were filled by lesbians (part-time, occasional, emerging, temporary, long-term and otherwise). This was a mutual love affair of lesbians for feminism (the idea that women matter) and of feminism for the essence of the lesbian vision (women are first in time, emotional interest, and political commitment). The slogan that "feminism is the theory and lesbianism the practice" may not be perfectly true, but its emotional validity brought the two movements together. In addition, most feminist organizations during this period attempted to include both heterosexuals and lesbians. On the subject of the body, the motto of feminism was "Our Bodies, Our Selves," which was not just a health slogan but also a call for self-determination, expressed in forms ranging from self-examination to sexual experimentation. Not surprisingly, "political lesbianism" was born in this milieu.

In a concrete sense, what combined aspects of the movements—and especially linked lesbians to feminism—was precisely what had drawn lesbians to work with women and girls throughout the nineteenth and twentieth centuries in the United States. Feminism, and in particular feminist institution building, represented the opportunity to express a lesbian's love of women both at work and in politics, even where the work and politics said "women" and not the subcategory "lesbians." This sort of work-for-women-and-girls provides the opportunity for a universalistic sublimated love, which can exist in a universe parallel to one's private life and particularistic love. With this match, lesbians became the leaders in many of the feminist institutions formed in the seventies: the women's health movement, with its self-examination and self-help movements, its collectives and health centers; the feminist press; bookstores; restaurants; music. It is through the work of such women that these feminist institutions have survived into the eighties and nineties.

In many cases, the language of the movement itself conflated women and lesbians. For example, during the mid-seventies, as lesbian culture went public, it was labeled "women's culture" by its promoters; for example, "women's music," which was really lesbian music, of course, and music for a predominantly white, college-educated audience at that. That this conflation still exists is shown by the fact that Olivia Records, the primary vector for lesbian/women's music, now sells "women's cruises" (no pun acknowledged), which are designed for lesbians, not for "feminists" or women in general.[2]

The feminist movement and the lesbian movement were parallel and interconnecting; they were also linked to other movements and had considerable diversity within them, which is often lost in more superficial reporting.[3] For example, there is a widespread notion that the "women's movement" was white and middle class,[4] but as I experienced it, it was intentionally cross-class and multiracial. Feminists and lesbians in all segments of the population were active in prison reform and organizing, especially the segment that worked with women; battered women's shelters; antiracist organizing; ethnic liberation struggles; school board fights; and reproductive rights that addressed sterilization abuse.[5]

Despite some invisibility in the eyes of the white Left and to many white gay men, it was during the seventies that both lesbians and women (at least the feminists in the name of women) "went public."[6] Gaining experience in their own movements, as well as in other struggles, they began to create new sets of institutions for women. As a result, for lesbians, alternate and additional institutions emerged, beyond women's bars and the sports clubs associated with them. Separatist settings and services for women (health clinics, therapy services, restaurants, book stores, retreats, land groups, classes, caucuses) were suddenly everywhere. Women's studies courses and programs were invented. Gay and straight women mingled. Lesbianism was presented as a legitimate option for women; many lesbian-inclined women chose it and did so openly, in ways that their older sisters could not have done so easily.

Feminism helped make this development of women's "spaces" and of lesbian lifestyle and culture possible, because it brought the energies of women of all sexual persuasions together in the name of women, therefore making available many more resources than either straight women or lesbians alone could generate by themselves. Each group had access to different types of resources. In a certain way, the reason why lesbians have led the women's movement and its institutions is that lesbians provide more labor, more focused attention, and less distraction: they are not so torn by the need to return to men. On the other hand, the connections of straight women to men brought a different set of resources, especially financial aid. Since women's salaries ranged from 59 to 63 percent of men's during this period, a woman with a man was almost inevitably in a wealthier household than a woman with a woman.

GAY LIBERATION

The movement for gay liberation, which emerged as a powerful force in 1969 and spread internationally within a few years, further affected lesbian visibility, politics, economics, and culture. While men dominated the movement, women were assertive in many of its political organizations and other institutions. The movement's effects on lesbian-gay solidarity varied by location. In larger urban areas, men dominated the economy and the institutions of the gay community; socializing by men and women was predominantly segregated and reflected different sexual, political, and social values. Lesbian culture, in both its older and its new institutions, was characterized by a more socially critical stance—beyond lesbian/gay assertion. Because women had fewer institutions to call their own, their gathering places continued to be more mixed racially and in terms of class than were male institutions, which, as they multiplied, replicated the class and race character of the larger society more thoroughly than did women's institutions. Lesbians were also just plain worse off economically than gay men; consequently their interests, alliances, and culture reflected this difference.

Gay male culture, except for that segment affected by groups such as the Radical Fairies, the Gay Liberation Front, and a few other groups, was more a celebration of male and gay culture without the radicalizing addition of feminism.[7] A major distinction between lesbians and gay men, as articulated in publications and politics of the seventies, was in their differing notions of what sexual freedom meant. In fact, to understand lesbians and the AIDS epidemic, it is important to spend some time looking at these different meanings.

LESBIANS AND GAY MEN: SEXUAL DIFFERENCE IN THE SEVENTIES

Models of sexuality for lesbians which dominated the seventies came from women's socialization and feminism. It has been argued by recent theorists that female development moves in the direction of a relational orientation in contrast to male developmental emphasis on individuation and separation.[8] Gilligan, for example, argued that, within Western culture, male moral development has emphasized an ethic of justice, whereas that of women has greater emphasis on caring. Even though some feminist theorists emphasize the role of oppression in developing this orientation in women,[9] it is still true that, regardless of the structural sources, almost all women, including lesbians, have been strongly affected by a pattern of socialization that emphasizes the importance of relationships and networks, as well as caregiving and nurturance. Even though lesbians may have a demonstrated ability to resist certain aspects of female socialization (males as sexual object choices for example), they are not immune from these cultural pressures.

Common wisdom in lesbian culture of the late seventies and early eighties asserted that lesbians form couples and model their coupleship on romantic love and enduring relationships. This popular notion was complemented and perhaps strengthened by research on "fusion" in lesbian relationships, which emphasizes the tendency to blur boundaries between self and other and identifies female socialization as a source of this tendency.[10] A second pervasive aspect of female socialization has been the historical and contemporary emphasis on monogamy, tied partly to patriarchal possessiveness but also to the risk of pregnancy and the need for legitimate fathership.

In contrast to these two aspects of female socialization (relatedness and monogamy as values and life orientations), male socialization has emphasized individuation and nonmonogamy. While gay men, like lesbians, challenge traditional sex roles, they are, similarly and simultaneously, drawn to them. Gay male sexuality in the seventies was historically marked by less emphasis on the creation of family or on sexual monogamy. The impact of gay liberation movements on gay male sexuality has been discussed in many venues, primarily because of the belief that patterns of sexuality among gay men have been responsible for the rapid spread of the epidemic.[11] Although a detailed look at this topic is outside the scope of this chapter, gay male and lesbian sexualities and the value systems associated with them were important sources of separation between men and women within the community.

For women who emerged as lesbians in the seventies, feminism had several sexual messages: communication, equality, androgyny, and nonviolence. Nonmonogamy was not one of the explicit messages of feminism, nor did monogamy suffer a serious critique. Gay liberation provided the opportunity for lesbians to be more "out," while female socialization seemed to ensure that they would move primarily in the directions women are expected to: seeking long-term close relationships. The critique of male-female sexual relationships led to an emphasis on equality and, for some women (both lesbian and straight), a fear of repeating the same oppressive forms found between men and women in traditional nonfeminist couples. This concern and its expression in feminist literature and theory eventually led to the "sex wars" of feminism, in which struggles against sexism, sexual abuse, and oppression were pitted against struggles for freedom to have one's own sex life and to be creative without being censored.[12] Lesbians who were out before the seventies reacted variously to these messages and conflicts depending on their interest, class, ethnicity, education, and commitment to previous patterns.

Differences within lesbian and feminist communities concerning sexual expression created major divisions which lingered into the nineties. One strand of feminists gravitated toward a severe critique of power; some became involved in the antipornography movement which supported censorship and regulation.[13] Other feminists rallied to protect free speech and self expression as cornerstones of women's right to determine their own sexuality. The conflicts escalated in the late seventies and early eighties, especially among the more political and academic segments of the feminist world. Lesbians were actively engaged in this debate. In addition, lesbians involved in femme-butch and the growing S/M community felt attacked by those who emphasized androgyny and equality as the only proper expressions of female sexuality.[14]

The message of gay liberation for men, however, was more one of self-expression of male socialization within the arena of gay sex. This meant multiple partners, self-assertion, and "individuation," or experimentation. Gay male sexuality had involved multiple sex partners before gay liberation; the gay movement, which basically legitimized gay life "as it was," focused on gaining full rights (again, a male theme of justice) for gay men to live their lives—and discover them—as they wished. In the early seventies, gay male liberation provided a critique of traditional male sexuality. This critique included the presentation of the possibility that gay men might form their own families, whether communal or more nuclear versions. By the end of the decade, more gay men had created families (in some cases linked to lesbians), which included children. However, as the gay movement became institutionalized, it lost much of its radical critique of sexism. There was no movement comparable to feminism to effectively challenge male socialization—although some segments of the gay male community adopted the critique of domination and oppression. They applied this critique to the position of gay male relations as well as to those between gay men and lesbians.

The seventies saw a rapid increase in public gay male culture, institutions, and political influence (including the first candidate, Harvey Milk, to be elected on a gay rights platform). Within these new institutions, struggles over the appropriate nature of gay male life appeared: What was the meaning and appropriateness of camp? of "super-masculine" behavior? of clone culture? Writers began to speak of gay identity and community replacing homosexual behavior and populations. Whereas gay men were in some cases able to claim actual locations—the Castro, the Village—for their community centers, lesbians existed more as a relational or fictional community, often on the geographical fringe of gay men's areas, but usually spread more widely and less distinct as a community.

While lesbians were especially connected to the feminist community and institutions, it seems that gay men were more connected to heterosexual life in its more traditional forms, including its "use" of women familially, socially, and economically. Possibly, this lack of challenge by gay men of sexism made it easy for them to appreciate the nurturing they received from lesbians and straight women during the epidemic, but harder to acknowledge women as intellectual equals.

Thus, when the seventies ended and the AIDS epidemic exploded, most lesbians and gay men were living essentially parallel lives, organized primarily around the separate themes of female values and feminism for the women and masculinity and justice for the men.

THE AIDS EPIDEMIC

Although AIDS has struck men in higher numbers than women, women have been among the ill since the beginning. They have also been involved as caretakers, educators, physicians, public health officials, and community activists. As a diverse social group linked by gender in an epidemic where gender and sexuality are key, women and lesbians in particular have played powerful symbolic, sexual, and social roles.

From the start, lesbians were involved not only in their occupational functions as nurses, activists, social workers, they were also present as women and lesbians, two potential master statuses. Simultaneously active and self-conscious, lesbians were often seen as representing a feminist stance. Their social-psychological backgrounds, the nature of the lesbian-gay community, and the broader social and political context of the early eighties affected the roles that lesbians could, and did, play in the epidemic. These roles have changed substantially over the first decade of AIDS activism.

The basic arenas of AIDS activity might usefully be sorted into five institutional foci: medical (including research), public health, educational, caring services, and political. As the eighties began, women in the United States (including lesbians) were occupationally placed in large numbers where they would be likely to encounter men with HIV. In medical settings, they comprised most nurses, as well as a significant proportion of nurses aides, home health workers, medical clerical staff, and an increasing number of physicians. Women also dominated the frontline work force in social work and therapy. They were well represented in public health, especially in health education. Within the lesbian and gay community, many of the service organizations that were cosexual had numerous female staff, because women outnumber men in the helping professions.

The above-noted professional roles, whether in straight or gay institutions, draw on traditional nurturing and service models for female activity. Though some lesbians may have been completely traditional in their attitudes toward their work, most had been recently affected by the enormous changes in lesbian culture and institutions that occurred in the seventies.

Within these institutions, and especially among activist segments in the political arena, we can delineate four dominant lesbian perspectives in the eighties on whether and how to make AIDS a social priority:

1. Women/lesbians make a distinctive contribution.
2. Equal rights for women/lesbians within the AIDS world.
3. Lesbians and gay men must form coalitions.
4. Lesbians need separatism.

These phrases summarize four approaches, which are best understood as ideal types. I have constructed this typology inductively on the basis of my field research and participation in AIDS work over the past ten years. The typology is complemented and supplemented by the findings of other researchers, although they may not use my language.[15] These perspectives have developed somewhat chronologically during the course of the epidemic, as women have participated in various institutional and social movement responses.[16]

In addition to these four primarily feminist approaches to AIDS, there are the nonfeminist and antifeminist conservative approaches to AIDS, some of which have specific positions on women and AIDS . Conservative approaches argue, for example, that certain infected adults (such as gay men, prostitutes, drug users, and "the promiscuous") deserve their infection and death. The holder of such a view may argue for quarantine of the "guilty" infected; in California, for example, prostitutes who test positive for HIV become felons instead of the misdemeanants they would be if uninfected. These conservative positions are less common among lesbians who are involved in public responses to AIDS and are therefore not explored in depth in this chapter.

In addition, there are some lesbians who have been called "nonfeminists" because they were too "femme," or too "into roles" or "power," or "soft" on pornography. In fact, most of these women did identify as feminists and were critical of those whom they call "lesbian feminists." The sex radicals (as some members of this group call themselves) felt rejected by lesbian separatist and lesbian feminist organizations, many of which were dominated by the philosophy of androgyny and equality. Their interest in AIDS politics and the organizational milieu of AIDS work was fueled by a belief that AIDS organizations would be locations that were more open about sexual diversity. Some were drawn to these gay organizations rather than to the lesbian organizations where they felt invisible or criticized. Strictly speaking, they are feminists, and their activity is included in the discussion of rationales listed below.

1. Women/Lesbians Make a Distinctive Contribution

This approach characterized the first few years of the epidemic and was (and continues to be) most commonly expressed by women working in the medical and caring services. Shorthand versions of this approach are "AIDS needs women" and "To get the best man for the job, call a woman." Distinctive contributionists argue that women have special skills to bring to the AIDS response, which should be brought and taught or shared with "the guys," our gay brothers.

In this model, what do women bring? They bring compassion, women's health movement experience, health skills, nurturing skills; experience with illness; ability to express emotions; relational abilities for organizational growth and change. Many lesbians did bring these skills and styles with them to their work in AIDS. The dominant organizations for the first half of the decade (1981 to 1986) were medical, caring, and education organizations. Initially, most of the clients were men. Within these organizations, lesbians played a variety of nurturing and relational roles. In some cases, women acted as leaders; their contribution has generally been underreported and underrated.

The Women's AIDS Network (WAN), located in the San Francisco Bay Area, was founded by a mixed group of lesbians and straight women in 1982 at an early national AIDS conference. Members of the organization, led primarily by lesbians, were overwhelmingly highly educated AIDS professionals[17]: nurses, doctors, therapists, health educators. Similar to the women in Melissa McNeill's study of 19 prominent lesbian AIDS activists,[18] almost all WAN members arrived with experience in feminism, health organizing, and/or lesbian and gay civil rights work.

They began by giving all they could from what they knew. Such an approach, giving all you've got, is compatible with conservative feminism and with "neoconservative" or "postmodern" feminism. In fact, some of the lesbians who worked at the San Francisco AIDS Foundation, as either staff or volunteers, are most appropriately described as nonfeminists and in some cases hostile to feminists. They saw feminism itself as hostile to gay men (because feminism criticized the men for "camp," or sexual promiscuity) or opposed to individual success. Their involvement was more often a result of connection to the gay male community and less a result of a political analysis. These women were sometimes unsympathetic to their more feminist coworkers, especially when they presented feminist agendas concerning services for women, interpreting such behavior as uncaring toward men.[19]

Most of the lesbians who got involved in AIDS research, service, and policy work in the early years, however, were both feminists and nurturers who saw themselves connected politically and ethically to the various populations at risk for AIDS.

The idea that women have special nurturing skills has frequently been expressed and appreciated in AIDS organizations, including those dominated by men. But the special skills associated with women's organizational experience was less acknowledged. This finding held true in McNeill's study as well as in my own research in San Francisco.

2. Equal Rights for Women/Lesbians Within the AIDS World

Soon after women became engaged in the work of the epidemic, a second perspective began to be expressed: that women, as AIDS workers and as people at risk for AIDS, were the victims of sexism and secondary status.

This perspective holds that we need to examine every AIDS response strategy to make certain that women's unique needs are met and that potential oppression and/or exploitation are prevented. Reproductive rights; civil liberties issues; the role of motherhood; HIV and maternal transmission; the scapegoating of prostitutes; equal access of women—and children—to AIDS education, treatment, social services, and food banks—these are all issues addressed by lesbians and straight women in the epidemic. They saw the equal rights approach as necessary because most AIDS policy was being determined by and for men, whether it was set within community based organizations (CBOs) or governmental organizations.

One example of such sexism played out in the San Francisco AIDS Foundation in 1985 and 1986. At that time, I was the coordinator of the women's program and the supervisor of educational materials development and distribution. I had supervised the development of most of the brochures for the foundation which were being distributed nationally: the first HIV test brochures (English and Spanish versions); a multiracial heterosexual brochure (English/Spanish); "sex, drugs, and AIDS"; a women and AIDS brochure (drafted by the Women's AIDS Network); and other materials for people with AIDS. The Women's AIDS Network agreed to work jointly with the foundation to produce what would be the first brochure specifically for lesbians. However, when I went to my supervisor, a gay man (and southerner) who was director of the education department, to show him the text and get formal permission for printing, for the first time in my work at the foundation I was told that my brochure would not be approved for printing because, in this case, unlike the others, "Lesbians are not at risk for AIDS." Needless to say, I was shocked by his response. Within a week, WAN was using its contacts within and without the organization to reverse the decision, and eventually (after three months of lobbying), the brochure was published. One rationalization that the director held onto was "Well, lesbians aren't really at risk, but since they are working so hard in AIDS services, they deserve a brochure." Thousands of copies were distributed or sold within the first year. The conflict indicated how invisible lesbians were as women at risk, as activists, and as experts.

In North American AIDS work, championing the equal rights focus for women often means emphasizing class and race issues because most women with HIV are poor and of either African-American or Latino descent. Lesbians, who have often been the primary representatives of straight women as well as themselves, often walked a fine line when they spoke about their own need for visibility. What did it mean to speak for "women" if one were also lesbian? Lesbian networking (through organizations like WAN), as well as direct service by lesbians to women of all sorts, has resulted in a situation in which straight women have increasingly championed lesbian needs as well as their own in terms of HIV/AIDS advocacy. As the international demographic and epidemiological facts have hit home (although slowly) in the United States, heterosexual women are receiving consistently more attention. Lesbians, though, lag far behind. Formal definitions of risk categories for HIV reflect this lesbian invisibility. For example, until 1993, the U.S. Centers for Disease Control (CDC) excluded any woman from its "lesbian" category if she had sex even once with a man since 1977.

The last two major stances held by lesbians in regard to the epidemic emerged most strongly during the second half of the decade, although, as will be seen, they (like the equal rights approach) also have their roots in feminist activist movements that flourished in the seventies.

By the middle of the first decade of AIDS, many AIDS organizations had begun to feel the stress of inadequate funding. Additionally, the dream of quick medical solutions and rapid research advances had faded. As a result, direct action tactics became more popular. ACT-UP and its clones were born and spread rapidly throughout the United States and Europe.

3. Lesbians and Gay Men Must Form Coalitions

Coalition lesbians argue that lesbians (and for that matter, everyone) should work on improving AIDS policies (even if the particular policy will benefit men primarily) because the public repressive response to the epidemic is a response to communities and populations that include lesbians as well as gay men. Therefore, it is in the interest of women, as well as the more often affected men, to have better AIDS policies.

AIDS is often seen by such women as a "homosexual" issue. They argue that many recent civil rights restrictions are based on homophobia and justified because of AIDS. Furthermore, the concomitant rise in antigay violence and the loss of community leaders, friends, and family through illness and death all affect lesbians as well as gay men. An additional argument is that focusing on AIDS discrimination is the best strategy for ending discrimination against gay people because the two discriminations (AIDS discrimination. and homophobia), as well as the prejudice, stigma, and marginalization associated with both, are completely entangled, and there is funding and some political interest in dealing with AIDS discrimination. Therefore, one can reach antigay discrimination by working on AIDS.[20]

Many AIDS activist women who share the coalition perspective also view the AIDS epidemic as an opportunity to move toward broader social agendas: national health care, local housing and shelters, effective and humane drug policy, and others. They see these changes as key to improving the role of women and gay people in society. .

This approach to AIDS work is often associated with an activist position. McNeill found that, of the half of her sample who were primarily involved in ACT-UP and OUT! (the Washington, D.C., version of ACT-UP), a major appeal was the activism. Many stated positions indicating that they saw AIDS work as a way of approaching the broader society and making changes in it. In my own interviews with lesbian members of ACT-UP New York, all stated that they saw their work as part of coalition politics. All were feminists and aligned with the sexual radical side of feminism.

Divisions with the ACT-UP organizations of several cities indicate that the definition of coalition politics varies. Whereas some women support the narrow definition of lesbians, gay men, and others working together around AIDS (the initial perspective of ACT-UP New York), others are more attuned to the broader critique of society and to the branches of ACT-UP that have taken on the wider health issues beyond AIDS.

It is out of the bonds between lesbian and gay male AIDS activists, symbolized in organizations like ACT-UP, that Queer Nation, gay antiviolence patrols, and queer culture have been formed. This new culture, in which women fill many leadership roles and which is explicitly multicultural, speaks primarily with the voice of the second generation since Stonewall—women and men who have come of age during the eighties. However, the legacies of racism and sexism have not been overcome in these organizations; they continue to break apart over challenges to the maintenance of white male systems of power.

While these political developments emerged, a previously traveled route was being explored by the "older generation" of lesbians: withdrawal and separatism.

4. Lesbians Need Separatism

"AIDS—Later for women!" This last perspective has strong roots in lesbian and feminist separatism. Separatist lesbians holding this perspective argue that both feminist and lesbian health priorities should be focused, not on AIDS, but on other, worse problems affecting women. For example, breast cancer strikes and kills many more women than does AIDS.[21] And our poverty and powerlessness are more serious health problems than HIV disease. This is the perspective presented in Jackie Winnow's speech at the 1988 Lesbians and AIDS conference in San Francisco which was reprinted in *Out/Look* magazine.[22] Although her comments were directed primarily at lesbians, she argued that all women suffer from the current AIDS funding and organizing focus, due to loss of funds for and diminished attention to women's health issues.

Additionally, some lesbians argue that, even if they themselves see AIDS as a major threat to their communities, this is not the way the average person feels in communities that are not primarily gay-identified, such as African-Americans, Latinos, the homeless, and poor whites. Therefore, AIDS-focused organizing is not an effective way to move toward organizing these communities, including their lesbian members, for survival.

While some lesbians may have stayed "out of AIDS" from the beginning because they were unconnected to gay men, did not see themselves at risk, or just wanted to avoid the whole thing, others who were engaged have left full- time work, some to work in other areas, some to do part-time volunteer activity. Of McNeill's subjects, despite their leadership roles, 25 percent (5) were turning their attention elsewhere. By 1991, 15 were working primarily on women and AIDS issues, as well as other health issues affecting women and lesbians.[23]

No matter what size or type of AIDS response organization one examines, these four perspectives appear. We are more likely to find the coalitionists in the more radical activist organizations, like the ACT-UP chapters, but in three months of visiting with ACT-UP New York in 1989, I found that the "distinctive contribution" idea was one of the strongest motivators for highly political women. Their distinctive contribution happened to be their organizing experiences gained in other direct action and civil disobedience movements. Consistently these were identified as feminist organizing "inventions," such as consciousness raising and affinity groups and various techniques to assure participatory democracy.

There is no one predominant lesbian perspective on AIDS. Even within fairly cohesive AIDS organizations with explicit values and priorities concerning the epidemic and women, there is considerable variation.

The priorities of women who have been active in AIDS response organizations have been undergoing considerable change as the organizations themselves grow, and shrink, and as the nature of the epidemic and the federal, state, and local responses to it have changed. We should expect these transformations in priorities to continue.

GENERATIONAL DIFFERENCES

Of lesbians who got involved in the AIDS epidemic in the first five years, some have stayed within the field, even if they have moved to other organizations (as many gay men have done). They have become career AIDS professionals. A second group has moved into other allied fields (health education, public health, systems management), in some cases with a focus on women. A third group has left AIDS and health altogether, an option that as far as I can tell, is being pursued primarily by those women who were more tangentially or "accidentally" engaged, either because of a single friendship or a coincidence of employment (a lesbian takes a job in a food bank in an AIDS agency, but really wants to be a graphic designer and eventually succeeds at this).

While some have become simultaneous AIDS professionals and direct action activists, this does not seem to be common. McNeill found considerable hostility between the professionals and the activists in her sample. The professionals referred to the activists as irresponsible and illinformed, while some of the activists thought that the professional women were co-opted. I would argue that, although there may have been the traditional hostility between members of the movement and the institutionalized service sector, there is also a generational split, reflecting major societal change in the last twenty years and its impact on these groups.

The differences between the older lesbians and the younger generation are deep, widespread in the lesbian community, and in many cases quite antagonistic. They affect how and why lesbians do—or don't do—AIDS work. They also affect how lesbians not involved with AIDS view the epidemic, sex (including safe sex), and lesbians who are connected to HIV and AIDS issues. Although the epidemic itself has helped to shape these differences, other social, economic, and cultural factors have also been at work. To explain this, I will conclude with comments on the two generations as they have emerged in this study of women engaged in AIDS activity.

The first group of lesbians (predominantly in their thirties and forties) grew up in the sixties, where they were influenced both by more traditional female socialization and by the radical activism of the civil rights movement, antiwar demonstrations, and nascent feminism. In the seventies, when many came of age and came out, feminism was strong, and the opportunity to be "out" relatively easily as a lesbian was new. For many of these women, simply "being" a lesbian and being public about it was a revolutionary sexual step.

The second generation, on the other hand, has come of age—and come out—in the eighties, a decade marked by explicit sexuality debates, a much greater openness about what would have been called deviant behavior ten years ago, broad female access to education, a deepening depression, and a growing radicalism among both gay men (as the epidemic remains "uncured" and the failed health economy slams into their lives) and other segments of the population. They have less faith in education or government, less of a sense of individual futures, and their sexual radicalness goes beyond being a lesbian. Being able to be a lesbian is more of a given than it was even ten years ago, and for many lesbians of the current generation, it is a very limiting identity.

During the eighties, gay men explored "safe sex" and brought everything from fisting, dildoes, and rimming to nipple rings, golden showers, and S/M scenes into public discussion—especially within the gay community, which by now had a shared press read by both men and women. Increasingly, lesbians, especially the younger ones, have sought access to this world of experimentation. Sexual activity that goes far beyond the feminist notions of equality and nonviolence have become exciting options to the new generation. While some older feminist lesbians look on in disappointment, younger women (and a few of their older friends) attend Faster Pussycat, the G-Spot, and the Ecstacy Lounge, where cruising, S/M, public sex, and such skills as the safe use of dildoes, are being (re)introduced to a new generation.

The current generation of AIDS activist lesbians carries a different psychology, culture, politics, and sexuality from those who came to the movement in the early eighties. The younger activists are connected to the older women by the term *lesbian* and by some similarities of sexual practice. Many, however, see their elders as sexually repressed, conservative, and somewhat anti-male.

The two groups may be separated by certain common sources of cross-generational conflict (the inevitable activist mellowing that comes with age and the fact that the older women can be—and in some cases are—the parents of the younger women). But it is the social changes of the eighties that have provided a different sexual and political framework and have led to a new sexuality and its political expression. The new sexuality includes an ever more pointed critique of sexual identities and practices that are organized through the dichotomous categories of male and female. Rebellion by the next generation comes to us all.

NOTES

[1]Doug McAdam, John McCarthy, and Meyer Zald, "Social movements," in *Handbook of Sociology* (New York: Sage, 1988).

[2]In 1987 I went on a one-week women's kayak trip, attended by a nonfeminist, recently divorced, 53-year-old straight woman who was shocked that everyone but her and the tour guide were lesbians. "What did she expect?" one dyke kayaker asked.

[3]See especially Alice Echols, *Daring to Be Bad: Radical Feminism in America, 1967–1975* (Minneapolis: University of Minnesota, 1989), for an excellent analysis of the radical side of seventies' feminism.

[4]This approach, which obscures the activity of those who do not command major amounts of resources and media, is repeated in the histories of many movements, where the roles of the poor, the oppressed, and the companions of the powerful are

repeatedly denigrated or made invisible because they have produced fewer material records of their role (fewer books, films, newspapers, paintings) which are easily accessible to historians and journalists of dominant classes and races. They are then proclaimed nonexistent as activists and creators.

[5]See B. Epstein, "Lesbians lead the movement," *Out/Look* (Summer 1988): 27–32.

[6]It is interesting that, when straight white men write the history of the seventies, again and again they record the death of "the movement." What movement do they mean? Perhaps it is "their" movement (the antiwar movement built on the civil rights movement), which was moribund. Of the active movements of the seventies, which they did not lead, they seem to see little, perhaps because they were not in their center. Feminism, gay rights, movements in Latino and Native American communities, the rise of mass-based antinuclear activism, and environmentalism seem to have passed them by, until they were labeled "identity politics" and somehow defused into "culture" and no longer "real" politics. Defining these movements as being primarily about identity gives the incorrect impression that they are simply about the assertion of community, and not about structural issues at all.

[7]John D'Emilio, "The gay community after Stonewall," in *Making Trouble* (New York: Routledge, 1992); Estelle Freedman and John D'Emilio, *Intimate Matters: A History of Sexuality in the United States* (New York: Harper & Row, 1988).

[8]Carol Gilligan, *In a Different Voice: Psychological Theory and Women's Development* Cambridge, Mass.: Harvard University Press, 1982).

[9]S. Hoagland, *Lesbian Ethics* (Palo Alto: Institute of Lesbian Studies, 1988).

[10]See B. Burch, "Psychological merger in lesbian couples: a joint ego psychological and systems approach," *Family Therapy* 9 (1982): 201–277; J. Krestan and C. Bepko, "The problem of fusion in the lesbian relationship," *Family Process* 19 (1980): 277–289; and S. Smalley, "Dependency issues in lesbian relationships," *Journal of Homosexuality* 14 (1987): 125–136.

[11]Cf. Randy Shilts, *And the Band Played On* (New York: St. Martin's, 1987), Larry Kramer, *Faggots* (New York: Random House, 1978) and *Reports from the Holocaust: The Making of an AIDS Activist* (New York: St. Martin's, 1989), among other works.

[12]See especially A. Snitow, C. Stansell, and S. Thompson, eds., *Powers of Desire: The Politics of Sexuality* (New York: Monthly Review Press, 1983), and Carole S. Vance, ed., *Pleasure and Danger: Exploring Female Sexuality* (Boston: Routledge 1984), to get a sense of the nature of these debates.

[13]See works by Andrea Dworkin, such as *Pornography: Men Possessing Women* (New York: Perigee, 1981), and Catharine MacKinnon for the detailed expression of this perspective.

[14]The best accounts of this conflict and the confusion experienced by femmes and butches of the seventies and eighties is found in Joan Nestle's excellent anthology, *The Persistent Desire: A Femme-Butch Reader* (Boston: Alyson, 1992).

[15]Cf. Melissa A. McNeill, *Who Are "We"? Exploring Lesbian Involvement in AIDS Work* (Master's Thesis, Smith College School of Social work, 1991).

[16]The alert reader will note the parallelism between my typology and recurrent value constructs concerning appropriate women's roles: traditionalism, liberal feminism, socialist feminism (coalition building), and radical/separatist/lesbian feminism.

[17]By this term I mean people who received their primary income from AIDS activities and who meet the sociological definition of a professional, someone whose primary value is in his or her education and receives honorific payment.

[18]McNeill, p. 50.

[19]Interestingly, in 1992, the notion that lesbians have little risk from AIDS and are suffering from "virus envy," resurfaced in England, where it is evident in writing by Simon Watney and in the most recent posters from the Terrence Higgins Trust, which proclaim that "Oral sex is very low risk, so throw away those dental dams." Lesbian inventors of the posters claim that safe-sex emphasis for lesbians is part of a combined negative attitude toward sex and a desire by some to be a greater part of the epidemic. See also Watney, *Policing Desire: Pornography, AIDS and the Media* (Minneapolis: University of Minnesota Press, 1987).

[20]Interview with Katy Taylor of the New York Human Rights Commission (1989).

[21]"About 142,000 American women develop [breast cancer] each year and 43,000 die of it. Only lung cancer causes more cancer deaths among American women." *New York Times*, 9 November 1989, p. B22, referring to an article in *NEJM* for 11/9/89.

[22]Jackie Winnow, "Lesbians working on AIDS: Assessing the impact on health care for women," *Out/Look* 5 (1989): 10–18.

[23]McNeill, p. 55.

Marcy Fraser and Diane Jones

The Role of Nurses in the HIV Epidemic

We bring to the writing of this chapter the premise that nursing and nurses are an integral and indispensable part of the health care delivery system, in particular of the HIV/AIDS care system. Critical issues facing nurses in this epidemic are the political challenges in maintaining quality of care, access to health care, and treatment and safety for providers.

We are not academicians nor are we researchers. We are two nurses, each with 10 years of experience in the HIV epidemic. We have noted the resounding absence of nurses' voices in chronicling the epidemic, yet we know that nurses have had a profound effect on the system within which we work. On a personal level, AIDS has changed nursing and each of us who has experienced its ravages in fundamental ways.

Our work experience has been in the San Francisco Bay Area, where the epidemic has predominantly affected gay men. We have worked primarily within the public and nonprofit health care system, and our patients have often been poor, homeless, and with few or no resources. We met in 1983 working on the AIDS ward at San Francisco General Hospital, the first inpatient AIDS ward in the United States.

When we undertook the writing of this chapter, we called a gathering of our peers to get feedback on the issues. Since we are both women and lesbians, and therefore prone to such egalitarian activities, we chose to throw a dinner and invite about 25 of our colleagues from various backgrounds to brainstorm with us. The group was representative of the variety of roles nurses play in the full spectrum of HIV care. It was inspiring to be in a room full of nurses who choose to work with people with AIDS.

Nurses work in all areas of the health care delivery system: in hospitals, home care, hospices, clinics, street outreach, public health nursing, education, administration, and management. Nurses work as program directors for community-based HIV programs and as managers in private organizations. Nurses' educational levels and job descriptions range from certified nursing attendants or aides to nurse practitioners or clinical nurse specialists, licensed vocational nurses and registered nurses. However, there are only two overarching categories: nurses who do "hands-on care" and nurses who "don't do that any more but did."

The distinction between these two categories parallels that in other fields between direct service providers and administrators; for example, the differences between teachers and school administrators who were at one time classroom teachers themselves. For nurses, this is the distinction between the bedside nurse and other nurses classified as supervisors, managers, or administrators. It is a complex and frustrating relationship, one often focused on the allocation of scarce resources.

The bedside nurse is directly involved with meeting the needs of and advocating for very sick people. Nurses who aren't at the bedside are responsible for supporting the systems that support the patient care environment: personnel management, quality assurance, fund raising, safety, budgeting, and responding to the myriad state and federal regulatory agencies that define our health care system.

The consensus of the dinner group was that, overall, nurses have had a positive impact on the health care system's ability to care for people with HIV/AIDS. Although nurses have been among the many health care providers who have responded with fear and paranoia to this epidemic, and have been guilty of refusing to care for patients with HIV disease, we have also been among its most invisible and unrecognized champions. Many of the caregiving systems and units that evolved to meet the needs of people with AIDS were created by nurses and to this day are "nurse-driven." As a result, the entire structure of health care delivery has been transformed.

Nurses have always known that this is not work for the "lone ranger" practitioner. This is work best done with a multidisciplinary team. The physical and emotional demands are such that nurses working together with other professionals (physicians, social workers, counselors, psychiatrists, rehab therapists, nutritionists) will serve patients most effectively.

Our focus in this chapter is on the nursing experience of hands-on care. The physical, emotional, and spiritual aspects of that experience form a strong bond among all nurses in HIV care. The memories of those experiences remain fresh.

Nurses who work directly with patients represent the greater number of us in the profession. For a very long time, 80 percent were working in hospitals. That figure has changed as the health care system has changed, so that now the majority of us work outside of hospitals: in clinics, hospices, and home health care. We do hands-on care outside of the hospital setting.

Nurses' unique perspective has grown from our constant and historical presence in all the different places within the health care system. We are at the sides of patients who benefit from the most sophisticated technology available, as well as those individuals who are the most alienated and compromised by the system's inefficiencies and inequities.

As a disease, AIDS has challenged our health care system to expand the definition of what it means to meet the needs of sick people. Nurses have been a critical voice in redefining those needs. Not only hospital and medical care, but housing, meals, transportation, legal assistance, and help with the activities of daily living must be included. The need for the full continuum of care has been dramatically revealed as the epidemic moves into communities of color and other populations where access to health care has been marginal at best. Nurses have served as important links in that continuum, providing services in nonhospital settings within communities.

Despite all of this presence, we have been traditionally and historically invisible. Nursing is a profession that is overwhelmingly female, greater than 90 percent. In the shadow of male physicians, female nurses have been portrayed as handmaidens. Women in our dinner group could recall being instructed to give up their chairs at the hospital nursing station when a doctor approached.

The challenge to nursing reflects the challenges faced by women in a sexist society. In the field of AIDS, there are now many male nurses, primarily gay men, working alongside female coworkers, both heterosexual and lesbian. Sometimes our motivation for being in this field, as women, has been called into question by our gay colleagues. They have been suspicious of our ability to truly care, since they perceive that we have not been truly affected by AIDS. Lesbians have been "grandmothered" into the "truly caring" circle because, they feel, we probably know what homophobia is about. However, the motivations of heterosexual women caring for gay men are often suspect.

Although many female nurses, heterosexual and lesbian, have commented on the relief they experience working in an environment where their gay male patients don't come on to them, garden-variety sexism remains alive and well. As recently as a few years ago, a male patient asked one of us as we arrived in his room, "Are you my waitress for today?" And one of the nurse practitioners in our group was asked in 1993, "Can ladies be doctors here?"

We have been put in our place by other healthcare professionals who see us as second class providers, charged with caring for bodily functions. The irony is that we are trusted with the most intimate and complex procedures, but not with long-term strategic planning or budgetary decisions.

Nurses can muster great influence in many settings, but we have little real authority. Despite the inherent sexism built into our status as professionals, the AIDS epidemic has attracted many nurses motivated by longstanding traditions of fighting for social justice and equality. These nurses stepped forward just as many in our profession were refusing to care for people with AIDS and embraced two socially disenfranchised populations: gay men and injection drug users. This combination has fueled an intensely political environment which in itself is attractive to many who want to grapple with the relationship between science and politics.

THE POLITICS OF HIV NURSING

As health care providers, we have a sorrowful legacy to overcome: that of working in an industry that has historically failed to serve gay men, lesbians, women, addicts, poor people, and people of color. Because of the demographics of the AIDS epidemic in the United States, these forces are played out in daily dramas at the bedside, in clinic waiting rooms, and in management meetings.

As health care workers, we have to cope with how we have internalized this legacy. In the play *Miss Evers' Boys,* by David Feldshuh, the public health nurse employed by the infamous Tuskegee syphilis experiment vividly epitomizes the catch-22 in which nurses have found themselves for years. This government-funded study was designed to follow the course of untreated syphilis among African-American men in the South. It began in 1932 and continued long after the discovery of penicillin in the 1940s. The play focuses on an African-American public health nurse who was the ultimate foot soldier in this despicable experiment. The play portrays the nurse's agony as she listens to her patients, their hopes for treatment and cure, knowing all the while that her efforts to advocate on their behalf are futile. Her physician supervisors, determined to sacrifice the patients in the interest of "scientific knowledge," withheld treatment in order to study the natural course of the disease to its end point—death. Without her complicity, the experiment would have failed. She was the crucial link between the physician-researchers and the "research subjects."

In the struggle to find effective treatment for HIV infection, clinical trials for experimental drugs were initially available only to a select group of participants. Women and people of color were not included in these studies for many years. Nurses, patients, and AIDS activists publicly pressured the pharmaceutical companies and research institutes. The deeply conservative traditions of research were debated, challenged, and changed by this public examination. Because of these efforts, drug studies are now more open, access to treatment has increased, and activists and patients are invited to give input to the actual study designs.

Nurses have been increasingly affected by the poverty connected with this disease. Last year, a nurse who had been working on the AIDS ward at San Francisco General Hospital for over eight years expressed this vividly when he commented, "We used to be seen as little angels of mercy. What happened? Our patients all seem to hate us." An adversarial or frustrating relationship is what we often experience. Patients frequently come into the health care system with distrust bred by years of neglect and abuse. Accustomed to being treated with condescension and disrespect, they respond with hostility to mask the fear and apprehension that once again they will not be cared for. They come with no feeling of empowerment, no training in advocacy or experience to negotiate their way through the health care morass. They run into nurses (and other health care providers) who themselves lack the training, skills, and understanding to overcome these historical legacies. As one nurse crudely put it, "It's not as fun anymore."

The problems patients are facing often go far beyond HIV disease. When a patient is homeless, no amount of tender loving care on the part of a committed and dedicated nurse will be able to change that fact. Instead, the nurse is seen as an accomplice to an unjust system that allows people with terminal diseases to be discharged to homeless shelters and addicts to go untreated for their addiction while receiving the latest and most expensive AIDS drugs. Nurses must learn to cope with these contradictions and not simply internalize the frustration and anger they feel.

As other fields began shrinking as the result of massive health care and social service cutbacks of the 1980s, the "AIDS industrial complex" was spawning new jobs and programs with funds that were wrestled from the federal government to combat the growing epidemic.

The field of AIDS has generated many high-paying jobs and career opportunities. A few years ago, while attending a national AIDS conference, reflecting on the careerism and grandstanding we encountered (and after one too many cups of coffee), we named the phenomenon we observed APES (AIDS provider ego syndrome). We were not immune to what happened in other fields of medicine. We witnessed the rapid professionalization of AIDS. The agencies spawned by early responses of community-based agencies were being replaced with traditional medical model approaches to care. Sadly, and somewhat cynically, we noted the changes.

The grassroots movement of the early 1980s was becoming part of the medical industrial machine. There was money to be made on the HIV epidemic, and the health care and research industries were gearing up. The traditional roles of doctor, nurse, and patient were revived and renewed. Many women wonder, if similar job opportunities existed in the field of women's health (if there were a better-financed response to the epidemic of breast cancer), how many of us would be there instead?

Lesbians and gay men emerged at the forefront of nurses willing to take on the assignments of caring for people with AIDS. By "seizing the moment," these nurses provided necessary role modeling and risk taking (long before much of what we know today about HIV) for health care workers in general. To this day, the proportion of lesbians and gay men in AIDS nursing is high. For many people, the epidemic has provided their first opportunity to be "out" on the job. In fact, being lesbian or gay sometimes added value and credibility to our professional status. Nurses with a personal background and experience with the challenge of recovery from drug and alcohol addiction were being sought out. How ironic that to be gay, lesbian, or an ex-junkie could actually make you more marketable in the AIDS workforce! However, lest we become delusional, the glass ceiling is as thick and strong in AIDS as elsewhere. Very few of the AIDS health care leaders on the national scene are other than white, heterosexual men, primarily physicians. In 1993 Kristine Gebbie, a nurse, was appointed by President Clinton to be the "AIDS czar," but she had no real power and no budget.

Beginning in the late 1980s, political battles were being waged on the streets. ACT-UP and other AIDS activists demonstrated before the giant pharmaceutical companies and outside the CDC and the FDA (later, they would move inside). Quieter and more personal battles were taking place in the corridors of clinics and hospital wards. Nurses were often the central characters in these dramas. At stake was a revolutionary redefinition of the role that patients (otherwise known as clients and consumers) were to play in the course of their illness. "ACT UP, FIGHT BACK!" became the battle cry. From treatment choices, to how aggressively they wanted to be treated, to opting for stopping treatment altogether and choosing the time and place of their death, gay male patients were negotiating a new relationship with their physicians and nurses. These men helped create a new standard and awareness among all consumers of health care. Their contributions will forever change the way victims become activists.

The impact on nurses' roles has been profound. Schooled in their role as "patients' advocates," nurses had to be willing to suspend judgment and their own opinions and feelings to become partners with their patients, and with their patients' lovers and families, in battling not only HIV disease but also unresponsive and archaic institutions. New concepts, such as "patient-centered care," were piloted on hospital AIDS wards.

The AIDS epidemic changed a lot of definitions and assumptions. In more progressive health care settings, old policies that restricted access to hospitalized patients were thrown out. The patient became the ultimate definer of his or her reality: Who constitutes the "family"? Who is the next of kin? Who will participate in decisions about the course of the illness? Who gets to spend the night with a dying patient? And, for many nurses, the newest challenge (as members of transsexual and transgender communities are becoming ill): Who gets to define the gender identity of the patient?

For every nurse in this epidemic willing to listen to her or his patient, be the voice that couldn't be heard, or argue with a team of doctors with long white coats, we can see a health care system that becomes more patient focused rather than physician dominated. Policies can become responsive to human needs; new standards can emerge to help change performance; and ultimately, the patient receives better care. Nurses celebrated these innovations and enjoyed some credit for their creation.

THE RISKS OF OCCUPATIONAL EXPOSURE

While we were basking in the excitement of our new sense of empowerment and accomplishment, we lived and worked in denial about any possible risk to ourselves.

In 1987, a nurse at San Francisco General Hospital became HIV-positive following a needlestick she had sustained six weeks earlier. The news sent shockwaves through the hospital staff and the entire community. For four years, the focused energy had been on convincing the world that working in this field was safe and the risk of exposure minimal. Nurses compared their record of needlesticks almost as trophies, and each new exposure became proof that concerns and fears among health care workers were mere AIDS hysteria.

The nurse, known as Jane Doe, waged a lonely and difficult battle with the San Francisco city bureaucracy to retain anonymity and collect workers' compensation for her medical expenses. Protecting her privacy and future employment proved to be an exhausting and lengthy struggle. It wasn't until nearly two years later, after a nurses' union intervened, that the city relented and agreed to set up procedures that would allow her to maintain confidentiality.

The risks to nursing personnel were not taken seriously. Action was not swift. To protect the workers meant acknowledging it was real. It would take three years before the hospital moved dirty needle disposal boxes out of the patients' bathrooms to the bedside, thereby reducing the risks that nurses and others would have of sustaining a needlestick like Jane Doe's.

Jane Doe led us to break with denial. We lacked any conscious realization of the relative risk involved in occupational exposure to HIV. The fact was that little was being done at the national level to assist health care workers with occupational risk. We expected our health institutions to take care of us. Through informal networks we heard about nurses in other parts of the country who had become HIV-positive through the actions or negligence of others. We felt frightened, outraged, and appalled—after all, we were only doing our jobs.

Many of our colleagues believe that there is underreporting of occupationally acquired HIV infection. In the San Francisco Bay Area alone, we have heard of no less than 10 nurses becoming HIV infected on the job. However, if a nurse belongs to any of the recognized "risk groups" for HIV and is infected on the job, the chances of being recognized and compensated for an occupational exposure are practically nil. The case reporting and definitions are rigid and limited.

In the United States, there are 100,000 reported needlesticks per year. If we use the current seroprevalence data of 2 percent HIV-positivity in the patient population, that means that 2,000 of the needlesticks are from HIV-positive sources. At the current rate of seroconversion of 0.03 percent, the result would be 8 health care workers becoming HIV-positive each year.

The CDC has reported 12 nurses with "documented on-the-job transmission" in 10 years. Another 14 nurses are classified as "possible" on the job transmission. The criteria set by the CDC to be classified as a "documented exposure" is so rigorous that few pass the test. In addition, there is considerable nonreporting due to a realistic fear that confidentiality and privacy will not be maintained. The experience of our patients demonstrated all too clearly the unfortunate results when health benefits or employment are endangered.

Many in our profession are critical of the poor response and lack of leadership from our federal health agencies with regard to occupational exposure. Nurse Jane Doe expressed outrage when she compared the CDC's handling of health care worker occupational exposure risk to their handling of the possible HIV transmission from a dentist to six patients in Florida.

In 1990, Kimberly Bergalis became nationally known as an "innocent victim." She advocated for mandatory testing of health care workers and mandatory reporting of HIV-infected health care workers. The CDC did little to lead the public out of its mass hysteria and counter the ravings of a few men on the congressional floor. Longstanding advocates of mandatory testing and reporting (under the predictable leadership of Senator Jesse Helms of North Carolina) were in charge of the Senate hearings on this subject. The CDC's willingness to release information and speculate as to how transmission took place in the Bergalis case (which to this day is still in dispute) came as an insult to all of us in the profession who believe the CDC consistently underreports the number of health care workers infected on the job. An added concern may be that many health care workers would be unwilling to work with patients with AIDS if honest information about rates of on-the-job transmission were regularly released.

The final straw came in the summer of 1991 when the Senate voted 99 to 1 to force states to adopt CDC recommendations that included a policy of "voluntary" disclosure of HIV status by health care workers to their patients. The impact on nurses was profound: when had the Senate voted 99 to 1 at any time and for anything in the history of this epidemic? Where was the leadership to inform the public of where the real risks were? In fact, once all the posturing was done and both Dr. Acer (the Florida dentist) and Kimberly Bergalis (his patient) were buried, after the news media had long lost interest in the story, the CDC changed its position and began to reassert that the risk posed by HIV-positive health care workers to their patients was minimal. No other case such as Dr. Acer's has ever been reported.

Jane Doe is struck by the irony that, in pregnancy, the risk to women over 35 of having a Down's syndrome baby is 1 in 1,000. As a result, the community standard is to recommend amniocentesis to all pregnant women over 35. Occupational exposure via needlesticks, resulting in seroconversion, is three times greater a risk (3 in 1,000). Why is there not a national standard mandating that all steps be taken to protect health care workers and accurately track the incidence and circumstances of seroconversion? Other threats to health care workers exist: hepatitis B and C, cytomegalovirus, and repeated exposure to toxic chemotherapeutic agents, to name a few.

Given the longstanding tradition in health care of discouraging workers from lobbying for a safer workplace, and the economics involved in investing in new, safer technologies, there is little material incentive for the health industry to make an honest reckoning with what is happening to its providers.

New and safer equipment ("needleless" syringes and IV access, better masks and improved gloves) is often priced at many times the cost of the traditional low-bid equipment in general use. As profits have begun to shrink throughout the health care industry, purchasing newer, safer, more expensive equipment seems less likely.

"NOTHING HAS GIVEN ME THE SATISFACTION THAT AIDS NURSING HAS"

Despite the risks of occupational exposure, we know of few nurses who have left this field of work once they start. So what *is* it that keeps so many of us working with people with HIV/AIDS?

In our caregiving to HIV/AIDS patients, we have experienced the most extreme highs and lows our profession has to offer. The compelling, exhausting, fulfilling emotional nature of the work has kept us here. The exposure to gay men's sensibilities and humor, the richness of how all the many cultures approach illness and death, the incredible grace and intimacy we have shared with our patients have kept us here. Our nearness to the mysteries of life and transitions to death has kept us here. We put up with low status, long hours, physically demanding work, and oceans of diarrhea in exchange for those moments we experience as packed with meaning.

On a day-to-day basis, we are not dealing with the overwhelming nature of an epidemic. It is the individual who is sick. In the face of tremendous loss and grief, we believe we can alleviate some of the suffering of those who are ill, by what we have to offer in the simplest way: by touching them. Nurses spend time touching people, bathing, drying, massaging, shampooing, combing, dressing, and feeding. We also spend time poking and prodding patients, preparing them for procedures in which perhaps neither the patient nor the nurse has any faith.

Outside of hospitals, nurses spend time arranging and coordinating care for patients. We lobby insurance carriers to pay for needed care that may technically be outside of a patient's benefit, but is clearly cost-effective. Coordinating volunteers and others to provide rides, meals, and assistance are tasks that offer tremendous satisfaction to the nurse and relief for a client whom science has little to offer in the way of medicine.

Often, nurses find themselves in the traditional female role of being in the middle. We are the bridges between physicians and patients, explaining to each what the other is trying to communicate. We facilitate interactions between patients and family members, between parents and lovers, between administrators and their peers. In nursing schools, we are trained to advocate for our patients, sticking up for them when they are unable to do it for themselves. We try to represent them, encourage and empower them to make decisions that are informed. Frequently, we find ourselves at odds with physicians who see us as underlings, meddling in their "orders."

We are also the keepers of secrets; secrets from family members, from physicians, and even from county coroners. When confronted by a patient determined to end a life that has become severely limited and painful, many physicians simply will not intervene. More often than not, it is the nurse who finds the patient dead, or who becomes the confidant of the patient's suicide plan. A nurse's license to practice, not to mention her personal ethics, can be jeopardized.

Nursing people with AIDS is about mortality. The nearness to dying and loss, the mystery of the last heartbeat between life and death attracts us. We prepare patients as best we can for the transition, and we wait. Bearing witness to the very powerful moment of death and sharing those mysteries keeps many of us working in this field. It is an honor and a privilege not lost on AIDS nurses.

This work has brought about exponential personal growth. We have been challenged by patients who ask, "Am I dying now?" or by mothers taking their sons or daughters home to die who want to know "What will it be like? What will happen?" and "Will it hurt?" We have tried to answer these questions to soothe loved ones and comfort our patients, and to deal with the inevitable questions of our own living and dying. Some of us have felt a new appreciation for life. Some of us have started doing things we were always afraid to do—taking risks in case we, too, run out of time.

Many nurses identify with patients who have been oppressed and, conversely, have difficulties with patients with whom they do not identify. Patients with long histories of psychiatric illness or addictions or who have been otherwise marginalized or abused since childhood challenge us to care and to learn different ways of giving. One must trust in order to feel cared about. Learning to approach someone who has not had a single positive experience with social institutions works our hearts and our nerves. We were humbled by one of our patients who said it so well: "Remember, anger is really fear in drag."

As intimate caregivers, we develop intense relationships with our patients and with each other. We enjoy the feeling of these relationships; they are described by words like *primal*. We are attracted to the passion, the drama, the humor, and the opportunity of human experience. We are present for the transactions in abusive family and partner relationships, as well as complete unconditional love between people. We have seen our patients' loved ones rise to the occasion and provide exhaustive care, and we have seen them sink to abandonment and regret. It is a rich environment of human experience, behavior, lifestyle, and culture.

AIDS brings a certain continuity between providers and patients. Many of us have known our patients over a period of years, from diagnosis to death. Patients confide in us, bring us to their most essential private places, and talk about the deeply felt issues of the human soul. We value these long-term relationships and know that they are therapeutic for both patient and caregiver.

The relationships that nurses develop with each other can be equally profound. It is necessary to bond and to trust in order to accomplish our jobs and support one another to go through these experiences. For most of us, the only people in our lives who understand or relate to what we do are other nurses. Our families can tolerate only a little of the story, but get a group of nurses together and the storytelling can go on late into the night . . . with great detail and considerable delight.

We are frequently asked how we live with burnout and continue doing this work for many years. Supportive work environments and individuals who are self-aware and know how to take care of themselves are key. We don't find the work inherently depressing. It is sad and stressful, challenging both personally and politically, but we agree that we get more out of it than we could ever put into it.

Last year, 1993, marked the ten-year anniversary of the opening of the HIV/AIDS program at San Francisco General Hospital. For many, it was also a personal tenth anniversary working with people with AIDS. It gives us pause to consider this fact. Early in the epidemic, some nurses were convinced (even hopeful) that they would be out of work in a few years, that a cure would be found. Passing this ten-year mark, and the ten thousandth death in San Francisco (which has a total population of less than 700,000) is an event with significant implications for our well-being as health care workers. We, too, have lost lovers, friends, and coworkers. HIV/AIDS crosses all the traditional protective boundaries of professional caregivers, as the professional distance gives way.

CONCLUSION

Looking into the future, it's impossible to imagine the historic global impact that the AIDS epidemic will have had when it runs its course. Already it has had a transforming effect on the health care system and on the role of nurses in particular. When we try to project what this next decade will look like, we have to take into account the context and impact of health care reform. We are in the beginning stages of massive changes whose outcomes are unpredictable. How responsive will health care institutions be to the needs of patients/consumers under "managed competition"? How would nursing as a profession fare under a system of universal access? Over the past ten years, the payers of medical bills (insurance companies, HMOs, and the government) have increasingly determined standards of care. They are making health care decisions together with their physician-consultants. Nurses, patients, and in many cases primary care providers, are not at the decision-making table. The realities of the bedside are thus absent when critical decisions are being made.

If nurses' depth of knowledge and expertise are to be counted, we need to become literate in the economics of health and claim a place in the national debate for health care reform. Armed with a growing sense of empowerment, having proven ourselves again in the AIDS epidemic (and in every other field of health care), we have a far-reaching perspective that, in its better moments, can advocate, articulate, pressure, and produce the quality health care that is the right of every individual in society.

Our experience on the front lines gives us the ability to discern what the points of effectiveness and efficiency are. In the absence of a cure for AIDS, effective and efficient care means acceptance of and respect for the individual regardless of transmission category or health insurance coverage. It means commitment to providing comfort and care, to relieve pain and suffering, and to assist the dying.

So what is our message? It is simply that we value our work, our patients, and our contribution. The spiritual aspects of our job, the social activism, the connections with human souls in need, and the opportunity to practice exquisite caring are all part of the payback we receive.

It is an honor to share this struggle with the thousands of people with HIV/AIDS we have known.

NOTE

[1]See James H. Jones, *Bad Blood: The Tuskegee Syphilis Experiment.* New York: The Free Press, 1993.

PART IV

Problems and Policies for Women in the Future

Helen Rodriguez-Trias and Carola Marte

Challenges and Possibilities: Women, HIV, and the Health Care System in the 1990s

THE AMERICAN HEALTH CARE SYSTEM: NOT MADE FOR WOMEN

A dvocates waging struggles to provide preventive, diagnostic, and clinical care services for HIV-infected women encounter a health care system ill equipped to meet even the barest needs of much of the population. Structural elements seriously hamper the efforts of advocates, clinicians, and researchers to provide a majority of people with acceptable levels of care. The basis of the system is the market. Based on the premise that health care is a commodity, the distribution, development, financing, and delivery of services respond to market forces rather than to people's needs.

The HIV epidemic began to affect women as the failures of the American health care system became increasingly evident even to conservative thinkers. Advocates for HIV-infected women recognized that they were dealing with a costly, inequitable system that excludes tens of millions of Americans from access and that two-thirds of the adults without health coverage were women. Most advocates realized that, to meet the needs of ever-larger numbers of low-income women, fundamental reform was necessary. Not surprisingly, as they fought for care for women with HIV, women also became core activists in the current movement for radical change in health care delivery.

The past decade's experience of organizing, lobbying, and legislating serves women well in the effort to forge policies and programs that are centered on women's concerns. The theoretical and practical basis for health care reform by women developed from their experiences of discomfort, humiliation, and abuse at the hands of medical practitioners and from their marginalization as health workers. Women have effectively organized and spearheaded the movement for reproductive rights. More than any other group involved in the movement for health care reform, women challenged the basic cultural core of medicine and its power structure.[1] Consider some examples. In resistance to the medicalization of childbirth, women have fought for birthing centers and the right of lay midwives to train and practice. From solid experience in community-based programs for battered women and in academia, women have succeeded in placing the problem of violence on the agenda of the medical community. From years of powerlessness and exclusion, women have fought for informed consent and increased patient participation in decision making. As women of color became more engaged in struggling for health rights and advocating for themselves and their communities, they raised issues such as racism and class biases that affect medical practice. Such issues were not always initially recognized or understood by the largely white middle-class women's health movement. As women have struggled together to understand one another's experiences and points of view, they have forged a movement for health care reform that contains the seeds of equity. The resulting dialogues among advocates advance the effectiveness and unity of the movement toward health care for all. None of this has come easily, as the same barriers of class, race, ethnicity, and education that divide the society plague all movements.

The higher prevalence of HIV is among women of color and of lower income, those who are already undervalued and marginalized.[2] Still, HIV-infected women are emerging as greatly effective leaders in the epidemic, challenging professionals' stereotypes of women and substance abuse, low-income women, lesbian women, and women of color. They participate in organizations and coalitions of women health providers, advocates, and public health workers, bringing a sense of urgency and reality to others. With their intimate knowledge of health care, HIV-infected women keep the focus of health care reform on improved services.

A weakness in the current debates on health care is a narrow focus on personal services; that is, services provided by doctors and other health professionals at their offices, clinics, or hospitals. The health of women, like that of all people, is ultimately more a function of public health policies and services than of personal health services. In no way does public health diminish the importance of personal health services for HIV-infected women. But public health emphasizes prevention and concerns itself with developing an environment, social and economic as well as physical, that fosters health. Advocates in the field of HIV make the distinction between personal health services and public health issues very clear. To address HIV we must also address inequities in life circumstances. For almost all preventable diseases, poor people fare worse. Indicators of the public's health in a state by state comparison show a clear correlation with poverty.[3] Women of color are overrepresented among the poor, as indeed they are among those infected by HIV. The immediate need and opportunity for reform of the health care delivery system should not sidetrack us from addressing the larger issues of the socioeconomic determinants of health. The struggles for public health reform and empowerment must occur simultaneously with struggles for health care reform around a universal system of accessible, acceptable, and appropriate services.

HEALTH CARE PROBLEMS AND WOMEN'S PERSPECTIVES

Briefly stated, the health care system in the United States shows signs of dysfunction in several major areas: cost, waste, inequities, fragmentation, maldistribution, and grossly uneven quality. Most of these problems are longstanding, affect most people, and have created almost insurmountable barriers for people fighting the HIV epidemic.

Cost and Waste

A majority of Americans want changes in health care. Although discussions in the media and in legislatures center on runaway costs, most people express greater concern about access and quality of care. From a consumer perspective, it seems evident that the "U.S. is already spending enough to bring every citizen high-quality, high-tech medical care—if we stop squandering our resources."[4] But it is not only consumer dissatisfaction that takes the debate on reform to its present high pitch. Rising costs, to over 13 percent of the gross national product, are the highest in the world. They translate to over $800 billion. Employers, government, workers and their representatives, all the components of the vast health care industry, and insurance companies all want to avoid paying a bigger portion or facing reductions in benefits or profits. In ways mostly obscure to the public, the bitter conflicts about who pays and who gains underlie the plethora of legislative proposals that purport to address the situation.

Health care activists agree on several points. There is considerable waste in the system from useless and frequently harmful treatment; administrative inefficiency creates losses; profits for insurance, pharmaceutical companies, and some providers are excessive; payment mechanisms allow for fraud. Translated to percentage of health expenditures, all this avoidable waste may be as high as one-quarter of the health bill.[5]

Women and children comprise a large proportion of the over 40 million who are uninsured or only very partially insured. In 1991, 12.5 percent of women and 12.7 percent of children under 18 years had no coverage. Medicaid provided coverage for nearly 11 percent of the total population.[6] Who receives Medicaid benefits varies markedly from state to state and in most cases is limited to the very poor. African Americans, Latinos, Native Americans, and Asian Americans are markedly overrepresented among those without health coverage. During all or part of 1989, 33 percent of Latinos (over 6 million persons) and 19 percent of African Americans were uninsured compared to about 12 percent of whites.[7] Women, particularly women with low incomes and women of color, therefore, have a strong stake in health reform that controls costs and provides universal coverage but that also controls unnecessary procedures, fraud, and red tape.

Women's concern about unnecessary procedures is well justified. Aware that they are often the subjects of unnecessary surgery, women have taken the lead in questioning the excessive performance of hysterectomies and Caesareans. In some instances, they have succeeded in gaining support from providers and lowered rates, thus decreasing the incidence of complications as well.

Besides their contribution to red tape, insurance companies harm women in many ways, specifically by their limitation of spousal benefits; lack of coverage for much routine and necessary care, such as gynecological exams; exclusion of persons with preexisting conditions; requirement of copayments; and complicated benefit packages. Women's organizations are increasing their support for health care legislation, termed "single payer," that will markedly limit the role of the insurance companies as a first step toward a national health system that will establish health care as a right.[8]

Inequities

As provided in the United States, health care mirrors the inequities inherent in the socioeconomic system and sustained by the culture. Poor people, persons from ethnic or racial minorities, persons with disabilities, those living in rural or isolated areas, persons who are homeless are among the many who are excluded from the benefits of our highly stratified system. The inequities affecting women go beyond race, ethnicity, and socioeconomic status. Medicine and the medical profession have long been male bulwarks. The ideology, research, and practice of medicine retain marked sex biases as well. Women of color confront racism and sexism as well as class biases.

Because data on health status seldom includes class as an identifier, there is little specific information on the effects of low income on the health status of women. Mortality rates and some health indicators such as limited activity do show differences according to social class above and beyond ethnicity.[9] Women who are poor are hit hard by unequal access to services. From late diagnosis for breast cancer,[10] to unavailable abortion services, to obstetricians who refuse to accept Medicaid for childbirth services, inequities hit hard.

The health care facilities, the quality of care they deliver, the range of services they provide, the attitudes of the health workers are class determined. Most women with low incomes in larger cities must rely on public hospitals or Medicaid clinics for their health care. In smaller towns and rural areas, there may be no available health care at all. For HIV-infected women, the situation is yet more dire; some need to travel hundreds of miles to reach any provider who is skilled and willing to see them.

Fragmentation

Health care, under the best of circumstances, includes prevention, diagnosis, treatment, and services to help restore function (rehabilitation). Without excessive inconvenience, people should be able to obtain acute care (needed within and for a short period of time), as well as long-term or chronic care. Facilities and staff should be equipped to provide on site, or within a reasonable distance, primary, secondary, and tertiary care. These terms refer to the level of specialization and availability of doctors, nurses, dentists, nurse practitioners, and other health care providers, but also to the level of care clinics or hospitals provide. For instance, a physician who in her office is able to care for an HIV-infected woman is providing primary care. Primary care is carried out in offices, clinics, or community settings. If the woman with HIV develops a complication that requires hospitalization, her doctor may need to get a consultation. The consultant and the hospital staff are providing a secondary level of care. Should she need intensive care, she might need to go to a tertiary care unit in that same hospital or transfer to another. Tertiary care is that rendered by highly specialized staff using equipment and facilities most often found in hospitals associated with medical schools, referred to as teaching hospitals. Fragmentation of services occurs because the various levels of services are in different places, the people rendering the services do not communicate effectively, and the paperwork is different from one service unit or hospital to another and invariably cumbersome. Further, in teaching hospitals, discontinuity of medical staff is the rule, since most are trainees who rotate through the different services. Proposals for case managers—that is, individuals who coordinate all the various aspects of care—spring from the recognition that, without someone to guide people and their health care workers, confusion will reign.

Maldistribution

Health care facilities and health care personnel are located not on the basis of the needs of communities, but for reasons of convenience for already-existing medical institutions such as schools or large hospitals or because investors followed markets. Many hospitals in cities are like housing, old and decrepit, long neglected as the earlier white inhabitants moved out and the people of color moved in. City, county, and state-run facilities are considered public, while those owned by individuals or corporate entities are private. In fact, all hospitals, regardless of ownership, receive large amounts of public funds for their operation. Doctors' offices and clinics, with a few exceptions such as federally funded health centers, are likewise located, not on the basis of need, but to maximize income. In poor urban communities of the sixties, physicians were a scarce commodity until the advent of government funding for services through Medicaid. The decades following saw a proliferation of city Medicaid clinics, derogatorily known as "Medicaid mills," which provided services in volume to maximize their gain. Rural America continues to be largely bereft of physicians and other health workers. The low density of the population does not sustain a high enough turnover to encourage practitioners to accept Medicaid. The federal government must fund and staff a network of rural and migrant health centers in an effort to fill some of the serious gaps in health care.

Large city hospitals that had undergone considerable reduction in bed capacity during the late seventies and early years of the eighties, were overwhelmed by the needs of people beset by drug addiction, accidents, assaults, homelessness, and then HIV. What had been barely tolerable deficiencies in physical plant, personnel, and equipment are now life threatening. Partly by default of the privately owned system of health care and partly because of tradition, state, county, city, and other local public health departments also provide clinic and in-hospital care for people of low income and for all who seek their specific services. These may include diagnosis and treatment for sexually transmitted diseases and tuberculosis, immunizations, prenatal care, and a host of other personal health services. The spread of the HIV epidemic in the same communities that receive care at public health clinics has taxed many beyond their capacity to deliver acceptable care. Women advocates of health care reform propose participation of public health professionals, community, representatives, government, and industry in assessing community needs in order to plan deployment of health care facilities and staff. Basing health care on needs will lead to evaluation of the efficacy of health care delivery to communities as well as individuals. Women recognize that only by broad and consistent participation of the women served can appropriate planning take place.

Uneven Quality

Good quality, or even what is termed "minimally acceptable quality," in health care is an elusive goal. Much depends on the internal standards of practice set by the professions, review procedures in institutions, and, ultimately, training, skills, motivation, and honesty of practitioners. Regulations or reviews set up by external bodies such as utilization groups or state agencies yield relatively little. The same fragmentation and maldistribution of health care providers and facilities, enmeshed in a commercial culture of health care that frustrates efforts at improving access, undermines those trying to ensure acceptable quality of care throughout the United States.

Women advocates maintain that ongoing reviews are necessary and that these must involve those who are using the services, both in setting standards and assuring that they are met. For health care reform to address issues of quality, we need directed research efforts to craft better measurements of the efficacy of diagnostic and treatment interventions.

WOMEN AND HIV: NEW CRISES FOR OLD PROBLEMS

The problems that HIV-infected women confront in the health care system are not new. Fragmentation of services, neglect of women's health research, and reproductive rights abuses have been issues of major concern to the women's health movement for decades. Criminalization of chemical dependency and abortion have always affected primarily the most disenfranchised persons, poor women and women of color. Criminalization of HIV transmission and mandatory HIV testing of selected populations, especially immigrants, prisoners, and the pregnant poor, are now added to the list. Different and unequal access to health care for the affluent compared to the working poor and the unemployed has earned growing attention as health reform becomes an item on the national economic agenda. A related issue that has received less attention than it should is the appalling shortage of substance abuse and family services for women in poor communities. Without access to such services, what medical care does exist in their communities may prove to be a wasted resource for many women.

Fragmentation of Services

The separation of gynecologic and obstetric services from other medical care is deeply ingrained in medical training and practice in the United States. Fragmentation of women's medical services is especially pernicious for women with HIV disease. Specialized infectious disease clinics, the most common setting for HIV care, are even less likely to offer gynecologic care than general medical clinics and medical practices. Conversely, many gynecologists are unwilling to treat HIV-infected women, and few have made themselves expert in gynecologic manifestations of HIV infection.

The result is that women with known HIV status are not adequately treated for often-severe gynecologic conditions, and untested women are not referred for counseling and testing, despite gynecologic problems that clearly indicate the presence of HIV infection. In addition, a large number of clinicians falsely attribute HIV risk to stereotyped groups (prostitutes, injection drug users) rather than to risk-taking behaviors (any unprotected vaginal and anal sex, any sharing of drug "works"). In our own experience, many HIV-infected women have continued without a correct diagnosis and without treatment despite seeking help. It is not unusual for a woman to be told by her physician that she does not need HIV testing because she was not the "type" to get infected, even when she has otherwise unexplained gynecologic symptoms characteristic of HIV disease.

One solution to the neglect of gynecology is for public health officials to mandate its inclusion in HIV care. The AIDS Institute of New York State's Department of Health has done so by including gynecologic protocols in its standard of care guidelines. The state's significantly enhanced Medicaid reimbursement rates for HIV care require compliance with its prescribed standards of care. Linking quality of care to reimbursements is a potentially powerful mechanism, because most HIV-infected individuals, especially women, are dependent on Medicaid or other publicly funded health care.

Ironically, women with private health insurance may be at even greater disadvantage than those who use publicly funded clinics. In New York City, where one-quarter of the nation's HIV-infected women reside, finding an acceptable gynecologist is a serious problem for women with insurance plans. It is far easier for uninsured and Medicaid-insured women than for privately insured women to locate a gynecologist or obstetrician who is willing to take them on as patients and, in addition, offers competent and nonstigmatizing care.

Broadening the Health Care Research Agenda

Hand in hand with neglect of health care services is neglect of health care research on issues of special concern to HIV-infected women, for instance, HIV-related gynecologic symptoms. The focus of the first decade of HIV/ AIDS research was almost exclusively on men. Women were rarely enrolled in research cohorts, and issues affecting primarily women were not studied. Therefore, although AIDS has been recognized in women since the beginning of the 1980s, we still know little about the course of HIV infection in women.

Significantly, a fundamental shift in federal policy on clinical trials and new medications is evolving because of the HIV epidemic. The media have publicized the successful advocacy efforts by ACT-UP and other mostly gay organizations to speed up approval of experimental drugs by "fast tracking" and other means. A problem for women, however, has been gaining access to even the already-approved medications. For example, a major question has been why so many retrospective studies from hospitals and health departments have noted a shorter survival time for women with AIDS than for men. Is this a biological and gender-related difference in our bodies' response to HIV? The answer seems to have more to do with economics and with institutionalized sexism and racism than with biology. Fewer women than men, especially women of color, have received AZT according to federally recommended guidelines.[11] Women with access to health care and antiretroviral therapy comparable to that of male study subjects derive the same survival benefits as do men.[12]

Other less publicized but equally fundamental changes in research design will have far-reaching effects on future health care research and policy. From the beginning of the epidemic, HIV and AIDS research on experimental drug regimens has taken place in AIDS clinical trials groups (ACTGs). ACTGs are located in academic medical centers and follow the conventional model of clinical research. They have been undersubscribed for a number of reasons. Individuals who do have access to such research centers but can afford buying experimental drugs on their own often prefer avoiding the frequent visits and multiple procedures that normally accompany enrollment in a research trial. Women and others from poor communities have always been significantly underrepresented in research trials, largely because they have had very limited access to health care to begin with. Child care, transportation, and competing social service appointments (public assistance, food stamps, housing crises) have also played a large role and, together with stigmatization, have constituted the traditional barriers for women and the poor. In addition, communities of color, especially African Americans, harbor a deep distrust of any official research. The story of the Tuskegee syphilis study on rural blacks is well known, and the theory that HIV itself is a conscious experiment in genocide by the federal government is widely held.[13]

Because the HIV epidemic is increasingly centered in poor communities with limited health care services, public health officials have been faced with the dilemma of how to include women, injection drug users, and others from such communities in research efforts. A parallel research track to ACTGs, the community programs for clinical research on AIDS (CPCRAs), were introduced in late 1989 both to answer charges of inequity in access to research and to ensure large and representative enough enrollments in HIV research for scientifically acceptable data. Simplified procedures and blood tests, as well as incentives such as meals, transportation costs, social service supports, and direct cash payments, have been introduced. In particular, offering access to comprehensive health care services has permitted women to enroll in research trials and disprove the stereotype that welfare recipients and women of color are themselves to blame for substandard health care.[14] At Harlem Hospital, for instance, 41 percent of the CPCRA research subjects are women,[15] a much higher proportion than in New York City, where 21 percent of people with AIDS are women. Similarly, high standards of gynecologic care, combined with a "user-friendly" approach, in a study of cervical dysplasia in HIV-infected and uninfected women at a New York City methadone program has reached full enrollment of 150 women in one year. Many women have been recruited by others already in the study, and 85 percent of the women are returning for six-month followup visits.[16]

Neglected Issues in the HIV Health Agenda

Apart from the lack of enrollment of women in research trials, the research agenda itself for HIV/AIDS has some glaring omissions that have a direct impact on the health care of HIV-infected women. The majority of "natural history" studies—that is, studies of the overall manifestations of HIV infection from a medical perspective—have been on cohorts of gay men and have therefore excluded women. In natural history studies of special groups, such as injection drug users, women have been underrepresented, and these studies have not included gynecologic manifestations of HIV. To show how skewed the research bias is, in July 1992, at the 8th International Conference on AIDS, none of the studies at a panel on "Gender-Related Variations in Natural History" included gynecologic manifestations of HIV. Funding that targets comprehensive research on the natural history of HIV infection in women, including gynecologic manifestations, became available from federal agencies only in late 1993, well into the second decade of HIV/AIDS in women.

Funding for the study of specific topics has also been lacking, which means that we do not know how to evaluate or treat a large number of problems experienced by HIV-infected women. Menstrual irregularites are experienced by many HIV-infected women, but we still know nothing about the hormonal consequences of HIV or how (and whether) to treat them. Conversely, virtually nothing is known about the effects of hormonal interventions, for instance, oral contraceptives, on the course of HIV infection despite their widespread use and the importance to HIV-infected women of being able to choose safe and effective contraception.

Research on abnormal Pap smears in HIV-infected women is the first and still the only gender-related issue to be investigated in any depth. Increased rates of cervical dysplasia (abnormalities of the cervix noted on Paps or on cervical biopsies) did not enter the medical literature at all until 1987, although many prevalence studies have shown that an HIV-infected woman's risk for dysplasia is at least five times higher than an uninfected woman's. A large, systematic, and prospective study of the relation of HIV to cervical disease began in late 1991. To date, cervical dysplasia is the only gender-related condition to have received such thorough attention.

Contraception and HIV Prevention

Woman-controlled methods of sexually transmitted disease (STD) and pregnancy prevention are of critical importance. The fact that women have not had women-controlled barrier methods or nonbarrier methods to prevent or even to reduce the risk of HIV transmission ("safer sex") underlines the failed priorities of national policy.[17] Both federally and privately funded research has been heavily directed to "hard sciences" like pharmacology and virology, disciplines that are seeking the magic bullet of medical cure for those already infected.

A major problem for women is that, with the exception of latex condoms, effective contraceptive methods do not prevent HIV transmission. Norplant, in particular, has the disturbing potential of becoming viewed as an ideal "solution" for prevention of perinatal HIV transmission and unplanned pregnancies among the poor. Norplant has been court-ordered in some cities as forced sterilization in HIV-infected women. Policy makers and providers need to become as concerned about horizontal transmission of HIV *to* women as they are about vertical transmission from women to their children. Women are in danger of losing what control they had gained over their own bodies through IUDs and birth control pills because these highly effective contraceptives do not protect against HIV and other STDs. "Safe sex" in the

HIV era means condoms, and behavioral studies suggest that there has been little change in women's difficulty negotiating the use of condoms by their male partners.

Female condoms, designed to be worn internally by women, very recently (Spring 1993) gained approval by the Food and Drug Administration (FDA). Concerted lobbying by National Women's Health Network and HIV and other women's advocacy groups played a major role in reversing the FDA's prior rejection. For the first time, an effective barrier protection for both pregnancy and HIV/STD infection can be worn by women. However, female condoms will be of limited use to the many women who either cannot afford them or whose male partners refuse to engage in sex with any condom in place.

It is difficult to envision that any type of condom can gain widespread use without revolutionary changes in men's attitudes or women's empowerment. A virucide capable of providing HIV protection for women would be easier to use without a partner's consent and despite his objections. Development of a virucide that is not also a spermicide (as nonoxynol-9 is) would offer women the ability to choose to bear children without risking either becoming HIV-infected or infecting their partners. Today, no proven virucide exists. Nonoxynol-9 was developed as a spermicide, and its efficacy or risks with respect to HIV are not known. The omission of research and services to address women's needs is glaring. Women advocates and legislators are working together for Congressional appropriation of funds designated for virucide research and other prevention efforts specifically meant for women.

Protecting women from sexual transmission of HIV is a discouraging area of HIV policy. But prevention is a women's issue also in a larger sense. HIV prevention for women requires more than education and awareness. Prevention programs must take into account that difficult social and economic conditions are in themselves obstacles to the full exercise of choices for many women, especially those who as poor women and women of color are at highest risk for HIV infection.[18]

Most women who are at risk for HIV transmission still do not know it. One reason is that health professionals, government leaders, and the media focus on false stereotypes of supposed risk groups, as if only sex workers and chemically dependent mothers of newborns need be concerned about acquiring or transmitting HIV. A second reason is that, even where a more realistic understanding of HIV risk exists, conventional education and prevention efforts are ineffective and fail to reach the women who need to hear, especially in communities where risk is increased for everyone because of high seroprevalence rates. A third problem is credibility. Most people trust peers from within their communities rather than outside authorities. This is not acknowledged in official prevention efforts and policy.

Relatively little of the federal HIV/AIDS budget goes for prevention.

Figures from the Office of the Budget show that, for every federal dollar spent on research, only 30 cents goes to prevention efforts. This ill-advised policy disproportionately affects women because increasing rates of heterosexual transmission are not matched by comparable gains in resources or strategies in the affected communities. Undervaluation of prevention services is compounded by the relative neglect of research on prevention. Just over half the 1992 federal contribution to the HIV/AIDS research budget was apportioned to studies of therapeutic agents and vaccines, compared to 14 percent for all behavioral research (of which prevention is only one segment).[19] Research on prevention, sexual behavior, and the social conditions and beliefs that influence behavior are therefore greatly underfunded. These, however, are the issues that need to be examined if we are to learn how to effect the social changes that will enable women to protect themselves and their families.

Understanding and Changing Behavior

For the most part, official policy has approached the need for behavioral changes in the HIV era as an educational problem to which the solution is the increased dissemination of information. In fact, little is known about what conditions are powerful enough to influence us to make different choices. For example, an understanding of the determinants of sexual behaviors is as important for preventing HIV transmission as research on medical interventions like virucides. Interactions between sexual partners represent negotiations in the context of complex social relationships. Although a great deal of data have been collected on anatomic choices in sexual encounters (especially for gay men), these data do not expose the social and behavioral factors that explain what motivates specific sexual encounters, or how sexual partners view benefits and risks or reach decisions on risk-taking and risk-reducing behaviors. In a society where sexism influences patterns of sexual relationships as well as policies that affect sexual practices (such as arresting women sex workers but not their clients), women will continue to be especially vulnerable. The existence of effective biological agents to prevent disease transmission will be secondary in many women's lives.

Reproductive choice is one behavioral issue that always occupies a central position in women's health policy and has, not surpisingly, also entered the official HIV research agenda. It had been assumed by health care professionals and researchers that HIV-infected women would not want to carry a pregnancy to term if they understood the risk to their infant from perinatal transmission. However, several studies have demonstrated that HIV-infected women choose to terminate or continue pregnancies in the same proportions and give the same reasons for their choices as uninfected women.[20] Women from inner-city communities have pointed out that there are higher priorities than HIV and health care for women struggling to shield themselves and their children from homelessness, violence, separation, and other dangers of urban poverty.

Most studies frame the question in medical terms: whether HIV status does or does not determine individual reproductive choices. This model does not reveal which life experiences do have an influence on reproductive decision making. By exploring in detail the family and residence histories of HIV-infected and uninfected women from inner-city neighborhoods, medical anthropologist Anitra Pivnick has taken a different approach. She found that a major determinant of reproductive choice proved to be whether or not a woman had been able to live with at least one of her children for most of that child's life. An HIV-infected woman who had been able to sustain a maternal relationship was significantly less likely to bear another child.[21]

The difference between these two research approaches is crucial. The context in which research is framed and its results interpreted, medical or social, can lead to divergent health policies and have a significant impact on women's lives. For example, studies documenting that HIV infection does not change reproductive behavior have been used to justify policies calling for mandatory HIV testing for pregnant women as a select population. They are also used to rationalize sterilization abuse and the increasing numbers of actions in which local law enforcement agencies and state legislatures have tried to criminalize childbirth in HIV-infected women on the grounds that they transmitted a deadly disease to their offspring.

If it is true that there are, in fact, identifiable social conditions informing the reproductive decisions made by HIV-infected women, positive interventions become a real possibility. If a woman's need for an enduring relationship with her child is recognized, offering access to the appropriate resources and support services can result in her ability to preserve or restore her family. In many cases, this will mean chemical dependency services or family support and skills training, neither of which currently exists outside of a few demonstration model programs. But the financial cost to society and the cost in human suffering to families by placing a higher value on punishment is as obvious as the cost-effectiveness of a child welfare and social service policy that favors keeping a woman and her child together rather than supporting the costs of foster care and multiple residences for each.

Significant changes are taking place in prevention and education services for HIV-infected women at the grassroots level. An increasing number of peer organizations are being developed by women themselves in their communities throughout the country. Key to the success of groups such as Sisterlove in Atlanta or the Women's Center in the Bronx is replacement of a hierarchical model staffed by professionals with a peer model supported and staffed by HIV-positive and other women from the community.

Women's peer organziations differ in how they started and how they are organized. In many cases, they have grown out of women's advocacy groups or HIV-positive women's support groups. A number have developed from culturally specific community-based organizations (CBOs) or as adjuncts to extant health and social service agencies in the community. However, all take their origin in a response to unmet needs of the women in their communities. A shared premise is that peer support creates a community that is essential for empowerment and that empowerment is an essential step for effective education and prevention efforts among women, especially those who suffer from racism and the stigma of poverty.

Peer education and outreach organizations are learning how to do what the health care establishment has not. Health care agencies in urban areas affected by the HIV epidemic are increasingly aware that they will have to learn from and work with peer organizations in order to reach women who would otherwise be invisible and excluded from health care.

In many communities, the HIV epidemic has provided the first common ground around which women have been empowered to organize. This has also drawn in affected family members and provided a starting point for many women to take over control of their lives. The number of women who, in confronting their own HIV infection, have found the strength to become drug free, win back their children from foster care, and work long hours to build networking agencies and services for their sisters is impressive.

Women as Caretakers

Overall, market-driven health care caters to individuals, especially wage earners. Lack of a family-centered model of health care in the United States has aggravated the exclusion of millions of women and children from more than minimal services, or any health care at all. HIV policies and services similarly focus on individuals, not families, and the higher visibility of males in the epidemic has intensified this trend. The effect on women is profound. The reality is that, in most families, women are the primary caretaker and parent. In HIV-affected families this can be an overwhelming role.

In poorer communities that are hardest hit by the HIV epidemic, the same women who must work for the family's financial survival, usually in low-paying jobs without paid time off for medical appointments or child care crises and without medical benefits, are exactly those women who are increasingly called on to fill the caretaking role for HIV-infected partners and relatives and for children from HIV-affected families.

For every HIV-infected child left orphaned by HIV, 2 or 3 other uninfected children will also be orphaned (the rate of perinatal transmission is, on average, 1 in 4). There will be an estimated 25,000 young children and 21,000 adolescents orphaned by AIDS in 1995; 75,000 AIDS orphans are projected by the year 2000.[22] So far, no public policy addresses this issue.

Planning by a parent for permanent placement of her own children after her death requires experienced legal advocacy and is an emotionally and socially complex issue. A few agencies are beginning to develop a model for such services, and many are finding that the stigma a woman feels about dying of AIDS and leaving her children behind is internalized as guilt and denial. This means that, once again, issues of self-validation will need to be solved before the objective task of legal advocacy in an area of complex regulations can begin. Children continue to be moved into malfunctioning, often abusive, foster systems. Many children are placed in foster care because of their mother's chemical dependency. However, awareness of their HIV diagnosis is a turning point for many women. The desire to look after their children is a powerful motive for dealing with chemical dependency and related issues. Nonetheless many service agencies continue to criminalize women rather than provide the social services and psychological supports that would permit them to restore their families.

Official disregard for the family and caretaker role of both HIV-infected and affected women will become one of the costliest arenas of the HIV epidemic unless these policies are revised. For those of us in clinical or social service positions, it is a common experience to watch our clients lose their jobs and income when they enter the world of frequent medical appointments and HIV-induced crises. HIV infection initiates a financial and social slide downward for whole families—far more than is apparent from the official statistics collected on HIV-infected individuals.

Comprehensive Women-Centered Services

The pressure to include HIV-infected women in the HIV health policy agenda is growing, if only because their numbers are increasing and they are perceived as "vectors" of HIV disease to men and children. This has created a dilemma for the current health care system because it has not developed service models or policies capable of solving the many problems of health care access for the uninsured, especially for women. But because of the pressure to do so in the case of HIV, the door has opened to develop and fund certain types of innovative service programs for women.

Advocates for women's health have long argued that the best remedy for the fragmentation of services for women is to create comprehensive services in a single location. Some infectious disease programs now have an internist, and sometimes also a gynecologist, available to mothers who bring their children to a pediatric clinic, recognizing that many women put their children's needs first and are more likely to attend a pediatric clinic than their own. A small amount of funding has become available for "demonstration models" of multiservice clinics, rationally designed to meet women's needs. Such comprehensive clinics can offer one-stop health care to women and their families. Ideally, this model would include mental health services, treatment for chemical dependency, and a full range of social services and legal advocacy, all in one site.

The spectre of AIDS has elicited funding for alternative models of care that would be useful for all women, not just HIV-infected women. HIV has provided the first opportunity to develop such models for this otherwise neglected population. For inner-city women who face daily experiences of poverty, physical violence, chemical dependency, and resulting social and family disintegration, medical services isolated from these social realities are insufficient.

The first comprehensive woman-centered HIV clinic, the Women and Children's Project at Cook County Hospital in Chicago, was started in 1988 as a direct response to the needs of HIV-infected women who were receiving no care. From the beginning it was more than a conventional medical clinic. It started as a small service that offered peer support groups and medical care to chemically dependent, HIV-infected women and their children. With the aid of Robert Wood Johnson funding, a fully comprehensive, women-centered program has evolved under the leadership of its medical director, Mardge Cohen. Many of its services—for instance, advocacy with the city's child welfare bureau (one of its first ancillary services) or relapse prevention groups and coed partner groups—have been developed in response to specific needs and requests of the women who use the clinic. This is a model that has proven effective, whose value is recognized by both clinicians and patients, and that should be replicated widely.

Networking and New Coalitions

The policies and networks of the women's health movement itself are undergoing some measure of transformation as a result of the HIV epidemic. In a number of cities and regions, task forces and other groups have been organized to address the special needs of women with HIV and to advocate for health policies and services that include HIV-positive women along with persons working on their behalf. Most of these organizations bring together women who have not previously worked closely with one another: HIV-positive women, women workers from community-based organizations, and women professionals. Although the distance between these different constituencies has not been closed, HIV women's advocacy groups are exceptional in moving toward building a networking movement that cuts across class lines and brings diverse women together around a common goal.

HIV-positive women are increasingly taking active roles in such organizations and becoming important spokespersons on issues that affect them. HIV-positive women, in particular, have taken leadership in advocating for improved services for all individuals in poor communities at risk. Many are becoming full-time activists, advocates, and policy makers. They are beginning to be visible in the media not just as "victims" and "patients" during interviews with professionals, but as articulate spokespersons drawing attention to services that are lacking and policies that discriminate against women or the poor.

Another type of coalition that is being formed under the pressure of the HIV epidemic and that has already had a significant effect on policy is the working relationship of lawyers, physicians and advocates to achieve equitable services and policies for their women clients by a combination of legal and advocacy pressure directed toward government agencies that set policy.

In the early 1980s, AIDS was stereotyped as a disease of gays. The original CDC case definition for AIDS was relevant primarily to males, generally more affluent gay males, for and about whom it was written. The most recent CDC revision was promulgated at the beginning of 1993 after more than a year of often-acerbic debate. Specific conditions disproportionately affecting women and poorer populations (tuberculosis, common bacterial pneumonia, cervical cancer) were included belatedly and with evident reluctance, and only after a second public hearing was held, largely in response to the efforts of women's advocates and activists. Here again, women were the chief spokespersons for the poorer communities at large. The importance of the surveillance definition was far reaching because it is used officially and unofficially for nonsurveillance purposes, for example, as the criteria for disability determinations or the basis on which federal funds are distributed to states and cities (as the case of Ryan White).

The partnership of legal and medical professionals working together with HIV-positive women advocates and activists has also been effective in direct legal action. *S.P., et al., v. Sullivan* (NY, NY; 90 Civ. 6294) is a class action suit brought by attorney Theresa McGovern against the Social Security Administration and Health and Human Services Department on behalf of HIV-infected women and other residents of poor communities. At issue was whether disability determinations should be based on the same strict criteria used for the CDC surveillance definition. Since the CDC criteria did not include gynecological or other gender-related conditions, it was difficult for women with these conditions to collect disability. Many persons with less disabling conditions did not have difficulty in obtaining disability status because their ailments were included in the CDC definition. (Pre-1993 CDC definitions were limited to conditions thought to be unusual or rare unless associated with HIV infection. Diseases such as ordinary tuberculosis were not included because they were not considered definitive of HIV, even though known to be associated with HIV disease and to be widespread in HIV-afflicted populations.) The Disability Administration agreed to revise its criteria in response to the suit and advocacy efforts.

Discriminatory exclusion of women of childbearing potential from access to research drugs is a practice that long predates the HIV era and has been official FDA policy since 1977. In April 1993, the FDA announced that it would abolish this policy, again in direct response to the protests of HIV-positive women and activist groups working closely with concerned health care physicians and lawyers and with professional advocacy groups such as the Washington, D.C.–based Women and AIDS Coalition. The effect of this policy change will be far reaching and is among the major advances that HIV advocacy has accomplished for women's health issues.

IMPACT OF HIV ON FUTURE WOMEN'S HEALTH POLICY

All this said, it remains uncertain to what extent the many women's health policy changes achieved by and for HIV-infected women will be mainstreamed in the 1990s. Many veterans of former battles to improve health care policies and to increase access to care for poorer populations have moved into HIV work as advocates or professionals. Many of us reasoned that HIV was attracting enough attention and resources to open the door for necessary policy changes and improvements for all women, especially because, for the most part, HIV-infected women are from the same underserved communities and are facing the same problems whose roots are in sexism and racism. Our hope was that the changes effected because of HIV could be institutionalized as an improved infrastructure for services to these communities, apart from HIV.

Concern is now growing that, in fact, we will increasingly be confronted with the problem of "AIDS exceptionalism." Rather than dealing with the epidemic at the level of the community, much of the funding infusion is restrictively tagged for HIV-infected persons only. Thus, services for noninfected women from the community at large are left as they were because funding for the innovative services is earmarked for HIV-infected women. This has far-reaching consequences. For example, comprehensive one-stop-shopping health care centers are often not available to women until they get infected. Special licensing waivers and funding arrangements are often created for "demonstration" programs. But, in the current system, medical care, mental health, social services, and alcohol/substance abuse agencies and funding streams are administered by separate bureaucracies at the federal level and in most states. Funding and regulatory agencies, concerned with protecting their own turf, have generally not supported efforts to mainstream programs such as comprehensive women's health services patterned on the demonstration models.

In New York City and many other communities, health care paid for by Medicaid, housing for the homeless, and a multitude of additional social services have become a privilege available only to those already HIV-infected. In New York City, if a homeless family acquires housing through the Division of AIDS Services, the family must move out when the HIV-infected family member dies.

The most disastrous effect of a policy of AIDS exceptionalism, and one that penalizes women especially, is that little funding is available for HIV prevention efforts geared to uninfected or untested individuals, especially in poorer communities. In New York City, for instance, federal Ryan White funding is a major source of financial support for community-based HIV "early intervention" programs in high-risk neighborhoods but cannot be used for outreach or other HIV prevention programs. Yet one of the most urgent needs is to reach the large number of women in these neighborhoods who do not realize they are at risk or do not have contact with the health care system.

Analogously, AIDS is prioritized over early HIV disease as well as prevention. A computer literature search for 1989 through 1991 showed 179 studies on cohorts of AIDS patients compared to 72 on HIV-infected cohorts. Out of 261 studies of specific populations, there were 6 of commercial sex workers, 9 of vertical transmission of HIV to children by their mothers, but only 1 of women with HIV. On behavioral issues, there were 156 studies of commercial sex workers and HIV/AIDS compared to 115 on general health behavior with respect to HIV/AIDS.[23]

Related to the issue of AIDS exceptionalism is the policy debate of whether to concentrate resources in the communities at highest risk of HIV. Despite the high media visibility of AIDS and the extraordinary costs of AIDS care and pharmaceuticals, AIDS currently represents a very modest share of the federal health care budget (less than 1 percent). If HIV care is perceived as a problem of a few, heavily populated, impoverished communities, it is likely to continue underfunded no matter what health care reforms are enacted.

CONCLUSION

Women have been infected and part of the HIV epidemic since its beginning in the 1980s but have been excluded from services and research until now, well into the 1990s. Awareness of this by health care professionals and policy makers is a recent event. And it is still the case that health care policy takes an interest in HIV-infected women primarily as vectors of transmission, as sex workers or chemically dependent mothers targeted for special interventions or controls.

Whether women will gain a voice or continue to be invisible and underserved as in the past will in part depend on whether we can continue to build on the new momentum of networking and organizing by professionals, policy makers and women from the communities working together. The slow and hard-won gains we are now achieving toward recognition of women's importance in the HIV epidemic, both as HIV-positive women and as caretakers and organizers, at least provides a base from which to fight for major changes in how resources are distributed. Equally important is the fight for radical changes in the priorities and policies that govern family service and social service systems.

What we have learned and wrested from the tragedy of women's silent HIV epidemic could become the energy to drive major changes in health care systems and policies that affect all women. The fiscal crisis in health care in the United States has moved health care reform onto the national agenda. This opens the door for dialogue on the most substantive issues: reintegrating health care for women and their families; redirecting reproductive rights policies; establishing prevention as a health care priority; replacing punitive with supportive policies for the social problems of the poor.

The women who have emerged as leaders in the HIV epidemic have substantial experience and concrete achievements to offer in the national health care dialogue. They have developed effective models of comprehensive one-stop care, of peer support and outreach, and of advocacy efforts that are strengthened by crossing the usual professional lines. Underlying this work is a crystal-clear consensus that women are central to health care, and that health care is about families and prevention more than about biomedical technology and individual patients/consumers. The challenge for us as women is to be sure that what we have achieved becomes widely recognized and informs our future health care system.

NOTES

[1]H. Rodriguez-Trias, "The women's health movement: Women take power," in *Reforming Medicine*, ed. V. W. Sidel and R. Sidel (New York: Pantheon Books, 1984), 107–126.

[2]From the report of the U.S. National Commission on AIDS, 1993.

[3]The American Public Health Association, *America's Public Health Report Card, A State-by-State Report on the Health of the Public* (Washington, D.C.: U.S. Government Printing Office, 1992).

[4]*Consumer Reports: Wasted Health Care Dollars*, July 1992, pp. 435–448.

[5]Public Citizen Health Research Group, "Health care problems and solutions," *Health Letter* 8(1992):7–9.

[6]D. U. Himmelstein, J. P. Lewontin, and S. Woolhandler, "New data on uninsured Americans," *Physicians for National Health Program Newsletter*, November 1992, pp. 10–15.

[7]General Accounting Office, *Hispanic Access to Health Care, Significant Gaps Exist*, January 1992, p. 10.

[8]National Women's Health Network Newsletter, May/June, 1992.

[9]V. Navarro, "Race or class versus race and class: Mortality differentials in the United States," *Lancet* 386(1990):1238–1240.

[10]B. L. Wells, and J. W. Horm, "Stage at diagnosis in breast cancer: Race and socioeconomic factors," *American Journal of Public Health* 82(1992):1383–1385.

[11]Michael D. Stein, John Piette, Vincent Mor, Tom J. Wachtel, John Fleishman, Kenneth H. Mayer, and Charles C. J. Carpenter, "Differences in access to zidovudine (AZT) among symptomatic HIV-infected persons" *J. Gen. Intern. Med.* 6(1991):35–50.

[12]George F. Lemp, Anne M. Hirozawa, Judith B. Cohen, Pamela A. Derish, Kevin C.

McKinney, and Sandra R. Hernandez, "Survival for women and men with AIDS" *J. Infect. Dis.* 166(1992):74–79.

[13]Harlon Dalton, "AIDS in blackface," *Daedalus* (Summer 1989): 205–228; Stephen B. Thomas and Sandra Crouse Quinn, "The Tuskegee syphilis study, 1932 to 1972: Implications for HIV education and AIDS risk education programs in the black community," *American Journal of Public Health* 81(1991):1498–1505.

[14]Wafaa El-Sadr and Linnea Capps, "The Challenge of Minority Recruitment in Clinical Trials for AIDS," *JAMA* 267(1992):954–957.

[15]Wafaa El-Sadr, personal communication.

[16]Carola Marte, unpublished data.

[17]Zena A. Stein, "HIV Prevention: The need for methods women can use," *Am. J. Public Health* 80(1990):460–462.

[18]Kathryn Carovano, "More than mothers and whores: Redefining the AIDS prevention needs of women," *Intl. J. of Health Services* 21(1991): 131–142.

[19]U.S. Office of the Budget/ASMB, April 6, 1993.

[20]Frank D. Johnston, Linda MacCallum, Ray Brettle, J. M. Inglis, and John F. Peutherer, "Does infection with HIV affect the outcome of pregnancy?" *Br. Med. J.* 296(1988): 467; Peter Selwyn, Rosalind J. Carter, Ellie E. Schoenbaum, Verna J. Robertson, Robert S. Klein, and Martha F. Rogers, "Knowledge of HIV antibody status and decisions to continue or terminate pregnancy among intravenous drug users," *JAMA* 261(1989): 3567–3571; Ann Sunderland, "Influence of Human Immunodeficiency Virus infection on reproductive decisions," *Obstet. Gynecol. Clinics North Am.* 17(1990): 585–594.

[21]Anitra Pivnick, "Reproductive decisions among HIV-infected, drug-using women: The importance of mother-child coresidence," *Med. Anthropol. Quarterly* 5(1991): 153–169.

[22]David Michaels and Carol Levine, "Estimates of the Number of Motherless Youth Orphaned by AIDS in the United States," *JAMA* 268(1992): 3456–3461.

[23]Jonathan Mann, Daniel J. M. Tarantola, and Thomas W. Netter, eds. *AIDS in the World* (Cambridge, Mass.: Harvard University Press, 1992), 258–260.

Cheri Pies

AIDS, Ethics, Reproductive Rights:
No Easy Answers

T he reproductive decisions and behaviors of pregnant women have come under intense and unrelenting scrutiny during the past several years.[1] Discussions of maternal-fetal conflict, fetal rights, trafficking drugs to a minor in utero, and fetal neglect have become commonplace. At the same time, considerable attention has been focused on the criminalization of pregnancy through the punitive sentencing of women convicted of substance use while pregnant or at the time of delivery. It is not surprising, then, that the medical, social, political, and economic concerns raised by the reproductive choices of pregnant HIV-infected women have served to intensify this scrutiny, catapulting women's reproductive lives into an already explosive arena of spirited discussion, contentious debate, and governmental regulation.

Health care providers, legislators, policy makers, and the general public have been drawn into this debate in a number of ways—sometimes through their direct contact with HIV-infected women, but more often through an array of human interest media stories, news reports on the growing incidence of HIV/AIDS among women and children, newspaper editorials, and professional journal articles. Their responses to this debate and their subsequent actions are of primary concern as we move through the second decade of this epidemic; they will be pivotal in ensuring the design and implementation of ethically sound policies.

This chapter addresses some of the compelling yet troubling ethical dilemmas that the intersection of HIV infection and pregnancy has posed. It explores some of the societal values being promoted and preserved by those individuals and groups making health care and policy decisions and raises key questions that must be considered if we are to engage in a meaningful and constructive dialogue on issues of reproductive rights in this age of AIDS.

To date, the public health community has responded to the questions raised by the reproductive choices of HIV-infected women with both conflicting and opposing actions. Some health care practitioners and policy makers have initiated efforts to make HIV antibody testing a routine part of all prenatal care, while others have taken steps to ensure that testing remains voluntary. State and local health officers in some jurisdictions have issued policy directives strongly urging women who are at risk for HIV or who are HIV-infected to "delay or postpone" childbearing until a later date, while others have cautioned that discouraging childbearing is not an effective tool in disease prevention. Several legislatures have proposed and passed laws making the transmission of HIV infection from one person to another a punishable offense, while others have argued for education and prevention, as opposed to criminalization and incarceration. Many physicians, nurses, social workers, counselors, and others have employed directive counseling techniques in their work with HIV-infected women who are making decisions concerning pregnancy, while others have chosen to remain nondirective in their interventions.

What is driving these decisions, choices, and subsequent actions? What values have influenced the thinking and perceptions of these individuals concerning the reproductive rights of HIV-infected women as the epidemic has progressed? And, most importantly, what are the consequences of proposed policies for women?

EARLY POLICIES ON HIV AND PREGNANCY

> The history of public health and disease control is marked by assumptions that certain women carry disease, overshadowing the fact that they suffer from diseases as well.[2]

Since the beginning of the AIDS epidemic, discussions related to HIV infection among women have included repeated references to women as "vessels" or "vectors" of disease, "incubators of sick babies," "wives" or "sexual partners," "prostitutes," and "mothers." Furthermore, many of the social and medical issues have been "explained in terms of the other people in her life who she is thought to have put in danger."[3] Not surprisingly, therefore, greater attention to HIV infection in women has come about, not as a result of the increasing numbers of women who are diagnosed with AIDS, but instead as a result of the increase in pediatric AIDS cases over the past few years. This focus reinforces the perception of women primarily as childbearers, "despite the fact that pregnancy lasts a relatively short period of time and most of the serious AIDS related illnesses in women occur outside of pregnancy."[4]

In 1985, long before the epidemiology of AIDS among women and children was well understood or well documented, the Centers for Disease Control (CDC) issued a recommendation concerning women who were infected with HIV or who had AIDS. It stated that this group of women should "be advised to consider delaying pregnancy until more is known about perinatal transmission of the virus."[5] Less than three years later, as suggestions for routine HIV antibody testing of women in their reproductive years were being debated, and considerable uncertainty remained about the rate of maternal transmission of HIV, James Curran, the director of the CDC AIDS program stated:

> There is no reason that the number of cases [of pediatric AIDS] shouldn't decline. Someone who understands the disease and is logical will not want to be pregnant and will consider the [HIV antibody] test results when making family planning decisions.[6]

Inherent in these statements is a worldview that reasons that discouraging women from becoming pregnant or carrying their pregnancies to term will prevent the births of many or most HIV-positive infants and that defines as "logical" any behavior that follows this advice and "illogical" any behavior that does not.

The 30 percent chance of HIV transmission from mother to child provides an influential argument for some people for preventing pregnancies in HIV-infected women. However, the statistical uncertainties surrounding the chance of maternal transmission of HIV infection to infants must also be considered. As Carol Levine and Nancy Dubler observed in 1990,

> Given the current state of knowledge [about HIV], there is no way to predict whether an HIV-infected woman will infect her fetus (the chances are in fact that she will not), no reliable way to determine in utero or at birth whether a baby is infected (unless it is born with symptoms), and no way to foretell the likely course of the disease (for the mother or the child) over time.[7]

CURRENT SENTIMENTS AMONG PUBLIC HEALTH PROVIDERS

Despite these uncertainties, there is widespread sentiment among health care providers that HIV-infected women should avoid pregnancy or, if pregnant, should not carry the pregnancy to term. Chavkin, Marte, Bland, and others[8] have documented that physicians and other health care practitioners frequently have "a tendency to coerce HIV-infected women into having abortions."[9] According to Anastos and Marte,

> Many doctors and other health care providers feel that it is not only their right but their responsibility to counsel and persuade an HIV infected woman to abort her pregnancy, even in the face of clear statements by the woman that she does not want to choose an abortion.[10]

It has also been noted by Susan Holman, a nurse who coordinated an NIH-funded study on perinatal transmission, that "health care practitioners who care for children find it especially difficult to understand why an HIV positive woman would not choose to abort."[11]

For other health care providers, however, there are many gray areas. While they may be acutely aware of the persuasiveness of an argument based on the projected rate of maternal-to-fetal transmission, they also strongly believe that women are individuals with moral agency and that their personal decisions concerning reproduction must be respected. Others fear that programs that offer HIV antibody testing in order to prevent pregnancies or births, rather than for HIV prevention, education, and counseling, could easily result in coercive actions on the part of health care providers and other public health practitioners.[12] One outspoken advocate of this perspective, Janet Mitchell, a clinician working with HIV-infected women at Harlem Hospital in New York City, explains it this way:

> Those of us who care for these women are most concerned by the lack of understanding of the importance of childbearing in these populations and the persistence of attitudes that deny women the right to make their own reproductive health choices. . . . We must be cautious in how we approach our need to do good, to do no harm.[13]

LEGISLATIVE ACTIONS AND AMBIGUITIES

During the past few years, disputes about the reproductive choices of HIV-infected women have embroiled numerous state legislatures. As suggested earlier, these debates have arisen in a climate in which women have been charged and sentenced for child abuse and neglect resulting from their use of illicit substances during pregnancy.[14]

As of 1993, if a woman lived in Arkansas, Illinois, Louisiana, Missouri, Oklahoma, or a number of other states and carries the fetus to term, she committed a felony against the child under broadly drawn state statutes on criminal transmission of HIV.[15] Interestingly, these laws encourage HIV-infected women to terminate their pregnancies in order to avoid committing a crime. Closen and Isaacman, two attorneys concerned by this turn of events, point out the irony of this situation by suggesting that, "while abortion is 100% certain to kill a fetus, about 40% to 80% of children born to HIV-infected mothers would be uninfected and would live."[16]

Another irony exists as well. While the federal government, represented by the voice of the CDC, does not directly discuss the option of abortion for preventing births of HIV-infected infants, this option is thought to be implicit in their recommendations. At the same time, however, it is virtually impossible in several states to obtain an abortion unless the pregnancy occurred as a result of rape or incest. Further complicating this situation is the stark reality that numerous clinics performing abortions have refused to provide care to women who are HIV-infected.[17] Thus, women are simultaneously cast as criminals, on the one hand, for potentially transmitting the virus, and on the other, for having an abortion.

Katherine Franke, an attorney credited with uncovering routine discrimination against HIV-infected women seeking abortions in New York City, further exposes the contradictory nature of federal policy regarding fetal "rights," abortion, and HIV infection. Suggesting that the antiabortion stance of the present administration is motivated by far more than a simple moral stance, she writes:

> The compelling state interest in fetal survival seems to evaporate when the mother and/or fetus have been exposed to HIV. When HIV infections become a factor in the abortion decision, the state's duty to defend potential life shifts to the interest of protecting society from the possibility of another person with AIDS.[18]

UNDERLYING COMPETING VALUES

The issues raised by these actions with regard to HIV and pregnancy pose tough questions. There are no simple, straightforward, or obvious answers. Based on what one considers right or wrong, good or bad, just or unjust, good reasons and debatable consequences exist for any given choice. Competing values are at stake, and moral ambiguities dominate. The privacy of individual choice is challenged by what is perceived to be in the best interests of society. At the same time, repeated threats are made on the right to autonomy, privacy, and confidentiality.

A reexamination of these conflicts in terms of their ethical components illustrates the dominant societal values that many seek to promote and preserve, as well as the alternate values that others draw on. For example, the deep concern felt by many about the children who will be born to HIV-infected women—the "innocent victims" of the epidemic—can be linked to the value that every child has a right to a healthy life. The belief that HIV-infected women are irresponsible, irrational, and immoral for choosing to become pregnant or continue a pregnancy supports the value that certain women are "fit" to be mothers. Conversely, the view that all women, regardless of their HIV status, have the right to make their own decisions regarding conception and childbearing, reflects the value that women must have the freedom to choose what they believe to be best for themselves, given their particular life situation.

The value stance that encourages HIV-infected women to avoid or terminate their pregnancies draws on the ethical precepts of "doing no harm" and "promoting the common good." On the one hand, this value stance can be seen as one designed to "prevent harm." That is, by discouraging HIV-infected women from childbearing, it contends that countless unborn children are being saved from possible harm. Yet it is important to ask, "Does this constitute acting in the patient's best interest?" and, if it does, for what type of patients generally, and for which patient specifically—the mother or the fetus? Moreover, who is deciding what "best interest" means?

The other side of this stance suggests that society values lives that have the potential to be productive, not those that will cost society or be supported by the productivity of others. As a society, should we only support reproduction when it produces children who are likely to be healthy, and not when it may contribute to illness, dependency, or even death? Furthermore, what is our moral obligation in light of the actions of public health officials and health care providers who believe they know what is best for individual women or for society and, by enforcing their views, are in effect reinforcing the paternalism that has plagued women's reproductive health care since the advent of Western medicine?

In the absence of certainty about the rate of maternal-fetal transmission early in the epidemic, it is critical to ask how people's values caused them to emphasize one point of view over another. For example, was a 50 percent chance of maternal-fetal transmission described as "bad" odds for a healthy baby or "good" odds? All too often, society's esteem for scientific knowledge is pitted against its judgment of what constitutes reasonable risk—and frequently the decision depends on which people are taking that risk. For example, if the HIV-infected women choosing to become pregnant and carry their pregnancies to term had been predominantly the wives of hemophiliacs, might the dominant interpretation of risk been different?

THE SOCIAL, CULTURAL, AND POLITICAL CONTEXT

The reproductive decisions of HIV-infected women cannot be isolated from the sociocultural, economic, political, and behavioral context in which their pregnancy decisions are made.[19] We must be careful not to assume that the day-to-day reality and moral universes of those treating HIV-infected women and those making policy about the lives of HIV-infected women are the same as those of the women who are infected with HIV and directly experiencing this disease.

The women who are represented in the U.S. HIV/AIDS statistics are basically the same population of women who are frequently overrepresented in every adverse outcome of pregnancy. Their reproductive behaviors have received and continue to receive intense public scrutiny, while their access to health care, welfare benefits, education, and employment has been systematically reduced.[20] Predominantly poor, disproportionately women of color,[21] they are familiar with threats to their reproductive rights. They have inherited the legacies of sterilization abuse, population control, and eugenics that have plagued reproductive health care throughout the past century in the United States.

Recognition of this context permits shifting the focus to a different set of ethical questions, questions that acknowledge the influence of an individual's life circumstances on their behaviors, choices, and actions. Results of studies designed to evaluate the influence of a woman's knowledge of HIV antibody status on reproductive decisions strongly suggest that a complex array of social, cultural, and personal factors influence pregnancy choices and that a strategy of attempting to prevent pediatric AIDS by preventing pregnancy is not and will not be effective.[22]

HIV-infected women are not making random, irresponsible, or irrational decisions concerning their lives and their pregnancies.[23] Each has a unique and complex moral system at work. Interestingly, knowledge of HIV infection, while cited in certain cases as a reason for terminating a pregnancy, was not found to have a significant effect on most women's reproductive decisions. For many women, religious considerations are paramount:

> As a devout Catholic . . . [i]t is very difficult when you are faced with [your own] death. If I terminated the pregnancy, I was afraid I would be condemned, that I would not be with God at the end of this world.[24]

For others, the 30 to 50 percent chance of having an HIV-infected infant is weighed against the realities of a life that might be filled with countless risks of even greater frequency.

> Women's risks—of abuse, violence, loss of housing, illness, discrimination—are daily fare. To them, AIDS is just another, and less immediate, risk.[25]

Certainly, a 50 to 70 percent chance of having a healthy child seems reasonable odds in this context.

For still others, childbearing plays a vital role in ensuring survival within one's community. Decisions to continue pregnancies are based, in part, on the importance of pregnancy and motherhood in achieving status in the community, a desire to replace children who have died, fears of genocide, pressure exerted by a partner and/or family members, and assurances from extended family that care will be provided for the child.[26]

In a recent study with HIV-infected drug-using women in the New York City area, Pivnik et al. found that the continuity of mother-child coresidence, previous abortion experience, and duration of knowledge of HIV-positive antibody status were significantly associated with reproductive decisions of HIV-infected women. Of special interest is the finding that HIV-infected women who had a child living in the home were more apt to choose to terminate their pregnancies than those whose children had been removed from the home for foster care or other social service placements.[27]

Finally, her expectations about the response of health care workers to her decision concerning her pregnancy may significantly influence the HIV-infected woman's choices. For example, because she is dependent on the health care provider for help, support, and care, she may fear that choosing to continue her pregnancy could result in compromised care or possibly neglect or harassment. Conversely, if she chooses to terminate her pregnancy, she may fear threats of sterilization, refusals by health care personnel to perform the abortion, or an absence of funding to assist with the medical procedure.

INCLUDING MEN IN THE MORAL EQUATION

> An attentive witness to the public debate over AIDS and reproductive responsibility could easily conclude that men have nothing to do with either the problem or its solution.[28]

Where do men fit in the moral equation when it comes to women's reproductive choices? For all intents and purposes, women are seen as the source of the problem. The primary focus on women and their ability to transmit HIV to their newborn is puzzling when a woman is only capable of infecting one child through pregnancy in a nine-month period of time, yet an HIV-infected man could infect any number of partners during that same period.[29] In addition, it is alarming that HIV prevention education encouraging condom use is targeted largely toward women who attend family planning and prenatal care clinics, thus suggesting that women are responsible for seeing to it that their male partners use condoms.

Where are the men? They are present as the policy makers at locations such as the Centers for Disease Control, physicians in hospitals, lawyers and judges in courts, and researchers at large academic institutions. Some are the fathers, frequently from the same class and ethnic background as the women they have infected. Without a doubt, these men are a part of the moral equation. Their understanding of the issues and their actions play a significant role in determining how the reproductive behaviors of HIV-infected women are viewed and treated. This is especially true for the policy makers and professionals whose values and opinions have wide impact.

WOMEN'S ROLES IN THE POLICY DIALOGUE

The current policies on HIV and pregnancy offer guidelines for the so-called "universal" woman. They are written to apply across the board to any woman, regardless of her life circumstances. They fail to take into account the nuances of women's lives, the circumstances under which their decisions are made, and the realities of their day-to-day existence. They assume that HIV-infected women who do not follow the CDC logic are choosing to willfully neglect the best interests of their potential children and the costs these children will bring to bear on society. This has not proven to be true.[30]

Policies that dictate what women should and should not do regarding pregnancy, or who should and should not have babies, leave little room for constructive dialogue with those to whom they are directed. Traditionally, reproductive policies have directed choices rather than posed questions to consider. Instead of dictating choices, perhaps we should consider instituting policies that identify a specific list of questions and issues to be addressed with clients and another set of questions and issues clinicians are responsible for addressing with one another. Clinicians, health care providers, and other auxiliary staff need to explore the ways in which their values and viewpoints affect their decisions and actions as they continue their work in this field. Moreover, they have a responsiblity to carefully examine their behavior and motivation in order to uphold their first mandate: do no harm. The situations are not likely to become easier.

If, as some commentators have suggested, this epidemic threatens the ethos of the privacy of each woman's decision concerning pregnancy,[31] how will we arrive at community standards that guarantee freedoms for individual differences in this matter of HIV and reproductive choice? This can only be realized though dialogue and discussion with all involved, including the pregnant woman, and with policies that serve to encourage such dialogue, not by determining a course of action with no discussion.

Because of the challenging and pressing nature of these dilemmas, it is imperative that many people, from consumers and interested citizens to policy makers and legislators, representing diverse perspectives and audiences, engage in an ongoing dialogue about these issues. While there is no single solution, we must identify strategies for bringing HIV-infected women and women at risk for HIV into the discussion, so that their voices, perspectives, and perceptions can be heard. Ideally, every task force, legislative or institution-based body dealing with issues of this nature should include HIV-infected women and/or their advocates. Everyone concerned with this problem has a great deal to learn from this group of women, and these women in turn have a lot to learn from each other—about their lives, their choices, the reasons for their choices, the logic and values that drive their decisions, the isolating nature of this disease.

Though essential, this inclusion is no easy task. On the one hand, institutional traditions as well as the resistance and paternalism of powerful groups will make such integration a challenging undertaking. On the other hand, because HIV-infected women do not comprise a coherent, singular community, finding ways to "represent" their voices will be require concerted effort.[32] Nevertheless, AIDS researchers, health care providers, educators, policy makers, journalists, and activists can no longer ignore what the women who are actually living these reproductive choices on a day-to-day basis have to say. Their absence from the dialogue has been tolerated far too long, and without their input, a discussion of the ethical considerations concerning HIV infection and pregnancy would be morally questionable.

ETHICS IN THE CONTEXT OF INEQUALITY

As long as a significant percentage of women live in poverty; as long as unemployment continues to rise and extension of unemployment benefits is denied; as long as women are denied an opportunity to education, job training, and equal pay for equal work; as long as these same women are denied welfare benefits for having children or are finding those benefits reduced due to state budget cutbacks; as long as poor women are denied access to abortion (while they can barely afford to support the children they do have); as long as our society expects everyone to make a "reasonable" choice—and what is reasonable is determined by those in power—any efforts to find resolution to the many compelling ethical issues discussed above must involve a broader social, political, and economic view of the problem of HIV infection and pregnancy. Discussions of ethical concerns that fail to take into account the social, cultural, and political context of HIV infection and pregnancy at best are inadequate and at worst harm women, children, and our society.

The ethics of reproductive choice for HIV-infected women is not a single-issue struggle. AIDS is not simply a disease that developed and exists in a vacuum. It is a symptom of larger problems in society; a disease of poverty, homophobia, institutionalized racism and sexism, and neglect.

As we are all well aware, the HIV/AIDS epidemic has served to expose the inequities in an already-inadequate health care system here in the United States. We must keep in mind that, if we are truly committed to addressing the compelling ethical questions raised by HIV-infected women and their reproductive choices, we must also consider the ethical implications of the larger sociopolitical context in which HIV disease and scrutiny of women's reproductive behavior have flourished. Without such an analysis, we will continue to lack just approaches to these problems.

NOTES

[1]J. Terry, "The Body Invaded: Medical Surveillance of Women as Reproducers," *Socialist Review* 19(1989): 13–43; K. Pollitt, "A New Assault on Feminism," *The Nation*, 26 March 1990; J. Gallagher, "Prenatal Invasions and Interventions: What's Wrong with Fetal Rights," *Harvard Women's Law Journal* 10(1987); W. Chavkin, "Drug Addiction and Pregnancy: Policy Crossroads," *American Journal of Public Health* 80(1990): 483–487.

[2]Terry.

[3]K. Franke, "Turning Issues Upside Down," in *AIDS: The Women*, ed. I. Rieder and P. Ruppelt (San Francisco: Cleis Press, 1988).

[4]K. Anastos and C. Marte, "Women—The Missing Persons in the AIDS Epidemic," *Health/PAC Bulletin*, Winter 1989, pp. 6–13.

[5]Centers for Disease Control, "Recommendations for Assisting in the Prevention of Perinatal Transmission of Human T-lymphotropic Virus Type III/Lymphadenopathy-associated Virus and Acquired Immunodeficiency Syndrome," *Morbidity and Mortality Weekly Report* 34(1985):721–732.

[6]Centers for Disease Control.

[7]C. Levine and N. N. Dubler, "Uncertain Risks and Bitter Realities: The Reproductive Choices of HIV-infected Women," *The Milbank Quarterly* 68(1990).

[8]H. Amaro, "Women's Reproductive Rights in the Age of AIDS: New Threats to Informed Choice" (Paper presented at the 97th Annual Convention of the American Psychological Association, New Orleans, 1989); Anastos and Marte, W. Chavkin, "Preventing AIDS, Targeting Women," *Health/PAC Bulletin*, Spring 1990, pp. 19–23; J. L. Mitchell, "Women, AIDS, and Public Policy," *AIDS and Public Policy* 3(1988); B. Santee, "HIV-Positive Women Have Rights Too—and They're Often Denied," *Women and AIDS Resource Network*, 1988; A. Bland, ed., "Respect for Women's Rights Comes Before Personal Values," *AIDS Alert* 6(1991).

[9]Bland.

[10]Anastos and Marte.

[11]L. Abraham, "Pregnant Women Face AIDS Dilemma," *American Medical News* 3(1988):34–35.

[12]Levine and Dubler.

[13]Mitchell.

[14]Terry; Amaro.

[15]M. L. Closen and S. H. Isaacman, "Are AIDS Transmission Laws Encouraging Abortion?" *Journal of American Bar Association,* December 1990.

[16]Closen and Isaacman.

[17]K. Franke, "Discrimination in Access to Reproductive Health Services" (Paper presented at Institute of Medicine Conference on Prenatal and Newborn Screening for HIV Infection, May 1990).

[18]Franke.

[19]Levine and Dubler.

[20]Mitchell.

[21]N. E. Kass, "Reproductive Decision Making in the Context of HIV: The Case for Nondirective Counseling," in *Women, AIDS, and the Next Generation,* ed R. Faden, G. Geller, and M. Powers (Cambridge: Oxford University Press, 1991); M. Gwinn, M. Pappaioanou, J. R. George, et al., "Prevalence of HIV Infection in Childbearing Women in the United States: Surveillance Using Newborn Blood Samples," *Journal of the American Medical Association* 265(1991); R. M. Selik and S. Y. Chu, "Surveillance for AIDS and HIV Infection Among Black and Hispanic Children and Women of Childbearing Age, 1981–1989," *Morbidity and Mortality Weekly Report* 39(1991); C. Marte and K. Anastos, "Women—The Missing Persons in the AIDS Epidemic," Part II, *Health/PAC Bulletin,* Spring 1990, pp. 11–18.

[22]Abraham; A. Sunderland, "Influence of Human Immunodeficiency Virus Infection on Reproductive Decisions," *Obstetrics and Gynecology Clinics of North America* 17(1990); F. D. Johnstone, R. P. Brettle, L. R. MacCallum, et al., "Women's Knowledge of Their HIV Antibody State: Its effect on Their Decision Whether to Continue the Pregnancy," *British Medical Journal* 300(1990):23–24; A. Pivnik, A. Jacobson, K. Eric, M. Mulvihill, M. A. Hsu and E. Drucker, "Reproductive Decisions Among HIV-Infected, Drug-Using Women: The Importance of Mother-Child Coresidence," *Medical Anthropology Quarterly* 5 (1991): 153–169; K. Nolan, "Ethical Issues in Caring for Pregnant Women and Newborns at Risk for HIV Infection," *Seminars in Perinatology* 13(1989):55–65.

[23]Sunderland; Johnstone; Pivnick.

[24]Abraham.

[25]Levine and Dubler.

[26]S. Holman, M. Berthaud, A. Sunderland, et al. "Women Infected with Human Immunodeficiency Virus: Counseling and Testing During Pregnancy," *Seminars in Perinatology* 13(1989):7–15; Pivnik.

[27]Pivnik.

[28]J. D. Arras, "AIDS and Reproductive Decisions: Having Children in Fear and Trembling," *Milbank Quarterly* 68(1990).

[29]H. S. Kaplan, *The Real Truth About Women and AIDS* (New York: Simon and Schuster 1987).

[30]P. A. Selwyn, R. J. Carter, E. E. Schoenbaum, et al., "Knowledge of HIV antibody Status and Decisions to Continue or Terminate Pregnancy Among Intravenous Drug Users," *Journal of the American Medical Association* 262(1990): 3567–3571; Sunderland; Marte and Ánastos; Pivnick.

[31]F. Hecht, "Counseling the HIV Positive Woman Regarding Pregnancy" (Letter to the Editor), *Journal of the American Medical Association* 257(1987); R. Bayer, "Perinatal Transmission of HIV Infection: The Ethics of Prevention," *Clinical Obstetrics and Gynecology* 32(1989).

[32]L. E. Dorfman, P. A. Derish and J. B. Cohen, "Hey Girlfriend—An Evaluation of AIDS Prevention among Women in the Sex Industry," *Health Education Quarterly* 19(1992):25–40.

REFERENCES

Ades, A. E., M. L. Newell, C. S. Peckham, et al. "Children Born to Women with HIV-1 Infection: Natural History and Risk of Transmission." *Lancet*, 337(1991).

Alexander, V. "Feds, Meds Cold-Shoulder Women with AIDS." *Guardian* 43(1991):7.

Allen, M. H., "Primary Care of Women Infected with the Human Immunodeficiency Virus." *Obstetrics and Gynecology Clinics of North America* 17(1990).

Andiman, W., B. J. Simpson, B. Olsen, et al. "Rate of Transmission of Human Immunodeficiency Virus Type 1 Infection from Mother to Child and Short-Term Outcome of Neonatal Infection." *American Journal of Diseases of Children* 144(1990):758–766.

Banzhaf, M., T. Morgan, and K. Ramspacher. "Reproductive Rights and AIDS: The Connections." In *Women, AIDS, and Activism*, edited by The ACT-UP/New York Women and AIDS Book Group. New York: South End Press, 1990.

Bayer, R. "AIDS and the Future of Reproductive Freedom." *Milbank Quarterly* 68(1990):179–204.

Bell, N. K., "AIDS and Women: Remaining Ethical Issues." *AIDS Education and Prevention* 1(1989):22–30.

Benson, J. D., and C. Maier. "Challenges Facing Women with HIV." *Focus: A Guide to AIDS Research and Counseling* 6(1990).

Carovano, K. "More Than Mothers and Whores: Redefining the AIDS Prevention Needs of Women." *International Journal of Health Services* 21(1991):131–142.

CDC. "Curran Supports Testing, Counseling for Pregnant Women." *AIDS Weekly*, 3 October 1988.

"Current Trends: First 100,000 Cases of AIDS—United States." *Morbidity and Mortality Weekly Report* 38(1989):561–563.

Ellerbrock, T. V., and M. F. Rogers. "Epidemiology of HIV Infection in Women in the United States." *Obstetrics and Gynecology Clinics of North America* 17(1990).

Faden, R. R. "HIV Infection, Pregnant Women, and Newborns." *Journal of the American Medical Association*, 264(1990):2416–2420.

Franke, K. "HIV-related Discrimination in Abortion Clinics in New York City." AIDS Discrimination Division, New York City Commission on Human Rights, 1989.

Fried, M. "Transforming the Reproductive Rights Movement: The Post-Webster Agenda." In *From Abortion to Reproductive Freedom: Transforming a Movement*, edited by M. Gerber Fried. New York: South End Press, 1990.

Hardy, L. M., ed. *HIV Screening of Pregnant Women and Newborns*. Committee on Prenatal and Newborn Screening for HIV Infection, Institute of Medicine. Washington, D.C.: National Academy Press, 1991.

Howe, E. G. "Societal and Clinical Approaches to Preventing Pediatric AIDS: Some Ethical Considerations." *AIDS and Public Policy* 5(1990).

Kleinig J. "The Ethical Challenge of AIDS to Traditional Liberal Values." *AIDS and Public Policy Journal* 5(1989).

Kolbert, K. "A Reproductive Rights Agenda for the 1990s." In *From Abortion to Reproductive Freedom: Transforming a Movement*, edited by M. Gerber Fried. New York: South End Press, 1990.

Landesman, S. H., A. Wilioughby, and H. L. Minkoff. "HIV Disease in Reproductive Age Women: A Problem of the Present." *Journal of the American Medical Association* 261(1989).

Levin, B. W. "Ethics and AIDS in the Neonatal Intensive Care Unit." Paper presented at American Public Health Association Meeting, Chicago, October 1989.

Mann, J. "Women, Mothers, Children and the Global AIDS Strategy." Paper presented at the International Conference on the Implications of AIDS for Mothers and Children, Paris, November 1989.

Manuel, C., P. Enel, J. Charrel, D. Reviron, M. P. Larher, X. Thirion, and J. L. Sanmarco. "The Ethical Approach to AIDS: A Bibliographical Review." *Journal of Medical Ethics* 16(1990):14–27.

Mitchell, J, L. "Drug Abuse and AIDS in Women and Their Affected Offspring." *Journal of the National Medical Association* 81(1989).

Nolan, K. "Human Immunodeficiency Virus Infection, Women, and Pregnancy: Ethical Issues." *Obstetrics and Gynecology Clinics of North America* 17(1990).

Osterholm, M. T., and K. L. MacDonald. "Facing the Complex Issues of Pediatric AIDS: The Public Health Perspective." *Journal of the American Medical Association* 258(1987).

Rapp, R. "Counseling Women at Risk: Models, Myths, Ambiguities." Paper presented at Hastings Center, December 1987.

Roe, K. "Private Troubles and Public Issues: Providing Abortion Amid Competing Definitions." *Social Science and Medicine* 29(1989):1191–1198.

Ryder, R. W., and S. E. Hassig. "The Epidemiology of Perinatal Transmission of HIV." *AIDS* 2(1988):S83–89.

Walters, L. "Ethical Issues in the Prevention and Treatment of HIV Infection and AIDS." *Science* 239(1988):597–603.

Mabel Bianco

How AIDS Changes
Development Priorities

I n the course of its 10 years of existence, the perception of AIDS as an
illness confined to minority groups has changed to a recognition of it as a
risk for the entire population, regardless of sex or nationality. Women,
who in industrialized countries were hardly infected at first, have suffered
increasing incidence of the disease during the latter half of the 1980s. In
many geographical areas, the men-to-women infected ratio is already 1:1, as
in Africa, or 1:2, as in the Caribbean.[1]

The increasing number of female AIDS patients is connected to the
growing importance of heterosexual transmission relative to other forms of
transmission; it is estimated that 3 out of 4 cases in the world are currently
infected through heterosexual relations. Another tendency over the last few
years is the higher rate of AIDS among the poor. In the city of New York, a
strong correlation has been found between the population lacking basic
needs and the number of AIDS cases. In the United States, although the black
and Hispanic communities represent only 20 percent of the total population,
the AIDS cases from those groups, which suffer the highest levels of poverty,
constitute 43 percent of the total number of AIDS cases.[2]

Estimates and projections carried out by the World Health Organization
regarding the changing profile of AIDS patients predict that, in the year 2000,
90 percent of the cases will come from developing countries. While the
incidence of AIDS cases toward the middle of the 1990s will stop increasing
in North America and western European nations, the incidence of AIDS in
developing countries will continue to rise.

This pandemic has affected the mortality rate of young adults, men, and
women all over the world. In 1983 in the United States, mortality rates in
men between 25 and 44 stopped declining. In 1987, the upward trend in
mortality due to AIDS was approximately 11.3 percent. This rate is expected
to reach its peak in 1995. In women between 15 and 44 years old in the United
States, AIDS has contributed to a rise in the mortality rate from 0.6 per
100,000 in 1985 to 2.5 per 100,000 in 1987, and it is predicted that, in the year
2000, AIDS will constitute the third leading cause of death in this age group
among black and Latino women.[3]

In Africa, the World Health Organization estimates that life expectancy will decrease and in the year 2010 will be less than that of 1985. This is because AIDS affects the mortality rates not only of young adults but also of children and infants under 5 years old through perinatal transmission. These predicted demographic changes will be reflected not only in mortality rates, but also in fertility rates, which are expected to decline. There will be fewer women of reproductive age due to their higher mortality, and those who remain will tend to reproduce less because many of them will be ill or HIV-infected. This has already begun to happen in some African countries.[4] Changes in the world's health situation, especially in developing countries, will mean a lower quality of life. Although this cannot be attributed exclusively to AIDS, it is undeniable that this disease is an important contributing factor.

The fact that AIDS affects young adults, men, and women; the prolonged period between infection and the physical manifestation of the disease; and the psychological and biological effects of awareness of the illness all result in decreased productivity. Some economic consequences are cutbacks in production, deterioration of families' standards of living, and an increase in the need for items that are very expensive, such as medical supplies, hospitalization, nurseries for orphans, and lodging for terminal AIDS patients without families or whose families cannot support or assist them.

In developing countries, such demands are made on health and social services, which have already been reduced and impoverished by structural adjustment policies implemented over the last few years. These policies diminish the budgets assigned to social sectors and do not cater to the new demands generated by HIV and its consequences, both direct and indirect. This leads to more social pressures and friction within these countries.

AIDS has created a series of new conditions which have further exacerbated the already-existing inequities in our world. The gap between privileged groups and those with unsatisfied basic needs, especially in developing countries, will continue to widen as a result of this pandemic. In addition, the decrease of productivity due to the illness and death of young people will cause higher levels of poverty, which will have an even more damaging effect on the available social and health services. Greater numbers of old people and children will have to replace young adults in work positions. Most developing countries will become trapped in a vicious circle if nothing is done.

Within the new framework, new diseases will coexist with the old ones. The reappearance of cholera in Latin America and tuberculosis elsewhere are two examples. Poverty is the common factor in all these types of illnesses. AIDS is already a "disease of the poor."[5] It is poverty that will draw the line between the more and less affected. The widening of the gap over the last few years between the poor and the rich, between sectors of over- and underconsumption has coincided with the appearance of AIDS. It was in the last years of the 1970s, when the World Health Organization made a call for "Health for All in the Year 2000," that AIDS appeared. The changes that followed have not only made "Health for All in the Year 2000" totally impossible but have actually diminished the existing health situation for much of the world population.

Socially speaking, AIDS creates a power conflict in the personal, family, and social environments. It brings to the surface some of the most common but also most neglected inequalities, such as the power difference between a man and woman. Although women's submission and subordination to men has undergone many changes due to repeated demonstrations against discrimination by women all over the world, women's rights remain neglected when it comes to social and political decisions. Will AIDS be the detonator needed to bring this inequality to an end?

Other social inequities between rich and poor all over the world which became more evident with AIDS are differences in purchasing power and in access to education, health, recreation, and other benefits. Perhaps the only positive contribution of AIDS to the evolution of mankind is the possibility of bringing these conflicts to a boiling point and exposing them for what they are.

I believe there is an urgent need to reevaluate the current model for development, which is based on consumption as the key to individual and social well-being and as the driving force behind production. By making consumption a priority in most of the world, we have created a hierarchy in which economic issues take precedent over social issues. As a natural consequence, values such as solidarity and ethics have been lost and replaced by success, unlimited competition, individualism, and opportunism.

How can we fight all this? AIDS has brought us face to face with this challenge by bringing to the surface the weak and vulnerable points of our models of development and productivity. These models do not promote more equity and suitable forms of life for the majority of the global population. If we continue to conceive of development only as economic growth, neglecting and devaluing the redistribution of resources and the creation of acceptable living standards for all human beings, "sustainable development" will remain an empty phrase.

The social conflicts that take place from day to day in various countries, in both the developed and the developing world, make it more than plain that relying on economic factors alone to measure the success of social and political processes is insufficient and unreliable. If these processes do not improve the quality of life, social instability will eventually cause those economic factors to deteriorate. Despite the efforts of economic ministers and authoritarian models, this process will act as a weight that will eventually drag the privileged sectors down as well. All of us are involved.

As Guimaraes says, "Proposals in order to overcome the crisis cannot be confined to purely economic considerations."[6] Just as AIDS patients cannot continue to be considered individually and outside of a family and social context, the world's inequalities cannot be characterized as individual phenomena; they are social problems. It is not a matter of guaranteeing better access to existing health services, education, and other individual needs, but to create and perform collective practices, based on solidarity, which provide a real solution to problems of health, education, and other social areas. Just as the free market alone cannot regulate social areas such as health,[7] the new international order "will have to consider poverty as the main source of chaos in the world," to quote Galbraith.[8] And whatever this new international order turns out to be, it would imply a growing and continuous flow of resources from rich countries to poor countries.

The question that arises is where the resources will come from, given the current world economic crisis. It is clear that this situation calls for a worldwide redistribution of resources, a redistribution that requires a reduction of military expenditures and of unnecessary investments which are often harmful to the environment, including many transport, production, and agricultural systems prompted by the current model of exploitation of resources. In this sense, the reduction of excessive consumption by privileged groups both in rich and poor countries is a prerequisite if our aim is the conservation of the planet and mankind.

From this new perspective, the possibility of growth with equity, we cannot forget efficiency, because without efficiency, there will be no equity. In the field of health services, it will be necessary to reevaluate and modify most current models of provision of services, which more often than not place the fulfillment of particular group interests above the common good and waste resources on pointless services as a result of ignorance, negligence, and old habits.

In relation to AIDS, for example, it is necessary to improve information and education, which are the main preventive tools.[9] Instead of promoting massive screening, with its higher costs and low results and its potential for increased discrimination and marginalization of ill or infected people, what we need are collective proposals based on solidarity.[10] In order to achieve this, we should promote more participation by all sectors, regardless of sex, race, or social status. This implies the socialization of power, enabling sectors until now excluded from the decision-making process, such as women, to take part once and for all. Civil participation has its limitations. If that participation is not considered, societies could fall prey to the imposition of political will, which only contributes to an appearance of participation and democratization of power. According to Guimaraes, "a qualitative change in the field of proposals is necessary in order to make possible a model of development with equity in Latin America,"[11] qualitative change which, in my opinion, will be possible only when those who today are deprived of power are allowed to participate. This is easier to accept for those who have less power and have lived for centuries in a condition of submission and subordination, as is the case for women, but it is not so simple for those who have traditionally held power. The matter is also defined in terms of countries. The developed countries will take some time to agree to change the current balance of power and share not only their wealth but also their decisions regarding investments and priorities. However, this is the only peaceful, safe, and effective means to achieve the goal.

I realize that this is utopian but it is the vision of utopia that has enabled the world to grow and develop. Utopia never dies; it changes and is renewed. Let us work together to make this utopia a reality, so we can control not only AIDS but other current dangers in the world as well. This will be the best legacy we can leave to future generations.

NOTES

[1]J. Mann, D. J. M. Tarantola, and T. W. Netter, eds., *AIDS in the World: A Global Report* (Cambridge, Mass.: Harvard University Press, 1992).

[2]C. Levine, "AIDS and changing concepts of family," *Milbank Quarterly* 68 (1990):33–58.

[3]J. Chin, "Present and future dimensions of HIV/AIDS pandemic," *Science Challenging AIDS*, ed. by G. B. Rossi (Switzerland: Karger, 1992), 35–50.

[4]R. Anderson, *Clarin Newspaper* (Nairobi, Kenya, from DPA) 11 August 1992.

[5]E. M. Ankrah, "The impact of AIDS on social, economic, health and welfare systems," in Rossi, 175–187.

[6]R. Guimaraes, "Desarrollo con equidad. Un neuvo cuento de hadas para los años '90," *CEPAL: CC/R*, 755, 20 April, 1990.

[7]A. Neri, "Economical Development and Health," *Saitama Public Health Summit*, September 1991.

[8]J. K. Galbraith, "Poverty: the new order enemy," *Le Monde*, (Paris), July 1991.

[9]"Función del PNUD en la lucha contra el HIV/SIDA: Marco de la política del PNUD para combatir el HIV/SIDA," Doc. Marzo 1992.

[10]V. Ramalingaswami, "The implications of AIDS in developing countries," in Rossi, 24–34.

[11]R. Guimaraes, "Desarrollo social de América Latina: Políticas y restricciones institucionales," *Socialismo y Participación* 44 (1988): 33–59.